T0234616

Lecture Notes in Computer Science 10410

Commenced Publication in 1973
Founding and Former Series Editors:
Gerhard Goos, Juris Hartmanis, and Jan van Leeuwen

More information about this series at http://www.springer.com/series/7409

Andreas Holzinger · Peter Kieseberg
A Min Tjoa · Edgar Weippl (Eds.)

Machine Learning
and Knowledge Extraction

First IFIP TC 5, WG 8.4, 8.9, 12.9
International Cross-Domain Conference, CD-MAKE 2017
Reggio, Italy, August 29 – September 1, 2017
Proceedings

 Springer

Editors
Andreas Holzinger
Medical University Graz
Graz
Austria

Peter Kieseberg
SBA Research
Vienna
Austria

A Min Tjoa
Vienna University of Technology
Vienna
Austria

Edgar Weippl
SBA Research
Vienna
Austria

ISSN 0302-9743 ISSN 1611-3349 (electronic)
Lecture Notes in Computer Science
ISBN 978-3-319-66807-9 ISBN 978-3-319-66808-6 (eBook)
DOI 10.1007/978-3-319-66808-6

Library of Congress Control Number: 2017951440

LNCS Sublibrary: SL3 – Information Systems and Applications, incl. Internet/Web, and HCI

Printed on acid-free paper

This Springer imprint is published by Springer Nature
The registered company is Springer International Publishing AG
The registered company address is: Gewerbestrasse 11, 6330 Cham, Switzerland

Preface

The International Cross Domain Conference for Machine Learning and Knowledge Extraction, CD-MAKE, is a joint effort of IFIP TC 5, IFIP WG 8.4, IFIP WG 8.9, and IFIP WG 12.9 and is held in conjunction with the International Conference on Availability, Reliability, and Security (ARES).

CD stands for Cross-Domain and means the integration and appraisal of different fields and application domains to provide an atmosphere to foster different perspectives and opinions. The conference is dedicated to offering an international platform for novel ideas and a fresh look at the methodologies for putting crazy ideas into business for the benefit of the human. Serendipity is a desired effect, cross-fertilizing methodologies and transferring algorithmic developments.

MAKE stands for MAchine Learning and Knowledge Extraction. Machine learning studies algorithms that can learn from data to gain knowledge from experience and to make decisions and predictions. A grand goal is to understand intelligence for the design and development of algorithms that work autonomously and can improve their learning behavior over time. The challenge is to discover relevant structural and/or temporal patterns ("knowledge") in data, which is often hidden in arbitrarily high dimensional spaces, which is simply not accessible to humans. Machine learning as a branch of Artificial Intelligence is currently undergoing kind of Cambrian explosion and is the fastest growing field in computer science today. There are many application domains, e.g., smart health, smart factory, etc. with many use cases from our daily life, e.g., speech recognition, autonomous driving, etc. The grand challenges are in sense-making, in context understanding, and in decision making under uncertainty. Our real-world is full of uncertainties, and probabilistic inference has enormously influenced Artificial Intelligence generally and statistical learning specifically. The inverse probability allows us to infer unknowns, to learn from data, and to make predictions to support decision making. Whether in social networks, health, or Industry 4.0 applications, the increasingly complex data sets require efficient, useful, and useable solutions for knowledge discovery and knowledge extraction.

To acknowledge here all those who contributed to the organization and stimulating discussions would be impossible. Many people contributed to the development of this volume, either directly or indirectly, so it would be sheerly impossible to list all of them. We herewith thank all colleagues and friends for all their positive and supportive encouragement. Last but not least we thank the Springer management team and the Springer production team for their smooth support.

Thank you to all! Let's make it!

August 2017

Andreas Holzinger
Peter Kieseberg
Edgar Weippl
A Min Tjoa

Organization

International Cross Domain Conference for Machine Learning and Knowledge Extraction (CD-MAKE 2017)

CD-MAKE Conference Organizers

Andreas Holzinger   Med. University and Graz University of Technology, Austria
Peter Kieseberg   SBA Research, Austria
Edgar Weippl   SBA Research, Austria (IFIP WG 8.4 Chair)
A Min Tjoa   TU Vienna, Austria (IFIP WG 8.9. Chair, Honorary Secretary IFIP)

Program Committee

Rakesh Agrawal   Microsoft Search Labs, USA
Amin Anjomshoaa   SENSEable City Laboratory, Massachusetts Institute of Technology, USA
Joel P. Arrais   Centre for Informatics and Systems, University of Coimbra, Portugal
John A. Atkinson Abutridy   Department of Computer Science, Universidad de Concepción, Chile
Chloe Agathe Azencott   Centre for Computational Biology (CBIO), Mines Paris Tech, France
Alexandra Balahur   European Commission Joint Research Céntre, Italy
Smaranda Belciug   Department of Computer Science, Faculty of Mathematics & Computer Science, University of Craiova, Romania
Mounir Ben Ayed   Research Group Intelligent Machines, Ecole Nationale d'Ingenieurs de Sfax, Tunisia
Mattia G. Bergomi   Champalimaud Centre for the Unknown, Portugal
Elisa Bertino   Department of Computer Science, Purdue University, USA
Michele Bezzi   Security Research, SAP Labs France, France
Jiang Bian   College of Medicine, Health Outcomes and Policy, University of Florida, USA
Chris Biemann   Language Technology Group, FB Informatik, Technische Universität Darmstadt, Germany
Miroslaw Bober   Department of Electronic Engineering, University of Surrey, UK

Aryya Gangopadhyay — UMBC Center of Cybersecurity, University of Maryland, USA

Panagiotis Germanakos — Department of Computer Science, University of Cyprus, Cyprus

Randy Goebel — Centre for Machine Learning, Department of Computer Science, University of Alberta, Canada

Michael Granitzer — Media Computer Science, University of Passau, Germany

Dimitrios Gunopulos — Knowledge Discovery in Databases Lab, Department of Informatics, University of Athens, Greece

Marie Gustafsson Friberger — Computer Science Department, Malmö University, Sweden

Siegfried Handschuh — Insight Centre for Data Analytics, NUI Galway, Ireland

Helwig Hauser — Visualization Group, University of Bergen, Norway

Julian Heinrich — Biodata Visualization Team, CSIRO, Australia

Kristina Hettne — BioSemantics Group, Department of Human Genetics, Leiden University Medical Center, Netherlands

Rainer Hofmann-Wellenhof — Division of General Dermatology, Graz University Hospital, Austria

Andreas Hotho — Data Mining and Information Retrieval Group, University of Würzburg, Germany

Jun Huan — Computational Knowledge Discovery Lab, University of Kansas, USA

Anthony Hunter — Intelligent Systems Group, Department of Computer Science, University College London, UK

Barna Laszlo Iantovics — Department of Mathematics and Informatics, Petru Maior University, Romania

Sara Johansson Fernstad — Computer Science and Digital Technologies, Northumbria University, UK

Igor Jurisica — IBM Life Sciences Discovery Centre, and Princess Margaret Cancer Centre, Canada

Andreas Kerren — ISOVIS Group, Department of Computer Science, Linnaeus University, Sweden

Negar Kiyavash — Department of Industrial and Enterprise Systems, University of Illinois at Urbana-Champaign, USA

Lubos Klucar — Bioinformatics Lab, Institute of Molecular Biology, Slovak Academy of Sciences, Slovakia

Natsuhiko Kumasaka — Center for Genomic Medicine (CGM), RIKEN, Japan

Robert S. Laramee — Data Visualization Group, Department of Computer Science, Swansea University, UK

Nada Lavrac — Department of Knowledge Technologies, Joszef Stefan Institute, Slovenia

Sangkyun Lee — Artificial Intelligence Unit, Dortmund University, Germany

Lenka Lhotska — Department of Cybernetics, Faculty of Electrical Engineering, Czech Technical University Prague, Czech Republic

Chunping Li	School of Software, Tsinghua University, China
Haibin Ling	Center for Data Analytics and Biomedical Informatics, Temple University, USA
Luca Longo	Knowledge & Data Engineering Group, Trinity College Dublin, Ireland
Andras Lukacs	Institute of Mathematics, Hungarian Academy of Sciences and Eoetvos University, Hungary
Ljiljana Majnaric Trtica	Department of Family Medicine, Medical School, University of Osijek, Croatia
Donato Malerba	Dipartimento di Informatica, Università degli Studi di Bari Aldo Moro, Italy
Vincenzo Manca	Dipartimento di Informatica, University of Verona, Italy
Ernestina Menasalvas	Data Mining Group, Polytechnic University of Madrid, Spain
Yoan Miche	Nokia Bell Labs, Helsinki, Finland
Silvia Miksch	Centre of Visual Analytics Science & Technology, Vienna University of Technology, Austria
Antonio Moreno-Ribas	Intelligent Technologies for Advanced Knowledge Acquisition, Univ. Rovira i Virgili, Spain
Marian Mrozek	Computational Mathematics, Institute of Computer Science, Jagiellonian University, Poland
Nysret Musliu	Database and Artificial Intelligence Group (DBAI), Vienna University of Technology, Austria
Zoran Obradovic	Data Analytics and Biomedical Informatics Center, Temple University, USA
Patricia Ordonez-Rozo	Department of Computer Science, University of Puerto Rico Rio Piedras, Puerto Rico
Daniel O'Leary	School of Business, University of Southern California, USA
Vasile Palade	School of Computing, Electronics and Mathematics, Coventry University, UK
Jan Paralic	Department of Cybernetics and Artificial Intelligence, Technical University of Kosice, Slovakia
Valerio Pascucci	Scientific Computing and Imaging Institute, University of Utah, USA
Gabriella Pasi	Laboratorio di Information Retrieval, Università di Milano Bicocca, Italy
Philip R.O. Payne	Institute for Informatics, School of Medicine, Washington University, USA
Roberto Perdisci	Institute for Artificial Intelligence, Computer Science Department, University of Georgia, USA
Armando J. Pinho	Departamento de Electrónica, Telecomunicações e Informática, University Aveiro, Portugal
Raul Rabadan	Biomedical Informatics, Columbia University, USA
Heri Ramampiaro	Data and Information Management Group, Norwegian University of Science and Technology, Norway

Fabrizio Riguzzi — Dipartimento di Matematica e Informatica, Università di Ferrara, Italy

Giuseppe Rizzo — Innovation Development, Istituto Superiore Mario Boella Turin, Italy

Lior Rokach — Department of Information Systems Engineering, Ben-Gurion University of the Negev, Israel

Timo Ropinski — Visual Computing Research Group, Ulm University, Germany

Jianhua Ruan — Computational Biology, Department of Computer Science, University of Texas, USA

Carsten Röcker — Fraunhofer IOSB-INA and Ostwestfalen-Lippe University of Applied Sciences, Germany

Pierangela Samarati — Dipartimento di Informatica, University of Milan, Italy

Giuseppe Santucci — Dipartimento di Informatica e Sistemistica, La Sapienza, University of Rome, Italy

Paola Sebastiani — Department of Biostatistics, School of Public Health, Boston University, USA

Christin Seifert — Media Computer Science, University of Passau, Germany

Bracha Shapira — Department of Information Systems Engineering, Ben-Gurion University of the Negev, Israel

Yongtang Shi — Center for Combinatorics, Nankai University, China

Neil R. Smalheiser — College of Medicine, Department of Psychiatry, University of Illinois at Chicago, USA

Axel J. Soto — National Centre for Text Mining (NaCTeM), Manchester Institute of Biotechnology, UK

Rainer Spang — Statistical Bioinformatics Department, Institute of Functional Genomics, University Regensburg, Germany

Irena Spasic — Health Informatics, School of Computer Science & Informatics, Cardiff University, UK

Jessica Staddon — Google Research and Computer Science Department, NC State University, USA

Jerzy Stefanowski — Institute of Computing Science, Poznan University of Technology, Poland

Ulrich Stelzl — Network Pharmacology Group, Institute of Pharmaceutical Sciences, Graz University, Austria

Gregor Stiglic — Stanford Center for Biomedical Informatics, Stanford School of Medicine, USA

Shiliang Sun — Pattern Recognition & Machine Learning Research Group, East China Normal University, China

Olof Torgersson — Applied Information Technology, Chalmers University of Technology, Sweden

Dimitar Trajanov — Department of Computer Science, Cyril and Methodius University, Macedonia

Shusaku Tsumoto — Department of Medical Informatics, Faculty of Medicine, Shimane University, Japan

Cagatay Turkay   Department of Computer Science, City University London,
                          UK
Karin Verspoor   Health and Life Sciences, National Information and
                          Communications Technology Australia, Australia
Jean Philippe Vert   Cancer Computational Genomics and Bioinformatics,
                          Mines ParisTech, France
Dmitry Vetrov   Bayesian Methods Research Group, Higher School
                          of Economics, Russia
Hubert Wagner   Institute for Science and Technology IST Austria, Austria
Byron Wallace   College of Computer and Information Science,
                          Northeastern University, USA
Daniel Weiskopf   Visualization and Interactive Systems Institute,
                          Universität Stuttgart, Germany
William B.L. Wong   HCI, Computing and Multimedia Department,
                          Middlesex University London, UK
Kai Xu   Visual Analytics, Computing and Multimedia Department,
                          Middlesex University London, UK
Jieping Ye   Center for Evolutionary Medicine and Informatics,
                          Arizona State University, USA
Pinar Yildirim   Department of Computer Engineering, Okan University,
                          Turkey
Ning Zhong   Knowledge Information Systems Laboratory,
                          Maebashi Institute of Technology, Japan
Xuezhong Zhou   Beijing Jiaotong University, China
Martina Ziefle   e-Health Group, RWTH Aachen University, Germany

Contents

MAKE VIS

MAKE AAL

MAKE Semantics

MAKE Topology

On Distance Mapping from non-Euclidean Spaces to Euclidean Spaces

Wei Ren[1], Yoan Miche[1(✉)], Ian Oliver[1], Silke Holtmanns[1], Kaj-Mikael Bjork[2], and Amaury Lendasse[3]

[1] Nokia Bell Labs, Karakaari 13, 02760 Espoo, Finland
yoan.miche@nokia-bell-labs.com
[2] Arcada University of Applied Sciences, Jan-Magnus Janssonin aukio 1, 00550 Helsinki, Finland
[3] The University of Iowa, Iowa City 52242-1527, USA

Abstract. Most Machine Learning techniques traditionally rely on some forms of Euclidean Distances, computed in a Euclidean space (typically $\mathbb{R}^d$). In more general cases, data might not live in a classical Euclidean space, and it can be difficult (or impossible) to find a direct representation for it in $\mathbb{R}^d$. Therefore, distance mapping from a non-Euclidean space to a canonical Euclidean space is essentially needed. We present in this paper a possible distance-mapping algorithm, such that the behavior of the pairwise distances in the mapped Euclidean space is preserved, compared to those in the original non-Euclidean space. Experimental results of the mapping algorithm are discussed on a specific type of datasets made of timestamped GPS coordinates. The comparison of the original and mapped distances, as well as the standard errors of the mapped distributions, are discussed.

1 Introduction

Traditionally, most data mining and machine learning have relied on the classical (or variations thereof) Euclidean distance (Minkowski distance with the exponent set to 2), over data that lies in $\mathbb{R}^d$ (with $d \in \mathbb{N}_+$). One problem with this approach is that it forces the data provider to process the original, raw data, in such a way that it is in $\mathbb{R}^d$, while it might not be natural to do so. For example, encoding arbitrary attributes (such as words from a specific, finite set) using integers, creates an underlying order between the elements, which has to be carefully taken care of. It also creates a certain distance between the elements, and the various choices in the conversion process are practically unlimited and difficult to address. We therefore look here into the possibility of not converting the data to a Euclidean space, and retain the data in its original space, provided that we have a distance function between its elements. In effect, we "only" require and concern ourselves, in this paper, with metric spaces, over potentially non-Euclidean spaces. With the fact that most data mining and machine learning methods rely on Euclidean distances and their properties, we want to verify

A. Holzinger et al. (Eds.): CD-MAKE 2017, LNCS 10410, pp. 3–13, 2017.
DOI: 10.1007/978-3-319-66808-6_1

that in such a case, the distances in a non-Euclidean metric space can behave close enough to the Euclidean distances over a Euclidean space. The reasoning behind this is that traditional Machine Learning and Data Mining algorithms might expect the distances between elements to behave in a certain manner, and respect certain properties, which we attempt to mimic with the following distance mapping approach.

A distance-mapping algorithm, in the context of this paper, is an approach that takes a set of objects as well as their pairwise distance function in the specific non-Euclidean space (so, a non-Euclidean metric space), and maps those pairwise distances to a canonical Euclidean space, in such a way that the distance distribution among the objects is approximately preserved in the mapped Euclidean space.

Distance-mapping algorithms are a useful tool in data applications, for example, data clustering and visualisations. Another good use case for distance-mapping, is mutual information [3,7,10], which is used to quantitatively measure the mutual dependence between two (or more) sets of random variables in information theory. Mutual information is most often estimated by constructing the k-nearest neighbors [7,10] graphs of the underlying data, which thus rely on the Euclidean distances. Hence, there is a strong need to re-calculate the distances over a potentially non-Euclidean space.

In the following Sect. 2, we first introduce basic notations to describe the distance mapping approach in Sects. 3, 4 and 5. After a short discussion about important implementation details in Sect. 7, we finally present and discuss results over a synthetic data set in Sect. 8.

2   Notations

As in the data privacy literature, one traditionally defines a dataset of N records by $X = [x_1, ..., x_N]^T$, the matrix of N samples (records) with d attributes $\{A^{(1)}, ..., A^{(d)}\}$. A record x_l is now defined as $x_l = [a_l^{(1)}, a_l^{(2)}, ..., a_l^{(d)}]$, $a_l^{(j)} \in \mathbb{X}^{(j)}$, where $\mathbb{X}^{(j)}$ is the set of all the possible values for a certain attribute $A^{(j)}$. Hence, we can see the vector $[a_1^{(j)}, a_2^{(j)}, ..., a_N^{(j)}]^T \in \mathbb{X}^{(j)}$ as a discrete random variable for a certain attribute over all the N samples.

Let us consider a metric space $\mathcal{X}^{(j)} = (\mathbb{X}^{(j)}, d^{(j)})$ using the set $\mathbb{X}^{(j)}$ explained above, endowed with the distance function $d^{(j)} : \mathbb{X}^{(j)} \times \mathbb{X}^{(j)} \longrightarrow \mathbb{R}_+$. Generally, $\mathcal{X}^{(j)}$ need not be an Euclidean metric space.

3   Distances over non-Euclidean Spaces

Now we consider two metric spaces $\mathcal{X}^{(i)} = (\mathbb{X}^{(i)}, d^{(i)})$ and $\mathcal{X}^{(j)} = (\mathbb{X}^{(j)}, d^{(j)})$. Let us assume $\mathcal{X}^{(i)}$ to be a canonical Euclidean space with the distance function $d^{(i)}$ the Euclidean norm and $\mathbb{X}^{(i)} = \mathbb{R}^d$, while $\mathcal{X}^{(j)}$ is a non-Euclidean space endowed with a non-Euclidean distance function $d^{(j)}$.

Assume $x^{(j)}$ and $y^{(j)}$ are two sets of discrete independent and identically distributed (iid) random variables for a certain attribute over $\mathbb{X}^{(j)}$. The distances within the metric space $\mathcal{X}^{(j)}$ can then be constructed by another set of random variable $z^{(j)}$:

$$z^{(j)} = d^{(j)}(x^{(j)}, y^{(j)}), \tag{1}$$

where the values of $z^{(j)}$ are over $\mathbb{R}_+$.

We denote by $f_{z^{(j)}}(d)$ the probability density function (PDF) of $z^{(j)}$, which describes the pairwise distance distribution over the non-Euclidean metric space $\mathcal{X}^{(j)}$. In the same way, we define $f_{z^{(i)}}(d)$ to be the distribution of pairwise distances over the Euclidean metric space $\mathcal{X}^{(i)}$.

We assume that there is a way to transform the distribution of the non-Euclidean distances $f_{z^{(j)}}(d)$ to $f_{z^{(j)}}^{map}(d)$ in such a way that $f_{z^{(j)}}^{map}(d)$ can be as close as possible to the Euclidean distance distribution $f_{z^{(i)}}(d)$:

$$\lim_{N \to \infty} f_{z^{(j)}}^{map} = f_{z^{(i)}}, \tag{2}$$

meaning that the two probability density function are equal at every point evaluated, in the limit case.

As we are using a limit number of realisations N of the random variables to estimate the distribution $f_{z^{(j)}}(d)$, the limit over N is based on the assumption that we can "afford" to draw sufficiently large enough number N of the variables to possibly estimate $f_{z^{(j)}}(d)$ to be close enough to $f_{z^{(i)}}(d)$. We present the mapping approach used in this paper in the following Sect. 4, by solving an integral equation so as to obtain equal probability masses.

4 Mapping Solution

We propose to use Machine Learning (more specifically, Universal Function Approximators [4]) to map the distribution $f_{z^{(j)}}$ of the non-Euclidean distance to the distribution $f_{z^{(i)}}$ of the Euclidean distance, with the fact that most Machine Learning techniques are able to fit a continuous input to another different continuous output.

We then want to make it so that given a certain distance $z = d^{(j)}(x, y)$ obtained over $\mathcal{X}^{(j)}$, we calculate α such that

$$\int_0^z f_{z^{(j)}}(t)dt = \int_0^\alpha f_{z^{(i)}}(t)dt, \tag{3}$$

We want to obtain α values so that the probability masses of the distances in the Non-Euclidean metric space $\mathcal{X}^{(j)}$ and the Euclidean metric space $\mathcal{X}^{(i)}$ are the same. The α value is the mapped distance over $\mathcal{X}^{(i)}$. To obtain α, firstly we need to calculate the integral in the left part of Eq. 3 with the given z; secondly we need to calculate the integral in the right part of Eq. 3 as a function of α; the α value can then be solved with Eq. 3.

The following Sect. 5 describes in practice the algorithm to achieve the distance mapping proposed.

5   Algorithm of Distance Mapping

To calculate the integral in the left part of Eq. 3, we first need to construct the distribution function $f_{z^{(j)}}$ using Machine Learning for functional estimates. The algorithm for distance mapping is explained as follows:

A.1 Draw as many samples as possible from $x^{(j)}$ and $y^{(j)}$ (random variables over $\mathbb{X}^{(j)}$);

A.2 Compute $z^{(j)} = d^{(j)}(x^{(j)}, y^{(j)})$;

A.3 Compute the histogram of $z^{(j)}$;

A.4 Use a Machine Learning algorithm to learn this histogram: this creates an un-normalized version of $f_{z^{(j)}}(t)$;

A.5 Compute the integral $f_{z^{(j)}}(t)$ over its domain to obtain the normalizing constant $C^{(j)}$;

A.6 Normalize the estimated function from 4. with the constant $C^{(j)}$;

A.7 This yields a functional representation $g^{(j)}(t)$ of $f_{z^{(j)}}(t)$ that behaves as an estimate of the PDF of $z^{(j)}$;

A.8 We can finally integrate $g^{(j)}(t)$ from 0 to z (which was the given distance value) to obtain a value we denote β:

$$\beta = \int_0^z g^{(j)}(t) \approx \int_0^z f_{z^{(j)}}(t)dt, \tag{4}$$

and this is also done numerically;

A.9 We assume the cumulative distribution function (CDF) of the Euclidean distances $\alpha = d^{(i)}(x, y)$ to be $F_{z^{(i)}}(\alpha)$. Solving Eq. 3 now becomes:

$$\beta = \int_0^z g^{(j)}(t) \approx F_{z^{(i)}}(\alpha), \tag{5}$$

$$\alpha = F_{z^{(i)}}^{-1}(\beta), \tag{6}$$

where $F_{z^{(i)}}^{-1}(\beta)$ is the inverse of the CDF in the mapped Euclidean space $\mathcal{X}^{(i)}$. The distances are then mapped from z to α.

Note that this algorithm is independent on the nature of $\mathcal{X}^{(i)}$: at this point, $\mathcal{X}^{(i)}$ can be any metric space. In the following, we look at the two possibilities of mapping a non-Euclidean space to a Euclidean space, or to another, non-Euclidean space (for completeness sake).

So, we are presented with two possibilities:

- $\mathcal{X}^{(i)} = (\mathbb{X}^{(i)}, d^{(i)})$ is the canonical Euclidean space, i.e. $\mathbb{X}^{(i)} = \mathbb{R}$ and $d^{(i)}$ is the Euclidean distance over $\mathbb{R}$;
- $\mathcal{X}^{(i)}$ is not the canonical Euclidean space, and the set of all necessary values $\mathbb{X}^{(i)}$ does not have to be $\mathbb{R}$, while $d^{(i)}$ is the Euclidean distance.

5.1 First Case

In the case of $\mathcal{X}^{(i)}$ being the canonical Euclidean space, we can find analytical expressions for $f_{\boldsymbol{z}^{(i)}}$ in Eq. 3, by making assumptions on how the variables $\boldsymbol{x}^{(i)}$ and $\boldsymbol{y}^{(i)}$ are distributed. If such assumptions are not acceptable for some reason, it is always possible to revert to the estimation approach mentioned above, or possibly solve analytically as below for other well-know distributions.

If $\boldsymbol{x}^{(i)}$ and $\boldsymbol{y}^{(i)}$ are normally distributed. We assume that $\boldsymbol{x}^{(i)}$ and $\boldsymbol{y}^{(i)}$ follow a normal distribution $\mathcal{N}(\mu, \sigma^2)$ with mean μ and variance σ^2. $\boldsymbol{x}^{(i)}$ and $\boldsymbol{y}^{(i)}$ are iid.

It is then clear that $\boldsymbol{z}^{(i)} = d(\boldsymbol{x}^{(i)}, \boldsymbol{y}^{(i)}) = |\boldsymbol{x}^{(i)} - \boldsymbol{y}^{(i)}|$ is distributed as a folded normal distribution of mean 0 and variance $2\sigma^2$: $\boldsymbol{z}^{(i)} \sim \mathcal{N}_f(0, 2\sigma^2)$. The probability density function of $\boldsymbol{z}^{(i)}$ can then be described as:

$$f_{\boldsymbol{z}^{(i)}}(t) = \frac{1}{\sigma\sqrt{\pi}} e^{-t^2/(4\sigma^2)}, \quad \text{for } t \geq 0 \tag{7}$$

Its CDF follows that

$$F_{\boldsymbol{z}^{(i)}}(\alpha) = \int_0^\alpha f_{\boldsymbol{z}^{(i)}}(t)dt = \mathrm{erf}(\frac{\alpha}{2\sigma}) \tag{8}$$

Finally, as we have calculated β in Eq. 5, we can solve easily

$$\alpha = 2\sigma \, \mathrm{erf}^{-1}(\beta). \tag{9}$$

If $\boldsymbol{x}^{(i)}$ and $\boldsymbol{y}^{(i)}$ are uniformly distributed. If we assume that $\boldsymbol{x}^{(i)}$ and $\boldsymbol{y}^{(i)}$ follow a uniform distribution $\mathcal{U}(a, b)$, with $(a \leq b)$, and are iid. The probability distribution of the distances $\boldsymbol{z}^{(i)}$ is then obtained that

$$f_{\boldsymbol{z}^{(i)}}(t) = \begin{cases} \frac{2}{b-a}\left(1 - \frac{t}{b-a}\right) & \text{if } 0 \leq t \leq b - a \\ 0 & \text{elsewhere} \end{cases} \tag{10}$$

which means that

$$F_{\boldsymbol{z}^{(i)}}(\alpha) = \int_0^\alpha f_{\boldsymbol{z}^{(i)}}(t)dt = -\frac{1}{(b-a)^2}\alpha^2 + \frac{2}{b-a}\alpha. \tag{11}$$

Solving as before, we finally have that

$$\alpha = (b - a)(1 - \sqrt{1 - \beta}), \tag{12}$$

given the fact that the other solution is not acceptable for our case (negative result for a distance value).

If the distances $|\boldsymbol{x}^{(i)} - \boldsymbol{y}^{(i)}|$ are Rayleigh distributed. A Rayleigh distribution often arises when the metric space is analyzed by the magnitude of the orthogonal two-dimensional vector components. If we assume the distances $\boldsymbol{z}^{(i)} = |\boldsymbol{x}^{(i)} - \boldsymbol{y}^{(i)}|$ follow a Rayleigh distribution with the scale parameter σ that

$$f_{\boldsymbol{z}^{(i)}}(t) = \frac{t}{\sigma^2} e^{-t^2/(2\sigma^2)}, \quad \text{for } t \geq 0. \tag{13}$$

The cumulative density then becomes

$$F_{\mathbf{z}^{(i)}}(\alpha) = \int_0^\alpha f_{\mathbf{z}^{(i)}}(t)dt = 1 - e^{-\alpha^2/(2\sigma^2)}. \tag{14}$$

The mapped distances α can then be solved by

$$\alpha = \sigma\sqrt{-2\log(1-\beta)}. \tag{15}$$

Other Distributions. We have discussed above the most common distributions of the distances $\mathbf{z}^{(i)}$ in the canonical Euclidean space $\mathcal{X}^{(i)}$. Certainly, the PDF of the distances $\mathbf{z}^{(i)}$ can exist in other less common fashions in certain specific circumstances. The implementation of the solution is not consummate so far. However, for the datasets used in practice with this work, which consist of timestamped GPS coordinates in the form of latitudes and longitudes, the discussed typical distributions are sufficient enough to illustrate the mapped distributions in the canonical Euclidean space. We will discuss about it in Sect. 8.

5.2 Second Case

In the second case, where $\mathcal{X}^{(i)}$ is not canonical Euclidean space, we basically have to perform the same estimate of $f_{\mathbf{z}^{(i)}}$ and its integral from 0 up to α, as we did for $f_{\mathbf{z}^{(j)}}$. The result is another function $G(\alpha)$:

$$G^{(i)}(\alpha) = \int_0^\alpha g^{(i)}(t)dt \approx \int_0^\alpha f_{\mathbf{z}^{(i)}}(t)dt. \tag{16}$$

We then have to solve numerically

$$G^{(i)}(\alpha) = \beta \tag{17}$$

for α.

6 Using ELM to Learn the Functional Distribution

We propose to use Extreme Learning Machines (ELM) [5,6] as the mapping tool between distance functions. The reason for choosing this specific Machine Learning technique is its excellent performance/computational time ratio among all the techniques. The model is simple and involves a minimal amount of computations. Since we are dealing with the limit problem of the number of records N to estimate the distribution $f_{\mathbf{z}^{(j)}}(d)$ (in Eq. 2), the ELM model is applicable in that it can learn the mapping in reasonable time for large amounts of data, if such a need arises. ELM is a universal function approximator, which can fit any continuous function.

The ELM algorithm was originally proposed by Guang-Bin Huang *et al.* in [6], and further developed, e.g. in [8,9,12], and analysed in [2]. It uses the structure of a Single Layer Feed-forward Neural Network (SLFN) [1]. The main concept behind the ELM approach is its random initialization, instead of a computationally costly procedure of training the hidden layer. The output weights matrix is then to be found between the hidden representation of the inputs and the outputs.

It works as following: Consider a set of N district observations $(\boldsymbol{x}_i, \boldsymbol{y}_i)$, with $\boldsymbol{x}_i \in \mathbb{R}^d$, $\boldsymbol{y}_i \in \mathbb{R}^c$, and $i = 1, ..., N$. In the case the SLFN would perfectly approximates the data, with the errors between the estimated outputs $\hat{\boldsymbol{y}}_i$ and the actual outputs $\boldsymbol{y}_i$ being zeros: $\hat{\boldsymbol{y}}_i = \boldsymbol{y}_i$. The relation between inputs, weights and outputs is then:

$$\sum_{j=1}^{n} \beta_j \phi(\boldsymbol{w}_j \boldsymbol{x}_i + b_j) = \boldsymbol{y}_i, \quad i \in [1, N], \tag{18}$$

where $\phi : \mathbb{R}^d \rightarrow \mathbb{R}^c$ is the activation function of the hidden neurons; $\boldsymbol{w}_j$ is the input weights; b_j is the biases; and β_j is the output weights. Equation 18 can also be written compactly as:

$$\boldsymbol{H}\boldsymbol{\beta} = \boldsymbol{Y}, \tag{19}$$

with $\boldsymbol{\beta} = (\beta_1^T, ..., \beta_n^T)^T$, and $\boldsymbol{Y} = (\boldsymbol{y}_1^T, ..., \boldsymbol{y}_n^T)^T$.

The output weights $\boldsymbol{\beta}$ can be solved from the hidden layer representation of inputs $\boldsymbol{H}$ and the actual outputs $\boldsymbol{Y}$:

$$\boldsymbol{\beta} = \boldsymbol{H}^\dagger \boldsymbol{Y}, \tag{20}$$

where $\boldsymbol{H}^\dagger$ is the Moore-Penrose generalised inverse [11] of the matrix $\boldsymbol{H}$.

The ELM training does not require iterations, so the most computationally costly part is the calculation of a pseudo-inverse of the matrix $\boldsymbol{H}$. This makes ELM an extremely fast Machine Learning method. Thus, we propose to use ELM to learn the distribution of the pairwise distances over non-Euclidean spaces $f_{\boldsymbol{z}^{(j)}}(t)$ or $F_{\boldsymbol{z}^{(j)}}(t)$.

7 Implementation Improvement

When implemented the mapping solution straightforwardly as in Sect. 5, the algorithm spends most of the CPU time on calculating the integral of $f_{\boldsymbol{z}^{(j)}}(t)$ over the distances $\boldsymbol{z}^{(j)}$ numerically as in Eq. 4. This consumes lots of computational time. This is because the number of the pairwise distances $\boldsymbol{z}^{(j)}$ is $N(N-1)/2$, which can obviously grow to a very large value when the data size N increases. Thus, we avoided the integration calculations by using machine leaning to learn the CDF $F_{\boldsymbol{z}^{(j)}}$, instead of learning the PDF $f_{\boldsymbol{z}^{(j)}}$ in A.4. This yields a function representation of $F_{\boldsymbol{z}^{(j)}}(t)$ (with the normalisation constant directly from $F_{\boldsymbol{z}^{(j)}}$). β can then be obtained straight from $F_{\boldsymbol{z}^{(j)}}(z)$.

The second most CPU consuming step in this algorithm is to find the most suitable described distribution of $f_{\boldsymbol{z}^{(i)}}(t)$ or $F_{\boldsymbol{z}^{(i)}}(t)$ in the Euclidean space $\mathcal{X}^{(i)}$. To choose whether the non-Euclidean distribution should best be mapped to a Normal, Uniform, Rayleigh, or other distribution, we have to fit the $F_{z^{(j)}}(t)$ to those well defined canonical Euclidean distances distributions and find the optimised parameters in the best suitable distribution with the least errors.

Again, if we use the pairwise distances $z^{(j)}$ in $F_{z^{(j)}}$ directly, the fitting computation is very heavy as we are trying to fit the data with $N(N-1)/2$ points. To make it easy, we use the functional representation of $F_{z^{(j)}}(t)$ with the user-defined distances in the pre-defined domain, with the purpose only to find the best distribution and its parameters (the functional presentation of $F_{z^{(i)}}(t)$). Then the mapped distance α can be obtained from Eq. 6 with the calculated β and the inverse functional representation of $F_{z^{(i)}}(t)$.

In the following Sect. 8, we present results over the typical data used for this work, GPS traces (latitude and longitude).

8   Experimental Results

We have tested the proposed mapping algorithm by mapping the pairwise distances in the dataset of GPS coordinates in the form of latitudes and longitudes, which is shown as the trajectory in Fig. 1. Assume we have a dataset $X = [x_1, ..., x_N]^T$ to depict the trajectory of one specific person, where the attributes of each record x_i explain the locations by latitude and longitude coordinates at the corresponding time t_i.

Note that the metric space of the GPS coordinates $\mathcal{X}^{(gps)} = (\mathbb{X}^{(gps)}, d^{(gps)})$ is a non-Euclidean space, because the distance $d^{(gps)}$ of two GPS coordinates (lat, lon) is the shortest route between the two points on the Earth's surface, namely, a segment of a great circle.

We first explore the limit condition on the number of records N in Eq. 2, in that N needs to be sufficiently large to possibly estimate $f_{z^{(j)}}$ (or $F_{z^{(j)}}$) to be close enough to $f_{z^{(i)}}$ (or $F_{z^{(i)}}$). We test on experimental datasets with various $N = 10, 30, 100, 1000$, within which each location record is randomly chosen along the introduced trajectory in Fig. 1.

Figure 2 illustrates the comparisons of the CDF $F_{z^{(j)}}(d)$ of the pairwise distances obtained from $\mathcal{X}^{(gps)} = (\mathbb{X}^{(gps)}, d^{(gps)})$, and the CDF $F_{z^{(i)}}(d)$ of the mapped distances in the Euclidean space, with $N = 10, 30, 100, 1000$ for the four subplots respectively.

It is clear to see that, in this specific simple case, with small N values of 10 and 30, there exists comparable disagreements of the CDF distributions between $\mathcal{X}^{(gps)}$ and the mapped Euclidean space. Meanwhile, with the larger N values of 100 and 1000, the limit condition on N is well satisfied, as it is plain to see that the non-Euclidean GPS metric $\mathcal{X}^{(gps)}$ behaves over its non-Euclidean space, accurately close to the mapped Euclidean metric over the mapped Euclidean space.

Thus, we can see that the number of record $N = 100$ is sufficient to closely estimate the distribution $f_{z^{(j)}}(d)$ to $f_{z^{(i)}}(d)$ in this very simple case. The Standard Errors (SE) of the mapped distribution $f_{z^{(i)}}$ are calculated, meanwhile selecting meticulously denser and broader N values from 5 to 5000, along the

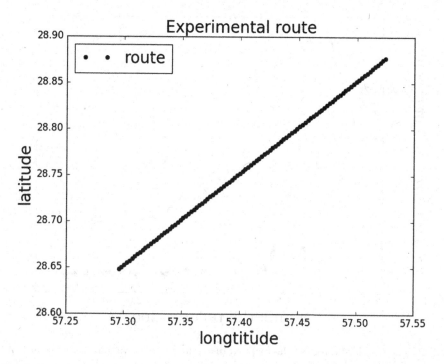

Fig. 1. Experimental dataset of locations in GPS coordinates with the form of latitudes and longitudes.

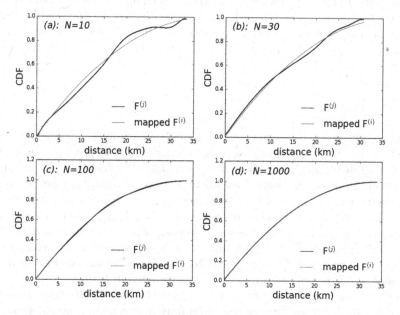

Fig. 2. The CDFs $F_{z^{(j)}}$ of the pairwise distances in the experimental dataset, and its corresponding mapped CDFs $F_{z^{(i)}}$, with $N = 10, 30, 100, 1000$.

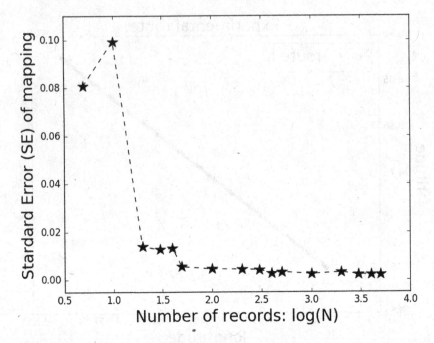

Fig. 3. The standard errors of the mapped distributions $F_{z(i)}$ vs. number of records n.

specific route. Figure 3 shows the SEs of the mapped distribution with the dependence on N. As the latitude and longitude coordinates are linearly altering in this simple case, the distances are mapped to a uniform distribution straightforwardly. The SE of the mapped $f_{z(i)}(d)$ converges closely to 0 at very small $N \simeq 50$.

9   Conclusion

We have developed and implemented a distance-mapping algorithm, which projects a non-Euclidean space to a canonical Euclidean space, in a way that the pairwise distances distributions are approximately preserved. The mapping algorithm is based on the assumptions that both spaces are actual metric spaces, and that the number of records N is large enough to estimate the pairwise distances $f_{z(j)}$ (or $F_{z(j)}$) to be close enough to $f_{z(i)}$ (or $F_{z(i)}$). We have tested our algorithm by illustrating the distance mapping of an experimental dataset of GPS coordinates. The limitation condition of N is discussed by the comparison of $F_{z(j)}$ and its mapped $F_{z(i)}$, using various N values. The standard errors of the mapped distance distribution $F_{z(i)}$ is also analyzed with various N.

Our distance mapping algorithm is performed with the most common canonical Euclidean distance distributions. Certainly, less common distributions are needed to be implemented as well, and might require specific adjustments. More diversified experimental examples are needed for completeness.

References

1. Auer, P., Burgsteiner, H., Maass, W.: A learning rule for very simple universal approximators consisting of a single layer of perceptrons. Neural Netw. **21**(5), 786–795 (2008)
2. Cambria, E., Huang, G.-B., Kasun, L.L.C., Zhou, H., Vong, C.M., Lin, J., Yin, J., Cai, Z., Liu, Q., Li, K., et al.: Extreme learning machines (trends & controversies). IEEE Intell. Syst. **28**(6), 30–59 (2013)
3. Cover, T.M.: Elements of Information Theory. Wiley, New York (1991)
4. Cybenko, G.: Approximation by superpositions of a sigmoidal function. Math. Control Signals Syst. (MCSS) **2**(4), 303–314 (1989)
5. Huang, G.-B., Chen, L., Siew, C.K., et al.: Universal approximation using incremental constructive feedforward networks with random hidden nodes. IEEE Trans. Neural Netw. **17**(4), 879–892 (2006)
6. Huang, G.-B., Zhu, Q.-Y., Siew, C.-K.: Extreme learning machine: theory and applications. Neurocomputing **70**(1), 489–501 (2006)
7. Kraskov, A., Stögbauer, H., Grassberger, P.: Estimating mutual information. Phys. Rev. E **69**(6), 066138 (2004)
8. Miche, Y., Sorjamaa, A., Bas, P., Simula, O., Jutten, C., Lendasse, A.: OP-ELM: optimally pruned extreme learning machine. IEEE Trans. Neural Netw. **21**(1), 158–162 (2010)
9. Miche, Y., Van Heeswijk, M., Bas, P., Simula, O., Lendasse, A.: TROP-ELM: a double-regularized ELM using LARS and tikhonov regularization. Neurocomputing **74**(16), 2413–2421 (2011)
10. Pál, D., Póczos, B., Szepesvári, C.: Estimation of rényi entropy and mutual information based on generalized nearest-neighbor graphs. In: Advances in Neural Information Processing Systems, pp. 1849–1857 (2010)
11. Rao, C.R., Mitra, S.K.: Generalized Inverse of Matrices and Its Applications. Wiley, New York (1971)
12. Van Heeswijk, M., Miche, Y., Oja, E., Lendasse, A.: Gpu-accelerated and parallelized ELM ensembles for large-scale regression. Neurocomputing **74**(16), 2430–2437 (2011)

Some Remarks on the Algebraic Properties of Group Invariant Operators in Persistent Homology

Patrizio Frosini$^{(\boxtimes)}$ and Nicola Quercioli

Department of Mathematics, University of Bologna, Bologna, Italy
patrizio.frosini@unibo.it, nicola.quercioli@studio.unibo.it

Abstract. Topological data analysis is a new approach to processing digital data, focusing on the fact that topological properties are quite important for efficient data comparison. In particular, persistent topology and homology are relevant mathematical tools in TDA, and their study is attracting more and more researchers. As a matter of fact, in many applications data can be represented by continuous real-valued functions defined on a topological space X, and persistent homology can be efficiently used to compare these data by describing the homological changes of the sub-level sets of those functions. However, persistent homology is invariant under the action of the group Homeo(X) of all self-homeomorphisms of X, while in many cases an invariance with respect to a proper subgroup G of Homeo(X) is preferable. Interestingly, it has been recently proved that this restricted invariance can be obtained by applying G-invariant non-expansive operators to the considered functions. As a consequence, in order to proceed along this line of research we need methods to build G-invariant non-expansive operators. According to this perspective, in this paper we prove some new results about the algebra of GINOs.

Keywords: Natural pseudo-distance · Filtering function · Group action · Group invariant non-expansive operator · Persistent homology group · Topological data analysis

1 Introduction

Topological data analysis (TDA) is an emerging research field that is revealing important in managing the deluge of data of the present digital world. The ability of describing and comparing how data are connected to each other in a topological sense is a key point for their efficient comparison [3]. Persistent topology and homology are relevant mathematical tools in TDA, and many researchers are investigating these concepts both from a theoretical and an applicative point of view [6]. Their approach is based on the fact that datasets can be often represented by real-valued continuous functions defined on a topological space X [2].

© IFIP International Federation for Information Processing 2017
Published by Springer International Publishing AG 2017. All Rights Reserved
A. Holzinger et al. (Eds.): CD-MAKE 2017, LNCS 10410, pp. 14–24, 2017.
DOI: 10.1007/978-3-319-66808-6_2

The theory of persistence analyzes the properties of these functions that "persist" in presence of noise. In particular, this analysis can be done by studying the evolution of the k-dimensional holes of the sub-level sets associated with those functions. This theory admits also an extension to the case of functions taking values in $\mathbb{R}^m$ (cf., e.g., [4,5]).

Recently, this line of research has been inserted in a theoretical framework that could be of use to establish a link between persistence theory and machine learning [10]. The main idea consists in looking at shape comparison as a problem concerning the approximation of a given observer instead of the approximation of data. In this setting each observer is seen as a collection of suitable operators acting on the family of functions that represents the set of possible data. These operators describe the way the information is elaborated by the observer, on the basis of the assumption that the observer is not entitled to choose the data but only the method to process them.

The operators we consider often refer to some kind of invariance. Invariance is an important property in shape analysis, and "approximating an observer" usually means to understand not only the way she/he looks at data, but also the equivalences she/he refers to in data comparison. For example, in character recognition the observer is interested in distinguishing the symbols 6 and 9, so that the invariance group should not contain rotations, while this is no more true if the observer is interested in comparing spiral shells.

In presence of an invariance group, the natural pseudo-metric can be used as a ground-truth for shape comparison. Let us consider a set Φ of continuous $\mathbb{R}$-valued functions defined on a topological space X and a subgroup G of the group $\mathrm{Homeo}(X)$ of all self-homeomorphisms of X. We assume that the group G acts on Φ by composition on the right. Now we can define the *natural pseudo-distance* d_G on Φ by setting $d_G(\varphi_1, \varphi_2) = \inf_{g \in G} \|\varphi_1 - \varphi_2 \circ g\|_\infty$, where $\|\cdot\|_\infty$ denotes the sup-norm. Roughly speaking, d_G is based on the attempt to find the best correspondence between two functions of Φ. If $d_G(\varphi_1, \varphi_2)$ is small, by definition there exists a homeomorphism $g \in G$ such that $\varphi_2 \circ g$ is a good approximation of φ_1 with respect to the sup-norm. If φ_1 and φ_2 describe the results of two measurements of X (e.g., two pictures, two CT scans, or two financial series), the fact that $d_G(\varphi_1, \varphi_2)$ is small means that the considered measurements can be aligned well by the reparameterization expressed by a suitable homeomorphism g.

Unfortunately, d_G is usually difficult to compute. However, one can approximate the natural pseudo-distance by means of persistent homology and G-invariant non-expansive operators (GINOs).

We recall that persistent homology describes the k-dimensional holes (components, tunnels, voids, ...) of the sub-level sets of a topological space X with respect to a given continuous function $\varphi : X \to \mathbb{R}^m$. If $m = 1$, persistent homology is described by suitable collections of points called *persistence diagrams* [8]. These diagrams can be compared by a suitable metric d_{match}, called *bottleneck* (or *matching*) *distance* (see the appendix of this paper).

It is known that if we compute the classical bottleneck distance between persistence diagrams associated with the functions $F(\varphi_1)$, $F(\varphi_2)$ and let F vary in the set of all G-invariant non-expansive operators on the space Φ, we obtain the same information given by the natural pseudo-distance d_G [11]. Therefore, the goal of approximating d_G naturally leads to the problem of approximating the space $\mathcal{F}(\Phi, G)$ of all G-invariant non-expansive operators on Φ. In [11] it has been proved that this space is compact, if we assume that Φ is compact. This guarantees that, in principle, $\mathcal{F}(\Phi, G)$ can be approximated by a finite subset.

In order to proceed along this line of research we need general methods to build G-invariant non-expansive operators. According to the goal of realizing those methods, this paper is devoted to prove some new results about the algebra of GINOs.

Our work is organized as follows. In Sect. 2 we introduce our mathematical setting. In Sect. 3 we give some new results about G-invariant non-expansive operators: in particular, we show how we can produce new GINOs by composition, translation, weighted average, maximization and, more in general, by means of a 1-Lipschitzian function applied to pre-existing GINOs. A short appendix about persistent homology concludes the paper.

2   Our Mathematical Model

Let X be a non-empty compact metric space, triangulated by a finite (and hence compact) simplicial complex. We suppose that the k-th homology group of X is nontrivial. For $k = 0$ the homology group always verifies the last assumption. Since X could be embedded in a larger (finitely) triangulable space Y_k with non-trivial homology in degree k, and substituted with Y_k, for $k \geq 1$ the condition is not restrictive. Let us consider a subspace Φ of the topological space $C^0(X, \mathbb{R})$ of all real-valued continuous functions from X, endowed with the topology induced by the sup-norm $\| \cdot \|_\infty$. Since X is compact, the considered functions are uniformly continuous. We suppose that Φ contains at least the constant functions taking every finite value c with $|c| \leq \sup_{\varphi \in \Phi} \|\varphi\|_\infty$. Each function in the space Φ will be called an *admissible filtering function on X*. The space Φ contains the functions that the observer considers as acceptable data. We also assume that a subgroup G of the group $\text{Homeo}(X)$ of all homeomorphisms from X onto X is given, and that if $\varphi \in \Phi$ and $g \in G$, then $\varphi \circ g \in \Phi$. In other words, the group G acts on Φ by composition on the right. We do not require G to be a proper subgroup of $\text{Homeo}(X)$, so that the equality $G = \text{Homeo}(X)$ may hold. One can easily show that G is a topological group with respect to the topology of the uniform convergence, and that the right action of G on the set Φ is continuous.

Definition 1. *Assume that a space $\Phi \subseteq C^0(X, \mathbb{R})$ and a group $G \subseteq \text{Homeo}(X)$ are given. Each function $F : \Phi \to \Phi$ is called a G-invariant Non-expansive Operator (GINO) for the pair (Φ, G), if:*

1. *F is G-invariant: $F(\varphi \circ g) = F(\varphi) \circ g$, $\forall \varphi \in \Phi$, $\forall g \in G$;*
2. *F is non-expansive: $\|F(\varphi_1) - F(\varphi_2)\|_\infty \leq \|\varphi_1 - \varphi_2\|_\infty$, $\forall \varphi_1, \varphi_2 \in \Phi$.*

If Φ is the space of all normalized grayscale images represented as functions from $\mathbb{R}^2$ to $[0,1]$ and G is the group of rigid motions of the plane, a simple example of operator $F \in \mathcal{F}(\Phi, G)$ is given by the Gaussian blurring filter, i.e. the operator F taking $\varphi \in \Phi$ to the function $\psi(x) = \frac{1}{2\pi\sigma^2} \int_{\mathbb{R}^2} \varphi(y) e^{-\frac{\|x-y\|^2}{2\sigma^2}} \, dy$ (see Fig. 1).

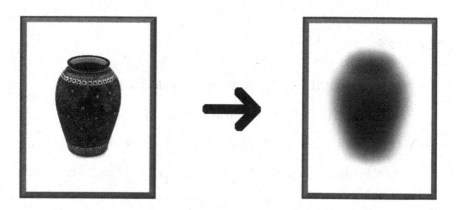

Fig. 1. The Gaussian blurring filter as an example of G-invariant non-expansive operator for G equal to the group of rigid motions of the plane.

For another approach to G-invariant persistent homology we refer the interested reader to [9].

3   Some New Results on Group Invariant Non-expansive Operators

In this section we will prove some new results about the algebra of GINOs, showing how new GINOs can be build by using pre-existing GINOs. The simplest one is based on functional composition.

Proposition 1. *If F_1, F_2 are GINOs for (Φ, G), then $F := F_2 \circ F_1$ is a GINO for (Φ, G).*

Proof. 1. Since F_1, F_2 are G-invariant, F is G-invariant:

$$F(\varphi \circ g) = (F_2 \circ F_1)(\varphi \circ g) = F_2(F_1(\varphi \circ g))$$
$$= F_2(F_1(\varphi) \circ g) = F_2(F_1(\varphi)) \circ g$$
$$= F(\varphi) \circ g$$

for every $\varphi \in \Phi$ and every $g \in G$.

2. Since F_1, F_2 are non-expansive, F is non-expansive:

$$\|F(\varphi_1) - F(\varphi_2)\|_\infty = \|(F_2 \circ F_1)(\varphi_1) - (F_2 \circ F_1)(\varphi_2)\|_\infty$$
$$= \|F_2(F_1(\varphi_1)) - F_2(F_1(\varphi_2))\|_\infty$$
$$\leq \|F_1(\varphi_1) - F_1(\varphi_2)\|_\infty$$
$$\leq \|\varphi_1 - \varphi_2\|_\infty$$

$\forall \varphi_1, \varphi_2 \in \Phi$.

$\square$

Let $F_1, \ldots, F_n$ be GINOs for (Φ, G). We can consider the function

$$\max(F_1, \ldots, F_n)(\varphi) := [\max(F_1(\varphi), \ldots, F_n(\varphi))]$$

from Φ to $C^0(X, \mathbb{R})$, where $[\max(F_1(\varphi), \ldots, F_n(\varphi))]$ is defined by setting

$$[\max(F_1(\varphi), \ldots, F_n(\varphi))](x) := \max(F_1(\varphi)(x), \ldots, F_n(\varphi)(x)).$$

Proposition 2. *Let $F_1, \ldots, F_n$ be GINOs for (Φ, G).*
If $\max(F_1, \ldots, F_n)(\Phi) \subseteq \Phi$, then $\max(F_1, \ldots, F_n)$ is a GINO for (Φ, G).

In order to proceed, we recall the proof of the following lemma (cf. [1]):

Lemma 1. *For every $u_1, \ldots, u_n, v_1, \ldots, v_n \in \mathbb{R}$ it holds that*

$$|\max(u_1, \ldots, u_n) - \max(v_1, \ldots, v_n)| \leq \max(|u_1 - v_1|, \ldots, |u_n - v_n|).$$

Proof. Without loss of generality we can suppose that $\max(u_1, \ldots, u_n) = u_1$. If $\max(v_1, \ldots, v_n) = v_1$ the claim trivially follows. It only remains to check the case $\max(v_1, \ldots, v_n) = v_i$, $i \neq 1$. We have that

$$\max(u_1, \ldots, u_n) - \max(v_1, \ldots, v_n) = u_1 - v_i$$
$$\leq u_1 - v_1$$
$$\leq |u_1 - v_1|$$
$$\leq \max(|u_1 - v_1|, \ldots, |u_n - v_n|).$$

Similarly, we obtain

$$\max(v_1, \ldots, v_n) - \max(u_1, \ldots, u_n) = v_i - u_1$$
$$\leq v_i - u_i$$
$$\leq |u_i - v_i|$$
$$\leq \max(|u_1 - v_1|, \ldots, |u_n - v_n|).$$

This proves the statement.

$\square$

Now we can prove the Proposition 2:

Proof. 1. Since $F_1, \ldots, F_n$ are G-invariant, $\max(F_1, \ldots, F_n)$ is G-invariant:

$$\begin{aligned}
\max(F_1, \ldots, F_n)(\varphi \circ g) &= [\max(F_1(\varphi \circ g), \ldots, F_n(\varphi \circ g)] \\
&= [\max(F_1(\varphi) \circ g, \ldots, F_n(\varphi) \circ g)] \\
&= [\max(F_1(\varphi), F_n(\varphi))] \circ g \\
&= \max(F_1, \ldots, F_n)(\varphi) \circ g
\end{aligned}$$

for every $\varphi \in \Phi$ and every $g \in G$.

2. Lemma 1 and non-expansivity of $F_1, \ldots, F_n$ imply that $\forall x \in X$ and $\forall \varphi_1, \varphi_2 \in \Phi$:

$$\begin{aligned}
&| \max(F_1(\varphi_1(x)), \ldots, F_n(\varphi_1(x))) - \max(F_1(\varphi_2(x)), \ldots, F_n(\varphi_2(x)))| \\
&\leq \max(|F_1(\varphi_1(x)) - F_1(\varphi_2(x))|, \ldots, |F_n(\varphi_1(x)) - F_n(\varphi_2(x))|) \\
&\leq \max(\|F_1(\varphi_1) - F_1(\varphi_2)\|_\infty, \ldots, \|F_n(\varphi_1) - F_n(\varphi_2)\|_\infty) \\
&\leq \max(\|\varphi_1 - \varphi_2\|_\infty, \|\varphi_1 - \varphi_2\|_\infty, \ldots, \|\varphi_1 - \varphi_2\|_\infty) \\
&= \|\varphi_1 - \varphi_2\|_\infty.
\end{aligned}$$

Since it holds for every $x \in X$, we obtain that $\| \max(F_1, \ldots, F_n)(\varphi_1) - \max(F_1, \ldots, F_n)(\varphi_2)\|_\infty \leq \|\varphi_1 - \varphi_2\|_\infty$. $\qquad \square$

Let F be a GINO for (Φ, G) and $b \in \mathbb{R}$. We can consider the function

$$F_b(\varphi) := F(\varphi) - b$$

from Φ to $C^0(X, \mathbb{R})$.

Proposition 3. *Assume that F is a GINO for (Φ, G) and $b \in \mathbb{R}$. If $F_b(\Phi) \subseteq \Phi$ then the operator F_b is a GINO for (Φ, G).*

Proof. 1. Since F is G-invariant, F_b is G-invariant too:

$$F_b(\varphi \circ g) = F(\varphi \circ g) - b = F(\varphi) \circ g - b = F_b(\varphi) \circ g$$

for every $\varphi \in \Phi$ and every $g \in G$.

2. Since F is non-expansive, F_b is non-expansive too:

$$\begin{aligned}
\|F_b(\varphi_1) - F_b(\varphi_2)\|_\infty &= \|F(\varphi_1) - b - (F(\varphi_2) - b)\|_\infty \\
&= \|F(\varphi_1) - F(\varphi_2)\|_\infty \\
&\leq \|\varphi_1 - \varphi_2\|_\infty
\end{aligned}$$

for every $\varphi_1, \varphi_2 \in \Phi$. $\qquad \square$

Let $F_1, \ldots, F_n$ be GINOs for (Φ, G) and $(a_1, \ldots, a_n) \in \mathbb{R}^n$ with $\sum_{i=1}^{n} |a_i| \leq 1$. We can consider the function

$$F_\Sigma(\varphi) := \sum_{i=1}^{n} a_i F_i(\varphi)$$

from Φ to $C^0(X, \mathbb{R})$.

Proposition 4. *Assume that $F_1, \ldots, F_n$ are GINOs for (Φ, G) and $(a_1, \ldots, a_n) \in \mathbb{R}^n$ with $\sum_{i=1}^{n} |a_i| \leq 1$. If $F_\Sigma(\Phi) \subseteq \Phi$, then F_Σ is a GINO for (Φ, G).*

Proof. 1. F_Σ is G-invariant, because $F_1, \ldots, F_n$ are G-invariant:

$$F_\Sigma(\varphi \circ g) = \sum_{i=1}^{n} a_i F_i(\varphi \circ g) = \sum_{i=1}^{n} a_i (F_i(\varphi) \circ g) = F_\Sigma(\varphi) \circ g$$

for every $\varphi \in \Phi$ and for every $g \in G$.

2. Since $F_1, \ldots, F_n$ are non-expansive and $\sum_{i=1}^{n} |a_i| \leq 1$, F_Σ is non-expansive:

$$\|F_\Sigma(\varphi_1) - F_\Sigma(\varphi_2)\|_\infty = \left\| \sum_{i=1}^{n} a_i F_i(\varphi_1) - \sum_{i=1}^{n} a_i F_i(\varphi_2) \right\|_\infty$$

$$= \left\| \sum_{i=1}^{n} a_i (F_i(\varphi_1) - F_i(\varphi_2)) \right\|_\infty$$

$$\leq \sum_{i=1}^{n} |a_i| \, \|(F_i(\varphi_1) - F_i(\varphi_2))\|_\infty$$

$$\leq \sum_{i=1}^{n} |a_i| \, \|\varphi_1 - \varphi_2\|_\infty \leq \|\varphi_1 - \varphi_2\|_\infty$$

for every $\varphi_1, \varphi_2 \in \Phi$.

$\square$

The last three results are generalized by the next one. Let $F_1, \ldots, F_n$ be GINOs for (Φ, G) and L be a 1-Lipschitzian map from $\mathbb{R}^n$ to $\mathbb{R}$, where $\mathbb{R}^n$ is endowed with the usual norm $\|(x_1, \ldots, x_n)\|_\infty = \max_{1 \leq i \leq n} |x_i|$. Now we consider the function

$$L^*(F_1, \ldots, F_n)(\varphi) := [L(F_1(\varphi), \ldots, F_n(\varphi))]$$

from Φ to $C^0(X, \mathbb{R})$, where $[L(F_1(\varphi), \ldots, F_n(\varphi))]$ is defined by setting

$$[L(F_1(\varphi), \ldots, F_n(\varphi))](x) := L(F_1(\varphi)(x), \ldots, F_n(\varphi)(x)).$$

Proposition 5. *Assume that $F_1, \ldots, F_n$ are GINOs for (Φ, G) and L is a 1-Lipschitzian map from $\mathbb{R}^n$ to $\mathbb{R}$. If $L^*(F_1, \ldots, F_n)(\Phi) \subseteq \Phi$, then $L^*(F_1, \ldots, F_n)$ is a GINO for (Φ, G).*

Proof. 1. The G-invariance of $F_1, \ldots, F_n$ implies that $L^*(F_1, \ldots, F_n)$ is G-invariant:

$$
\begin{aligned}
L^*(F_1, \ldots, F_n)(\varphi \circ g) &= [L(F_1(\varphi \circ g), \ldots, F_n(\varphi \circ g))] \\
&= [L(F_1(\varphi) \circ g, \ldots, F_n(\varphi) \circ g)] \\
&= [L(F_1(\varphi), \ldots, F_n(\varphi))] \circ g \\
&= L^*(F_1, \ldots, F_n)(\varphi) \circ g
\end{aligned}
$$

for every $\varphi \in \Phi$ and every $g \in G$.

2. Since $F_1, \ldots, F_n$ are non-expansive and L is 1-Lipschitzian, for every $x \in X$ and every $\varphi_1, \varphi_2 \in \Phi$ we have that

$$
\begin{aligned}
&|L(F_1(\varphi_1)(x), \ldots, F_n(\varphi_1)(x)) - L(F_1(\varphi_2)(x), \ldots, F_n(\varphi_2)(x))| \\
&\le \|(F_1(\varphi_1(x)) - F_1(\varphi_2(x)), \ldots, F_n(\varphi_1(x)) - F_n(\varphi_2(x)))\|_\infty \\
&= \max_{1 \le i \le n} |F_i(\varphi_1(x)) - F_i(\varphi_2(x))| \\
&\le \max_{1 \le i \le n} \|F_i(\varphi_1) - F_i(\varphi_2)\|_\infty \\
&\le \|\varphi_1 - \varphi_2\|_\infty.
\end{aligned}
$$

In conclusion,

$$
\|L^*(F_1, \ldots, F_n)(\varphi_1) - L^*(F_1, \ldots, F_n)(\varphi_2)\|_\infty \le \|\varphi_1 - \varphi_2\|_\infty.
$$

Therefore $L^*(F_1, \ldots, F_n)$ is non-expansive. $\square$

4   Conclusions

In this paper we have illustrated some new methods to build new G-invariant non-expansive operators from pre-existing ones. The ability of doing that is important to produce large sets of GINOs, in order to get good approximations of the topological space $\mathcal{F}(\Phi, G)$ and hence good approximations of the natural pseudo-distance d_G. The approximation of $\mathcal{F}(\Phi, G)$ can be seen as an approximation of the considered observer, represented as a collection of invariant operators.

In order to show the use of the approach based on GINOs, a simple demonstrator has been realized, illustrating how this technique could make available new methods for image comparison. The demonstrator is named GIPHOD–*G-Invariant Persistent HOmology Demonstrator* and is available at the web page http://giphod.ii.uj.edu.pl/index2/ (joint work with Grzegorz Jabłoński and Marc Ethier). The user is asked to choose an invariance group in a list and a query image in a dataset Φ^* of quite simple synthetic images obtained by adding a small number of bell-like functions (see Fig. 2). After that, GIPHOD provides ten images that are judged to be the most similar to the proposed query image with respect to the chosen invariance group (see Fig. 3). In this case study, the

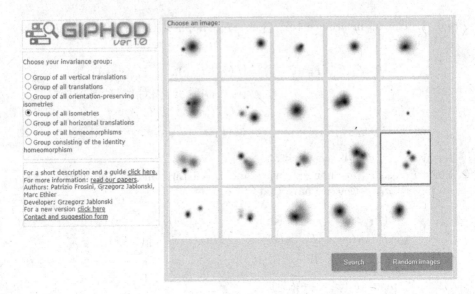

Fig. 2. GIPHOD asks the user to choose an invariance group in a list and a query image in a dataset.

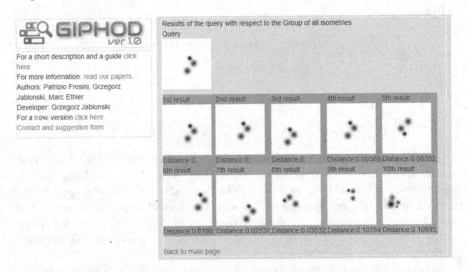

Fig. 3. GIPHOD provides ten images that are judged to be the most similar to the proposed query image with respect to the chosen invariance group.

dataset Φ^* is a subset of the set Φ of all continuous functions from the square $[0,1] \times [0,1]$ to the interval $[0,1]$. Each function represents a grayscale image on the square $[0,1] \times [0,1]$ (1=white, 0=black). GIPHOD uses a collection of GINOs for each invariance group G and tries to approximate d_G by means of the previously described technique, based on computing the persistent homology of the functions $F(\varphi)$ for $\varphi \in \Phi$ and F varying in our set of operators.

Many questions remain open. In particular, the extension of our approach to operators taking the pair (Φ, G) into a different pair (Ψ, H) should be studied. We are planning to do that in a forthcoming paper.

Acknowledgment. The research described in this article has been partially supported by GNSAGA-INdAM (Italy).

Appendix: Persistent Homology

We recall some basic definitions and facts in persistent homology. A more detailed and formal treatment can be found in [7]. In plain words, persistent homology describes the changes of the homology groups of the sub-level sets $X_t = \varphi^{-1}((-\infty, t])$ varying t in $\mathbb{R}$, for each real-valued continuous function $\varphi : X \to \mathbb{R}$. The parameter t can be seen as an increasing time, whose change produces the birth and death of k-dimensional holes in the sub-level set X_t. For $k = 0, 1, 2$, the expression "k-dimensional holes" refers to connected components, tunnels and voids, respectively.

The concept of persistence can be formalized by the definition of persistent homology group with respect to the function $\varphi : X \to \mathbb{R}$:

Definition 2. *If $u, v \in \mathbb{R}$ and $u < v$, we can consider the inclusion i of X_u into X_v. Such an inclusion induces a homomorphism $i_k : H_k(X_u) \to H_k(X_v)$ between the homology groups of X_u and X_v in degree k. The group $PH_k^\varphi(u, v) := i_k(H_k(X_u))$ is called the k-th persistent homology group with respect to the function $\varphi : X \to \mathbb{R}$, computed at the point (u, v). The rank $r_k(\varphi)(u, v)$ of this group is said the k-th persistent Betti number function with respect to the function $\varphi : X \to \mathbb{R}$, computed at the point (u, v).*

Remark 1. We can easily check that the persistent homology groups (and hence also the persistent Betti number functions) are invariant under the action of $\mathrm{Homeo}(X)$.

A classical way to represent persistent Betti number functions (up to subsets of measure zero of their domain) is given by multisets named *persistence diagrams*. The k-th persistence diagram is the multiset of all pairs $p_j = (b_j, d_j)$, where b_j and d_j are the times of birth and death of the j-th k-dimensional hole, respectively. When a hole never dies, we set its time of death equal to ∞. The multiplicity $m(p_j)$ says how many holes share both the time of birth b_j and the time of death d_j. For technical reasons, the points (t, t) are added to each persistence diagram, each one with infinite multiplicity.

Persistence diagrams can be compared by a metric δ_{match}, which is called *bottleneck distance* or *matching distance*. We recall here its formal definition, taking into account that each persistence diagram D can contain an infinite number of points, and that each point $p \in D$ has a multiplicity $m(p) \geq 1$.

For every $q \in \Delta^*$, the equality $m(q) = 0$ means that q does not belong to the persistence diagram D. In our exposition we set $\Delta := \{(x,y) \in \mathbb{R}^2 : x = y\}$, $\Delta^+ := \{(x,y) \in \mathbb{R}^2 : x < y\}$, $\bar{\Delta}^+ := \{(x,y) \in \mathbb{R}^2 : x \leq y\}$, $\Delta^* := \Delta^+ \cup \{(x,\infty) : x \in \mathbb{R}\}$ and $\bar{\Delta}^* := \bar{\Delta}^+ \cup \{(x,\infty) : x \in \mathbb{R}\}$. We endow $\bar{\Delta}^*$ with the pseudo-metric d^* defined by setting $d^*(p, p')$ equal to the minimum between the cost of moving p to p' and the cost of moving p and p' onto Δ, with respect to the max-norm. We observe that $d^*(p, p') = 0$ for every $p, p' \in \Delta$. If $p \in \Delta^+$ and $p \in \Delta$, then $d^*(p, p')$ equals the distance, induced by the max-norm, between p and Δ. Points at infinity have a finite distance only to other points at infinity, and their distance equals the Euclidean distance between their abscissas.

Definition 3. *Let D_1, D_2 be two persistence diagrams. We define the bottleneck distance δ_{match} between D_1 and D_2 by setting*

$$\delta_{match}(D_1, D_2) := \inf_{\sigma} \sup_{x \in D_1} d^*(x, \sigma(x))$$

where $\sigma : D_1 \to D_2$ is a bijection.

For further details about the concepts of persistence diagram and bottleneck distance, we refer the reader to [7].

References

1. Biasotti, S., Cerri, A., Frosini, P., Giorgi, D.: A new algorithm for computing the 2-dimensional matching distance between size functions. Pattern Recogn. Lett. **32**(14), 1735–1746 (2011)
2. Biasotti, S., De Floriani, L., Falcidieno, B., Frosini, P., Giorgi, D., Landi, C., Papaleo, L., Spagnuolo, M.: Describing shapes by geometrical-topological properties of real functions. ACM Comput. Surv. **40**(4), 12:1–12:87 (2008)
3. Carlsson, G.: Topology and data. Bull. Amer. Math. Soc. **46**(2), 255–308 (2009)
4. Carlsson, G., Zomorodian, A.: The theory of multidimensional persistence. Discrete Comput. Geom. **42**(1), 71–93 (2009)
5. Cerri, A., Di Fabio, B., Ferri, M., Frosini, P., Landi, C.: Betti numbers in multidimensional persistent homology are stable functions. Math. Meth. Appl. Sci. **36**, 1543–1557 (2013)
6. Edelsbrunner, H., Morozov, D.: Persistent homology: theory and practice. European Congress of Mathematics, pp. 31–50 (2013)
7. Edelsbrunner, H., Harer, J.L.: Persistent homology–a survey. Contemp. Math. **453**, 257–282 (2008)
8. Edelsbrunner, H., Harer, J.L.: Computational Topology. An Introduction. American Mathematical Society, Providence (2010)
9. Frosini, P.: G-invariant persistent homology. Math. Meth. Appl. Sci. **38**(6), 1190–1199 (2015)
10. Frosini, P.: Towards an observer-oriented theory of shape comparison. In: Ferreira, A., Giachetti, A., Giorgi, D. (eds.) Proceedings of the 8th Eurographics Workshop on 3D Object Retrieval, Lisbon, Portugal, pp. 5–8 (2016)
11. Frosini, P., Jabłoński, G.: Combining persistent homology and invariance groups for shape comparison. Discrete Comput. Geom. **55**(2), 373–409 (2016)

Decentralized Computation of Homology in Wireless Sensor Networks Using Spanning Trees

Domen Šoberl[1(✉)], Neža Mramor Kosta[1], and Primož Škraba[2]

[1] Faculty of Computer and Information Science, University of Ljubljana,
Večna pot 113, SI-1000, Ljubljana, Slovenia
{domen.soberl,neza.mramor-kosta}@fri.uni-lj.si
[2] Jožef Stefan Institute, Jamova Cesta 39, SI-1000, Ljubljana, Slovenia
primoz.skraba@ijs.si

Abstract. When deploying a wireless sensor network over an area of interest, the information on signal coverage is critical. It has been shown that even when geometric position and orientation of individual nodes is not known, useful information on coverage can still be deduced based on connectivity data. In recent years, homological criteria have been introduced to verify complete signal coverage, given only the network communication graph. However, their algorithmic implementation has been limited due to high computational complexity of centralized algorithms, and high demand for communication in decentralized solutions, where a network employs the processing power of its nodes to check the coverage autonomously. To mitigate these problems, known approaches impose certain limitations on network topologies. In this paper, we propose a novel distributed algorithm which uses spanning trees to verify homology-based network coverage criteria, and works for arbitrary network topologies. We demonstrate that its communication demands are suitable even for low-bandwidth wireless sensor networks.

Keywords: Wireless sensor networks · Coverage problem · Simplicial homology · Computational homology · Rips complex

1 Introduction

Wireless sensor networks (WSN) have in recent years become well-established ad-hoc networks with numerous applications in environmental and health care monitoring. Distributed nature of WSNs, random node deployment and frequent topology changes challenge the researchers to design special data mining techniques, suitable for WSNs [1]. Small sensing nodes, scattered over an area of interest, typically sample the domain in a point cloud fashion, making possible the use of computational geometry and algebraic topology to extract knowledge from the collected data [2]. An active field of research in WSN has been the

Published by Springer International Publishing AG 2017. All Rights Reserved
A. Holzinger et al. (Eds.): CD-MAKE 2017, LNCS 10410, pp. 25–40, 2017.
DOI: 10.1007/978-3-319-66808-6_3

problem of coverage [3], which is usually interpreted as how well a WSN monitors its area of interest. Substantial research has been done on how to assure coverage in WSN by manually deploying nodes [4–6]. In many cases, manual positioning is highly impractical or not possible at all, therefore a number of coverage verification methods had been introduced. Some of them employ geometric constructs based on Voronoi diagrams or Delaunay triangulation, and so rely on the geometric location of nodes [7–11]. Detecting geometric position is a difficult problem, requiring additional hardware such as GPS, which might not always be feasible (e.g. GPS does not work indoors). Other methods tend to verify coverage using relative node positions or angles between them [12–14]. These techniques rely on strengths of received signals and timing differentials.

Simple network devices mostly lack the ability to obtain their geometric layout. To provide a coverage verification feature for such low-cost networks, connectivity based solutions are required. We base our work on the work of Ghrist et al. [15–18], who introduced an innovative approach based on algebraic topology. They showed that under certain conditions regarding the ratio between the sensing range and the communication range of nodes in a WSN, a connection-based combinatorial construction called the *Rips complex* (also known as the Vietoris-Rips complex), captures certain information on sensing coverage. More precisely, the criterion derived from homological properties of the Rips complex states that a hole-free Rips complex over a WSN assures complete sensing coverage. Soon, decentralized implementations were proposed [19,20] which rely on distributed processing and storage of large matrices. Such algorithms impose a heavy communication load on the network to the extent, that their use for practical purposes is questionable. To mitigate this problem, partitioning of large networks using *divide-and-conquer* method has been proposed [21–24]. This led to more pragmatic approaches of coverage verification where holes in the Rips complex are detected by local message flooding or systematic network reduction [25,26]. To the best of our knowledge, all known algorithms assume certain topological limitations, most notably the demand for a circular *fence* made of specially designated and configured nodes.

In this paper, we propose a novel distributed algorithm for homological coverage verification that imposes no limitations on network topology and demands no special nodes to be designated and configured further, they are based on a common network structure, namely the *spanning tree*. We simulate the algorithm on networks of different sizes and demonstrate a low demand for data exchange, which should easily be handled even by low-bandwidth networks. The rest of the paper is organized as follows: in Sect. 2 we cover the basics of homological coverage verification in wireless sensor networks. In Sect. 3 we give a detailed description our algorithm. We then present the results of simulations in Sect. 4, and give our our final conclusions in Sect. 5.

2   Homological Coverage Criteria

We model a wireless sensor network as a collection of nodes scattered over a plane, each performing environmental measurements within the sensing radius

r_s, and communicating with other nodes within the the communication radius r_c. We define wireless sensor network as a triple $N = (V, r_s, r_c)$, where $V = \{v_1, \dots, v_k\}, k \geq 2$, is a set of planar points representing nodes. We adopt the following WSN properties from [18]:

P1. Nodes V lie in a compact connected domain $\mathcal{D} \subset \mathbb{R}^2$.
P2. Every node has its unique ID number which can be broadcast to all nodes within its communication radius r_c.
P3. The sensing and communication radii satisfy the condition $r_s \geq r_c/\sqrt{3}$.

To optimize the performance, the power of transmission should be adjusted close to $r_c = \sqrt{3} \cdot r_s$. Two nodes within the range r_c can communicate to each other, forming a link within the communication graph $\mathcal{G}_N = (V, E), E = \{(u, v) \in V \times V | u \neq v, d(u, v) \leq r_c\}$. The domain of interest is defined implicitly as the area spanned by connectivity graph $\mathcal{G}_N$ (see Fig. 1). The connectivity graph may assume arbitrary topology. In the case a network splits into disconnected sub-networks, the algorithm computes the coverage of each network independently.

Definition 1 (network domain). *Domain $\mathcal{D} \subset \mathbb{R}^2$ of network $N = (V, r_s, r_c)$ is the smallest contractible set which contains all line segments $\overline{uv}$, where $u, v \in V$, and $d(u, v) \leq r_c$.*

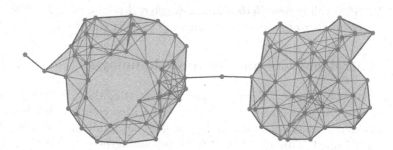

Fig. 1. Domain $\mathcal{D}$ assumes arbitrary topology. The failing of a node may split the coverage verification process into two independent tasks.

Each node covers a disk-shaped part of the domain within its sensing range r_s. We want to verify whether every point of domain $\mathcal{D}$ is within the sensing reach of at least one node.

Definition 2 (domain coverage). *Let $\mathcal{D}$ be the domain of network $N = (V, r_s, r_c)$. Domain $\mathcal{D}$ is covered if $\mathcal{D} \subseteq \bigcup_{v \in V} D_v$, where*

$$D_v = \{t \in \mathbb{R}^2 | d(v, t) \leq r_s\}. \tag{1}$$

Given a finite set of nodes V, a subset $\sigma = \{v_0, v_1, \ldots, v_k\} \subseteq V$ is called a *simplex*. Every subset $\tau \subset \sigma$ is also a simplex, called *face* of σ. A *simplicial complex* over V is a collection K of simplices with vertices in V, such that the faces of every $\sigma \in K$ are also contained in K (see [27,28]). We consider two types of simplicial complexes over V. One is the *Čech complex* $\check{C}(V) = \{\sigma \subseteq V | \bigcap_{v \in \sigma} D_v \neq \emptyset\}$, where D_v is as in (1). It has been shown that the Čech complex fully captures the homology of its underlying geometric shape [29]. This means that every hole in the coverage of network domain corresponds to a hole in $\check{C}(V)$. Unfortunately, the Čech complex is not computable by our WSN since geometric information is needed, as evident from (1). The second simplicial complex we consider is the *Rips complex* $\mathcal{R}(\mathcal{G}_N) = \{\sigma \subseteq V | \forall \{u, v\} \subseteq \sigma : (u, v) \in \mathcal{G}_N\}$, which is built on connectivity information. As shown in [26], under assumption **P3**, there are no holes in $\check{C}(V)$ if there are no holes in $\mathcal{R}(\mathcal{G}_N)$. The absence of holes in the Rips complex therefore guarantees the coverage of domain $\mathcal{D}$.

Simplicial homology provides a convenient way to describe *holes* of a simplicial complex K. Take a sequence of links in K, such that they form a cycle c. If a set of triangles can be found in K, such that the border of their union is exactly the cycle c, then c does not encircle a hole. On the other hand, if such a set of triangles does not exist, c can be taken as a representative of the hole (or the sum of holes) around which it is wrapped. Cycles representing the same set of holes are called *homologous* cycles, and are considered homologically identical. These cycles form the *first homology group* of K, denoted $H_1(K)$. The rank of $H_1(K)$ is called *first Betti number*, denoted $\beta_1(K) = \mathrm{rank}(H_1(K))$, and represents the number of holes in K. Domain $\mathcal{D}$ is covered if $\beta_1(\mathcal{R}(\mathcal{G}_N)) = 0$.

3   Decentralized Computation of Homology

In this section, we propose a novel approach to computing the first Betti number of the network's Rips complex. We construct the Rips complex distributively by merging smaller network segments into larger ones, until the complete Rips complex is obtained. This way, the parallel processing power of WSN can be exploited, requiring only local communication between nodes. We begin with the smallest segments which are hole-free, and if by merging two segments a hole is constructed, it is detected and considered only once. The process takes place in the direction of a precomputed spanning tree, from the leaves to the root. The final result is stored distributively, with each node holding the number of holes it discovered, and the global Betti number is obtained by simple summation of the local values up the tree.

The initial set of network segments is the set of all *closed stars* of nodes in $\mathcal{R}(\mathcal{G}_N)$. The *star* of node v, denoted $\mathrm{St}(v)$, is the set of all simplices that contain v, and is generally not a simplicial complex. The *closure* $\overline{S}$ of a set of simplices S is the smallest simplicial subcomplex of $\mathcal{R}(\mathcal{G}_N)$ that contains all simplices from S. The closure $\overline{\mathrm{St}}(v)$, called the *closed star* of v, is therefore the set of all simplices that contain v, together with all their faces, that is $\overline{\mathrm{St}}(v) = \{\tau \leq \sigma | v \in \sigma, \sigma \in \mathcal{R}(\mathcal{G}_N)\}$. Initially, every node constructs its own closed star by examining its local

2-hop neighborhood. This is done in two steps. First, every node broadcasts its ID to all its immediate neighbors. After nodes collect their list of neighbors, lists are then broadcast in the second step. The precomputed spanning tree needs not be minimal for the algorithm to work correctly, but a minimal spanning tree improves performance. Distributed algorithms for constructing a minimal spanning tree are well-established (e.g. [30]).

3.1   Network Segmentation and Merging

At any time during the execution of our algorithm, the network is partitioned into segments, which merge into larger segments, until finally, all parts of the network are merged into the complete Rips complex. Two segments can be merged only if their intersection is non-empty, assuring that every segment is connected.

Definition 3 (network segment). *Let $N = (V, r_s, r_c)$ be a wireless sensor network and $U \subseteq V$ such a subset of its nodes, that the simplicial complex $S = \bigcup_{u_i \in U} \overline{St}(u_i) \subseteq \mathcal{R}(\mathcal{G}_N)$ is connected. We call the complex S, a segment of network N.*

The process of merging begins with the set of closed stars as the smallest simplicial complexes, which are small enough to not allow any holes. Each node merges its star with the segments received from their children within the spanning tree. To describe the process of merging, we arbitrarily assign indices to segments that are being merged within a single node v. We shall call such ordered set of segments a sequence of segments and write $\{S_1, S_2, \ldots, S_n\}$.

Definition 4 (segment merging). *A sequence of segments $z = \{S_1, S_2, \ldots, S_n\}$ is mergeable if for every $1 \geq k < n$ holds $(S_1 \cup \cdots \cup S_k) \cap S_{k+1} \neq \emptyset$. Segment merging is the operation that maps a mergeable sequence $\{S_1, S_2, \ldots, S_n\}$ to simplicial complex $S = S_1 \cup S_2 \cup \cdots \cup S_n$.*

In a spanning tree, the distance between a node v and its children is one hop, therefore all segments received by v have a non-empty intersection with $\overline{St}(v)$. The order of merging can therefore be arbitrary if it begins with $\overline{St}(v)$.

3.2   Computing Betti Numbers

Each node captures the number of holes generated by merging smaller segments into larger ones. The information on holes is then discarded and the merged segment forwarded to the parent node as a hole-free segment. This assures that the holes discovered by one node are not discovered again later in the process. We say that a node computes the *local first Betti number*, so that the summation of all local Betti numbers gives $\beta_1(\mathcal{R}(\mathcal{G}_N))$. In this section, we propose an algorithm to capture the number of locally generated holes. We begin with the following proposition which we prove with the help of the Mayer-Vietoris sequence (see [27–29]).

Proposition 1. *Let A and B be network segments with nonempty intersection and trivial first homology group, that is $\tilde{H}_1(A) \cong \tilde{H}_1(B) = 0$, where $\tilde{H}$ denotes the reduced homology. Then there exists isomorphism*

$$\tilde{H}_1(A \cup B) \cong \tilde{H}_0(A \cap B). \tag{2}$$

Proof. Since A and B are network segments, they are by definition connected simplicial complexes, thus $\tilde{H}_0(A) \cong \tilde{H}_0(B) \cong 0$. The right tail of the reduced Mayer-Vietoris sequence of the triple $(A \cup B, A, B)$ is:

$$\underbrace{\tilde{H}_1(A) \oplus \tilde{H}_1(B)}_{\cong 0} \overset{\phi}{\longrightarrow} \tilde{H}_1(A \cup B) \overset{\partial}{\longrightarrow} \tilde{H}_0(A \cap B) \overset{\psi}{\longrightarrow} \underbrace{\tilde{H}_0(A) \oplus \tilde{H}_0(B)}_{\cong 0}.$$

Obviously, $\operatorname{im} \phi = 0$ and $\ker \psi = \tilde{H}_0(A \cap B)$. *Exactness* of the sequence implies $\ker \partial = 0$ and $\operatorname{im} \partial = \tilde{H}_0(A \cap B)$, and hence ∂ is an isomorphism. □

In other words, if we merge two segments which are free of holes, there is a correspondence between the holes in the union and the number of disjoint components in their intersection. This yields the following corollary.

Corollary 1. *Let A and B be network segments with nonempty intersection and $\beta_1(A) = \beta_1(B) = 0$. If $\#$ denotes the number of disjoint components of the simplicial complex, that is $\#K = \beta_0(K) = \tilde{\beta}_0(K) + 1$, then:*

$$\beta_1(A \cup B) = \#(A \cap B) - 1. \tag{3}$$

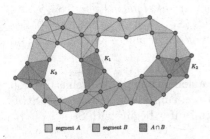

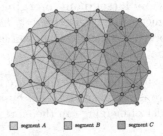

Fig. 2. Holes are formed by merging two segments.

Fig. 3. A false hole can be formed by segments A and C.

When merging two segments, the above rule is used to count the number of holes in their union, as demonstrated in Fig. 2: The intersection of segments A and B consists of three components, namely K_0, K_1 and K_2, and their union contains two holes. Usually, more than two segments are being merged within a single node, therefore in the remainder of this section we consider extending this rule to an arbitrary mergeable sequence of segments. We address the following three problems:

1. When a hole is formed by merging two segments, the produced union is not a hole-free segment. In Sect. 3.3 we show that if such a segment is merged again higher in the spanning tree, the rule from Corollary 1 on counting the holes still applies.
2. The order in which segments are merged can produce fake holes, which are filled later in the process by succeeding segments (see Fig. 3). In Sect. 3.4 we show how such fake holes can be detected and excluded from computation of local Betti numbers.
3. Branches of the spanning tree may intersect, therefore a node is not guaranteed to receive the full information on segments local to its branch. In Sect. 3.5, we show that a node can detect the lack of such information. In such cases merging is done only partially, and instead of a single segment, a set of unmerged segments is forwarded to the parent node. Segments are then merged at the higher level, where the missing information becomes available. Our simulations show that in practice such scenarios occur infrequently.

3.3 Merging Within a Spanning Tree

We divide every network segment into two regions - the *core* and the *frame*. The core can be seen as the internal part of the segment where holes, if they exist, reside. The frame can be seen as the outer layer, where segments intersect when merged up the spanning tree.

Definition 5 (core and frame). *Let* $S = \bigcup_{v \in M} \overline{\mathrm{St}}(v)$ *be a network segment. We call the smallest simplicial complex that contains all nodes* $v \in M$, *the* core *of segment* S, *and denote* $\mathcal{C}(S)$. *We call the closure of its complement* $\overline{S \backslash \mathcal{C}(S)}$, *the* frame *of segment* S, *and denote* $\mathcal{F}(S)$.

Recall that the closure $\overline{S}$ of a collection of simplices S is defined as the smallest simplicial complex that contains all simplices from S. The smallest segment core is the singleton $\{v\}$ within a closed star $\overline{\mathrm{St}}(v)$. As two stars, $\overline{\mathrm{St}}(v)$ and $\overline{\mathrm{St}}(u)$, are being merged, new segment $\overline{\mathrm{St}}(v) \cup \overline{\mathrm{St}}(u)$ is formed, its core now containing u and v, while both stars cease to exist as separate network segments. Proceeding with the process up the spanning tree, each produced network segment is the union of closed stars that belong to a certain tree branch, and its core comprised of the nodes within that branch. At any time, each node belongs to the core of exactly one recorded network segment. This guarantees $\mathcal{C}(A) \cap \mathcal{C}(B) = \emptyset$ for any two segments A and B.

Proposition 2. *Let* A *and* B *be mergeable network segments, such that* $\mathcal{C}(A) \cap \mathcal{C}(B) = \emptyset$. *Then*

$$A \cap B = \mathcal{F}(A) \cap \mathcal{F}(B). \tag{4}$$

Proof. First, let us show that $\mathcal{F}(A) \cap \mathcal{C}(B) \subseteq \mathcal{F}(A) \cap \mathcal{F}(B)$. We will do this by proving (i) $\mathcal{F}(A) \cap \mathcal{C}(B) \subseteq \mathcal{F}(A)$, and (ii) $\mathcal{F}(A) \cap \mathcal{C}(B) \subseteq \mathcal{F}(B)$. Statement (i) is obvious. To prove (ii) suppose there exists a $v \in \mathcal{F}(A) \cap \mathcal{C}(B)$, such that

$v \notin \mathcal{F}(B)$. Since v is not in $\mathcal{F}(B)$, all its neighbors must also be in $\mathcal{C}(B)$. Recall that segments are composed of closed stars of their core nodes. Since $v \in A$, at least one of its neighbors has to be in $\mathcal{C}(A)$. This contradicts $\mathcal{C}(A) \cap \mathcal{C}(B) = \emptyset$, therefore $v \in \mathcal{F}(B)$. So we have proven (ii). In the same way we show that $\mathcal{F}(B) \cap \mathcal{C}(A) \subseteq \mathcal{F}(B) \cap \mathcal{F}(A)$. Finally, we deduce:

$$
\begin{aligned}
A \cap B &= (\mathcal{C}(A) \cup \mathcal{F}(A)) \cap (\mathcal{C}(B) \cup \mathcal{F}(B)) \\
&= \underbrace{(\mathcal{C}(A) \cap \mathcal{C}(B))}_{=\emptyset} \cup \underbrace{(\mathcal{F}(A) \cap \mathcal{C}(B))}_{\subseteq \mathcal{F}(A) \cap \mathcal{F}(B)} \cup \underbrace{(\mathcal{C}(A) \cap \mathcal{F}(B))}_{\subseteq \mathcal{F}(A) \cap \mathcal{F}(B)} \cup (\mathcal{F}(A) \cap \mathcal{F}(B)) \\
&= \mathcal{F}(A) \cap \mathcal{F}(B)
\end{aligned}
$$

$\square$

To obtain the intersection of two segments, only the intersection of their frames is required. This significantly lowers the amount of data needed to represent a segment within the network, since only their frames need to be forwarded from children to parent nodes. Intersected components are used as the basis to compute the local Betti number (3), after which they are discarded, as they join the core of the produced segment. Information on the discovered hole is lost, so the same hole cannot be discovered again higher in the tree.

3.4   Merging Multiple Segments

Consider a sequence of mergeable segments $z : \{S_1, S_2, \ldots, S_n\}$ being merged at some node in the spanning tree. As seen from example in Fig. 3, temporary holes can be produced by an unfortunate ordering of segments. We propose the following equation to compute the local first Betti number when merging multiple segments:

$$
\beta_1(z) = \sum_{k=1}^{n-1} \left(b_1^k(z) - \delta_1^k(z) \right). \tag{5}
$$

where

$$
b_1^k(z) = \# \left(\bigcup_{i=1}^{k} S_i \right) \cap S_{k+1} - 1, \tag{6}
$$

and $\delta_1^k(z)$ is the function that returns the number of false holes produced by $b_1^k(z)$. Note that (6) is the rule from Corollary 1, applied at the k-th step of merging the sequence z. Here we discuss how to implement function δ_1 algorithmically.

Consider the operation of merging two segments A and B, as shown in Fig. 2. Each hole can be represented as a pair of distinct components $\{K_i, K_j\} \in \mathcal{K}$, for instance, one hole can be represented by $\{K_0, K_1\}$ and the other by $\{K_1, K_2\}$. These two pairs represent a possible choice of generators for group $H_1(\mathcal{R}(\mathcal{G}_N))$. When such a pair represents a false hole, it must be removed from the set of possible generators. This is done by connecting both components, which results in lowering the rank of the group $H_1(\mathcal{R}(\mathcal{G}_N))$ by 1. Say we detect $\{K_0, K_1\}$ as a false hole. We connect $K_{01} = K_0 + K_1$ and end up with only one choice of group generators, which is $\{K_{01}, K_2\}$.

Suppose a node merges a sequence of segments and computes $\beta_1(z)$ by (5). Denote by A, B, and C three segments to be merged in that particular order. Suppose segments A and B form two holes, one of which is being covered by C, as shown in Fig. 4. To check the hole represented by $\{K_0, K_1\}$, we consider the following four sets:

$$M_a = A \cap C, \qquad M_b = B \cap C,$$
$$k_0 = K_0 \cap C, \qquad k_1 = K_1 \cap C. \tag{7}$$

Recall that all segments intersect at their *frames*, therefore the information needed to compute the above intersections is available at the node. We are interested whether C spans over the hole g. This is true if and only if a path from k_0 to k_1 exists through M_a and separately through M_b. Both paths are verified by the standard flooding algorithm. If both paths exist, hole g is a false hole. Note that we are not interested, neither possess the information on possible holes within C, for they have been treated and recorded elsewhere.

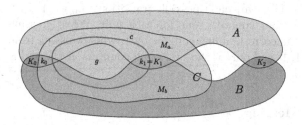

Fig. 4. The false hole of $A \cup B$ is covered by segment C.

Now consider the case of four or more segments, for instance a sequence $z : \{A, B, C, D\}$, where A and B are being merged, and the discovered hole g needs to be checked with C and D. This differs from the scenario of three segments in the fact, that we have to account for possible holes constructed by the union of C and D. The algorithm is the following:

1. Use the previous algorithm to check g with C and D separately. Continue only if g was not eliminated.
2. Construct the union $S = C \cup D$ and check g with S. If S contains holes, continue.
3. Let h be a hole in S, represented by disjoint components $\{L_0, L_1\}$ as shown in Fig. 5. Determine the scenario (a) or (b). Cycle c was constructed in the previous step. If scenario (a), g is a fake hole. If scenario (b), continue.
4. Elements g and h are homologous. Hole g is false if and only if hole h is false. If more than four segments, test hole h recursively with the remaining segments, e.g. $E, F, G, \ldots$

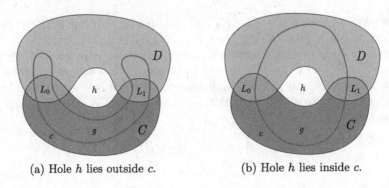

(a) Hole h lies outside c.   (b) Hole h lies inside c.

Fig. 5. Testing hole g against union $C \cup D$.

The problem is now reduced by one element. We repeat the process on sequence $z_1 : \{(A \cup B), C, D, \ldots\}$ until all segments are merged.

In step 3 of the above algorithm, scenario (a) or (b) from Fig. 5 must be determined. We do this in the following way. Pick a node inside L_0 and travel from there around the cycle c once, observing the transitions between regions A, B, L_0 and L_2. There are eight possible transitions: $L_0 \leftrightarrow A$, $L_0 \leftrightarrow B$, $L_1 \leftrightarrow A$, $L_1 \leftrightarrow B$. Define four counters, one for each pair. When crossing from left to right, increase the corresponding counter by 1, when crossing from right to left, decrease it by 1. If and only if the sum of all counters at the end is nonzero, the hole h lies inside the cycle c.

3.5   Partial Merging

In the preceding section we assumed that the sequence $z : \{A, B, C, D, \ldots\}$ contained all segments which are needed to verify hole g. This assumption held in the vast majority of our simulations. However, there were some cases where crucial information was sent to a different branch of the tree. A node must be able to detect such a case and postpone a critical merging, until the missing segment is received higher in the tree. It can, nevertheless, still merge non-critical segments. It comes down to the question whether a hole that appears to be true according to the locally available information, is actually a hole in $\mathcal{R}(\mathcal{G}_N)$. The following proposition states the criteria by which the lack of information can be verified.

Proposition 3. *Let $\{S_1, \ldots, S_n\}$ be a mergeable sequence of locally available network segments. Denote $S = S_1 \cup \cdots \cup S_n$. If for every mergeable pair $\{S_i, S_j\}$ holds:*

$$\forall \{v\} \in S_i \cap S_j : \{v\} \in \mathcal{C}(S), \tag{8}$$

then every cycle $c \in H_1(S)$ which is not a border is also not a border in $H_1(\mathcal{R}(\mathcal{G}_N))$. Or in other words, every true hole in S is also a hole in $\mathcal{R}(\mathcal{G}_N)$.

Proof. We prove the proposition by contradiction. Suppose a cycle c is nontrivial in $H_1(S)$ and trivial in $H_1(\mathcal{R}(\mathcal{G}_N))$, and (8) holds. Without loss of generality suppose the hole, represented by c, was constructed by merging segments S_i and S_j, as depicted in Fig. 6. Because c is trivial in $H_1(\mathcal{R}(\mathcal{G}_N))$, a disk $D \subset H_1(\mathcal{R}(\mathcal{G}_N))$ exists, such that $\partial D \cong c$. Consider now all nodes $v_i \in c$ and their closed stars $\overline{\mathrm{St}}(v_i)$. Obviously, every such star contains at least one node in D and is therefore not fully contained in S. Nodes v_i are therefore not contained in the core $\mathcal{C}(S)$. Circle c is contained in S_i and S_j, so a node v_0 on c exists which is also in the intersection $S_i \cap S_j$. We have thus proven the existence of $\{v_0\} \in S_i \cap S_j$, $\{v_0\} \notin \mathcal{C}(S)$, which contradicts (8).   □

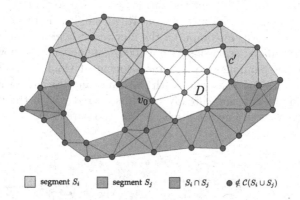

Fig. 6. The structure of $\mathcal{C}(S)$ carries information about the missing D.

Suppose a node v receives segments $S_1 \cup \cdots \cup S_n$ from its subtree. To use the above property, the core of segment $S = S_1 \cup \cdots \cup S_n$ needs to be known, or more precisely, its nodes. Withing a spanning tree, the set of core nodes at v is exactly the set of all descendants of v, which can easily be obtained by child − parent communication. Recall that each hole g which appears by merging $S = S_i \cup S_j$ is represented by a pair $\{K_i, K_j\}$ of disjoint components $K_i, K_j \subset S_i \cap S_j$. If all nodes of K_i and K_j belong to $\mathcal{C}(S)$, node v possesses enough information to verify it. Otherwise S_i and S_j are forwarded to the parent node unmerged.

4   Results

We tested the algorithm in a simulated environment using a single processor system. To simulate the parallel computing feature of wireless sensor network, we ran each node in a separate thread, and used inter-thread communication to simulate wireless communication channels. The goals of simulations were the following:

1. To asses computational complexity on a parallel system.
2. To estimate the communication burden of algorithm on a WSN.
3. To measure the computational and communicational burden distribution between the nodes.
4. To measure the frequency of partial merging.

We ran the algorithm on 1000 randomly generated networks, grouped in 10 classes by size. The i-th class contained 100 networks of size $100 \cdot i$ nodes. We kept the density of nodes constant for all classes at an average of 8.9 neighbors per node with standard deviation of 0.3. Holes were formed by restricting node deployment at random parts of the domain. To verify the correctness of the algorithm, we compared the output of each simulation with the actual number of holes in the coverage. We kept the ratio $r_c/r_s = \sqrt{3}$ so that the holes in the coverage exactly matched the holes in the Rips complex. It turned out that in all 1000 cases the algorithm computed the number of holes correctly.

   One of our simulated scenarios with a 1000-node network is shown In Fig. 7. Arrows depict the spanning tree. A large segment at the first level of the tree can be seen (root resides at level 0), with the frame and the core visibly distinct. The hole within the core has already been discovered within this tree branch. The three holes at the frame are discovered by the parent.

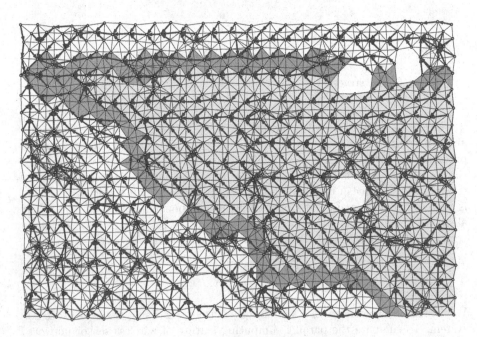

Fig. 7. Simulation with a 1000-node network.

   To asses computational time complexity on a distributed system, we identified the longest sequential computational path for each network. That is the branch within the spanning tree which performs the maximum number of operations and therefore takes the longest to finish. We chose functions of *union* and *intersection* of simplicial complexes on the level of nodes as basic operations. A number of n operations means that n nodes are input to the *union* or *intersection* function. Both these functions can be implemented in linear time [31], if the elements are kept sorted.

Our results are shown in Table 1. Column **OP** shows the average number of operations, i.e. the number of nodes participating in each operation of union or intersection. Column **C** is the normalization of **OP** by the size of the network. The trend shows a near linear correlation between the size of the network and the computational demand, which is heavily influenced by the number of partial mergings. The latter is a matter of the established topology and especially the shape of the constructed spanning tree. The average number of actual holes per simulation is displayed in column **HOLES**. All the holes were correctly detected by our algorithm, forming very few fake ones in the process, of which all we correctly classified as false. As seen from the column **FALSE** in the table, the algorithm in general is not prone to forming false holes. Column **PART** shows how often per simulation only partial merging had to be performed due to missing data. In the last column, we can see the average amount of data transmitted per node, for the purpose of our algorithm. Each data unit is a number, representing a node ID. A single number is needed to represent a node and a pair of numbers to represent a link. If we suppose 32-bit IDs, 1024 units implies 4 KB of transmitted data per node. The increase is obviously logarithmic with respect to the network size, since the size of the segments increase with the depth of the spanning tree.

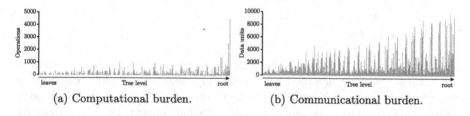

(a) Computational burden.   (b) Communicational burden.

Fig. 8. Distribution of computational and communicational burden in a 1000 node network.

Computational and communicational burdens are not distributed equally between the nodes. We expect the nodes with larger subtrees to generally receive a larger amount of data and consequently be forced to carry out more processing task. Figure 8 shows distribution of computational and communicational share between nodes in relation to their level in the spanning tree, in a typical 1000-node network. Each vertical bar represents the load of a single node. A steady climb towards the root can be seen in the case of data exchange (Fig. 8b), with many shorter branches joining in throughout the whole path. The amount of

Table 1. Simulation results: averages of 100 simulations.

Size	OP	C	HOLES	FALSE	PART	DATA
100	2443	24.4	1	0.00	0.06	727
200	4144	20.7	1.66	0.03	0.28	880
300	6068	20.2	1.92	0.02	0.57	926
400	7832	19.6	2.53	0.12	1.28	861
500	12798	25.6	3.03	0.12	2.22	1017
600	12267	20.4	3.26	0.13	2.49	953
700	15550	22.2	4.04	0.07	2.71	969
800	14919	18.6	5.04	0.40	2.75	919
900	20419	22.7	5.24	0.54	4.64	1016
1000	27594	27.6	4.69	0.23	6.37	1087

Size - number of nodes in the network; **OP** - average number of basic operations; **C** - coefficient OP/Size; **HOLES** - average number of holes; **FALSE** - average number of false holes; **PART** - average occurrence of partial merging. **DATA** - sent data per node;

transmitted data never exceeded 10,000 units per node, which in the case of 32-bit IDs, means the maximum demand was 40 KB per node. In the case of computational distribution (Fig. 8a), a severe load increase is usually observed at the root node. This is due to the fact, that at the root level, the complete information is available and therefore many partially merged sequences finished there.

5   Conclusions

In this paper we presented a novel algorithm for coverage verification in wireless sensor networks using homological criteria. The algorithm exploits distributed computational power of WSN to compute the first Betti number of the underlying Rips complex, which encodes information on domain coverage. We introduced the concept of network segments as the basic building blocks of the Rips complex and showed that by systematically merging them up the spanning tree, its homology can correctly be computed. Our simulations confirm the correctness the algorithm and show its computational time on a distributed system to be linear with the size of the network, but under significant influence of established network topology. There is still, however, room for improvement on the parallelization of tasks. Each node could begin its task as soon as some data becomes available, rather than wait until all the data is received. The costly hole verification process could at least partially be distributed down the spanning tree to the child nodes which have already finished their tasks. The high computational burden at the root node could be lowered by constraining the upper part of the spanning tree to a lower branching factor. As far as the communicational load is concerned, we believe our solution is efficient enough to run even in networks with low data bandwidth.

References

1. Raut, A.R., Khandait, S.P.: Review on data mining techniques in wireless sensor networks. In: 2015 2nd International Conference on Electronics and Communication Systems (ICECS). IEEE, February 2015
2. Holzinger, A.: On topological data mining. In: Holzinger, A., Jurisica, I. (eds.) Interactive Knowledge Discovery and Data Mining in Biomedical Informatics. LNCS, vol. 8401, pp. 331–356. Springer, Heidelberg (2014). doi:10.1007/978-3-662-43968-5_19
3. Fan, G., Jin, S.: Coverage problem in wireless sensor network: a survey. J. Netw. 5(9), 1033–1040 (2010)
4. Bai, X., Kuma, S., Xua, D., Yun, Z., La, T.H.: Deploying wireless sensors to achieve both coverage and connectivity. In: Proceedings of the Seventh ACM International Symposium on Mobile ad hoc Networking and Computing. ACM Press (2006)
5. Bai, X., Yun, Z., Xuan, D., Lai, T.H., Jia, W.: Deploying four-connectivity and full-coverage wireless sensor networks. In: IEEE INFOCOM 2008 - The 27th Conference on Computer Communications. IEEE, April 2008
6. Li, X., Frey, H., Santoro, N., Stojmenovic, I.: Strictly localized sensor self-deployment for optimal focused coverage. IEEE Trans. Mob. Comput. 10(11), 1520–1533 (2011)
7. So, A.M.-C., Ye, Y.: On solving coverage problems in a wireless sensor network using voronoi diagrams. In: Deng, X., Ye, Y. (eds.) WINE 2005. LNCS, vol. 3828, pp. 584–593. Springer, Heidelberg (2005). doi:10.1007/11600930_58
8. Wang, G., Cao, G., Porta, T.L.: Movement-assisted sensor deployment. IEEE Trans. Mob. Comput. 5(6), 640–652 (2006)
9. Zhang, C., Zhang, Y., Fang, Y.: Localized algorithms for coverage boundary detection in wireless sensor networks. Wirel. Netw. 15(1), 3–20 (2007)
10. Zhang, C., Zhang, Y., Fang, Y.: A coverage inference protocol for wireless sensor networks. IEEE Trans. Mob. Comput. 9(6), 850–864 (2010)
11. Kumari, P., Singh, Y.: Delaunay triangulation coverage strategy for wireless sensor networks. In: 2012 International Conference on Computer Communication and Informatics. IEEE, January 2012
12. Huang, C.F., Tseng, Y.C.: The coverage problem in a wireless sensor network. In: Proceedings of the 2nd ACM International Conference on Wireless Sensor Networks and Applications. ACM Press (2003)
13. Wang, X., Xing, G., Zhang, Y., Lu, C., Pless, R., Gill, C.: Integrated coverage and connectivity configuration in wireless sensor networks. In: Proceedings of the First International Conference on Embedded Networked Sensor Systems. ACM Press (2003)
14. Bejerano, Y.: Simple and efficient k-coverage verification without location information. In: IEEE INFOCOM 2008 - The 27th Conference on Computer Communications. IEEE, April 2008
15. Ghrist, R., Muhammad, A.: Coverage and hole-detection in sensor networks via homology. In: IPSN 2005. Fourth International Symposium on Information Processing in Sensor Networks. IEEE (2005)

16. de Silva, V., Ghrist, R., Muhammad, A.: Blind swarms for coverage in 2-d. In: Robotics: Science and Systems I. Robotics: Science and Systems Foundation, June 2005

17. de Silva, V., Ghrist, R.: Coverage in sensor networks via persistent homology. Algebraic Geom. Topol. **7**(1), 339–358 (2007)

18. Iyengar, S.S., Boroojeni, K.G., Balakrishnan, N.: Coordinate-free coverage in sensor networks via homology. Mathematical Theories of Distributed Sensor Networks, pp. 57–82. Springer, New York (2014). doi:10.1007/978-1-4419-8420-3_4

19. Muhammad, A., Jadbabaie, A.: Decentralized computation of homology groups in networks by gossip. In: 2007 American Control Conference. IEEE, July 2007

20. Tahbaz-Salehi, A., Jadbabaie, A.: Distributed coverage verification in sensor networks without location information. IEEE Trans. Autom. Control **55**(8), 1837–1849 (2010)

21. Kanno, J., Selmic, R.R., Phoha, V.: Detecting coverage holes in wireless sensor networks. In: 2009 17th Mediterranean Conference on Control and Automation. IEEE, June 2009

22. Chintakunta, H., Krim, H.: Divide and conquer: localizing coverage holes in sensor networks. In: 2010 7th Annual IEEE Communications Society Conference on Sensor, Mesh and Ad Hoc Communications and Networks (SECON). IEEE, June 2010

23. Arai, Z., Hayashi, K., Hiraoka, Y.: Mayer-vietoris sequences and coverage problems in sensor networks. Jpn. J. Ind. Appl. Math. **28**(2), 237–250 (2011)

24. Chintakunta, H., Krim, H.: Distributed localization of coverage holes using topological persistence. IEEE Trans. Signal Process. **62**(10), 2531–2541 (2014)

25. Dłotko, P., Ghrist, R., Juda, M., Mrozek, M.: Distributed computation of coverage in sensor networks by homological methods. Appl. Algebra Eng. Commun. Comput. **23**(1–2), 29–58 (2012)

26. Yan, F., Vergne, A., Martins, P., Decreusefond, L.: Homology-based distributed coverage hole detection in wireless sensor networks. IEEE/ACM Trans. Netw. **23**(6), 1705–1718 (2015)

27. Hatcher, A.: Algebraic Topology. Cambridge University Press, Cambridge (2002)

28. Edelsbrunner, H., Harer, J.: Computational Topology - An Introduction. American Mathematical Society, Providence (2010)

29. Bott, R., Tu, L.W.: Differential Forms in Algebraic Topology. Springer, New York (1982). doi:10.1007/978-1-4757-3951-0

30. Khan, M., Pandurangan, G.: A fast distributed approximation algorithm for minimum spanning trees. Distrib. Comput. **20**(6), 391–402 (2007)

31. Aho, A.V., Hopcroft, J.E., Ullman, J.: Data Structures and Algorithms, 1st edn. Addison-Wesley Longman Publishing Co. Inc, Boston (1983)

Detecting and Ranking API Usage Pattern in Large Source Code Repository: A LFM Based Approach

Jitong Zhao and Yan Liu[✉]

School of Software Engineering, Tongji University,
Cao'an Road 4800, Jiading District, Shanghai, China
{1410787,yanliu.sse}@tongji.edu.cn

Abstract. Code examples are key resources for helping programmers to learn correct Application Programming Interface (API) usages efficiently. However, most framework and library APIs fail in providing sufficient and adequate code examples in corresponding official documentations. Thus, it takes great programmers' efforts to browse and extract API usage examples from websites. To reduce such effort, this paper proposes a graph-based pattern-oriented mining approach, LFM-OUPD (Local fitness measure for detecting overlapping usage patterns) for API usage facility, that recommends proper API code examples from data analytics. API method queries are accepted from programmers and corresponding code files are collected from related API dataset. The detailed structural links among API method elements in conceptual source codes are captured and generate a code graph structure. Lancichinetti et al. proposed an overlapping community detecting algorithm (Local fitness measure, LFM), based on the local optimization of a fitness function. In LFM-OUPD, a mining algorithm based on LFM is presented to explore the division of method sequences in the directed source code element graph and detect candidates of different API usage patterns. Then a ranking approach is applied to obtain appropriate API usage pattern and code example candidates. A case study on Google Guava is conducted to evaluate the effectiveness of this approach.

Keywords: Graph mining · Source code mining · API usage recommendation · Data analytics

1 Introduction

Open source libraries and frameworks has mushroomed in the nearly ten years. Modern software industry cumulatively depends on third-party APIs provided by open source organizations [22]. Inevitably, programmers extensively leverage Application Programming Interfaces (APIs) to implement functionality and perform various tasks, which support code reuse and help unify programming

© IFIP International Federation for Information Processing 2017
Published by Springer International Publishing AG 2017. All Rights Reserved
A. Holzinger et al. (Eds.): CD-MAKE 2017, LNCS 10410, pp. 41–56, 2017.
DOI: 10.1007/978-3-319-66808-6_4

experience. However, it is a tough task to select and utilize an appropriate API, as APIs have grown exponentially and become more inseparable from software development current days. For instance, to build a primary website using Spring-MVC framework, programmers need to invoke dozens of APIs, including data storage API, Java Messaging Service (JMS), ServletAPI and so on. The scope of all these APIs' skill sets are so broad that even the most experienced programmers need to spend lots of time to gain a thorough understanding of each API. Furthermore, various barriers factors [6,13] cause APIs hard to learn, such as insufficient or inadequate examples, unspecified issues with API's structural design, uncompleted or ambiguous documentation. Therefore, it is a critical job for assisting programmers to fully comprehend APIs effectively and efficiently with less effort.

Figure 1 shows the current state of practice: if programmers have questions about an API, they have to browse the documentation or code examples even articles on Internet for solutions manually. Also, they try to use APIs or ask colleagues sometimes.

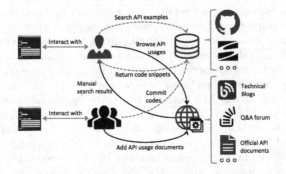

Fig. 1. Current state of practice

In these cases, source code examples often emerge as a acknowledged resource for programmers while learning usages of APIs [13]. This is also evident by the rapid development of code search engines (CSEs). While the results returned by CSEs are usually too massive for programmers to follow, so more researches have been done on various clustering and ranking algorithms in the stage of API usage results filter. Recent work [3,11,12,15] has helped programmers alleviate burden and better understand individual APIs. These approaches focus on GitHub source code analyzing, API usage mining, API pattern clustering and code candidates ranking.

API code usage information scatters on Internet including GitHub, official documents, and Stack overflow, however there is not a systematic knowledge base for this. These information usually suffers from deficiencies of irregular structure, which is similar to a social network. In this situation network community discovery methods are suitable to explore the programming information raw data. In this paper, we propose an approach LFM-OUPD (Local fitness measure for detecting overlapping usage patterns) for API usage facility from data analytics perspective to help recommend proper code examples. We extract corresponding API method sequences from dataset, and construct links among API method elements, storing as graph structure. A mining algorithm based on Local fitness measure (LFM) is provided to detect usage patterns. After identifying and ranking API usage pattern with various features, we select the most appropriate code snippet for the programmers. At last, we conduct a comparison experiment between LFM, LFM-OUPD and MAPO [22], using a Google Guava[1] API case study. The results demonstrate that LFM-OUPD is more effective and adopted to actual APIs compared with the other two approaches.

The remainder of this paper is organized as follows. Section 2 summarizes related work including various recommending systems and technologies. Section 3 proposes an approach, LFM-OUPD, to detect and rank API usage pattern in software repository and recommend proper code examples for programmers. A case study on Google Guava is conducted to evaluate the effectiveness of this approach in Sect. 4. Lastly, we conclude this paper in Sect. 5.

2   Related Work

Helping programmers to learn how to use an API method has gained a considerable attention in recent year research. Several recommendation systems [3,11,12,15] have been designed to suggest relevant API usage examples for supporting programming tasks. They can be organized in the categories according to the data-mining mechanisms of their proposed techniques.

Some researches try to extract related information from numerous web pages, then deliver uniform views to programmers. APIExamples [18] performs in-depth analysis on the collected code snippets and descriptive texts from web pages, including usage examples clustering and ranking. It provides two kinds of user interaction style: an IDE plug-in and a web search portal.

Other contributions tried to leverage modern Q&A websites to provide efficient recommendations. Various technology forums offer concise answers and rich technical contexts including executable code snippets. Example Overflow [21] uses built-in social mechanisms of the popular technical forum, Stack Overflow[2] to recommend embeddable and high quality code.

The most related contributions are those interested in mining API usage pattern from common online code search engine and code snippet recommender. Current CSEs nearly wholly leverage text-oriented information-retrieval(IR) techniques that disregards inherent structure of source code. To address this problem, researchers have presented numerous approaches [9,14,15,17,19] to improve CSEs, further more, new recommendation engines are proposed. These are generally designed to work in the form of integrated development environment (IDE) plug-in to interact with programmers. MAPO [22] mines API usage

---

[1] https://github.com/google/guava.
[2] http://stackoverflow.com/.

pattern from large number of code snippets gathered by online code search engines such as Google Code Search.[3] In particular, based on the BIDE algorithm, MAPO combines frequent subsequence mining with clustering to mine closed sequential pattern. In addition, it provides a recommender integrated with Eclipse IDE.

The main limitations of all the contribution mentioned above are that they can't detect common API usage patterns, and do not performs in-depth analysis on the code graph structure. Our approach tries to resolves these limitations and presents a new dimension of the API usage pattern detection. First, we collect multiple API clients programs of the target studied API which help construct a graph structure. Then, a graph-based approach is presented to identify candidates of different API method sequences and rank them with three appropriateness metrics. Finally, our approach detects common API usage patterns which are used frequently in the same way by client programs and recommends them to the programmers.

3   LFM-OUPD: An Approach for Proper API Usage Pattern Recommendation

Aiming at addressing the issues during finding proper API code examples, we propose a recommendation approach, LFM-OUPD (Local fitness measure for detecting overlapping usage patterns). In LFM-OUPD, implicit API usage dependencies is modeled by API method call sequences, which are extracted from the API implementation code. As its name implies, API method call sequence is a series of API methods, which are used together to realize a specific function. LFM-OUPD takes these API usage dependencies as the basis of recommendation, which can make the suggested API usage patterns (Sect. 3.1) more appropriate for developers.

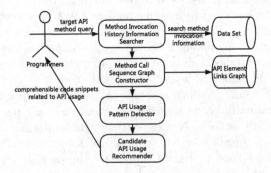

Fig. 2. Overview of LFM-OUPD

---

[3] http://www.google.com/codesearch.

Figure 2 shows the overview of LFM-OUPD. At beginning, an API programmer specifies the name of an API method that needs code examples as a query. Then, the API method invocation history information of target API method is collected from the existing dataset. LFM-OUPD utilizes a method call sequence graph constructor (Sect. 3.2) to capture the detailed structural links among API method elements in conceptual source codes and generate a code graph structure. An API usage pattern detector (Sect. 3.3) is proposed for classifying and mining different API usage patterns from the method call sequence graph. An optimized candidate API usage recommender (Sect. 3.4) is also required in processing and generating API usage pattern ranking list quickly. Finally, the most comprehension-friendly code snippets, which are related to the optimized API usage, are selected and recommended to the API programmers (Sect. 3.5).

3.1 API Usage Pattern

Before interpreting approach LFM-OUPD, we provide a detailed definition of API usage pattern. Our approach defines an API Usage Pattern (UP) as a sequence of API method calls. These API method calls have co-appeared relations, namely, they are always located closely in the client programs. Every API usage pattern is an exclusive subset of API call methods.

A fixed sequence of API method calls are usually located in different code snippets, which have the same co-appeared relations and are expected to be concluded into an API usage pattern. However, it is impossible to detect all the possible target method usage scenarios. An approach is required to identify possible API Usage Patterns from large amount of API's client programs and detect API's usage scenarios. Therefore, our approach is designed to capture out co-appeared relations among API's methods, and offer proper code examples relevant to the target API Usage Pattern.

3.2 Method Call Sequence Graph Constructor

Preparing Dataset. For most APIs with rich set of client code on Internet, potential sources files with code examples can be directly collected from existing data source. Client code hosted on GitHub can provide enough valuable scenarios on how to use various API methods. We need to collect code usage information from GitHub at project level for detecting APIs across projects and extract the references between methods of the client programs and the public methods of APIs based on Eclipse's JDT compiler [1]. The API usage dataset published by Sawant and Bacchelli [16] just meets our basic requirement. This dataset contains information about 5 APIs and how their public methods are utilized over the course of their entire lifetime by 20,263 projects. Thus, we utilized it in our approach to analyse the relevant API method usage information among code snippets.

Generating API Method Call Sequences. This section aims at generating API method call sequences of target query. In our approach, we consider the code locations as API method calls when there is a super constructor call, a method call or a class instance creation. To keep the issues simple, this paper does not consider method overloading situation in user code, and more research will be done in further.

Accepting the API method query from programmers, our approach performs search on API usage dataset to obtain target API method invocation history information. We locate all the class files where target API method ever appeared and collect these method invocation information in the class file level. We generate a method call sequence for each class file, which performs a sequential traversal to collect API method calls. For example, the corresponding method call sequence of statement 'static Cache<Integer, String> cache = CacheBuilder.newBuilder().expireAfterWrite(5, TimeUnit.SECONDS).build();' is as follows.

```
com.google.common.cache.CacheBuilder.newBuilder
com.google.common.cache.CacheBuilder.expireAfterWrite
com.google.common.cache.CacheBuilder.build
```

In addition, the information about class name, project name, url access of Github and so on are also collected and stored.

Constructing Links Among API Method Elements. After generating corresponding API method call sequences, the detailed structural links among API method elements in conceptual source codes are captured and generate a code graph structure illustrated in Fig. 3.

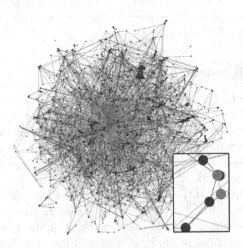

Fig. 3. Method sequence call graph

Intuitively, the method call sequences across different java class files compose a method call sequence graph together, with the linear method call sequence in one file regarded as a sub-graph. In addition, the edge between two method nodes in this graph is weighed by the frequency of their co-appearance.

Nodes in the graph represent API methods, e.g., 'com.google.common.cache. CacheBuilder.newBuilder()'. The edge in this directed graph represents sequential flows from method to method based on the collected API method call sequences. Take for example, if there are three methods in a statement 'method1(); method2(); method3();', we construct a graph structure as 'method1() -> method2() -> method3()', which means method2() appears followed by method1() and method3() appears followed by method2() in this statement. In this case, method1() -> method3() is not allowed, which should strictly follow the appearance location sequence.

Also, the weight of the edge represents the time count that two methods are used together. The weight of edge is an important metric to evaluate the tightness of two API method, which contributes to detect API usage pattern in the latter section. Figure 4 shows an example of method call sequence graph. Method 'com.google.common.cache.CacheBuilder.maximumSize()' is located followed by method 'com.google.common.cache.CacheBuilder.newBuilder()' in java programs and the weight of their edge is 20. This means method newBuilder() and maximumSize() are used together and located closely in 20 java class files.

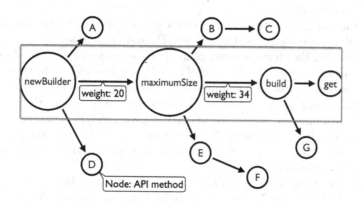

Fig. 4. Method sequence call graph demo

3.3 API Usage Pattern Detector

The method call sequence graph can be treated as a directed weighted complex network. We transfer the API usage pattern detecting question to the exploration question of high weight and high density method call sequences. Recent years, researchers propose many classical community detecting algorithms [5,8,10,20] to investigate complex networks and their natural characteristics. Lancichinetti et al. [7] proposed an overlapping community detecting algorithm (Local fitness measure, LFM), based on the local optimization of a fitness function. In this section, we propose a local extension algorithm of detecting overlapping usage patterns (LFM-OUPD) based on LFM.

Directed Degree Centrality of Method Node. In the directed weighted code graph, the large directed degree centrality of a method node usually means that the node is in the center of overall code network, and this node is also densely connected to the neighbouring method nodes. This kind of node is called core seed node of the directed source code graph. The directed degree centrality of one node is affected by weighted in-degree and out-degree of the node. We introduce a definition of directed degree centrality C_i of node i as follows,

$$C_i = \omega C_i^{in} + (1-\omega) C_i^{out} \tag{1}$$

where C_i^{in} represents the weighted in-degree of $node_j$, C_i^{out} represents the weighted out-degree, and ω is the weight parameter, which is used to adjust the weight of in-degree and out-degree in the directed degree centrality.

Neighbourhood Calculation Rules. LFM-OUPD utilizes the idea of detecting communities through a local optimization of some metric, which has already been applied earlier [2,4]. This approach selects a core seed node as the initial sub-graph, and continuously extends this sub-graph by adding neighbour node until the fitness function of the usage pattern community reaches the maximization. Thus, It is helpful to introduce the neighbourhood calculation rules of a sub-graph community.

Assuming UP_i is the ith element in a set of UPs, the neighbour nodes of UP_i is identified as successor of leaf nodes in UP_i, and predecessor of root nodes in UP_i. Considering the characteristics of method sequence diagram, we don't take successor or predecessor of other nodes in UP_i into consideration when finding neighbour nodes. As the code snippets are naturally existing as a single directed method chain diagram, the mined results are expected to be a method sequence diagram, which only one-way direction flow is permitted. It is noteworthy that, if there is a sub-ring in the method sequence call graph, we treat the sub-ring as a whole to determine whether it is a root or leaf node, and find their common successor or predecessor.

Figure 5 interprets the neighbourhood calculation rules. For a Usage Pattern with three API methods B, C and D, its leaf node is method D, and its root node is method B, so its neighbourhood are method A1, A2, E1 and E2. For a Usage Pattern with three API methods B, C and F, there is a sub-ring in it, that is method C and D. Here we treat method C and F as a whole leaf method node, so its neighbourhood are method A1, A2 and G.

Directed Fitness Function of API Usage Patterns. Directed Fitness Function of API Usage Patterns $f(UP_i)$ is utilized to measure the extent of impact when a node joins the API usage pattern UP_i. The basic assumption behind our algorithm is that the internal nodes in an API usage pattern is much more densely connected to each other compared with the relationships of other nodes. Thus, when $f(UP_i)$ reaches the peak, optimal division of a method sequence UP_i is produced. If one node has a significant impact on its neighbourhood sequences, the node is divided into multiple API usage patterns, and then the overlapping

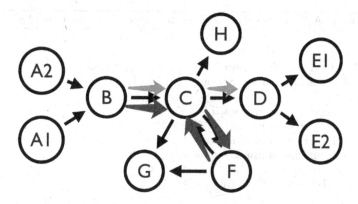

Fig. 5. Neighbourhood calculation example

method sequence structure is formed. Consider the characteristics of directed weighted edge graph structure, $f(UP_i)$ is defined as follows,

$$f(PU_i) = \frac{W_{all}^{in}}{(W_{all}^{in} + W_{leaf}^{in\_out} + W_{root}^{out\_in})\alpha} \qquad (2)$$

where W_{all}^{in} represents total weight of edges between nodes in UP_i, $W_{leaf}^{in\_out}$ represents total weight of edges directed from leaf nodes of UP_i to neighbour nodes, $W_{root}^{out\_in}$ represents total weight of edges directed from neighbour nodes to root node of UP_i, and α is the threshold parameter used to control the size of the API usage pattern produced. Considering the characteristics of method call sequence graph and neighbour nodes calculation rules, the method sequence list is required to be single directed. Thus, the fitness function only cares about the edges directed to the root node of UP_i from external nodes, and the edges directed from leaf nodes of UP_i to the external nodes, when calculating weights between edges of UP_i and outside.

API Usage Patterns Detecting Algorithm. Based on LFM, the core idea of our algorithm is to start from the core seed nodes in the API method call sequence graph, and constantly merge the neighbour to produce the API usage pattern. Firstly, the node with the largest directed degree centrality is found as the core seed node, and then the neighbour nodes with the greatest influence on the directed fitness function $f(UP_i)$ are merged continuously. Finally, the API usage pattern UP_i is produced until the merging process comes to convergence. After forming a usage pattern, select the core node in the rest nodes to continue the next division of the usage pattern, and ultimately all the nodes in the graph are partitioned into usage patterns. Algorithm 1 describe the overall process of detecting API usage patterns.

Algorithm 1. API usage patterns detecting algorithm based on LFM

Input: Method sequence call graph $G(V, E, M)$, $\alpha = 0.3$;
Output: Usage patterns set UP;
1: **for all** Method node $v_i \in V$ **do**
2:     Calculate the directed degree centrality C_i of v_i;
3: **end for**
4: Initialize the Usage patterns set $UP = \varnothing$;
5: Initialize the current usage pattern $UP_j = \varnothing$, $j = 0$;
6: Initialize the current method node set $V_c = V$;
7: Initialize the maximum fitness function $f_{max} = 0$;
8: **for** $V_c \neq \varnothing$ **do**
9:     Set the seed node $v_s = \{v_i \mid \max\limits_{v_i \in V_c} C_i\}$
10:    Set $UP_j = v_s$;
11:    Calculate the set of all neighbor nodes of UP_j, denoted by V_n;
12:    **for all** $v_i \in V_n$ **do**
13:        Add v_i to UP_j and calculate $f(UP_j)$;
14:        Set $l = 0$;
15:        **if** $f(UP_j) \geq f_{max}$ **then**
16:            $f_{max} = f(UP_j)$, $l = i$;
17:        **end if**
18:        Delete v_i from UP_j;
19:    **end for**
20:    **if** l==0 **then**
21:        Add UP_j to UP, $j = j + 1$;
22:    **else**
23:        Add v_l to UP_j;
24:        Do step 11-25;
25:    **end if**
26:    Update the current method node set $V_c = V_c - UP_j$
27: **end for**
28: **return** UP

3.4   Candidate API Usage Recommender

After usage patterns are detected by our approach, we select UP results containing user query(the target API method chose by the user) as API usage pattern candidates. Candidate API patterns ranking mechanism is also required to evaluate the score of usage pattern candidates and assist to pick appropriate ones. There are three appropriateness metrics, cohesiveness, availability and representation to calculate the final score, which is positive correlated with the ranking of an API usage pattern. The range of these three metrics is all between 0 and 1. The final score is the sum of these three metrics. The higher this score values, the more appropriate the API usage is for recommendation. After usage pattern candidate lists are recommended according to the ranking phase, users can select an interested usage pattern to browse related code examples.

Cohesiveness. The cohesiveness metric evaluates the aggregation of API method calls within a usage pattern. A usage pattern with higher cohesiveness is tended to be more frequent and significant. The cohesiveness metric for a usage pattern UP is determined by the weight of the usage pattern $W_{all}^{in}(UP)$ and the total weight of the method call sequence graph $TotalWeight(G)$. For example, if there is a usage pattern, whose $W_{all}^{in}(UP)$ is 49, and the $TotalWeight(G)$ of the method call sequence graph is 200, the $cohesiveness(UP)$ is 0.245. The formulation for cohesiveness is shown as follows.

$$cohesiveness(UP) = \frac{W_{all}^{in}(UP)}{TotalWeight(G)} \tag{3}$$

Availability. The availability metric evaluates the significance of a usage pattern. A usage pattern with higher availability is tended to be more universal for demonstrating a specific API method usage scenario. The availability metric for a usage pattern UP is determined by $CSNum(UP)$ and $CSNum(TargetQuery)$. $CSNum(UP)$ represents the number of code snippet (CS) where all the API method calls of the API usage pattern are used in. $CSNum(TargetQuery)$ represents the number of code snippet where the target method query call is ever used in. The formulation for availability is shown as follows.

$$availability(UP) = \frac{CSNum(UP)}{CSNum(TargetQuery)} \tag{4}$$

For example, the target method call is 'method1()' and there are 40 code snippets including 'method1()'. The detected usage pattern is the method call sequence 'method1, method2, method3()', and there are 15 code snippets containing these three methods. Then the *availability* is 15/40, that is 0.375.

Representation. The representation metric evaluates the portion of third-party method calls in the usage pattern calls. Methods invoked by a developer's own class will decrease the representation of a usage pattern. A usage pattern with higher representation is tended to be more representative and comprehensible. For a usage pattern with higher representation, the developer can filter useful information out of the noise during code review with less effort. The representation metric for a usage pattern UP is determined by the number of third-party method calls $ThirdPartyMCNum(UP)$ and the total number of method calls $MCNum(UP)$ appearing in the UP.

$$representation(UP) = \frac{ThirdPartyMCNum(UP)}{MCNum(UP)} \tag{5}$$

3.5   Candidate Code Examples Recommender

We use the following recommendation mechanism to rank code examples of target API usage pattern and pick the code snippets with the best demonstrative effect: we prefer code snippet with less lines; prefer examples containing more comments; prefer code examples using less API methods apart from those in the target API usage pattern.

For a target API usage pattern, code snippets containing all the corresponding methods are gathered from the existing dataset. To select appropriate code snippet, we use three criterion, number of code lines $LineNum(CS)$, descriptive textural comments $CommentNum(CS)$ and number of API method calls of usage pattern $MCNum(UP)$ to calculate the ranking score. The formula is shown as follows.

$$Score(CS) = \frac{MCNum(UP)}{LineNum(CS)} + \frac{MCNum(UP)}{MCNum(CS)} + \frac{1}{CommentNum(CS)} \quad (6)$$

In addition, if there is not a comment in code snippet, we set default value as 0.5. The lower this score values, the more appropriate the code snippets are for recommendation.

4   Case Study

We conducted an experimental case study on LFM, MAPO and LFM-OUPD. The case study is performed to investigate whether LFM-OUPD can assist programmers to figure out API usage patterns and locate code examples effectively.

4.1   Setup

To establish the current graph dataset, we focus our effort on one programming language, Java, and select one specific API library, Google Guava (see Footnote 1). This made our data collection and processing more relevant and manageable. We utilized dataset offered by Sawant and Bacchelli [16], which extracts method invocation and annotation references information about Google Guava API from 3013 projects.

LFM and LFM-OUPD are realized using Python language. LFM-OUPD implementation supports the recommendation of code snippets for a framework API implemented in Java. All experiments are carried out on a machine with CPU 2.7 GHz Intel Core i5, 8 GB RAM.

4.2   CacheBuilder Method Case

The CacheBuilder class[4] in Google Guava provides support to actually construct cache instances and set the desired features. It uses fluent style of building and provides various options of setting properties on the cache.

We conducted a comparison experiment study on LFM, MAPO and LFM-OUPD. The study aims to investigate whether LFM-OUPD can assist programmers locate API pattern and code snippet examples of interest efficiently. LFM

---

[4] https://google.github.io/guava/releases/17.0/api/docs/com/google/common/cache/CacheBuilder.html.

Table 1. API usage patterns returned by LFM

PID	Cohesiveness	Availability	Representative	Mapped API usage
1	0.82	0	1	Non-representative API usage
2	0.84	0	0.83	Non-representative API usage
3	0.62	0.15	0.67	CacheBuilder set testing timed eviction
4	0.44	0.1	0.87	CacheBuilder set size-based eviction
5	0.25	0	0.92	Non-representative API usage

returns 2484 API usage patterns from the API method-based sequences graph. There are 16 API usage patterns containing target API method. Table 1 illustrates the performance of top 5 API usage patterns. Obviously, their performance is not satisfying enough to support recommendation. Moreover, only two of them are valid usage patterns that correctly demonstrate CacheBuilder usages. However, these two method call sequences still miss approaches compared with representative code snippets.

LFM-OUPD returns 1712 API usage patterns from the API method-based sequences graph. There are 76 API usage patterns containing target API method CacheBuilder.newBuilder(). Table 2 illustrates the performance of top 10 API usage patterns sorted by ranking scores.

Table 2. API usage patterns returned by LFM-OUPD

PID	Cohesiveness	Availability	Representative	Mapped API usage
1	0.82	0.1	1	CacheBuilder set size-based eviction
2	0.78	0.102	1	CacheBuilder set timed eviction
3	0.77	0.1	0.875	CacheBuilder set testing timed eviction
4	0.62	0.104	1	CacheBuilder set reference-based eviction
5	0.67	0.65	1	Initialization mechanism from a CacheLoader
6	0.66	0.34	1	Initialization mechanism from a Callable
7	0.54	0.08	1	Mechanism of explicit removals
8	0.52	0.07	1	Mechanism of removal listeners
9	0.08	0.01	0.67	Sequence pattern contains developer's test code
10	0.05	0.01	0.43	Sequence pattern contains isolated approach

Column 'Mapped API Usage' interprets the mapping between detected API usage patterns and their mapped usage implementation mechanisms. There are eight valid usage pattern candidates that correctly demonstrate CacheBuilder usages. Method call sequence candidates from pattern 1 to 4 demonstrate mechanism of setting eviction cache features with different requestor objects and attributes. Method call sequence of pattern 5 demonstrates mechanism of initialization from a CacheLoader. API usage pattern 6 demonstrates mechanism of initialization from a Callable. API usage candidates 7 and 8 demonstrate mechanism of reference-based eviction.

Taking the mapped API usage 5 as an example, the corresponding method call sequence for 'initialization from a CacheLoader' usage is as follows.

```
com.google.common.cache.CacheBuilder.newBuilder
com.google.common.cache.CacheBuilder.maximumSize
com.google.common.cache.CacheBuilder.build
com.google.common.cache.LoadingCache.get
```

Code snippet of 'CacheBuilder.newBuilder' for this pattern recommended by LFM-OUPD is illustrated in Fig. 6. To better understand this API usage, method calls appearing in pattern 5 are marked in red lines. This is a code snippet helping programmers to study how to initialize a cache using a CacheLoader class.

```
01  LoadingCache<Key, Graph> graphs = CacheBuilder.newBuilder()
02          .maximumSize(1000)
03          .build(
04              new CacheLoader<Key, Graph>() {
05                  public Graph load(Key key) throws AnyException {
06                      return createExpensiveGraph(key);
07                  }
08              });
09
10
11  try {
12      return graphs.get(key);
13  } catch (ExecutionException e) {
14      throw new OtherException(e.getCause());
15  }
```

Fig. 6. Code snippet of 'CacheBuilder.newBuilder'

Table 3 presents a comparison of other two approaches and LFM-OUPD. As the table shows, for the given 8 API usages, LFM-OUPD could detect and recommend all related API usage patterns based on user query, while the other two approaches' recommended results are subset of usage patterns returned by LFM-OUPD. Thus, our approach performs better than LFM and MAPO.

The case study results demonstrate that LFM-OUPD is effective for assisting programmers to identify different API usages. Also, LFM-OUPD greatly help programmers pick up appropriate representative code examples transformed from API usage candidates with less selecting and modification effort.

Furthermore, comparing with LFM, LFM-OUPD approach enhances the cohesiveness, availability, representative metric dramatically and could offer more representative API usage patterns. This can help programmers figure out more usage examples of target method.

Table 3. API usage patterns returned by three approaches

PID	Mapped API usage	LFM-OUPD	LFM	MAPO
1	CacheBuilder set size-based eviction	Y	Y	Y
2	CacheBuilder set timed eviction	Y	N	Y
3	CacheBuilder set testing timed eviction	Y	Y	Y
4	CacheBuilder set reference-based eviction	Y	N	N
5	Initialization mechanism from a CacheLoader	Y	N	Y
6	Initialization mechanism from a Callable	Y	N	Y
7	Mechanism of explicit removals	Y	N	Y
8	Mechanism of removal listeners	Y	N	N

5 Conclusion

In this work, an approach, LFM-OUPD, is proposed to recommend proper code examples for assisting programmers learning API more efficiently. LFM-OUPD is a graph-based approach, using community detecting approach to detect API usage patterns, which exits as high weight and density sub-graph in the API method call sequence graph. The detailed structural links among API method elements in conceptual source codes are captured and stored as graph structure. In LFM-OUPD, a mining algorithm based on LFM is presented to detect candidates of different API usage patterns. Also three appropriateness metrics are provided to assist ranking and recommending usage pattern. The effectiveness of LFM-OUPD is evaluated through a comparison case study. The study results demonstrate that, given an API method, LFM-OUPD can detect its various usages and recommend reliable code examples.

References

1. Aeschlimann, M., Baumer, D., Lanneluc, J.: Java tool smithing extending the eclipse java development tools. In: Proceedings of the 2nd EclipseCon (2005)
2. Baumes, J., Goldberg, M.K., Krishnamoorthy, M.S., Magdon-Ismail, M., Preston, N.: Finding communities by clustering a graph into overlapping subgraphs. IADIS AC 5, 97–104 (2005)
3. Bosu, A., Carver, J.C., Bird, C., Orbeck, J., Chockley, C.: Process aspects and social dynamics of contemporary code review: insights from open source development and industrial practice at microsoft. IEEE Trans. Softw. Eng. 42, 302–321 (2016)
4. Clauset, A.: Finding local community structure in networks. Phys. Rev. E 72(2), 026132 (2005)
5. Gregory, S.: An algorithm to find overlapping community structure in networks. In: Kok, J.N., Koronacki, J., Lopez de Mantaras, R., Matwin, S., Mladenič, D., Skowron, A. (eds.) PKDD 2007. LNCS, vol. 4702, pp. 91–102. Springer, Heidelberg (2007). doi:10.1007/978-3-540-74976-9_12

6. Ko, A.J., Myers, B., Aung, H.H.: Six learning barriers in end-user programming systems. In: IEEE Symposium on Visual Languages and Human Centric Computing, pp. 199–206 (2004)
7. Lancichinetti, A., Fortunato, S., Kertész, J.: Detecting the overlapping and hierarchical community structure in complex networks. New J. Phys. **11**(3), 033015 (2009)
8. Malliaros, F.D., Vazirgiannis, M.: Clustering and community detection in directed networks: a survey. Phys. Rep. **533**(4), 95–142 (2013)
9. Mar, L.W., Wu, Y.C., Jiau, H.C.: Recommending proper API code examples for documentation purpose. In: 2011 18th Asia Pacific Software Engineering Conference (APSEC), pp. 331–338 (2011)
10. Newman, M.E., Girvan, M.: Finding and evaluating community structure in networks. Phys. Rev. E **69**(2), 026113 (2004)
11. Ponzanelli, L., Bavota, G., Di Penta, M., Oliveto, R., Lanza, M.: Prompter: a self-confident recommender system. In: 2014 IEEE International Conference on Software Maintenance and Evolution (ICSME), pp. 577–580. IEEE (2014)
12. Radevski, S., Hata, H., Matsumoto, K.: Towards building API usage example metrics. In: 2016 IEEE 23rd International Conference on Software Analysis, Evolution, and Reengineering (SANER), vol. 1, pp. 619–623. IEEE (2016)
13. Robillard, M.P.: What makes APIs hard to learn? Answers from developers. Softw. IEEE **26**(6), 27–34 (2009)
14. Saied, M.A., Abdeen, H., Benomar, O., Sahraoui, H.: Could we infer unordered API usage patterns only using the library source code? In: 2015 IEEE 23rd International Conference on Program Comprehension (ICPC), pp. 71–81 (2015)
15. Saied, M.A., Benomar, O., Abdeen, H., Sahraoui, H.: Mining multi-level API usage patterns. In: 2015 IEEE 22nd International Conference on Software Analysis, Evolution and Reengineering (SANER), pp. 23–32. IEEE (2015)
16. Sawant, A.A., Bacchelli, A.: A dataset for API usage. In: Proceedings of the 12th Working Conference on Mining Software Repositories, pp. 506–509. IEEE Press (2015)
17. Wang, J., Dang, Y., Zhang, H., Chen, K., Xie, T., Zhang, D.: Mining succinct and high-coverage API usage patterns from source code. In: 2013 10th IEEE Working Conference on Mining Software Repositories (MSR), pp. 319–328 (2013)
18. Wang, L., Fang, L., Wang, L., Li, G., Xie, B., Yang, F.: APIExample: an effective web search based usage example recommendation system for Java APIs. In: 2011 26th IEEE/ACM International Conference on Automated Software Engineering (ASE), pp. 592–595 (2011)
19. Wu, Y.C., Mar, L.W., Jiau, H.C.: CoDocent: support API usage with code example and API documentation. In: 2010 Fifth International Conference on Software Engineering Advances (ICSEA), pp. 135–140 (2010)
20. Xie, J., Kelley, S., Szymanski, B.K.: Overlapping community detection in networks: the state-of-the-art and comparative study. ACM Comput. Surv. (CSUR) **45**(4), 43 (2013)
21. Zagalsky, A., Barzilay, O., Yehudai, A.: Example overflow: using social media for code recommendation. In: 2012 Third International Workshop on Recommendation Systems for Software Engineering (RSSE), pp. 38–42 (2012)
22. Zhong, H., Xie, T., Zhang, L., Pei, J., Mei, H.: MAPO: mining and recommending API usage patterns. In: Drossopoulou, S. (ed.) ECOOP 2009. LNCS, vol. 5653, pp. 318–343. Springer, Heidelberg (2009). doi:10.1007/978-3-642-03013-0_15

MAKE Smart Factor

Towards a Framework for Assistance Systems to Support Work Processes in Smart Factories

Michael Fellmann[1(✉)], Sebastian Robert[2], Sebastian Büttner[3],
Henrik Mucha[3], and Carsten Röcker[2,3]

[1] Chair of Business Information Systems,
University of Rostock, Rostock, Germany
michael.fellmann@uni-rostock.de
[2] Fraunhofer-Institute of Optronics,
System Technologies and Image Exploitation,
Application Center Industrial Automation (IOSB-INA), Lemgo, Germany
{sebastian.robert,
carsten.roecker}@iosb-ina.fraunhofer.de
[3] Ostwestfalen-Lippe University of Applied Sciences, Lemgo, Germany
{sebastian.buettner,henrik.mucha}@hs-owl.de

Abstract. Increasingly, production processes are enabled and controlled by Information Technology (IT), a development being also referred to as "Industry 4.0". IT thereby contributes to flexible and adaptive production processes, and in this sense factories become "smart factories". In line with this, IT also more and more supports human workers via various assistance systems. This support aims to both support workers to better execute their tasks and to reduce the effort and time required when working. However, due to the large spectrum of assistance systems, it is hard to acquire an overview and to select an adequate system for a smart factory based on meaningful criteria. We therefore synthesize a set of comparison criteria into a consistent framework and demonstrate the application of our framework by classifying three examples.

Keywords: Assistance systems · Smart factory · Production processes

1 Introduction and Motivation

Automation of production processes is a trend that traces back to the industrial revolution or even beyond. In today's industrial production, machines are an integral part and its importance will even rise in future [7]. With the further digitalization and interconnection of production systems, which is sometimes referred to as *Industry 4.0* [8], *Smart Industry* or *Smart Manufacturing* [11], the role of human work changes significantly. Tasks of production worker and knowledge worker, such as product development and production planning will intertwine and manual production work will shift to planning, control and monitoring tasks for machines and processes [7]. But even manual production work won't vanish: with decreasing lot sizes caused by shorter product-lifecycles and higher product variations (mass customization), manual work processes will still be required. However, processes will become more complex and

© IFIP International Federation for Information Processing 2017
Published by Springer International Publishing AG 2017. All Rights Reserved
A. Holzinger et al. (Eds.): CD-MAKE 2017, LNCS 10410, pp. 59–68, 2017.
DOI: 10.1007/978-3-319-66808-6_5

error-prone, since human workers need to be able to produce more different product variations and consequently will have to master a larger variety of single work steps.

Due to the aforementioned trends, complexity and required skills of tasks in industrial work environments will increase. Given the demographic shift [2] and reports about shortage of high-skilled labor in OECD countries [5], the question raises on how this more complex work can actually be handled in future. There is a strong need for supporting employees work in the future of manufacturing by making the complexity of the new industrial environments more manageable. Assistance systems have the potential to address this need. However, whereas in other domains such as car driving, navigation or computer configuration, assistance systems are already state of the art and widely accepted, assistance systems to support workers in industrial settings are still not in widespread use. This situation may change dramatically in the future due to the ever-increasing computation power, new sensors and actuators and new interaction technologies. These advances make smart environments in the context of production feasible [13] that are a requirement for advanced assistance systems. We will call these new smart environments "smart factories". Based on the definition of Lucke et al. [13], a smart factory is defined as "a factory that context-aware assists people and machines in execution of their task". This supportive environment spans different levels of the factory from the top floor to the shop floor. To establish a smart factory, a multitude of systems and subsystems are required. While Lucke et al. [13] distinguish between calm-systems (hardware) and context-aware-applications (software), we will focus only on one type of context-aware-applications in this paper, namely on assistance systems. We understand an assistance system in production as a *context-aware system consisting of hardware and software that supports a user with the execution of a task and adapts depending on the progress of the task* (cf. [1]). Potentially, the system can adapt to other context information, e.g. to specific users and their physical and emotional states or to objects in or the state of the physical environment.

In the last decades, a lot of assistance systems for industrial tasks have been proposed. However, the research landscape in this context is heterogeneous and a clear and coherent overview is missing. Lots of studies exist that present or evaluate specific systems, e.g. [10, 16, 17]. Surveys have been done with respect to a single aspect or with the focus on specific technologies, such as work on Industrial Augmented Reality (IAR) [6], work with a focus on Augmented Reality (AR) and Virtual Reality (VR) [3] or the consideration of Human-Machine Interaction (HMI) in the domain of Industry 4.0 [9, 14]. Still, to our knowledge, a holistic overview and classification of the previous research work on assistance systems in smart factories is missing. This is even more surprising as these systems become more and more relevant for industrial practice. Both researchers and practitioner would benefit from a clear and coherent set of attributes structured in a framework to compare work done in this research field. Scientists new to the field could get a quick insight into the field, others could use the overview work to retrieve relevant works from the mass of publications. Practitioners could derive more easy design decisions from existing work and evaluations by using the classification. Furthermore, they could use the overview work to get an insight into the possibilities that assistance systems could offer for the smart factories of the future. Last, but not least a coherent framework will establish a common ground for discussion in the field and help to identify open research topics and new research questions.

With this paper, we want to close the gap and provide the first framework for assistance systems in smart factories. The framework contains key characteristics of assistance systems and is meant for both researcher and practitioners. We achieve this goal by doing a morphological analysis based on existing work to construct our framework.

The rest of the paper is organized as follows. Section 2 is a methodical consideration about the creation of the framework. Section 3 describes and visualizes the framework. In Sect. 4 we will classify three research projects into our framework, followed by a conclusion and outlook in Sect. 5.

2 Methodological Considerations

In the following, we briefly introduce the research procedure that was executed to construct our framework for work assistance systems (cf. Fig. 1).

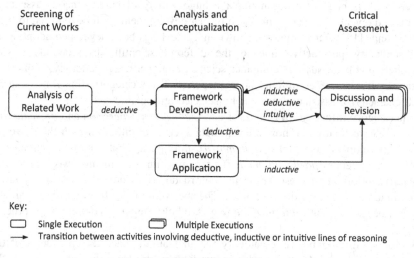

Fig. 1. Research procedure

The construction process can be divided in three main stages. At *screening of current works*, we analyzed related works. All five authors that are engaged in researching assistance systems contributed multiple research works from their academic knowledge base. We then performed a forward and backward search on these articles. At *analysis and conceptualization*, we constructed the framework and subsequently applied it to the description of existing assistance systems. We then entered the stage of *critical assessment* and discussed needs for revision which emerged from applying the framework. In line with [15], we furthermore applied all reasoning techniques being *deductive*, *inductive* and *intuitive*. Deductive reasoning (conceptual-to-empirical) was performed when the framework was initially constructed based on literature and in applying the framework. Inductive reasoning (empirical-to-conceptual) was performed when the framework application to real-world systems led to revisions. All reasoning techniques have been applied when moving back and forth between *framework development* (stage *analysis and conceptualization*) and *discussion and revision* (stage *critical assessment*). In order to continuously refine our framework, an incremental approach has been used in line with [15]. To do so, activities in the last two stages form a cycle. Moreover, we added an inner cycle via a bidirectional relation between *framework development* and *discussion and revision*. It was performed in several extensive discussion sessions. All objective and subjective ending conditions of the incremental process suggested in [15] have been met, except the criteria "All objects or a representative sample of objects have been examined". Since the knowledge bases of the researchers in conjunction with forward and backward search were used, we cannot guarantee representativeness and hence consider our framework preliminary.

3   Framework

A framework is helpful in organizing the huge variety of heterogeneous assistance systems and revealing the areas in which further developments will be required to meet user demands [18]. Our framework shown in Table 1 has been developed adopting an interdisciplinary perspective due to the different scientific backgrounds of the researchers involved, such as computer science, engineering, psychology, economics and design. It is organized in four major categories. These categories integrate features, which characterize assistance systems by selected attributes.

The category **information** is divided into the features *generation* and *presentation*. The first feature focuses on how relevant data is created; either through the power of software developers' algorithms (*automated*), through a combination of human and machine intelligence (*partly automated*) or mainly through manual work processes (*manually*). Information presentation in contrast describes how the passing of information in terms of complexity is realized. The spectrum ranges from *basic* (e.g. simple graphics, beeps), through *intermediate* (e.g. symbols, steps) to *complex* (e.g. process models).

We chose **intelligence** as a category for all features that sum up aspects of the system that are a result of data-driven predictions or decisions regardless of the underlying technique in use. Techniques might range from classical Artificial Intelligence approaches leveraging declarative or procedural knowledge representations to more recently discussed techniques such as collaborative interactive machine learning [20]. *State detection* refers to the ability of the assistance system to gather data about the current condition of *tools* (e.g. tool tracking), *machines* (e.g. log files), *products* (e.g. target/ actual comparison) and finally also the *user* (e.g. vital data). *Context sensitivity* partly builds on these data and describes the application in fields such as *task* (e.g. task-specific instructions), *environment* (e.g. adaption of the screen due to incidence of light) and *user* (e.g. individual knowledge and experience). The dichotomous feature *learning* aptitude finally characterizes the ability of the assistance system to learn from past data in order to improve future behavior.

The category **interaction** describes the specification of the interface between humans and the assistance systems. The feature *control* characterizes the execution of

Table 1. Framework

Information	
Generation	Presentation
Manual	Basic
Partly automated	Intermediate
Automated	Complex

Intelligence		
State detection	Context Sensitivity	Learning Aptitude
No	No	No
Tools	Task	
Machine / Product	Environment	Yes
User	User	

Interaction				
Control	User Involvement	Input	Output	Extent of Immersion
Human	Low	Traditional	Visual	None
Cooperation	Middle		Haptic / Tactile	Augmented Reality
Machine	High	Modern	Acoustic	Virtual Reality

System Characteristics		
Transportability	Robustness	Technology Readiness Level
Stationary	Low	Low (1-3)
Restricted	Middle	Middle (4-6)
Unrestricted	High	High (7-9)

the jobs and is therefore partitioned in the attributes *human*, *cooperation* and *machine*. Furthermore, the feature *user involvement* classifies the level of cognitive, visual and manual distraction and depends on characteristics of the used interaction mode (attributes *low*, *middle* and *high*). On the one hand, we classify the feature *input* into *traditional* input devices (e.g. keyboard, joystick, touchscreen) and *modern* (e.g. motion-based or touchless devices such as gesture control, speech recognition, eye-tracking). On the other hand, the feature *output* is grouped into *visual* (e.g. displays, projection), *haptic/tactile* (e.g. vibration/haptic technology) and *acoustical* (e.g. speaker, structure-borne sound). The feature *extent of immersion* describes the level to which the assistance systems are capable of delivering an inclusive, extensive, surrounding and vivid illusion of reality to the senses of a human participant [12]. For our field of work, the attributes *none*, *augmented reality* and *virtual reality* are of relevance.

The fourth category, **system characteristics**, specifies aspects concerning the construction of the assistance system. The *transportability* of the system is grouped in *stationary* (e.g. system integrated into machinery), *restricted* (e.g. transportation and setup requires some effort) and *unrestricted* (e.g. mobile devices such as tablet computers). We define *robustness* as the ability of the assistance system to withstand unintentional events (e.g. soft- and hardware actions) or the consequences of human error without being damaged (attributes: *low*, *middle*, *high*). Finally, we derive the *technology readiness level* for the technology maturity in accordance with the European Commission definition [2] in *low* (level 1–3), *middle* (level 4–6) and *high* (level 7–9).

All in all, the final framework resembles a faceted classification, since multiple properties (facets or features) with multiple values are captured. However, since facets normally represent "clearly defined, mutually exclusive, and collectively exhaustive aspects [...] of a class or specific subject" [19], it is not a faceted classification in a strict sense since we allow that multiple property values hold when a subject is classified.

4   Framework Application

In order to demonstrate the application of our framework, we selected and classified three assistance systems. We selected the systems such that the aspect of diversity concerning the selected systems is emphasized. With this, we want to showcase the generality of our framework. The result is presented in the following sub-sections.

4.1   Intelligent Worker Assistance (Büttner et al. 2017)

The first system, presented in [4], can be described as an intelligent assistance system supporting workers in stationary manual assembly by means of projection-based augmented reality (AR) and hand tracking. Using depth cameras, the system can track the hands of the user and notifies the user about wrong picking actions or errors in the assembly process. The system automatically adapts the digital projection-based overlay according to the current work situation. Such a system contributes to helping the worker in dealing with increasing requirements regarding quality, accuracy and clocking of the assembly processes. The system identifies the respective work piece via computer vision and provides the worker with the corresponding assembly instructions. Depth cameras that are fixed on the ceiling of the assembly station capture the worker's movements, the workspace and all objects that are situated in it, such as material boxes. This allows to monitor single steps (for example picking a component), intuitively control the production process by means of gesture recognition and successively ensures a correct assembly of the product. Visual aids in the form of text, graphics or video sequences can be displayed directly on the assembly workplace via projections. In connection with the gesture recognition by the depth camera system, the assistance system can also be operated via touch detection.

The generation of **information** is *partly automated* while its presentation is clearly *complex*. The system features a wide range of media from video to rich graphics to simple icons.

With regard to **intelligence**, the system features *state detection* in so far as it is capable of tracking *tools*, the *machine* or *product* and the *user* via its depth cameras. *Context sensitivity* applies to the *task* and the *user* because the system may identify false assembly steps by tracking user hand movements. *Learning aptitude* can be classified with *no*, since the system is not able to learn over time.

In terms of **interaction**, *control* is to be classified as *cooperation* because actions and commands can be initiated by both the human and the machine or system. *User involvement* is *low* since information are generated by the system. The input modalities are modern, e.g. soft buttons via projection, and the *output* is *visual*. The *extent of immersion* is clearly *Augmented Reality*.

Regarding **system characteristics**, the *transportability* is to be labelled as *stationary* while the robustness classifies as *middle*. The system's *technology readiness level* falls within the *middle* (4–6) category.

4.2   TeleAdvisor (Gurevich et al. 2012)

TeleAdvisor, presented in [10], supports remote assistance tasks by enabling live in-situ projections. The system comprises a video camera and a pico-projector mounted on top of a tele-operated robotic arm. Thus, using a desktop interface a remote expert can guide a worker through e.g. a maintenance task by annotating the workspace with visual information such as pointers and text. Active tracking of the projection space is employed in order to reliably correlate between the camera's view and the projector space. Using the robotic arm, the expert can also control the field of view.

All projected **information** is *generated manually* by the expert operating TeleAdvisor via the desktop interface. The expert may create annotations such as text, free-hand sketches, and choose from a set of images and icons, all available in different colours. Hence, information *presentation* classifies as *intermediate*.

The systems inherent **intelligence** does not feature *state detection* but allows for recognizing the *environment* in order to align the projection correctly (*context sensitivity*). The system is suitable for learning only in so far as it facilitates human-to-human mentoring (*learning aptitude: no*).

In terms of **interaction** the TeleAdvisor relies on *human* operation and control. The *user involvment* is *high* since all information is generated and processed by the users (expert and worker). *Input* can be described as *traditional* since the desktop interface is operated by mouse and keyboard while *output* modalities are restricted to *visuals* (the source does not mention acoustics). Because of the in-situ projection, the *extent of immersion* is clearly *augmented reality*.

Regarding **system characteristics**, the authors rate their system high in terms of *transportability*, however, we classify TeleAdvisor as *restricted* since the source does not mention battery supply which makes it bound to a power cord. Looking at *robustness* an assessment is difficult due to lacking information. Again, the creators describe the system as very robust (*high*), so we will follow this assessment. The *technology readiness level* scores in the *middle* category.

4.3   Smart-Glasses-Based Service Support System (Niemöller et al. 2017)

The prototype system presented in [16] aims to support service technicians in executing service tasks. It is motivated by the complexity of today's high-tech products that require an increasing amount of information during service work. In order to provide this information directly within the work process and to guide the service technician, information is displayed on smart glasses controlled via voice recognition. With that, the service technician can work hands-free and interference with manual tasks is minimized. The system is implemented with the glass development kit on Android.

All displayed **information** is *generated manually* by experts who can create contents for the Smart-Glasses-based Service Support System using a desktop computer. The expert can create step-by-step guidance and provide a detailed description for each step. Such information can comprise spare part information, pictures, wiring diagrams, videos and technical details. Due to these rich options for the presentation of information including multi-media, *presentation* of *complex* information is possible.

In regard to **intelligence**, neither *state detection* nor *context sensitivity* is implemented. However, a limited form of *learning aptitude* is indirectly available by using the features to easily provide feedback e.g. by making photos and commenting the pictures using voice recording. Such feedback can be processed and the information support could be improved on that basis which might be considered as a form of learning.

In terms of **interaction**, the *control* of the system can be considered as *cooperative* since the user triggers the display of information, but the system can also guide the user with step-by-step-descriptions. *User involvement* is *high* since all information belonging to an information object such as an activity has to be requested by the user whereby several requests may be required if the information is complex and must be displayed on multiple screens. *Input* can be made with *modern* interfaces such as voice recognition and touch displays attached to the side pieces of the smart glass. Regarding *output*, *visual* and *acoustic* output is possible. Since the smart glass create an information overlay to what is seen in reality, the *extent of immersion* is *augmented reality*.

Regarding **system characteristics**, *transportability* of smart glasses is *unrestricted* which is an advantage. However, in regard to *robustness*, such devices are prone to mechanical damage and hence have to be carried with caution. In terms of the *technology readiness level*, a distinction has to be made between hardware and software.

While maturity of hardware is *high* since smart glasses are offered from major vendors, software maturity is *low* since (as of now) it is an academic prototype.

5   Conclusion and Outlook

In this paper, we presented a framework for classifying assistance systems in the context of smart factories. The framework has been iteratively developed by five experts from different backgrounds (computer science, engineering, psychology, economics and design) based on an analysis of literature in the related field of research. The framework consists of four major categories: *information, intelligence, interaction* and *system characteristic*. Each of the major categories contains multiple features, where each of the features represents a certain aspect of the system that can be described with the attributes provided in the context of the feature. The selection of attributes is not mutually exclusive, so for some of the features, multiple attributes can be used to classify a certain system, e.g. for the major category *interaction* and the feature *output* the attributes *visual* and *acoustic* can be used mutually to describe an aspect of the system.

To verify the functionality of the framework, we described and classified three assistance systems that have been provided by previous research projects. For this presentation, we chose three systems from the related literature that were as diverse as possible and had only few attributes in common. The classification of the three systems demonstrates the functionality of the framework well and shows that the framework provides all major aspects that characterize the three systems.

With the framework, we pursue the following three objectives: First, we want to provide a tool for classifying existing and new systems to better understand the aspects of these systems and to identify common key characteristics of assistance systems. Second, we want to found a common vocabulary in the research field. Third, we want to support the identification of research gaps, which will be possible by looking for aspects that are not present in the current generation of assistance systems. These three objectives are not only valuable for researchers in the field. We also aim to provide a better understanding by practitioners in the field who are welcome to use the framework as input for the development process of new assistance systems.

In our future work, we plan to further validate and revise our initial framework by classifying a large set of systems and to identify patterns and common characteristics e.g. of more research-oriented systems and industry-oriented systems.

References

1. acatech – Deutsche Akademie der Technikwissenschaften: Kompetenzentwicklungsstudie Industrie 4.0 – Erste Ergebnisse und Schlussfolgerungen, München (2016)
2. Anderson, G.F., Hussey, P.S.: Population aging: a comparison among industrialized countries. Health Aff. **19**(3), 191–203 (2000)

3. Büttner, S., Mucha, H., Funk, M., Kosch, T., Aehnelt, M., Robert, S., Röcker, C.: The design space of augmented and virtual reality applications for assistive environments in manufacturing: a visual approach. In: Proceedings of the 10th ACM International Conference on PErvasive Technologies Related to Assistive Environments. ACM (2017)

4. Büttner, S., Sand, O., Röcker, C.: Exploring design opportunities for intelligent worker assistance: a new approach using projetion-based AR and a novel hand-tracking algorithm. In: Braun, A., Wichert, R., Maña, A. (eds.) AmI 2017. LNCS, vol. 10217, pp. 33–45. Springer, Cham (2017). doi:10.1007/978-3-319-56997-0_3

5. Chaloff, J., Lemaitre, G.: Managing Highly-Skilled Labour Migration. OECD Social, Employment and Migration Working Papers (2009). doi:10.1787/1815199X

6. Fite-Georgel, P.: Is there a reality in industrial augmented reality? In: 2011 10th IEEE International Symposium Mixed and Augmented Reality (ISMAR), pp. 201–210. IEEE (2011)

7. Ganschar, O., Gerlach, S., Hämmerle, M., Krause, T., Schlund, S.: In: Spath, D. (ed.). Produktionsarbeit der Zukunft – Industrie 4.0, pp. 50–56. Fraunhofer Verlag, Stuttgart (2013)

8. Geissbauer, R., Vedso, J., Schrauf, S.: Industry 4.0: Building the digital enterprise. PwC (2015)

9. Gorecky, D., Schmitt, M., Loskyll, M., Zühlke, D.: Human-machine-interaction in the industry 4.0 era. In: Industrial Informatics (INDIN) 2014, pp. 2896–294 (2014)

10. Gurevich, P., Lanir, J., Cohen, B., Stone, R.: TeleAdvisor: a versatile augmented reality tool for remote assistance. In: Proceedings of the SIGCHI Conference on Human Factors in Computing Systems 2012, pp. 619–622. ACM (2012)

11. Hermann, M., Pentek, T., Otto, B.: Design principles for Industry 4.0 Scenarios. In: HICSS 2016, pp. 3928–3937. IEEE (2016)

12. Jain, D., Sra, M., Guo, J., Marques, R., Wu, R., Chiu, J., Schmandt, C.: Immersive terrestrial scuba diving using virtual reality. In: Proceedings of the 2016 CHI Conference Extended Abstracts on Human Factors in Computing Systems, pp. 1563–1569. ACM (2016)

13. Lucke, D., Constantinescu, C., Westkämper, E.: Smart factory-a step towards the next generation of manufacturing. In: Mitsuishi M., et al. (eds.) Manufacturing Systems and Technologies for the New Frontier, pp. 115–118. Springer, London (2008)

14. Nelles, J., Kuz, S., Mertens, A., Schlick, C. M.: Human-centered design of assistance systems for production planning and control: The role of the human in Industry 4.0. In: Proceedings of the IEEE International Conference Industrial Technology (ICIT) 2016, pp. 2099–2104. IEEE (2016)

15. Nickerson, R.C., Varshney, U., Muntermann, J.: A method for taxonomy development and its application in information systems. Eur. J. Inform. Syst. 2013(22), 336–359 (2013)

16. Niemöller, C., Metzger, D., Thomas, O.: Design and evaluation of a smart-glasses-based service support system. In: Leimeister, J.M., Brenner, W. (eds.) Proceedings of WI 2017, pp. 106–120 (2017)

17. Röcker, C., Robert, S.: Projektionsbasierte Montageunterstützung mit visueller Fortschrittserkennung. In: visIT Industrie 4.0. Fraunhofer IOSB, Karlsruhe, Germany (2016)

18. Sprague, J.R., Ralph, H.: A framework for the development of decision support systems. MIS Q. 4(1), 1–26 (1980)

19. Taylor, A.G., Miller, D.P., Bohdan, S.W.: Introduction to Cataloging and Classification. Libraries Unlimited (2000)

20. Robert, S., Büttner, S., Röcker, C., Holzinger, A.: Reasoning under uncertainty: towards collaborative interactive machine learning. In: Holzinger, A. (ed.) Machine Learning for Health Informatics. LNCS, vol. 9605, pp. 357–376. Springer, Cham (2016). doi:10.1007/978-3-319-50478-0_18

Managing Complexity: Towards Intelligent Error-Handling Assistance Trough Interactive Alarm Flood Reduction

Sebastian Büttner[✉], Paul Wunderlich, Mario Heinz, Oliver Niggemann, and Carsten Röcker

Institute Industrial IT (inIT), OWL University of Applied Sciences, Lemgo, Germany
{sebastian.buettner,paul.wunderlich,mario.heinz, oliver.niggemann,carsten.roecker}@hs-owl.de

Abstract. The current trend of integrating machines and factories into cyber-physical systems (CPS) creates an enormous complexity for operators of such systems. Especially the search for the root cause of cascading failures becomes highly time-consuming. Within this paper, we address the question on how to help human users to better and faster understand root causes of such situations. We propose a concept of interactive alarm flood reduction and present the implementation of a first vertical prototype for such a system. We consider this prototype as a first artifact to be discussed by the research community and aim towards an incremental further development of the system in order to support humans in complex error situations.

Keywords: Alarm flood reduction · Machine learning · Assistive system

1 Introduction and Motivation

Currently the landscape of industrial production changes fundamentally. While in the past decades engineering in industrial production focused on the question on how to further automatize industrial production, the current development concentrates on the digitalization and connection of industrial components and whole factories to form so-called cyber-physical systems (CPS) [26]. The formed networks as well as the use of machine learning technologies to create intelligent production components will increase production efficiency and is therefore of huge economic value. A study of Germany's digital association Bitkom forecasts a value-added potential of 79 billion euros in the six major industrial branches of the German economy until 2025 [4]. With the changes of technologies and processes, human interactions with production systems and factories will also be transformed [30].

By creating new networks of industrial components and factories, complexity is induced into the system. This complexity can become an issue in case of

A. Holzinger et al. (Eds.): CD-MAKE 2017, LNCS 10410, pp. 69–82, 2017.
DOI: 10.1007/978-3-319-66808-6_6

errors, faults, failures, or security attacks of a single component that might influence other parts of overall CPS due to cascading failures [25]. While some of the cascading failures might be avoided by incorporating robustness principles into the design and implementation process of CPS (e.g. [43]), we assume that there will be always failure situations that will require human interventions. However, finding root causes in failure situations requires more effort and becomes costly, if systems are connected. Maintenance work in the new complex context of CPS requires interdisciplinary skills and high competencies, such as knowledge about the technologies, economic and legal factors, social and communicational skills and willingness to learn [33]. Based on these high requirements and the present shortage in highly-skilled workers it would be desirable to have intelligent systems that support humans in the analysis and handling of failures in CPS. With this paper, we want to focus on the question on how to help human users to understand root causes of complex failure situations. More specifically, we address the topic of interactive alarm flood reduction in CPS scenarios, an interactive machine learning (iML) approach to find root causes of complex failure situations. With this paper, we present a first prototype of an assistive system that can help users to find root causes of alarm floods by using machine learning technologies.

The rest of the paper is organized as follows. Section 2 gives an overview on related work in the research areas of assistive systems for error-handling, alarm flood reduction and iML. Section 3 shortly describes the research through design method that is the foundation for our research method. Section 4 proposes our concept of interactive alarm flood reduction. Section 5 describes our prototype in detail, followed by a discussion of the results, a conclusion and outlook in Sect. 6.

2   Related Work

In this section, we will provide an overview of the current research regarding three fields: First, we will present previous assistive systems in the context of error-handling. Second, we will show previous machine learning methods for alarm flood reduction and third, we will present the young research field of iML.

2.1   Assistive Systems for Error-Handling

There has been a lot of research work on the topic of assistive systems to support work processes in the future of industrial production and many overview works and surveys exist, e.g. on how to support users with Augmented Reality (AR) in industry [5,14]. However, only few proposed systems considered the support in complex error situations and focus mainly on a non-interactive visualization. Folmer et al. [15] present a system called Automatic Alarm Data Analyzer (AADA) that use machine learning algorithms to reduce alarm floods and a three-dimensional visualization to show only the most important information to an operator. In a similar way, Laberge et al. [24] analyzed different alarm summary display designs for the visualization of complex error situations. They compared a list-based presentation with a time-series presentation showing icons and summarized descriptions. According to their study, the latter presentation led to fewer false user responses. Another work in this domain by Renzhin et al. [31] analyses and visualizes communication data between machines in CPS in various way. By choosing the appropriate visualization, users are empowered to find errors more easily. Furthermore, the system can find deviations from the normal state of the system and reports such errors automatically to the user.

2.2   Alarm Flood Reduction

The topic of alarm flood reduction gained attention from the process industry after incidents like the explosion at the Texaco Refinery in Milford Haven [17]. As a result, the non-profit organization Engineering Equipment & Materials Users' Association (EEMUA) created the guideline EEMUA 191 [10]. The quasi-standard EEMUA 191 for alarm management recommends to have only one alarm per 10 min. Based on this, further standards such as ANSI/ISA-18.2-2009 [28] or IEC62682:2014 [9] have been developed. With the vision of industry 4.0 this topic has an increasing importance also for other industrial branches. Several approaches to address the topic of alarm floods exist. Most of them deal with clustering similar alarms together. A good overview about different approaches is provided by Wang et al. [39].

We want to focus on reducing alarm floods by identifying the root cause of the alarm flood. Therefore, we need a causal model which represents the dependencies of the alarms. Probabilistic graphical models, such as Bayesian nets, fault trees, or Petri nets are particularly suitable for this purpose. They were already used in the field of alarm flood reduction. Kezunovic and Guan [23] use a fuzzy reasoning Petri nets diagnose model to identify root causes. For this, they take advantages of an expert rule based system and fuzzy logic. Simeu-Abazi et al. [35] exploit dynamic fault trees to filter false alarms and locate faults from alarms. Guo et al. [16] develop an analytic model for alarm processing, which is based on temporal constraint networks. They use this model to find out what caused the reported alarms and estimate when these events happen. Wei et al. [41] apply a rule network for alarm processing. They can determine the root cause and also identify missing or false alarms. Wang et al. [37] combine association rules with fuzzy logic. They use a weighted fuzzy association rule mining approach to discover correlated alarm sequences. Based on this, they are able to identify root causes. Abele et al. [1] propose to combine modeling knowledge and machine learning knowledge to identify alarm root causes. They use a constrained-based method to learn the causal model of a factory represented by a Bayesian network. This enables faster modeling and accurate parametrization of alarm dependencies but expert knowledge is still required. Wang et al. [38] apply an online root-cause analysis of alarms in discrete Bayesian networks. They restrict the Bayesian Network to have only one child. The method is evaluated on a numerical example of a tank-level system. In [42] various approaches to learn a causal representation of alarms to identify the root cause are investigated. The concept for the reduction of alarm floods in this work is based on their findings.

2.3 Interactive Machine Learning (iML)

In the context of Machine Learning, iML is an approach that involves humans into machine learning processes to deliver better results than fully-automated systems. According to Robert et al. [32], the available iML system can be classified into the following three categories:

First, there are iML systems, where an appropriate data visualization helps humans to manually build a model. Still, the interference is done automatically based on the manually created model. Examples for this system are the perception-based classification (PBC) system presented by Ankerst et al. [2,3] and the work of Ware et al. [40].

Second, systems have been described under the term iML that involve humans into an evaluation-feedback loop to improve an automatically generated model. The created model is appropriately visualized to the user and the system contains a feedback channel, where users can assess the quality of a certain model. With this feedback, the system can improve the model iteratively. These systems require a very fast model generation to allow rapid improvement when feedback is given to the system. Examples for such systems are the system of Fails et al. [11] that allows interaction designers to rapidly build perceptual user interfaces (PUI) and the Wekinator[1] system that analyses human gestures in the context of music making [12].

The third type that is also named collaborative iML (ciML) is the newest of the approaches. ciML systems can be characterized as system, where humans can influence the model generation algorithm during runtime and work collaboratively with the algorithm to create a model. Examples for ciML systems are the decision tree generation system by Ankerst et al. [3] and interactive ant-colony algorithm to solve the traveling salesman problem (TSP) presented by Holzinger et al. [20].

In this paper, we understand iML as systems, were the user is involved into the feedback loop of iML systems, which is the second type in the classification above.

3 Method

To better understand, how to support users in handling complex failure situations, we decided to develop a first prototype of an interactive system for alarm flood reduction. This prototype can be seen as a research artifact to communicate and discuss ideas among the research community [27]. In this way, we follow the "research through design" approach proposed by Zimmerman et al. [44]. To develop the prototype, we chose an iterative approach and followed the human-centered design process specified in ISO 9241-210 (see [21], cf. [19]). This process

---

[1] http://www.wekinator.org/.

has proven to be very effective for designing interactive systems with a high usability and has been successfully applied in an industrial context as well [6].

The prototype presented in this paper is the result of the first iteration. It is a vertical prototype, so it does not contain all features of the system yet, but therefore contains the core functionality and shows the feasibility of our concept.

4   Concept

The general concept proposed in this paper is the use of a cloud-based machine learning system that monitors data from machines and becomes active in the situation of an alarm flood, which we define as an occurrence of more than ten errors per minute. This concept is shown in Fig. 1. Data, such as error messages and warnings from machines and factories are send to a cloud service and stored in a database. Based on this data, a machine learning algorithm builds up a model of the relation of different error messages and warnings. In case of an alarm flood the model is used to infer conclusions about the root cause of the current situation. The analysis is presented to the user in a suitable way (e.g. via an adaptive and responsive user interface). There are two types of user involvement in this concept: First, the users of the assistive system (usually the operators of factories or machines) report (explicitly or implicitly) feedback to the system, if a certain root cause was predicted correctly from the system. This feedback is stored in the database and used for the next iteration of the

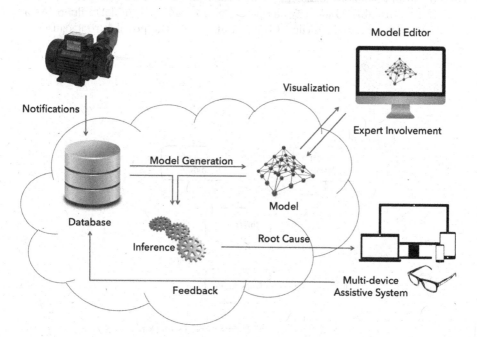

Fig. 1. Overall process of the interactive alarm flood reduction

model generation. Second, expert users can improve the model by using a model editor. By assessing, if a detected error correlation is a causal relation or not, the expert can manually change the model. The manual changes are kept when the model is rebuilt in following iterations.

This section will focus on the aspects of the conceptual development of the alarm flood reduction (algorithm) and the adaptive and responsive user interface.

4.1 Alarm Flood Reduction

The concept of the alarm flood reduction is depicted in Fig. 2. The concept can be divided into two steps. As an initial step a causal model from the gathered data in the alarm log is learned. In the alarm log the alarms of the factory or CPS are listed with information about timing, description and status. The status represents if the alarm is active or inactive. Based on the information of the alarm log a causal model of the alarms is learned. Probabilistic graphical models are suitable for as a causal model. We decide to use Bayesian Networks to represent the dependencies of the alarms as a causal model. Bayesian networks are a class of graphical models which allow an intuitive representation of multivariate data. A Bayesian network is a directed acyclic graph, denoted $B = (N, E)$, with a set of variables $\boldsymbol{X} = \{X_1, X_2, \ldots, X_p\}$. Each node $n \in N$ is associated with one variable X_i. The edges $e \in E$, which connect the nodes, represent direct probabilistic dependencies. In a second step, we use the current alarms and the learned causal model of the alarms to infer the root cause. Because of the learned relations, we are able to identify the possible root cause of an alarm flood. As a consequence, we can reduce the amount of alarms to the possible root cause.

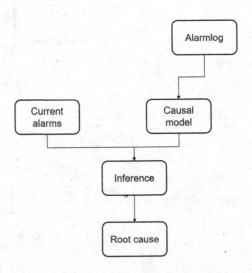

Fig. 2. Concept of alarm flood reduction

4.2   Adaptive and Responsive User Interface

We distinguish between two separate user interfaces: the interface of the assistive system and the model generator.

The user interface of the assistive system should be highly flexible to support different users and work situations. Therefore, we propose an adaptive and responsive user interface, that can be used with various technologies and interaction concepts. As a basic user interface, we use a responsive web application that adapts to different devices. While responsive web applications are the current state of web technology, they are limited to (two-dimensional) graphical user interfaces. With this interaction concept, we go beyond this limitation. The web application is the base visualization; however, if a user needs further assistance, such as support in a repair scenario, where free hands are required, the user can switch to an augmented reality (AR) visualization based on head-mounted displays (HMD) (such as [29]) or mobile in-situ projections (such as [7]). Beyond the visualization, the user needs to have a way of giving feedback to the system, while and after doing maintenance work. Especially the results of an obtained repair task are important to check, whether the model is accurate or need to be improved. Therefore, we included a feedback channel to the system to report, whether the root cause was detected correctly. This feedback channel could be explicitly by users' approvals or implicitly (cf. [34]) by the recognition of the users' activities and tasks.

The model generator is used by experts to manually adapt the model. This interface presents the model in the form of a large graph. Due to the large data sets that might be involved, this interface is shown on large computer displays. Expert users can mark edges that represent causalities of errors or remove edges from the model, that are no causal relations.

5   Prototype

In the context of the human-centered design process (compare section Method), a first prototype has been developed iteratively. This prototype represents a vertical prototype, so it does not contain all features of the system yet. However, it contains the core functionality and shows the feasibility of our proposed concept. This section will describe the implementation of the prototype system.

5.1   Architecture

The high-level architecture of the presented system is shown in Fig. 3. For the basic infrastructure, we use Amazon Web Services (AWS), which provides services, such as virtual servers, a database (DynamoDB), and supports the development of application programming interfaces (APIs) that follow the principles of representational state transfer (RESTful APIs). We provide a web server with a generic RESTful API, where different machines can be connected to. Since industrial machines usually do not use web protocols but rather rely on machine

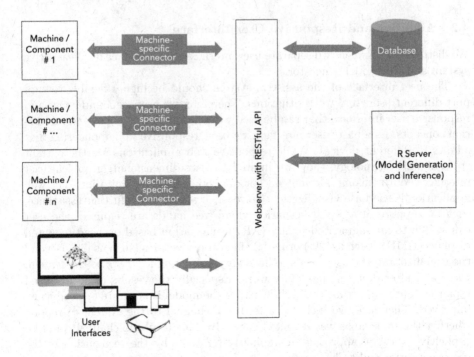

Fig. 3. High-level architecture of the system

to machine protocols, such as Open Platform Communications Unified Architecture (OPC UA), individual connectors need to be implemented for each of the specific machine types. The web server is connected to the AWS DynamoDB and to a server running an R environment[2] for executing the machine learning algorithms. The web server is also used to provide the current user interface to various devices. The following sections present the implementation of the machine learning algorithms and of the user interface in more detail.

5.2   Machine Learning Algorithms

The implementation of the machine learning algorithm contains three steps, namely structure learning, parameter learning and inference. We use the Max-Min Hill-Climbing which was developed by Tsamardinos et al. for learning the structure [36]. For a better understanding of the associated pseudo code, we need a few definitions. The dataset D consists of a set of variables ϑ. In the variable PC_x the candidates of parents and children for the node X are stored. This set of candidates is calculated with a Max-Min Parents and Children (MMPC) algorithm. The variable Y is a node of the set PC_x. The pseudo code of MMHC looks as follows: The algorithm first identifies the parents and children set of each variable, then performs a greedy Hill-Climbing search in the reduced space

---

[2] https://www.r-project.org/.

of Bayesian network. The search begins with an empty graph. The edge addition, removal, or reversing which leads to the largest increase in the score is taken and the search continues in a similar way recursively. The difference from standard Hill-Climbing is that the search is constrained to only consider edges which were discovered by MMPC in the first phase. The MMPC algorithm calculates the correlation between the nodes.

In a next step, the probabilities or parameters of the Bayesian network are learned. For this we use the maximum likelihood estimation (MLE) which was developed by R.A. Fischer and is a classical method in statistics [13]. Here, a parameter p is estimated to maximize the probability of obtaining the observation under the condition of the parameter p. In other words, the MLE provides the most plausible parameter p as an estimate with respect to the observation. If the parameter p is a probability in the Bayesian network and the historical data D represents the observations, the likelihood function is composed as follows:

Algorithm 1. MMHC Algorithm

1: **procedure** MMHC(D)
2:    Input: data D
3:    Output: a DAG on the variables in D
4:    % Restrict
5:    **for** every variable $X \in \vartheta$ **do**
6:        $PC_X = \text{MMPC}(X, D)$
7:    **end for**
8:    % Search
9:    Starting from an empty graph perform Greedy Hill-Climbing with operators add-edge, delete-edge, reverse-edge. $Y \rightarrow X$ if $Y \in PC_X$
10:   **Return** the highest scoring DAG found
11: **end procedure**

$$L(D|p) = \prod_{i=1}^{n} f(D|p) \tag{1}$$

The probability density function of D under the condition p is $f(D|p)$. With the learned structure and the probabilities, the inference can begin. The approximate method logic sampling (LS) is used for this purpose.

The Logic Sampling Algorithm is a very simple procedure developed by Max Henrion in 1986 [18]. In this case, a state is arbitrarily assumed per sample for the root nodes according to their probability table. Thus, a certain number of samples, which are determined, are carried out. Subsequently, the probability that e.g. a node X assumes the state True as follows:

$$P(X = True) = \frac{\text{Number of cases with X} = \text{True}}{\text{Number of all samples}} \tag{2}$$

This process always converges to the correct solution, but in very rare cases the number of samples required can become exorbitant [22]. The feedback of the expert is included with a whitelist and blacklist in the structure learning. The whitelist contains all predetermined relations and the blacklist contains all prohibited relations between the alarms.

5.3   User Interface

The current user interface is built on the basis of web technologies. Server-sided, the system provides a generic RESTful API for exchanging the data between the server and the end-users' devices. The actual client is built as a responsive web application. While the responsive assistive system is part of the current prototype, the model editor is ongoing work and therefore not further described in this section.

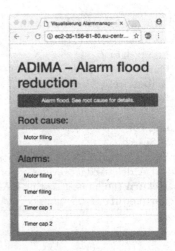

Fig. 4. Screenshots of the responsive web application with (a) normal situation without errors and (b) case of an occurring alarm flood. (Color figure online)

The webserver can be accessed to load the assistive system in form of a responsive web application that automatically adapts to the device of the user, such as computer screens, smartphones or tablet computers. The integration of other interaction devices, such as HMDs for hand-free operation is ongoing work. The user interface is implemented in HTML5 using the frameworks Bootstrap[3] and AngularJS[4]. To display the information on small screens, the content of the current user interface is limited to the most important information. It shows the occurring errors and (in case of an alarm flood) the root cause of the problem

---

[3] http://getbootstrap.com/.
[4] https://angularjs.org/.

(see Fig. 4b) or a huge green check mark if all machines are working properly (see Fig. 4a).

Since this responsive website cannot be displayed on devices without web browsers, such as HMDs, native applications will be provided in future that also make use of the generic API. According to our concept, there will be more detailed assistance information to display not only the root cause but rather various types of media (images, videos) that help users to fix a specific cascade of errors, which is a topic for future work.

6 Discussion, Conclusion and Outlook

In this paper, we proposed our concept of a system for interactive alarm flood reduction for determine root causes in complex failure situations. Such a system will be beneficial for finding errors in complex industrial environments, e.g. in the future of production, when CPS become omnipresent. Contrary to previous work, we do not only focus on automatic machine learning concepts for alarm flood reduction, but rather want to establish a feedback channel to empower users to give feedback of the results of the alarm flood reduction to the system. Having this possibility, the model representing the causal relations of alarms can iteratively be improved.

We presented a first vertical prototype of our concept consisting of a machine learning system based on the Max-Min Hill-Climbing algorithm of Tsamardinos et al. [36] and the maximum likelihood estimation of Fischer [13] as well as a responsive web application as user interface based on web technology. This prototype has been developed in an iterative design process. While a formal evaluation of our prototype is outstanding and future work, we discussed the results with experts from industry. However, the prototype shows the feasibility of our proposed concept.

Future work will focus on the improvement of the system to give better predictions of root causes as well as a deeper integration of human feedback. Furthermore, additional features will be added to the very basic user interface described in this paper. The responsive web application will be extended in the way to actually realize an assistive system; this will be achieved by not only showing the error but rather guide users through the process of repair or maintenance in a similar way to assistive systems in manufacturing, such as [8]. For this purpose, the system will be extended to also allow for connecting other interaction devices, e.g. HMDs. While the interface of the web server is designed in a way to cover this process, a specific scenario containing machines and related maintenance and repair manuals needs to be created. Parallel to this technical development, we plan to evaluate the overall systems repeatedly during the iterative development process.

As already stated our system is in an early stage. However, the current prototype is a first artifact to communicate our vision and to discuss ideas among the research community (cf. [27,44]). The further development and evaluation will give more insight into the question on how to help human users to understand errors in complex interconnected systems, such as CPS.

Acknowledgments. This work is funded by the German Federal Ministry of Education and Research (BMBF) for project ADIMA under grant number 03FH019PX5.

References

1. Abele, L., Anic, M., Gutmann, T., Folmer, J., Kleinsteuber, M., Vogel-Heuser, B.: Combining knowledge modeling and machine learning for alarm root cause analysis. IFAC Proc. Vol. **46**(9), 1843–1848 (2013)
2. Ankerst, M., Elsen, C., Ester, M., Kriegel, H.-P.: Visual classification: an interactive approach to decision tree construction. In: Proceedings of the Fifth ACM SIGKDD International Conference on Knowledge Discovery and Data Mining, pp. 392–396. ACM (1999)
3. Ankerst, M., Ester, M., Kriegel, H.-P.: Towards an effective cooperation of the user and the computer for classification. In: Proceedings of the Sixth ACM SIGKDD International Conference on Knowledge Discovery and Data Mining (KDD 2000), pp. 179–188, New York. ACM (2000)
4. Bauer, W., Horváth, P.: Industrie 4.0 - Volkswirtschaftliches Potenzial für Deutschland. Controlling **27**(8–9), 515–517 (2015)
5. Büttner, S., Mucha, H., Funk, M., Kosch, T., Aehnelt, M., Robert, S., Röcker, C.: The design space of augmented and virtual reality applications for assistive environments in manufacturing: a visual approach. In: Proceedings of the 10th International Conference on Pervasive Technologies Related to Assistive Environments, pp. 433–440. ACM (June 2017)
6. Büttner, S., Röcker, C.: Applying human-centered design methods in industry - a field report. In: Human-Computer Interaction-Perspectives on Industry 4.0. Workshop at i-KNOW 2016, Graz (2016)
7. Büttner, S., Sand, O., Röcker, C.: Extending the design space in industrial manufacturing through mobile projection. In: Proceedings of the 17th International Conference on Human-Computer Interaction with Mobile Devices and Services Adjunct, pp. 1130–1133. ACM (2015)
8. Büttner, S., Sand, O., Röcker, C.: Exploring design opportunities for intelligent worker assistance: a new approach using projetion-based AR and a novel hand-tracking algorithm. In: Braun, A., Wichert, R., Maña, A. (eds.) AmI 2017. LNCS, vol. 10217, pp. 33–45. Springer, Cham (2017). doi:10.1007/978-3-319-56997-0_3
9. International Electrotechnical Commission: En-iec 62682:2014 management of alarm systems for the process industries. Technical report, International Electrotechnical Commission
10. Engineering Equipment, Materials Users Association, Engineering Equipment, and Materials Users Association Staff: Alarm systems: a guide to design, management and procurement. EEMUA publication. EEMUA (Engineering Equipment & Materials Users Association) (2007)
11. Fails, J.A., Olsen Jr., D.R.: Interactive machine learning. In: Proceedings of the 8th International Conference on Intelligent User Interfaces, pp. 39–45. ACM (2003)
12. Fiebrink, R., Cook, P.R., Trueman, D.: Human model evaluation in interactive supervised learning. In: Proceedings of the SIGCHI Conference on Human Factors in Computing Systems (CHI 2011), pp. 147–156, New York. ACM (2011)
13. Fisher, R.A.: On an absolute criterion for fitting frequency curves. Messenger Math. **41**, 155–160 (1912)

14. Fite-Georgel, P.: Is there a reality in industrial augmented reality? In: 2011 10th IEEE International Symposium on Mixed and Augmented Reality (ISMAR), pp. 201–210. IEEE (2011)

15. Folmer, J., Pantförder, D., Vogel-Heuser, B.: An analytical alarm flood reduction to reduce operator's workload. In: Jacko, J.A. (ed.) HCI 2011. LNCS, vol. 6764, pp. 297–306. Springer, Heidelberg (2011). doi:10.1007/978-3-642-21619-0_38

16. Guo, W., Wen, F., Liao, Z., Wei, L., Xin, J.: An analytic model-based approach for power system alarm processing employing temporal constraint network. IEEE Trans. Power Deliv. **25**(4), 2435–2447 (2010)

17. Health and Safety Executive - GB: The Explosion and Fires at the Texaco Refinery, Milford Haven, 24 July 1994: A Report of the Investigation by the Health and Safety Executive Into the Explosion and Fires on the Pembroke Cracking Company Plant at the Texaco Refinery, Milford Haven on 24 July 1994. Incident Report Series. HSE Books (1997)

18. Henrion, M.: Propagating uncertainty in Bayesian networks by probabilistic logic sampling. In: Uncertainty in Artificial Intelligence 2nd Annual Conference on Uncertainty in Artificial Intelligence (UAI-86), pp. 149–163. Elsevier Science, Amsterdam (1986)

19. Holzinger, A., Errath, M., Searle, G., Thurnher, B., Slany, W.: From extreme programming and usability engineering to extreme usability in software engineering education. In: 29th Annual International Computer Software and Applications Conference (COMPSAC 2005), vol. 2, pp. 169–172. IEEE (2005)

20. Holzinger, A., Plass, M., Holzinger, K., Crişan, G.C., Pintea, C.-M., Palade, V.: Towards interactive machine learning (iML): applying ant colony algorithms to solve the traveling salesman problem with the human-in-the-loop approach. In: Buccafurri, F., Holzinger, A., Kieseberg, P., Tjoa, A.M., Weippl, E. (eds.) CD-ARES 2016. LNCS, vol. 9817, pp. 81–95. Springer, Cham (2016). doi:10.1007/978-3-319-45507-5_6

21. ISO 9241-210:2010: Ergonomics of human system interaction – part 210: Human-centred design for interactive systems. International Standardization Organization (ISO), Switzerland (2009)

22. Kanal, L., Lemmer, J.: Uncertainty in Artificial Intelligence 2. Machine Intelligence and Pattern Recognition. Elsevier Science (2014)

23. Kezunovic, M., Guan, Y.: Intelligent alarm processing: from data intensive to information rich. In: 2009 42nd Hawaii International Conference on System Sciences, pp. 1–8, January 2009

24. Laberge, J.C., Bullemer, P., Tolsma, M., Dal Vernon, C.R.: Addressing alarm flood situations in the process industries through alarm summary display design and alarm response strategy. Int. J. Ind. Ergon. **44**(3), 395–406 (2014)

25. Lee, E.A.: Cyber physical systems: design challenges. In: 2008 11th IEEE International Symposium on Object Oriented Real-Time Distributed Computing (ISORC), pp. 363–369. IEEE (2008)

26. Lee, J., Bagheri, B., Kao, H.-A.: A cyber-physical systems architecture for industry 4.0-based manufacturing systems. Manuf. Lett. **3**, 18–23 (2015)

27. Mucha, H., Nebe, K.: Human-centered toolkit design. In: HCITools: Strategies and Best Practices for Designing, Evaluating and Sharing Technical HCI Toolkits, Workshop at CHI 2017, Denver. ACM (2017)

28. International Society of Automation and American National Standards Institute: ANSI/ISA-18.2-2009, Management of Alarm Systems for the Process Industries. ISA (2009)

29. Paelke, V., Röcker, C., Koch, N., Flatt, H., Büttner, S.: User interfaces for cyber-physical systems. at-Automatisierungstechnik **63**(10), 833–843 (2015)
30. Rajkumar, R.R., Lee, I., Sha, L., Stankovic, J.: Cyber-physical systems: the next computing revolution. In: Proceedings of the 47th Design Automation Conference, pp. 731–736. ACM (2010)
31. Renzhin, D., Pantförder, D., Folmer, J., Vogel-Heuser, B.: Darstellungskonzepte für die zustandsabhängige Diagnose industrieller Kommunikationsnetzwerken für verteilte Automatisierungssysteme. In: MBEES, pp. 91–100 (2012)
32. Robert, S., Büttner, S., Röcker, C., Holzinger, A.: Reasoning under uncertainty: towards collaborative interactive machine learning. In: Holzinger, A. (ed.) Machine Learning for Health Informatics. LNCS, vol. 9605, pp. 357–376. Springer, Cham (2016). doi:10.1007/978-3-319-50478-0_18
33. Schenk, M.: Instandhaltung technischer Systeme: Methoden und Werkzeuge zur Gewährleistung eines sicheren und wirtschaftlichen Anlagenbetriebs. Springer, Heidelberg (2009). doi:10.1007/978-3-642-03949-2
34. Schmidt, A.: Implicit human computer interaction through context. Pers. Technol. **4**(2), 191–199 (2000)
35. Simeu-Abazi, Z., Lefebvre, A., Derain, J.-P.: A methodology of alarm filtering using dynamic fault tree. Reliab. Eng. Syst. Saf. **96**(2), 257–266 (2011)
36. Tsamardinos, I., Brown, L.E., Aliferis, C.F.: The max-min hill-climbing Bayesian network structure learning algorithm. Mach. Learn. **65**(1), 31–78 (2006)
37. Wang, J., Li, H., Huang, J., Su, C.: Association rules mining based analysis of consequential alarm sequences in chemical processes. J. Loss Prev. Process Ind. **41**, 178–185 (2016)
38. Wang, J., Xu, J., Zhu, D.: Online root-cause analysis of alarms in discrete Bayesian networks with known structures. In: Proceeding of the 11th World Congress on Intelligent Control and Automation, pp. 467–472, June 2014
39. Wang, J., Yang, F., Chen, T., Shah, S.L.: An overview of industrial alarm systems: main causes for alarm overloading, research status, and open problems. IEEE Trans. Autom. Sci. Eng. **13**(2), 1045–1061 (2016)
40. Ware, M., Frank, E., Holmes, G., Hall, M., Witten, I.H.: Interactive machine learning: letting users build classifiers. Int. J. Hum. Comput. Stud. **55**(3), 281–292 (2001)
41. Wei, L., Guo, W., Wen, F., Ledwich, G., Liao, Z., Xin, J.: An online intelligent alarm-processing system for digital substations. IEEE Trans. Power Deliv. **26**(3), 1615–1624 (2011)
42. Wunderlich, P., Niggemann, O.: Structure learning methods for Bayesian networks to reduce alarm floods by identifying the root cause. In: 22nd IEEE International Conference on Emerging Technologies and Factory Automation (ETFA 2017), September 2017
43. Yagan, O., Qian, D., Zhang, J., Cochran, D.: Optimal allocation of interconnecting links in cyber-physical systems: interdependence, cascading failures, and robustness. IEEE Trans. Parallel Distrib. Syst. **23**(9), 1708–1720 (2012)
44. Zimmerman, J., Forlizzi, J., Evenson, S.: Research through design as a method for interaction design research in HCI. In: Proceedings of the SIGCHI Conference on Human Factors in Computing Systems, pp. 493–502. ACM (2007)

Online Self-disclosure: From Users' Regrets to Instructional Awareness

N.E. Díaz Ferreyra[(✉)], Rene Meis, and Maritta Heisel

University of Duisburg-Essen, Duisburg, Germany
{nicolas.diaz-ferreyra,rene.meis,maritta.heisel}@uni-due.de
https://www.ucsm.info/

Abstract. Unlike the offline world, the online world is devoid of well-evolved norms of interaction which guide socialization and self-disclosure. Therefore, it is difficult for members of online communities like Social Network Sites (SNSs) to control the scope of their actions and predict others' reactions to them. Consequently users might not always anticipate the consequences of their online activities and often engage in actions they later regret. Regrettable and negative self-disclosure experiences can be considered as rich sources of privacy heuristics and a valuable input for the development of privacy awareness mechanisms. In this work, we introduce a Privacy Heuristics Derivation Method (PHeDer) to encode regrettable self-disclosure experiences into privacy best practices. Since information about the impact and the frequency of unwanted incidents (such as job loss, identity theft or bad image) can be used to raise users' awareness, this method (and its conceptual model) puts special focus on the risks of online self-disclosure. At the end of this work, we provide assessment on how the outcome of the method can be used in the context of an adaptive awareness system for generating tailored feedback and support.

Keywords: Social network sites · Adaptive privacy · Awareness · Heuristics · Risk analysis

1 Introduction

Nowadays, different SNSs support a wide and diverse range of interests and practices [4]. While sites like Facebook or Twitter serve as more general purpose platforms, others like LinkedIn or Researchgate provide a more specific structure designed for targeting the needs of particular groups of users (professionals and scientists, respectively) [15]. Independently of their aim, the anatomy of any SNS consists of a set of core features that allow users to share, co-create, discuss and modify different types of media content [15]. Through such features users share their interests, emotions, opinions and beliefs with a large network of friends and acquaintances within a few seconds.

A. Holzinger et al. (Eds.): CD-MAKE 2017, LNCS 10410, pp. 83–102, 2017.
DOI: 10.1007/978-3-319-66808-6_7

The act of revealing personal information to others is commonly known as "self-disclosure" [2]. This practice (which is common and frequent in both online and offline contexts) is key for the development and maintenance of personal relationships [31]. However, disclosures (specially in online contexts like SNSs) very often reveal detailed information about the user's real life and social relationships [14]. Furthermore, when revealing too much personal information users take the risk of becoming victims of privacy threats like stalking, scamming, grooming or cyber-bulling. These threats, together with negative consequences for the user's image, make online self-disclosure in many cases a regrettable experience.

There are diverse factors which contribute to engaging in online self-disclosure activities. A poor understanding of the size and composition of audiences, psychological factors like narcissism [27] and impression management [16,28], or low privacy literacy [26] are often discussed and analyzed as the main factors mediating in online self-disclosure. However, the role of computers as social actors and consequently the role of technology in shaping our perceptions of information privacy is often omitted [25]. Since private digital data is intangible and only perceived through the interfaces and physical materials of media technologies, such technologies modulate users' emotional perception and attachment towards their private information [25]. Nevertheless, media technologies are not succeeding in taking such emotional perception to the *visceral* level. This is, making the tie between users' feelings and data visible, tangible and emotionally appreciable so they can perceive (in a visceral way) the impact of their disclosures.

Since regrettable online self-disclosure experiences often come along with a *visceral reaction*[1], they can be considered as sources of privacy heuristics which can help the users in making better and more informed privacy decisions, as to contribute in the emotional attachment towards their digital data. Díaz Ferreyra et al. [8] propose an Instructional Awareness Software Architecture (IASA) that prescribes the components of an adaptive Instructional Awareness System (IAS), which provides tailored feedback on users' disclosures in SNSs. In line with this approach, this work proposes to encode the outcome of empirical research and everyday online self-disclosure experiences into the knowledge base of IAS. Taking regrettable user experiences as the starting point, this work introduces a method for the derivation of privacy heuristics (best practices) and their further incorporation into IAS.

The rest of the paper is organized as follows. In the next section we discuss preventative technologies in the landscape of privacy technologies. In Sect. 3 we discuss how empirical research on users' regrettable disclosures can be a rich source of privacy heuristics and serve for the development of preventative technologies. Next, Sect. 4 introduces the conceptual model and the method's steps for the derivation of privacy heuristics. In Sect. 5, we provide assessment towards the evaluation of the method and its outcome for the generation of instructional awareness. We next discuss the advantages and drawbacks of this

---

[1] A visceral reaction is an "instinctive, gut-deep bodily response to a stimulus or experience"[1]. For instance, a burning sensation in the stomach when loosing something of value (e.g. wallet, passport, etc.).

approach together with future work in Sect. 6. Finally, we conclude with an outline of the implications of our approach.

2   Related Work

Whether in or out of the context of SNSs, privacy is certainly a multifaceted and complex problem that receives the attention of researchers across a wide spectrum of disciplines. Online self-disclosure and its unwanted consequences have been discussed and treated by research in media psychology and computer science, among others. However, framing self-disclosure as a privacy problem may sound paradoxical since this is a voluntary act performed by the users, and it does not violate "the right of the individual to decide what information about himself should be communicated to others and under what circumstances" (which is Westin's definition of privacy [32]). Nevertheless, the privacy landscape is much broader and existing solutions rely on different technical and social assumptions as well as definitions of privacy [7].

2.1   Self-disclosure in the Privacy Landscape

Gürses and Díaz [7] describe the landscape of privacy technologies in terms of three paradigms: control, confidentiality and practice. Technologies located in the "control" paradigm understand privacy as Westin does (i.e. the ability to determine acceptable data collection and usage) and seek to provide individuals with control and oversight over the collection, processing and use of their data. In the "confidentiality" paradigm, technologies are inspired by the definition of privacy as "the right to be alone" and aim to create an individual autonomous sphere free from intrusions. Both paradigms, control and confidentiality, have a strong security focus but do not put much attention on improving transparency and enabling identity construction [7]. After all, privacy contributes widely to the construction of one's identity both at an individual and collective level. That is precisely the (implicit) notion of privacy that users put into "practice" when they self-disclose, namely "the freedom of unreasonable constraints on the construction of one's own identity". In order to support the users in building such constraints, technologies in the practice paradigm aim to make information flows more transparent through feedback and awareness [7].

2.2   Preventative Technologies

Many efforts have been put in raising privacy awareness among the users of SNSs in order to mitigate the unwanted consequences of online self-disclosure [6,8,9,11,29]. However, many of these preventative technologies rely on static and non adaptive awareness solutions, which in many cases hinders the engagement of the users towards such systems. Wang et al. [29] developed three plugins for Facebook which aimed to help the users to avoid regrettable disclosures. These plugins called "privacy nudges" intervened when the user was about to post a message in his/her biography either (i) introducing a delay, (ii) providing visual cues about the audience of the post, or (iii) giving feedback about the meaning (positive or negative) of the post. Despite its novelty, mixed reactions were observed when these nudges were tested against Facebook users: some users liked them and managed to engage with them, and some others did not. An explanation to this can be found in a qualitative study conducted by Schäwel and Krämer [23], which revealed that the engagement level of privacy awareness systems is tightly related with their ability of providing tailored feedback to the users.

To overcome the issues of static approaches, other preventative technologies focus on providing personalized feedback and guidance to the users though adaptive mechanisms. For instance, Caliki et al. developed "Privacy Dynamics", an adaptive architecture which uses Social Identity Theory (SIT) to learn privacy norms from the users' sharing behaviors [6]. Basically, the SIT postulates that people belong to multiple social identities. For instance, being *Sweedish*, being an *athlete*, or being a *researcher* are all examples of social identities/identity groups. Social identities and identity groups play an important role in the construction of people's privacy because they are tightly related to the targeted audience of the user's disclosures. This is, a user frequently has a mental conceptualization of the different social identity groups with whom he/she is interacting. However, there can be a misalignment between this mental model and the real audience, which can lead to a privacy violation. For instance, when disclosing a negative comment about one's workplace without thinking that a work colleague can be part of the post's audience. In this case the conceptualized audience is not including the work colleagues, while the actual audience is. To overcome this issue, "Privacy Dynamics" uses Inductive Logic Programming (ILP) to learn these privacy rules and consequently resolve the conflicts among them. Other adaptive solutions like the ones from Ghazinour et al. [11], and Fang et al. [9] follow similar supervised learning approaches. This work provides an instrument for the incorporation of user-centered privacy requirements into the design process of adaptive preventative technologies.

3   Theoretical Background

Regrettable online self-disclosure experiences are hardly taken into consideration for the development of preventative technologies. In this section we discuss the importance of such experiences for eliciting user-centered privacy requirements as for the generation of adaptive feedback and awareness. Likewise, we will discuss the role of regrets in the derivation of privacy heuristics and their incorporation into the design of preventative technologies.

3.1   Self-disclosure Privacy Concerns

Systems are developed on the basis of requirements that specify their desired behavior in a given environment. Privacy requirements represent the positions and judgments of multiple stakeholders with respect to privacy and transparency claims in a system-to-be [13]. In order to discuss privacy claims from a multiple stakeholders perspective, all the information that will be collected, used, processed, distributed or deleted by the system-to-be should be deemed relevant for privacy analysis [13]. Typically, in a requirements elicitation process, stakeholders are the ones who put the privacy claims on the table for their consideration and later realization into privacy preserving features of the system-to-be. However, online self-disclosure begins when the system is up-and-running and operated by its users. Thus, privacy requirements that arise as consequence of online self-disclosure activities are mostly manifested in the operating stage of the system-to-be. Moreover, the origin of a online self-disclosure privacy concern is often a regrettable experience encountered by the user or his/her inner circle of friends, family or acquaintances.

3.2 Regrets in SNSs

Basically a regret can be defined as an unwanted consequence (factual or potential) of an action which materializes an unwanted incident (such as stalking, identity theft, harassment, or reputation damage) and derives in a feeling of sadness, repentance or disappointment [30]. Wang et al. [30] conducted an empirical study over 321 active Facebook users in order to identify different regrettable scenarios. Such regrets were identified through online surveys and interviews where users answered the question "Have you posted something on Facebook and then regretted doing it? If so, what happened?". Users reported situations where posting about (a) alcohol and illegal drug use (b) sex (c) religion and politics (d) profanity and obscenity (e) personal and family issues (f) work and company and (g) content with strong sentiment, had lead them to negative online experiences. This suggests that online self-disclosure privacy requirements do not emerge as a concern per-se, but as a consequence of regrettable online activities. Therefore, the first step into a user-centered privacy analysis should be to consider regrettable self-disclosure experiences as explicit manifestations of privacy concerns.

3.3 Instructional Awareness

In line with the adaptive preventative technologies, Díaz Ferreyra et al. introduced the concept of IAS which consists in providing adaptive privacy guidance to the users when they intend to reveal private and sensitive information in a post [8]. IAS has its basis in IASA, which resembles principles of self-adaptation in order to satisfy the particular privacy concerns of the users. In order to provide personalized privacy guidance and feedback to the user, IASA senses the user's "post" events and identifies pieces of private and sensitive information contained in such messages. If information of such nature is indeed detected by IAS, the system proceeds to the generation of personalized feedback to inform the user about this situation. Such feedback consists in a warning message together with a recommendation about the possible preventive actions that the user can follow in order to protect his/her privacy. For example, if the user attempts to disclose his/her new phone number in a post, IAS will raise a warning message like "Your phone number is included in the post. Do you want to know how to protect your private data?" and recommend the user to restrict the post's audience (for instance to "friends only").

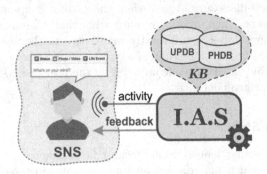

Fig. 1. Instructional Awareness System (IAS)

As shown in Fig. 1, IAS uses a Knowledge Base (KB) which is divided in two for the generation of adaptive feedback. The first one is a User Performance Data Base (UPDB) which tracks the privacy practices of the user's towards the recommendations delivered by IAS. This is, how many times the user has ignored/accepted the system's warnings, and how often the user discloses private and sensitive information, among other variables of adaptation. Such adaptation variables allow IAS to regulate the frequency and intensity of the feedback. The second part of the KB is a Privacy Heuristics Data Base (PHDB) which stores privacy knowledge encoded into constraints. Such constraints are privacy best practices which are evaluated when a "post" action takes place. Following the phone number example, if a constraint defined as "*if* post contains phone number *then* keep the audience not public" is violated, then IAS raises a warning message. As described, the UPDB and PHDB work closely together in detecting risky disclosures and recommending preventive actions to the user. In order to embody the design of IAS with user-centered privacy requirements, we propose to incorporate knowledge about online self-disclosure regrettable experiences inside the PHDB. This work will focus on the derivation of such knowledge in the form of privacy heuristics and their incorporation as the core components of IAS's PHDB.

4   Privacy Heuristics Derivation (PHeDer)

In this section we introduce the conceptual model for conducting self-disclosure privacy analysis, and our method for extracting of privacy heuristics from the users' regrettable online self-disclosure experiences. The method, called Privacy Heuristics Derivation method (PHeDer), starts with the identification of a regrettable scenario and concludes with one or more privacy heuristics defined as constraints for their later inclusion into IAS's PHDB.

4.1 Conceptual Model

In a traditional requirements engineering approach, a concern is basically raised due to actions performed over a piece of information that can lead to a privacy breach. Such actions, that when performed materialize a risk, are defined as privacy threats. The case of online self-disclosure has the particularity that the threat which exposes the user to a privacy risk is an action performed by the user him/herself. This is, the act of disclosing private or sensitive information in a post within a SNS. Thus, awareness mechanisms would enrich their performance by incorporating in their feedback engine the knowledge abut the risks of online-self disclosure. Consequently, by being informed about the possible risks of online self-disclosure, users can make more informed and wise decisions in order to protect their private information against their own actions.

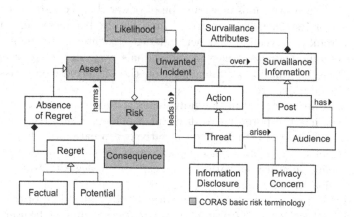

Fig. 2. PHeDer conceptual model

The conceptual elements that form the basis for the analysis of self-disclosure experiences are represented in the Unified Modeling Language (UML) [12] class diagram of Fig. 2. As said, *Threats* are *Actions* performed over pieces of *Surveillance Information* (SI) (see Sect. 4.1) in the system which can lead to an *Unwanted Incident* (such as identity theft, harassment, or reputation damage). A *Post* in a SNS is a type SI which is disclosed to a specific *Audience* and is composed by one or more *Surveillance Attributes* (SA) (see Sect. 4.1). As mentioned, *Information Disclosure* is the *Threat* of which we want to protect the user in order to avoid a regrettable online experience. Hence, the *Absence of Regret* is the *Asset* that must be protected. A *Regret* can be factual or potential in the sense that can be the result of concrete user experiences, or the result of conceptual (not yet reported by the users) self-disclosure scenarios.

The PHeDer conceptual model is based on the CORAS basic risk terminology [17]. Like in CORAS, a *Risk* in PHeDer is the *Likelihood* of an *Unwanted Incident* and its *Consequence* for the *Asset*. In this sense, a *Consequence* is a value on an impact scale such as *insignificant, minor, moderate, major* or *catastrophic*. Likewise, the *Likelihood* is a value on a frequency scale such as *rare, unlikely, possible, likely* and *certain*. CORAS considers that different *Assets* can be harmed by the same *Unwanted Incident* and cause different *Consequences*. Therefore CORAS models the relation between *Unwanted Incidents*, *Assets* and *Consequences* as a *Risk*. Since in our case, the only *Asset* that should be protected is the *Absence of Regret*, we will concentrate our analysis on the *Unwanted Incidents* and consider the *Risks* as such.

Risks. Performing a detailed risk analysis of online self-disclosure goes beyond the scope of this work, but certainly risks must be taken into consideration when describing a self disclosure scenario. Petronio [22] describes the most common types of self disclosure risks and groups them into five categories:

- *Security risks* are situations of disruption of power that jeopardize the safety of the user or its inner circle of friends and family. For instance, a mother may be careful on revealing that her underage daughter is pregnant for fear of negative repercussions. Likewise, individuals with HIV often keep their health status information private based on the perceived safety risks (e.g. harassment, job loss, etc.).
- *Stigma risks* are grounded in the individual's self-identity and involve information that has the potential to discredit a person. These risks are based on the assumption that others might negatively evaluate individuals' behaviors or opinions. For instance, sharing controversial opinions or thoughts (e.g. religious beliefs, political affiliation, etc.), can lead to negative evaluation and even exclusion from a group.
- *Face risks (self-image)* are associated with a potential feeling of embarrassment or loss of self-image. Therefore, these situations comprise the user's internal moral face (shame, integrity, debasement, and honor) and his/her external social face (social recognition, position, authority, influence and power). For example, revealing failing in a driving test can be embarrassing.
- *Relational risks* represent situations where the disclosure of a thought or opinion might threaten the status of a relationship. Relational risks may come in a variety of forms like hurting another person's feelings by expressing negative opinions towards him/her, or expressing the concern to a partner that he/she is having an affair.
- *Role risks* take place when the disclosure of intimate information jeopardizes the social role of an individual. These are situations where the revelation of private information is perceived as highly inappropriate by the receptors. For instance, a supervisor's leader role might be compromised if he/she asks for an advice regarding his/her marital status to a subordinate.

According to Petronio [22], the risk levels of self-disclosure episodes vary from individual to individual. This is, episodes that might be seen as highly risky for some users, may not be seen as such by others. In consequence, the risk levels of self-disclosure fluctuate along a range of values in a risk scale [22]. A risk level in CORAS is represented as a value obtained from the *Likelihood* and *Consequence* of an *Unwanted Incident* and expressed in a scale such as *very low, low, high* and *very high*. We will adopt this approach for the analysis of regrettable self-disclosure experiences and consequently for the derivation of privacy heuristics.

Surveillance Information. The risks of self-disclosure are often grounded in the audience to which the information is being disclosed and the type of information being disclosed. Therefore, defining which information should be considered for privacy analysis is a very important aspect for the derivation of privacy heuristics. In the context of SNSs, privacy concerns related to data aggregation, probabilistic re-identification of individuals, as well as undesirable social categorizations ought to be discussed by the stakeholders [13]. This means that information that might not be personal per-se (e.g. potentially linkable data) can raise privacy concerns. Consequently, any observable information, regardless if that information can be linked to individuals, groups or communities, should be considered for privacy analysis. Such information, which covers Personally Identifiable Information (PII) and more, is defined by Gürses [13] as "surveillance information" (SI). Because of its broad scope, we will adopt this terminology for the identification and analysis of the information disclosed by the users of SNSs.

Self-disclosure Dimensions. Equally important as the SI disclosed by the users, are the attributes enclosed in it. Petkos et al. [21] propose a taxonomy of personal data based on legal notions of personal information, as well as general perceptions of privacy and other state of the art definitions. This approach consists in organizing the user's private or sensitive personal attributes into different high-level categories called "privacy dimensions" (i.e. demographics, psychological traits, sexual profile, political attitudes, religious beliefs, health factors and condition, location, and consumer profile). This taxonomy, unlike other approaches that focus on the source of the data (e.g. Schneider et al. [24]), has a strong focus on the semantics of the data about the user and allows a semantic and intuitive representation of different aspects of the user's personal information [21]. Many of these dimensions keep a strong correlation with the regrettable scenarios reported by the users in the study conducted by Wang et al. [30] discussed in Sect. 3.2 (e.g. users reported that sharing information about their religious beliefs and profanity had lead them to a regrettable experience). Consequently, based on the regret categories proposed by Wang et al. and taking into account the concept of SI, we have refined the original privacy dimensions of Petkos et al. into what we call the "self-disclosure dimensions". These self-disclosure dimensions (Table 1), which are expressed as a set of "surveillance attributes" (SAs), allow us to analyze from a regret-oriented perspective the SI disclosed by the user in a post. Since the original categories were not covering

Table 1. The "self-disclosure" dimensions.

#	Dimension	Surveillance attributes
I	Demographics	Age, Gender, Nationality, Racial origin, Ethnicity, Literacy level, Employment status, Income level, Family status
II	Sexual profile	Sexual preference
III	Political attitudes	Supported party, Political ideology
IV	Religious beliefs	Supported religion
V	Health factors and condition	Smoking, Alcohol drinking, Drug use, Chronic diseases, Disabilities, Other health factors
VI	Location	Home location, Work location, Favorite places, Visited places
VII	Administrative	Personal Identification Number
VIII	Contact	Email address, Phone number
IX	Sentiment	Negative, Neutral, Positive

attributes like email address, phone number, personal identification number[2] and sentiment, we added three new dimensions (namely Administrative, Contact and Sentiment) to the original taxonomy.

4.2 Method

The PHeDer method consists of four sequential steps which are *regret acknowledgment*, *concern analysis*, *heuristics design*, and *constraint integration*. As depicted in Fig. 3, each stage of the method draws on different external inputs and generates the outputs for the next step. The final output of the method is an updated version of the IAS'PHDB.

Step 1: Regret Acknowledgment. The input for this step could be any evidence source of regret. Such evidence might come from regrettable experiences that the users reported themselves, or as the outcome of an empirical research like the one conducted by Wang et al. [30]. For the sake of simplicity, we assume that a single development group carries forward all the steps of the method and counts with the results of an empirical study about regrettable experiences. However, since these experiences can take place in any moment in time, it would be convenient to provide "offline" communication channels (i.e. outside of an empirical research instance) to the users for direct communication with the development team. In this step, a regrettable scenario should be described informally by the development team in terms of which information was disclosed, which was the unintended audience that it reached, and what where the unwanted incidents

---

[2] Examples of personal identification number are Social Security Number (SSN), passport number, driver's license number, taxpayer identification number, or financial account or credit card number [19].

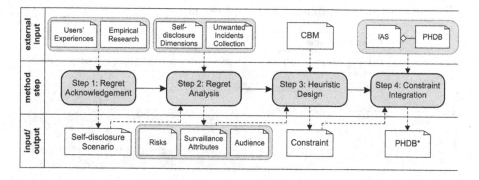

Fig. 3. PHeDer steps and artifacts

USER'S POST

"A typical day at the office. Lots of complaints and bad mood.
Cannot wait for the day to be over...!"

Actual Audience: PUBLIC.
Unintended Audience: The user's work colleagues, or superior.
Unwanted Incidents: Wake-up call from superior; bad image; job loss.

Fig. 4. Example of self-disclosure scenario

that lead the user to a feeling of regret. The output of this step can be represented as in Fig. 4 which describes a scenario where a user reported that he/she regretted to write a negative comment about his/her workplace in a public post.

Step 2: Regret Analysis. The post shared by the user in the example of Fig. 4 contains information related to his/her *employment status* and *work location*, together with a *negative* sentiment. According to Table 1, these are SAs of the *demographics*, *location* and *sentiment* self-disclosure dimensions respectively. Therefore, it is possible to trace a semantic correlation between the content of the post and one or more self-disclosure dimensions, and consequently express a regrettable scenario in terms of one or more SAs.

As previously mentioned, a regrettable scenario can lead to one or more unwanted incidents with a certain likelihood of occurrence (i.e. a risk). Consequently, a risk function must be defined to estimate the likelihood and the impact of the unwanted incidents of a regrettable scenario. Like in CORAS, such a function can be represented as a matrix similar to the one in Table 2. This matrix is divided in four sections, each representing one of the risk levels: *very low* (green), *low* (yellow), *high* (orange) and *very high* (red). A risk level is derived from the frequency of the unwanted incident (i.e. rare, unlikely, possible, likely or certain) and its consequence (i.e. insignificant, minor, moderate, major or catastrophic). We assume that knowledge about unwanted incidents which can or have occurred as consequence of online self-disclosure are stored in an

Table 2. Example of risk matrix.

		Consequence				
		Insignificant	Minor	Moderate	Major	Catastrophic
Likelihood	Rare					
	Unlikely					I3
	Possible				I1	
	Likely			I2		
	Certain					

"Unwanted Incidents Collection". Such a collection will help to build the risk matrix and consequently to analyze the potential risks of a regrettable scenario.

Let us assume that the scenario described in Fig. 4 by the development team has three unwanted incidents *wake up call from superior (I1)*, *bad image (I2)*, and *job loss (I3)*. One can consider that the frequency of such incidents is the same for every user in a SNS, and can therefore be determined in a global scale by a risk expert. Nevertheless, when it comes to the estimation of the consequences of each incident, global assumptions are harder to make. This is basically because, as mentioned in Sect. 4.1, users do not perceive the consequences of a self-disclosure act in the same levels. For instance, a bad image incident can be catastrophic for a certain user or group of users, or can be insignificant for others. Therefore, a risk matrix must be elaborated for every regrettable scenario and for every user or group of users with similar characteristics.

Clearly, to keep an individual risk matrix for every user is an unpractical and not efficient solution. Besides, different users can share the same severity perceptions towards a particular risk, meaning that they share the same privacy attitudes. Such similarities have been acknowledged by Westin who developed a "Privacy Segmentation Index" to categorize individuals into three privacy groups: *fundamentalists*, *pragmatists*, and *unconcerned* [32]. Privacy *fundamentalists* are at the maximum extreme of privacy concerns being the most protective of their privacy. Privacy *pragmatists* on the other hand evaluate the potential pros and cons of sharing information and make their decisions according to the trust they perceive towards the information's receiver. On the other extreme, privacy *unconcerned* are the less protective of their privacy since they perceive that the benefits of information disclosure far outweigh the potential negative consequences. These categories have been widely used to measure privacy attitudes and therefore could be beneficial for the elaboration of the risk matrix of regrettable scenarios. Users could be grouped into these three categories, which means that it would only be necessary to elaborate three risk matrices (one for each privacy attitude).

Step 3: Heuristic Design. This step consists in the codification of the outcome of Step 2 (risk matrix, SAs, and audience) into privacy heuristics. According to Díaz Ferreyra et al. [8], the domain knowledge of IAS should be encoded following principles of Constraint Based Modeling (CBM) which postulates that domain knowledge (i.e. privacy heuristics) can be represented as constraints on correct solutions of a problem (i.e. a self-disclosure scenario). Such correct solutions must satisfy a set of fundamental domain principles (encoded in constraints) that should not be violated. As long as the users never reach a state that is known to be wrong (i.e. a regrettable scenario), they are free to perform whatever actions they please. In this sense, a state constraint is a pair of *relevance* and *satisfaction* tests on a problem state, where each member of the pair can be seen as a set of features or properties that a problem state must satisfy [8].

In Snippet 1, *relevance* and *satisfaction* tests over a problem state are expressed as Horn Clauses in Prolog. The relevance condition consists of the left hand side of the *share* predicate, which acknowledges and evaluates an information disclosure event (in this case a post). Such event is modeled by the parameters [X|Xs] (a list of SAs where X is the first element), Au (the post's audience), and Usr (the user's id). Likewise, the satisfaction condition (right hand side of the predicate) evaluates the existence of a potential regrettable scenario associated with the disclosure of such SAs to a certain audience. In order to find out if the user's disclosure can derive in a regrettable scenario, the potential risks of the disclosure must be evaluated. This evaluation is carried out by the *regret* predicate which checks if there is an unwanted incident whose risk is not acceptable for the user. Since the risk acceptance depends on the user's privacy attitude, it is necessary to instantiate the Att variable with one of the *fundamentalist*, *pragmatist* or *unconcerned* values. This unification process consists of binding the content of the Att variable with an *attitude* predicate containing the same user's id. Following the same unification approach, the *srv_att_list* checks if [X|Xs] is not an empty list, and if it is composed by SAs.

```
share([X|Xs], Au, Usr):- srv_att_list([X|Xs]), audience(Au), user(Usr),
    attitude(Usr, Att), not regret([X|Xs], Au, Att).

regret([X|Xs], Au, Att):- unwanted_inc([X|Xs], Au, Att, Unwi),
    risk(Att, Unwi, Type, Cons, Freq, Level), not acceptable(Att, Level).

unwanted_inc([X|Xs], Au, Att, Unwi):-unw_incident([Y|Ys], Au, Att, Unwi),
    subset([Y|Ys],[X|Xs]).

srv_att_list([X]):- srv_att(X).
srv_att_list([X|Xs]):- srv_att(X), srv_att_list(Xs).
```

Snippet 1. Relevance and satisfaction conditions

Depending on the user's attitude, the impact of an unwanted incident can vary between *insignificant* and *catastrophic*. Therefore, the acceptance level of an unwanted incident also fluctuates between very low, low, high and very high, depending on the user's attitude. The *regret* predicate models the evaluation of the risks associated with the user's disclosure (i.e. the post) by taking into account his/her privacy attitude (Att), the list of SAs ([X|Xs]) and the audience (AU). First, the predicate invokes the *unw_incident* predicate, in order to find an unwanted incident (i.e. instantiate the Unwi variable) linked with the SAs disclosed in the user's post, his/her attitude, and the post's audience. Thereafter, the *risk* predicate is invoked with the attitude and unwanted incident as parameters (Att and Unwi respectively) to compute the risk level of the unwanted incident (i.e. unify the Level variable). If the risk level of an unwanted incident is not acceptable according to the user's attitude, then the post is considered as potentially regrettable. Therefore, the last step of the *risk* predicate consists on checking the risk's acceptance. This is done by matching the unified variables Att and Level with an *acceptable* fact which defines the acceptance level of risk for each privacy attitude. For this, we assume that for a fundamentalist only very low risks are acceptable, for a pragmatist very low and low risks, and for a unconcerned the risks which are very low, low and high. If the risk is not acceptable, then the user's disclosure is assessed as a potential *regret* and the satisfaction condition of the *share* predicate gets violated.

```
unw_incident([Employmentstatus, Worklocation, Negative], Work, Job_loss).
risk(Pragmatist, Job_loss, Relational, Catastrophic, Rare, High).


audience(Work).
user(John).
attitude(John, Pragmatist).
acceptable(Pragmatist, Low).
acceptable(Pragmatist, Very_low).
srv_att(Worklocation).
srv_att(Negative).
srv_att(Employmentstatus).
```

Snippet 2. Privacy heuristic example

In order to asses our disclosure scenario, a set of facts which encode one or more privacy heuristics are evaluated. The heuristic of Snippet 2 has been derived from the analysis performed over the regrettable scenario described in Fig. 4. Here, the content of the risk matrix is encoded in the facts *unw_incident* and *risk*. The first one states that a job loss is an unwanted incident which occurs if SAs related to the user's employment status and work location together with a negative sentiment are disclosed to an audience containing people from his/her workplace. The second one states that such unwanted incident (that can be cataloged as Relational according to the categories described in 4.1) is rare to occur, but has a catastrophic impact among users with a pragmatic privacy attitude. Consequently, the risk is assessed as "high" for pragmatic users. Therefore, if a user John, who is a pragmatist, shares "A typical day at the office. Lots of complaints and bad mood. Cannot wait for the day to be over...!", then the risk is evaluated as not acceptable and the post considered as potentially regrettable.

Step 4: Constraint Integration. Once the constraints are derived, we proceed to their incorporation in a PHDB like the one in IAS. As it is shown in the Fig. 3, the association between PHDB and IAS is "weak", meaning that the PHDB does not compleately depend on an IAS. This is because a PHDB can serve other purposes which are not necessarily the ones of IAS (e.g. other awareness or privacy recommender systems with similar characteristics). On the other hand, it will depend on the particular implementation of the data base on how the integration procedure is executed. If the PHDB is encoded in Prolog as in the example, then the command *asserta* can be used to incorporate new facts and predicates to the data base [10]. Nevertheless, different implementations will require specific solutions for this step.

5 Privacy Heuristics Evaluation in IAS

Once an iteration of the PHeDer method is completed, a new set of privacy heuristics are included in the PHDB of an IAS. As described in Sect. 3.3, an IAS uses the knowledge stored in the PHDB and the UPDB in order to deliver a feedback message to the user when he/she is about to disclose a piece of SI in a post. The Algorithm 1 (function *AnalyzePost*) describes how this process is executed at run time. First, a *DetectSurvAtt* function (line 2) is in charge of tracing a semantic correlation between the content of the post and one or more SAs. This can be achieved for example by using Support Vector Machines for developing a classifier which automatically derives the SAs contained in a post (similar to the proposal of Nguyen-Son et al. [20]). Once the post is expressed as a set of SAs, a *Share* function (like the one described in Snippet 1) assesses the potential risks of the disclosure and evaluates the scenario as *regrettable* or not (see line 5). If the post is considered as potentially regrettable for the user, then a feedback message must be raised informing about the risks of the disclosure and a set of possible actions to overcome this issue (for instance, hints on how to constraint the post's audience).

As explained in the previous section, both risk level and the level of acceptance depend on the user's privacy attitude. Therefore, the user's attitude is retrieved by the *GetUsrAttitude* function (line 7) to be later used by the *GetUnacRisks* to compute the set of unacceptable risks (line 8). For this, *GetUnacRisks* takes into account the SAs contained in the post, and the targeted audience in addition to the user's privacy attitude. Both functions, *GetUnacRisks* and *GetUsrAttitude*, can be easily implemented by querying the content of the PHDB. This is, using the predicates and facts of Snippets 1 and 2. Since the feedback must take into account how the user is performing regarding his/her privacy attitudes, a *GetUsrPerformance* function (line 9) collects such information from the UPDB as described in Sect. 3.3. The feedback generation concludes after calling the *GenFeedback* function (line 10), which taking into account the user's attitude, performance and unacceptable risks elaborates a tailored feedback message to the user. An implementation assessment for the generation of adaptive feedback goes beyond the scope of this paper and will be part of future work.

Algorithm 1. Pseudo-code of the AnalyzePost algorithm

```
1: function ANALYZEPOST(Post P, Audience Au, User Usr)
2:     Set[SurvAttr] SAs := DetectSurvAtt(P);
3:     String feedbackMsg;
4:     if SAs ≠ ∅ then
5:         bool regrettable := ¬Share(SAs, Au, U);
6:         if regrettable then
7:             Attitude Att := GetUsrAttitude(U);
8:             Set[Risk] Rsks := GetUnacRisks(SAs, Au, Att);
9:             Performance Perf := GetUsrPerformance(U);
10:            feedbackMsg := GenFeedback(Perf, Rsks, Att);
11:        end if
12:    end if
13:    return feedbackMsg;
14: end function
```

The study of Schäwel and Krämer [23] suggests that users of SNSs would engage with a system which holds the adaptive properties of IAS. Therefore, an implementation of IAS needs to measure the effectiveness of the heuristics and consequently of the PHeDer method in the practice. Considering that self-disclosure is an activity which can take place across different SNSs, and many of them like Facebook offer an API for connecting to its services, an application for smartphones (app) is a good implementation option. Having a prototype of such app, a use case scenario with a group of users can be set up in order to evaluate their privacy attitudes before and after using an IAS. Consequently, in-depth interviews can be conducted to get more insights about the user's reactions and acceptance of the recommendations. This evaluation stage is part of an ongoing work in progress and is expected to be extensively discussed in a future research study.

6   Discussion and Future Work

One of the drawbacks of some adaptive preventative technologies like the one from Caliki et al. [6] is that privacy knowledge is learned from the user's previous disclosures (i.e. in a "supervised learning" approach). This means that new users of the system will spend some time without support until the first set of privacy rules is learned. This leads to another drawback which is that such approaches also rely in the assumption that the user's sharing decisions (i.e. training set) where always consistent with his/her privacy norms (i.e. the user has never accidentally revealed content to an unintended audience). Since this is not always the case, these systems are likely to learn wrong sharing rules in a non-controlled operational environment. To overcome this issue, the PHeDer method could be applied to generate a privacy knowledge base-line so that new users can have support from the very beginning, develop a proactive behavior, and consequently make fewer mistakes when sharing their information.

On the other hand, PHeDer relies in the assumption that users can be clustered according to their privacy attitudes like proposed by Westin. Current research by Woodruff et al. has put the predictive potential of Westin's categories into question [33]. Basically, Westin's Privacy Segmentation Index consists of three questions and a set of rules to translate the answers into the three categories discussed in Sect. 4.2. However, these questions examine privacy attitudes about consumer control, business, laws, and regulations. Therefore, they capture broad generic privacy attitudes, which are not good predictors of context-specific privacy related behaviors. Moreover, the index seems to rely on the unstated assumption that individuals make privacy decisions that are highly rational, informed and reflective. This has been already questioned and documented in the so called "Privacy Paradox" [3] which revealed peoples' privacy attitude-behavior dichotomy. Consequently, and as suggested by Woodruff et al., future work should consider alternative instruments to better capture and predict the users's privacy attitudes such as the Internet Users' Information Privacy Concern (IUIPC) scale [18] or the Privacy Concern Scale (PCS) [5].

Another possible critic to PHeDer is that the method is executed offline (not at run-time) and requires a study about users' regrettable disclosures as input. This hinders the incorporation of new heuristics into the PHDB, basically because of the cost of conducting such type of studies. This is, the time and the resources needed to recruit the participants of the study, as well as for data conditioning and the application of the method's steps. Thus, a run-time approach for learning this privacy heuristics would be beneficial for keeping up to date the content of the PHDB. One possible way is to examine the deleted posts of a user in terms of the disclosed SAs. If such post contains one or more SAs, then it could be considered as a regret. Of course, then the question arises about which were the reasons (unwanted incidents) that made the user delete the post. A simple solution would be to ask directly to the user this question and try to estimate the risks. Such a run-time approach for learning privacy heuristics is also part of our future work.

7   Conclusion

Since online self-disclosure takes place at run-time and not prior to the system's development phase, regrettable experiences are hardly taken into consideration for shaping privacy requirements. Consequently, the implementation of awareness mechanisms which satisfy such privacy requirements is often neglected. The method presented in this work considers users' regrettable experiences as explicit manifestations of privacy concerns. Therefore, it can be seen as a user-oriented elicitation method of privacy requirements for SNSs. Consequently, the heuristics derived from the method can not only shape better awareness mechanisms and preventative technologies like IAS, but also improve the ones in the state of the art. We believe that using heuristics derived from the users' regrets to raise awareness is promising not only for promoting a proactive privacy behavior, but also for making the tie between the user and his/her digital data more emotionally appreciable. It is matter of future research to evaluate the effectiveness of such heuristics in a prototype of IAS, as to develop engagement mechanisms for making privacy awareness an ongoing and sustained learning process.

Acknowledgments. This work was supported by the Deutsche Forschungsgemein-schaft (DFG) under grant No. GRK 2167, Research Training Group "User-Centred Social Media".

References

1. Ackerman, A.: Visceral Reactions: Emotional Pay Dirt or Fast Track to Melodrama? May 2012. Retrieved March 2, 2017. http://www.helpingwritersbecomeauthors.com/visceral-reactions-emotional-pay-dirt/
2. Archer, R.L.: Self-disclosure. In: The self in social psychology, pp. 183–204. Oxford University Press, March 1980
3. Barnes, S.B.: A privacy paradox: social networking in the United States. First Monday bf 11(9), September 2006. http://dx.doi.org/10.5210/fm.v11i9.1394
4. Boyd, D.M., Ellison, N.B.: Social network sites: definition, history, and scholarship. J. Comput. Mediated Commun. **13**(1), 210–230 (2007). http://dx.doi.org/10.1111/j.1083-6101.2007.00393.x
5. Buchanan, T., Paine, C., Joinson, A.N., Reips, U.D.: Development of measures of online privacy concern and protection for use on the internet. J. Am. Soc. Inf. Sci. Technol. **58**(2), 157–165 (2007). http://dx.doi.org/10.1002/asi.20459
6. Calikli, G., Law, M., Bandara, A.K., Russo, A., Dickens, L., Price, B.A., Stuart, A., Levine, M., Nuseibeh, B.: Privacy dynamics: learning privacy norms for social software. In: Proceedings of the 11th International Symposium on Software Engineering for Adaptive and Self-Managing Systems, pp. 47–56. ACM, May 2016
7. Diaz, C., Gürses, S.: Understanding the landscape of privacy technologies (extended abstract). In: Proceedings of the Information Security Summit, ISS 2012, pp. 58–63, May 2012
8. Díaz Ferreyra, N.E., Schäwel, J., Heisel, M., Meske, C.: Addressing self-disclosure in social media: an instructional awareness approach. In: Proceedings of the 2nd ACS/IEEE International Workshop on Online Social Networks Technologies (OSNT). ACS/IEEE, December 2016
9. Fang, L., LeFevre, K.: Privacy wizards for social networking sites. In: Proceedings of the 19th International Conference on World Wide Web. WWW 2010, pp. 351–360. ACM, New York (2010). http://doi.acm.org/10.1145/1772690.1772727
10. Frühwirth, T., De Koninck, L., Triska, M., Wielemaker, J.: SWI Prolog Reference Manual 6.2. 2. BoD-Books on Demand (2012)
11. Ghazinour, K., Matwin, S., Sokolova, M.: YourPrivacyProtector: a recommender system for privacy settings in social networks. Int. J. Secur. Privacy Trust Manag. (IJSPTM) **2**(4), August 2013
12. Group, O.M: OMG Unified Modeling Language (OMG UML). OMG Document Number formal/2015-03-01, March 2015
13. Gürses, S.: Multilateral Privacy Rquirements Analysis in Online Social Networks. Ph.D. thesis, KU Leuven, Heverlee (2010)
14. Gürses, S., Rizk, R., Gunther, O.: Privacy design in online social setworks: learning from privacy breaches and community feedback. In: Proceedings of the International Conference on Information Systems, ICIS 2008, p. 90, December 2008

15. Kietzmann, J.H., Hermkens, K., McCarthy, I.P., Silvestre, B.S.: Social media? Get serious! understanding the functional building blocks of social media. Bus. Horiz. **54**(3), 241–251 (2011). http://dx.doi.org/10.1016/j.bushor.2011.01.005

16. Krämer, N., Haferkamp, N.: Online self-presentation: balancing privacy concerns and impression construction on social networking sites. In: Trepte, S., Reinecke, L. (eds.) Privacy Online, pp. 127–141. Springer, Heidelberg (2011). doi:10.1007/978-3-642-21521-6_10

17. Lund, M.S., Solhaug, B., Stølen, K.: Model-Driven Risk Analysis: The CORAS Approach. Springer Science & Business Media, Heidelberg (2010). doi:10.1007/978-3-642-12323-8

18. Malhotra, N.K., Kim, S.S., Agarwal, J.: Internet users' information privacy concerns (IUIPC): the construct, the scale, and a causal model. In: Information Systems Research, vol. 15, pp. 336–355. Informs, December 2004

19. McCallister, E., Grance, T., Scarfone, K.A.: Guide to protecting the confidentiality of Personally Identifiable Information (PII). DIANE Publishing (2010)

20. Nguyen-Son, H.Q., Tran, M.T., Yoshiura, H., Sonehara, N., Echizen, I.: Anonymizing personal text messages posted in online social networks and detecting disclosures of personal information. IEICE Trans. Inf. Syst. **98**(1), 78–88 (2015)

21. Petkos, G., Papadopoulos, S., Kompatsiaris, Y.: PScore: a framework for enhancing privacy awareness in online social networks. In: Proceedings of the 10th International Conference on Availability, Reliability and Security, ARES 2015, pp. 592–600. IEEE, August 2015

22. Petronio, S.: Boundaries of Privacy: Dialectics of Disclosure. Suny Press, Albany (2012)

23. Schäwel, J., Krämer, N.: Paving the way for technical privacy support: a qualitative study on users' intentions to engage in privacy protection. In: The 67th Annual Conference of the International Communication Association (2017)

24. Schneier, B.: A taxonomy of social networking data. IEEE Secur. Priv. **8**(4), 88–88 (2010)

25. Stark, L.: The emotional context of information privacy. Inf. Soc. **32**(1), 14–27 (2016)

26. Trepte, S., Teutsch, D., Masur, P.K., Eicher, C., Fischer, M., Hennhöfer, A., Lind, F.: Do people know about privacy and data protection strategies? Towards the "Online Privacy Literacy Scale" (OPLIS). In: Gutwirth, S., Leenes, R., Hert, P. (eds.) Reforming European Data Protection Law. LGTS, vol. 20, pp. 333–365. Springer, Dordrecht (2015). doi:10.1007/978-94-017-9385-8_14

27. Utz, S., Krämer, N.: The privacy paradox on social network sites revisited: The role of individual characteristics and group norms. Cyberpsychol. J. Psychosoc. Res. Cyberspace **3**(2) (2009). https://cyberpsychology.eu/article/view/4223/3265

28. Vitak, J.: Balancing privacy concerns and impression management strategies on Facebook. In: Proceedings of the Eleventh Symposium on Usable Privacy and Security, SOUPS 2015. USENIX, July 2015

29. Wang, Y., Leon, P.G., Scott, K., Chen, X., Acquisti, A., Cranor, L.F.: Privacy nudges for social media: an exploratory facebook study. In: Proceedings of the 22nd International Conference on World Wide Web, pp. 763–770. ACM (2013)

30. Wang, Y., Norcie, G., Komanduri, S., Acquisti, A., Leon, P.G., Cranor, L.F.: I regretted the minute I pressed share: a qualitative study of regrets on facebook. In: Proceedings of the Seventh Symposium on Usable Privacy and Security, SOUPS 2011. ACM (2011)

31. Wang, Y.C., Burke, M., Kraut, R.: Modeling self-disclosure in social networking sites. In: Proceedings of the 19th ACM Conference on Computer-Supported Cooperative Work & Social Computing, CSCW 2016, pp. 74–85. ACM, February 2016
32. Westin, A.F.: Privacy and freedom. Wash. Lee Law Rev. **25**(1), 166 (1968)
33. Woodruff, A., Pihur, V., Consolvo, S., Schmidt, L., Brandimarte, L., Acquisti, A.: Would a privacy fundamentalist sell their dna for $1000.. if nothing bad happened as a result? the westin categories, behavioral intentions, and consequences. In: Proceedings of the Tenth Symposium on Usable Privacy and Security, SOUPS 2014. USENIX (2014)

MAKE Privacy

Decision Tree Rule Induction for Detecting Covert Timing Channels in TCP/IP Traffic

Félix Iglesias[(✉)], Valentin Bernhardt, Robert Annessi, and Tanja Zseby

CN Group, Institute of Telecommunications, TU Wien,
Gusshausstra 25/E389, 1040 Vienna, Austria
felix.iglesias@nt.tuwien.ac.at
https://www.nt.tuwien.ac.at/research/communication-networks/

Abstract. The detection of covert channels in communication networks is a current security challenge. By clandestinely transferring information, covert channels are able to circumvent security barriers, compromise systems, and facilitate data leakage. A set of statistical methods called DAT (Descriptive Analytics of Traffic) has been previously proposed as a general approach for detecting covert channels. In this paper, we implement and evaluate DAT detectors for the specific case of covert timing channels. Additionally, we propose machine learning models to induce classification rules and enable the fine parameterization of DAT detectors. A testbed has been created to reproduce main timing techniques published in the literature; consequently, the testbed allows the evaluation of covert channel detection techniques. We specifically applied Decision Trees to infer DAT-rules, achieving high accuracy and detection rates. This paper is a step forward for the actual implementation of effective covert channel detection plugins in modern network security devices.

Keywords: Covert channels · Decision trees · Forensic analysis · Machine learning · Network communications · Statistics

1   Introduction

Network communication platforms and protocols have been devised with clear structures and policies to allow fluent data transmission between different actors in networks. Covert channels profit from such structures and policies to send information in ways that are not in compliance with the original design of the communication schemes. The purpose of this unorthodox communication is that the covert data transfer remains generally unperceived but for the sender and receiver of the covert information. Ultimately, the pragmatic goal is usually—although not always—fraudulent or illicit, such as data exfiltration, or malware communication. For this reason, modern Intrusion Detection systems (IDS) should incorporate covert channel detection capabilities to cope with those hidden communication methods.

© IFIP International Federation for Information Processing 2017
Published by Springer International Publishing AG 2017. All Rights Reserved
A. Holzinger et al. (Eds.): CD-MAKE 2017, LNCS 10410, pp. 105–122, 2017.
DOI: 10.1007/978-3-319-66808-6_8

In [11], detectors based on descriptive analytics of traffic (DAT) were presented as a broad-scope solution for covert channel identification in TCP/IP networks. DAT detectors operate by extracting meaningful information from network traffic and transform it into flow vectors. In such vectors, every susceptible TCP/IP field is represented by a set of features based on aggregations, statistics, autocorrelation, and multimodality estimations.

There exists a wide variety of ways to send covert information in IP networks. Diverse taxonomies and schemes to classify covert channels have been proposed in the literature over the years, e.g., [19,28,30]. More recent surveys are given in [11,24]. In [24], Wendzel et al. analyze 109 techniques developed between 1987 and 2013 and organize covert channel techniques as variations of 11 characteristic patterns. In [11], covert channels are differently classified from a detection perspective. The interested reader can find good overviews as well as links to multiple publications about the design and detection of covert channels in the cited papers. Beyond accurate classifications, from a global perspective covert channels were originally differentiated as: *timing* channels, if timing properties of communications mask the covert message, and *storage* channels, if covert data is somehow conveyed inside packets. In this work, we focus on *timing* channels.

In [11], DAT detectors were theoretically depicted. The evaluation was conducted with a proof of concept where the rules of a DAT detector prototype were adjusted solely based on experts knowledge, achieving moderate performance rates. Therefore, the main goals and contributions of this paper are:

1. To deeply evaluate DAT detectors for the specific case of covert timing channels. To this end, a testbed for generating and testing covert channels has been created. The evaluation has been conducted by implementing eight of the most popular covert timing techniques proposed in the literature.
2. To establish a methodology for tuning DAT detector parameters and rules based on Decision Trees learners.
3. To generalize a set of constituent rules for DAT detectors in the scope of covert timing channels, thus enabling the incorporation of DAT detectors in future IDS.

2   Related Work

Already in the '70s, covert timing channels were identified by the USA Air Force experts as a potential problem of secure communications even in end-to-end encryption scenarios [16]. Actually, devised without paying a special attention to security concerns, TCP/IP protocols entail many possibilities to conceal covert information. As a consequence, a considerable number of covert channel techniques have been presented in the related literature since then.

In the '90s, J.C. Wray noticed that the partition between *storage* and *timing* channels was not always appropriate, since there are covert channels that share properties of both types [25]. An example of half-timing half-storage channel is given in [8], where a little delay is introduced in the packet delivery to make the lowest bit of TCP timestamps—usually seemingly random—to coincide with the covert bit to send. In this case, information is hidden in a TCP field, but the method invariably affects time properties in the communication. Note that, in this case, even if it is not possible for a warden to decode the message without checking packet fields, the detection by only analyzing packet inter-arrival times (henceforth *iats*) is theoretically possible. Another *hybrid* technique was proposed by W. Mazurczyk and K. Szczypiorski, who developed a method that inserts covert data in the payloads of VoIP packets that were intentionally delayed and normally dropped [15]. In [9], C.G. Girling tested a covert timing channel assuming that a sender could address a number of hosts in a network, and a wiretapper in the middle would interpret destination addresses as codifications (e.g., 16 addresses can conceal 4 bits of information).

Nevertheless, covert timing channels do not usually involve using information of packet fields. The attention is normally focused on iats. For example, in [3] the sender and receiver of the covert communication are synchronized and agree on a fixed sampling time interval. The existence or absence of a packet in the interval transports the covert information. V. Berk, A. Giani and G. Cybenko show a timing channel technique where covert 1s and 0s are deduced from two different packet delays [2]. Authors also discuss the *bandwidth commitment* in the design and implementation of covert timing channels, i.e., a low bandwidth is undesired for transmitting information but makes the covert channel stealthier.

Packet delays are also manipulated in [18], where a Jitterbug slightly modifies the time behaviour (in a millisecond scale) of hacked input devices, such as a keyboard, in order to allow an eavesdropper to guess the introduced data by observing the generated time sequence. This is a good example of how different malware can exploit covert channels. Video stream data is proposed as a carrier for sending binary covert information in [5], and a threshold for packet-iats is used to differentiate between 0s and 1s at the destination. Video on Demand services are used in [31] to transport covert information also by carefully manipulating iat values. In [26] message redundancy is exploited by applying Huffman coding to transform covert symbols into packet delays.

Given that detection methods are often based on statistics and distributions of the network usage, in [7] covert timing channels are created by matching time-distributions generated by legitimate services. In [13], Kiyavash and Coleman study a method for interactive traffic that relies on encoding mechanisms, statistical structures of network queues and packet iat for sending covert information. A different time-based approach is proposed in [14]. Here, bursts of packets transport the covert information, and the total number of packets in the burst represents the covert symbol. Additional timing-based convert channel techniques can be consulted, for example, in [10], [23] or [1].

The detection of covert timing channels has been classically faced from the perspective of the analysis of statistical properties. For instance, in [3], in addition to present some covert timing techniques, the detection of the proposed channels is conducted by means of calculations on variance patterns and measuring similarity between adjacent iats. Entropy calculations are also used for such purpose, for example, Gianvecchio and Wang test entropy-based detection on three different techniques in [6]. More recently, in [4], *time-deterministic replay* has been introduced as a technique that can reproduce the precise timing of applications and, therefore, be used for disclosing covert timing channels. As for machine learning approaches, Support Vector Machines has been proposed for covert channel detection several times, e.g., in [21], and specifically for timing channels in [20], achieving good results against four popular timing techniques. Decision tree learners also obtain successful detection rates when tested with basic timing techniques in [29].

The detection framework presented in [11]—i.e., DAT detectors—focuses on the characterization of flows by means of a careful selection of statistical calculations and estimations. Therefore, it is a statistical approach in nature; nevertheless, in this paper we propose the application of machine learning to induce and adjust the rules embedded in DAT detectors, enhancing the basic proposal and making the most of the depicted framework. The excellent properties of Decision Trees for knowledge abstraction and generalization make them highly appropriated for the aimed purpose.

3   DAT Detector

DAT detectors are primarily introduced and widely described from a theoretical perspective in [11]. They are devised to be lightweight, fast traffic analyzers in network middleboxes. DAT detectors basically operate with descriptive analytics of traffic flows, creating flow vectors whose features are based on aggregations, statistics, autocorrelation, and multimodality estimations.

A DAT detector consists of three well-differentiated phases (Fig. 1): preprocessing (P), feature extraction and transformation (T), and flow labeling and covert channel detection (D).

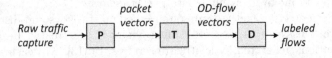

P – Preprocessing
T – Feature extraction and transformation
D – Flow labeling and CC detection

Fig. 1. DAT overall three-phase scheme.

1. *Preprocessing*
The first phase takes raw traffic captures as inputs (e.g., PCAP files). Traffic captures are parsed and packet vectors are formed with meaningful, homogeneous information for the subsequent analysis.

For the specific case of covert timing channels, the selected information must provide time characteristics and allow the identification of flows. Assuming that raw traffic is obtained as packet captures and a flow is simply defined by the source IP and destination IP tuple[1], the output of the preprocessing phase will contain packet vectors as shown in Eq. 1:

$$pkt_i = \{\text{timestamp}, \text{src.IP}, \text{dst.IP}\} \tag{1}$$

where pkt_i stands for the ith-captured-packet, "timestamp" refers to the actual time when packet i was captured, and "src.IP" and "dst.IP" correspond to the flow source and destination IP addresses respectively.

2. *Feature extraction and transformation*

In this step, packet vectors are transformed into flows. At the same time, predefined calculations and estimations are conducted upon the flows. Finally, new two-level structured *OD-flow* vectors are created (origin-destination flow vectors). The first level corresponds to the packet fields to explore (e.g., IP Protocol, Time to Live, TCP Window, iat[2]), and the second level contains the calculations and estimations performed for every analyzed field. The general set of features proposed in [11] are:

U	number of unique values.
S_k	number of multimodality distribution peaks.
w_S	relative width of the main distribution.
S_s	number of main symbols.
Mo	statistical mode value.
$p(Mo)$	number of packets (or iats) with the mode value (percentage).
ρ_A	sum of autocorrelation coefficients.
μ_Δ	mean of differences.
$pkts$	total number of packets.

The proposed features may vary depending on the field to analyze. In our experiments only iats are required, and we specifically redefine some features for the iat field. For example, μ_Δ and Mo are not used, and $\mu_{\omega S}$ is a novelty and replaces w_S. $\mu_{\omega S}$ is the mean of standard distributions of peaks obtained by kernel density estimations. Therefore, $\mu_{\omega S}$ allows to easily abstract the average distribution width. In addition, we add c, which depends on S_k and $pkts$. c is an estimation of the number of potential covert bytes and is calculated by means of simple ad-hoc tables [11]. In the cited work, c is incorporated in the last detection phase, but it can perfectly be estimated in the

---

[1] Note that the classic 5-tuple used to identify communication flows is not used here (i.e., *src.IP, dst.IP, Protocol, src.Port, dst.Port*). Unlike overt IP communications, covert channels can be constructed using different protocols, source and destination ports in the transmission of the same hidden message.

[2] *iat* is treated like a header field for DAT detectors.

OD-flow generation and included in the vector. Therefore, for the specific case of covert timing channel detection, a OD-flow vector is expressed as (Eq. 2)[3]:

$$\text{flow\_vec} = \{U, S_k, \mu_{\omega S}, S_s, p(Mo), \rho_A, pkts, c\} \tag{2}$$

The meaning of the features can be better understood with an example. Imagine a flow of 200 packets from host A to host B (i.e., 199 iats). The detected iat-distribution matches Fig. 2. Considering a granularity of 5 ms, out of 199 actual iats, the number of observed unique iat-values (U) is 25 (every bar of the frequency diagram or histogram). In Fig. 2, the kernel density estimation (red curve) shows two peaks ($S_k = 2$) with an average standard distribution ($\mu_{\omega S}$) close to 20 ms (i.e., average width between 40 ms and 50 ms). S_s equals 13 according to the main symbols calculation proposed in [11] (i.e., it is approximately the number of outstanding histogram bars). The statistical mode for captured iats is 30 ms, which occurs 20 times, then $p(Mo) = \frac{20}{199} \approx 0.10$. The iats series is highly chaotic, showing $\rho_A = 0.05$. With $S_k = 2$ and $pkts = 200$, a proper estimation of c is 28 (according to the methods in [11]). The OD-vector would remain:

$$\text{flow\_vec}_{A \rightarrow B} = \{25, 2, 19.3m, 13, 0.10, 0.05, 199, 28\} \tag{3}$$

3. *Flow labeling and covert channel detection*

A complete implementation of DAT detectors is expected to analyze traffic according to four different blocks or steps:

- A *Packet Compliance Checker*, which, according to a set of fixed policies, detects traffic that is corrupted or does not comply to standard practices.
- The *Intra-field Analysis* block, which checks TCP/IP header fields separately by examining the corresponding OD-flow vector values.
- The *Inter-field Analysis* block, which considers combinations of OD-flow vector values in different TCP/IP header fields.
- A *ML-based Detector* (machine-learning-based), which compares OD-flows by using a library that contains representative patterns (footprints) of OD-flows with covert channels. Such patterns are linked to known, published techniques.

Here we aim to detect solely covert timing channels, so only a single TCP/IP flow field is to be analyzed: iats. It also means that only the *Intra-field Analysis* block must be adjusted and tested. Considering the specific case of covert timing channels, the evaluation of the *Intra-field Analysis*, the validation of Decision Trees as rule extractor-learners, and the proposal of a set of rules for actual implementations are the goals of this work.

---

[3] Features in Eq. 2 should be annotated with the first-level field to which they correspond (i.e., U_{TTL}, $U_{src.Port}$, $U_{iat},...$). Since in this work we only use iats, we omit such subindices for the sake of clarity.

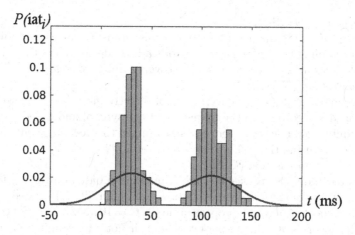

Fig. 2. iat-distribution of an example flow. *Probability* frequency diagram (blue) and kernel density estimation curve (red). (Color figure online)

4   Implemented Timing Techniques

We have created a testbed for the evaluation of covert channel detection techniques. Eight of the covert timing channels introduced in Sect. 2 have been implemented for the conducted experiments. We depict them with mnemonic names, using the first three letters of the author who originally published the technique and the corresponding reference. Note that covert channel generation manipulates packet delays in the communication source (aka inter departure times, henceforth abbreviated as *idts*), but detection uses iats; i.e., for two consecutive packets a and b, $iat_{ab} = idt_{ab} + (d_b - d_a)$, where d_a and d_b are the transmission delays of packet a and packet b.

The implemented covert timing techniques are:

- *Packet presence* (CAB)
  As presented in [3], the CAB technique requires synchronicity between the sender and the receiver, who agree on a fixed interval as sampling time. The absence or presence of a packet during an interval represents the binary symbol 0 or 1 respectively (Fig. 3). In [3], different implementations for ensuring synchronization are suggested.
- *Differential/derivative* (ZAN)
  This differential covert channel was originally proposed for the IP-packet Time to Live field [27], but can be easily implemented by using packet delays. Given a basic idt (t_b), whenever a 1 is to be send the previous idt is modified by adding or subtracting t_{inc}; in case of a 0, the last idt is kept the same, i.e., with no modification (Fig. 4).
- *Fixed intervals* (BER)
  Proposed in [2], this technique establishes fixed idts to represent 0s and 1s, respectively t_0 and t_1 (Fig. 5).

– *Jitterbug/modulus* (SHA)

The Jitterbug [18] manipulates an existing transmission. It establishes a ground sampling time interval ω and adds a little delay to idts to make them divisible by ω or $\omega/2$ according to the covert symbol to send (Fig. 6).

– *Huffman coding* (JIN)

This technique codes every covert symbol directly into a set of packets with different idts according to the frequency of the symbol and based on a Huffman codification. For the experiments we applied this technique only for plain text files and using the codification presented in [26] (Fig. 7).

– *Timestamp manipulation* (GIF)

By this technique [8], packet idts are manipulated based on the least significant bit (LSB) of the TCP timestamp. A minimum idt (t_b) between packets must be respected (authors propose, at least, $t_b = 10$ ms). If the LSB coincides with the covert symbol, the packet is sent; if not, the condition is checked again after a time t_w (Fig. 8).

– *One threshold* (GAS)

Devised for Android platforms and with video services as carriers, this technique establishes a threshold th for iats [5]. Delays above and below th will be considered 1s and 0s respectively (Fig. 9).

– *Packet bursts* (LUO)

By this technique presented in [14], packet bursts are sent separated by a waiting time interval t_w. The number of packets in a burst directly represents the covert symbol or piece of code to send. For example, three packets in a burst are used to send the symbol "3" (Fig. 10).

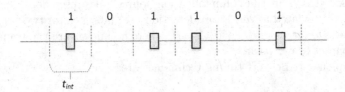

Fig. 3. CAB technique: presence or absence of a packet.

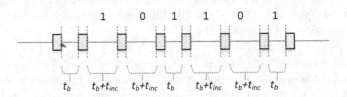

Fig. 4. ZAN technique: differential idt.

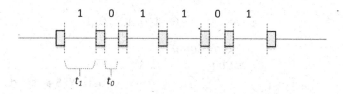

Fig. 5. BER technique: fixed idts.

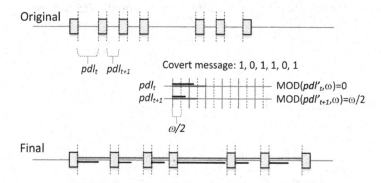

Fig. 6. SHA technique: jitterbug delay manipulation.

Covert message: "hi 5"

	frequency	time
"h"	normal	50ms + 70ms
"i"	high	140ms
" "	very high	60ms
"5"	low	80ms + 140ms

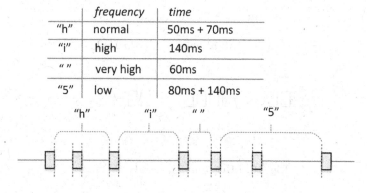

Fig. 7. JIN technique: Huffman coding.

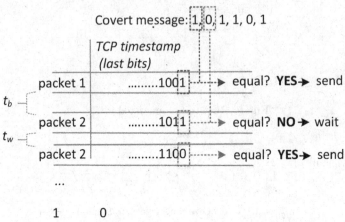

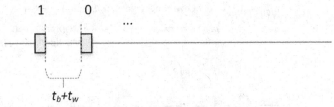

Fig. 8. GIF technique: timestamp manipulation.

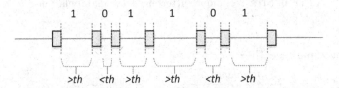

Fig. 9. GAS technique: one threshold.

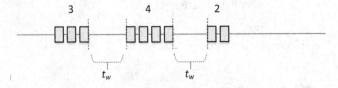

Fig. 10. LUO technique: packet bursts.

5   Experiments

The objective of the experiments was to create and refine DAT rules for the detection of covert timing channels. For this purpose, training and testing processes were performed with known—i.e., labeled—datasets. Figure 11 illustrates the training process, which consisted of three main phases: (1) dataset generation, (2) model obtaining, and (3) rule generalization.

1. *Dataset Generation*

   A testbed for traffic generation was built for creating IP flows containing covert channels as defined by the techniques published in the literature and briefly described in Sect. 4. In addition to selecting techniques, inputs included the files to covertly send and configuration parameters necessary for the setup. We have created two datasets (*cc_training* and *cc_testing*) with different files and random seeds. Selected files included different kinds of plain-text documents (poems, list of passwords, technical reports and programming scripts), images (PNG and JPEG), compressed files (in ZIP and GZ formats) and 3DES encrypted files. Parameters for the automated generation of flows with covert channels were randomly selected within the ranges defined in Table 1. The parameter ranges were adjusted according to the papers in which the techniques were originally presented or, if not documented, based on the knowledge of network traffic measurement experts. As for the training sets that are free of covert channels, real network data was downloaded from the MAWI Working Group Traffic Archive. In the MAWI database[4], 15 min of real backbone traffic is published every day for research purposes. We downloaded traffic corresponding to Sun Feb. 5, 2017, and divided into three 5-minute datasets, from which we used one dataset for training (*nocc_training*), one for testing (*nocc_testing*), and discarded the third one.

2. *Model Obtaining*

   During the second phase, OD-flows were extracted from the datasets, labeled, and jumbled before undergoing classification. To improve classification efficacy we filtered out some obvious non-suspicious traffic, i.e., all flows with less than one packet were already discarded in this phase. For all explored datasets (with and without covert channels), the maximum observation window for a OD-flow was set to five minutes (the rest was simply discarded). The interested reader can freely download the used OD-flow datasets from [22].

   The objective in this phase was to obtain a classification model that could differentiate flows with covert channels from flows without. Since generalization was desired, Decision Trees were selected as classifiers. Decision Trees are known to be efficient learners, with good accuracy rates and, more importantly, they allow easy interpretation and rule extraction from results [12]. We used basic Decision Tree algorithms based on recursive partitioning instead of more complex options (e.g., Random Forest) because they are more interpretable and predictions are easier to explain and generalize. Another characteristic of Decision Trees that make them eligible for the current application is that they are embedded feature selection methods [17], i.e., they can potentially ignore features that are redundant or irrelevant.

---

[4] http://mawi.wide.ad.jp/mawi/.

During the experiments, pre- and postpruning were performed to avoid overfitting and favor generalization.[5] In addition, a 10-fold cross-validation process was performed to reinforce disclosed models. During the training phase, models were obtained from the *cc_training* and *nocc_training* datasets.

3. *Rule Generalization*

In the final phase, rules were extracted from the Decision Tree *complete* model. These rules were manually checked later and adjusted according to generalization criteria. An enhanced set of rules was obtained and implemented in DAT detectors.

Once new rules were embedded, DAT detectors underwent an additional testing phase with reserved datasets. Such validation was conducted with completely new data (not used before): *cc_testing* and *nocc_testing*.

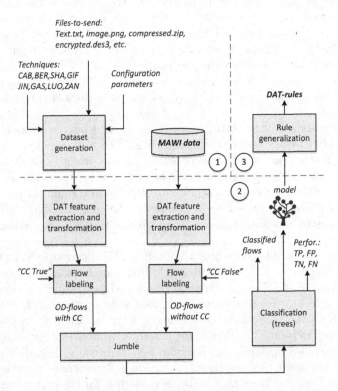

Fig. 11. Phases of the training process: dataset generation, model obtaining, and rule generation.

---

[5] Details of the conducted parametrization are: Decision Trees used Information Gain (i.e., entropy-based) as splitting criterion; the minimal size for splitting was four samples; the minimal leaf size was two samples, allowing a maximal tree depth of 20 levels; the minimal gain for splitting a node was 0.1; the confidence level used for the pessimistic error calculation of pruning was 0.25, whereas the number of prepruning alternatives was three.

Table 1. Parameters for the random generation of covert channels.

Technique	Parameters
d_i (delay)	By default, transmissions delays are modeled with a Lomax (Pareto Type II) distribution with $\alpha = 3$ ms and $\lambda = 10$ ms
CAB	$t_{int} \in [60, 140]$ ms
BER	$t_0 \in [10, 50]$ ms, $t_1 \in [80, 220]$ ms
SHA	pkt-dist.: Gamma with $k \in [40, 760]$ ms, $\phi \in [40, 360]$ ms $\omega \in [10, 90]$ ms
GAS	0-idts pkt-dist.: $t_0 = th - t_s$ 1-idts pkt-dist.: $t_1 = th - t_s + t_a$ $th \in [100, 300]$ ms, $t_s \in [60, 140]$ms, $t_a \in [20, 80]$ ms
JIN	Codification from [26]
LUO	$t_w \in [50, 250]$ ms Packets in a burst are sent every ms
ZAN	$t_b \in [30, 70]$ ms, $t_{inc} \in [30, 70]$ ms
GIF	$t_b \in [10, 30]$ ms, $t_w \in [4, 12]$ ms

It is worth remarking that, even not among the purposes of the current work, the presented testbed enables the modeling of covert timing channel techniques and the obtaining of patterns for the *ML-based Detector* block introduced in Sect. 3.

6   Results

The outcomes of the tests conducted in Sect. 5 were used to evaluate the performance of DAT detectors and the validity of the obtained constituent decision rules. Results were divided into two distinct phases:

1. Obtaining a rule-based decision model based on Decision Tree induction.
2. Validation of the generalized model with testing datasets.

6.1   Rule Extraction Experiments

Decision Trees generated the model illustrated in Fig. 12. The corresponding performances indices are shown in Table 2. Results in Table 2 discloses that Decision Trees were able to capture significant patterns to discriminate between flows with and without covert channels. Provided training data is representative enough, the use of cross validation ensures the robustness of the obtained model and indices.

One of the first aspects that draws attention from Fig. 12 is the absence of ρ_A, S_s and S_k in the solution model. Not using ρ_A is not surprising as iats time series are chaotic and low self-correlated regardless of the class. This is due to the fact that, given a sampling resolution of 1 ms, delays in generation and transport invariably entail scenarios with a considerable entropy. The absence of S_s is also understandable due to same reason, i.e., transmission delays make iats to take approximate but different values even when coming from the same idt by design. In this respect, S_k is a better estimation of main symbols for the iat-case but,

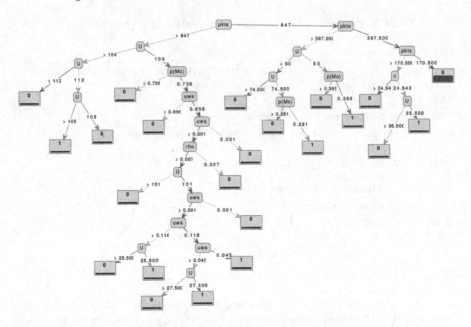

Fig. 12. Decision Tree obtained during the training phase. '1' corresponds to leaves that identify covert channels, '0' for leaves that identify normal traffic.

Table 2. Performance Indices of the complete model during training (datasets: *cc_training* and *nocc_training*).

	Predicted CC	Predicted Normal
Real CC	1015 (TP)	17 (FN)
Real Normal	7 (FP)	16302 (TN)

Accuracy	99.86% ± 0.05%
Precision	99.96% ± 0.04%
Recall	99.90% ± 0.06%
AUC (area under ROC)	0.996 ± 0.004

even so, it does not appear in the Tree either. Actually, S_k is indirectly affecting the model through other parameters, such as c and $\mu_{\omega S}$ (which depend on S_k). Decision Trees just avoided redundancy with respect to this variable (given to its capabilities for feature selection), but the use of multimodality by kernel density estimation was determinant for the detection.

6.2   DAT Testing After Generalization

The close examination of the model in Fig. 12 allows to carry out a rule generalization like the one exposed in Fig. 13. The generalized Decision Tree in Fig. 13

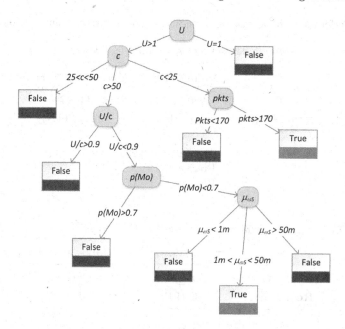

Fig. 13. Generalized decision tree implemented in final DAT detectors.

condenses the detection in two main common patterns (green leaves). One of these patterns corresponds to flows that, during the observation scope (5 min), show a considerable amount of packets ($pkts > 170$) but low potential covert bytes ($c < 25$). This is idiosyncratic of flows with most iats very close to one center value, making S_k and S_s equal one or close to one (for instance, the packet bursts technique, LUO). However, the behaviour emphasized by this decision branch can also be matched by some legitimate services and is prone to generate some false positives (see Table 3).

The second branch, which concentrates most of the discovered covert channels, reveals that covert channels show distributions where packet-iats are in a range between 1 ms and 50 ms around the center values; also, the iat-mode-value represents less that 70% of iats, the number of estimated possible covert bytes must be high ($c > 50$) and the number of unique values (in ms resolution) is somehow below the estimated covert bytes ($U/c < 0.9$). This revealing last property suggests the footprint of a structure behind iat-values, which are generated by algorithmic patterns.

Note that in Fig. 13 the $U > 1$ condition has been included, as such condition is not inferred by Decision Trees but previously imposed in the experiments (i.e., a flow with only one iat value cannot hide a covert timing channel). Except for this specific feature U, a certain fuzziness is naturally assumed when establishing rule thresholds. Therefore, in DAT detectors, instead of strictly applying the thresholds discovered by Decision Trees with a step function, the fitting of every feature to the given rules has been adjusted by using a smooth step

Table 3. Performance indices of the generalized model during evaluation and testing.

DATA: *cc_training* dataset and *nocc_training* dataset

	Predicted CC	Predicted Normal
Real CC	990 (TP)	33 (FN)
Real Normal	94 (FP)	16320 (TN)

Accuracy	99.23%
Precision	91.33%
Recall	96.77%

DATA: *cc_testing* dataset and *nocc_testing* dataset

	Predicted CC	Predicted Normal
Real CC	995 (TP)	42 (FN)
Real Normal	99 (FP)	16013 (TN)

Accuracy	99.18%
Precision	90.95%
Recall	95.95%

function. Later, the final evaluation is obtained with the product t-norm among the different branch conditions.

Table 3 shows the results for the final validation experiments. Indices are promising for detectors that are designed to be lightweight detection barriers, although reveal some false positives to be corrected in final applications. Future implementations will gain robustness by the incorporation of fuzzy controllers in the DAT-decision making, whose capabilities to deal with vague thresholds make them perfect for the application. Detection accuracy is also expected to improve by the complementary analysis carried out by the *ML-based Detector* block, which stores a library with patterns related to known covert channel techniques. The development of such pattern library can be easily performed by the same testbed used together with Decision Trees rule extractors.

7 Conclusion

This work tested and validated statistics-based framework—DAT detectors—for the detection of covert timing channels. To this end, multiple cover channels have been generated based on a set of eight popular covert timing techniques, which were then mixed up with real traffic captures. Decision Trees classifiers were used to infer rules from training data to embed in final implementations of the DAT detector decision making. The final testing with new datasets corroborated the fitness of DAT detectors. In short, this work complements and satisfactorily proves the theoretical foundations exposed in [11], paving the way for an easy integration of fast covert channel detection in modern IDSs.

Acknowledgments. The research leading to these results has been partially funded by the Vienna Science and Technology Fund (WWTF) through project ICT15-129, "BigDAMA".

References

1. Archibald, R., Ghosal, D.: A covert timing channel based on fountain codes. In: 2012 IEEE 11th International Conference on Trust, Security and Privacy in Computing and Communications, pp. 970–977 (2012)
2. Berk, V., Giani, A., Cybenko, G., Hanover, N.: Detection of covert channel encoding in network packet delays. Rapport technique TR536, de lUniversité de Dartmouth, p. 19 (2005)
3. Cabuk, S., Brodley, C.E., Shields, C.: IP covert timing channels: design and detection. In: Proceedings of the 11th ACM Conference on Computer and Communications Security (CCS 2004), pp. 178–187. ACM, New York (2004)
4. Chen, A., Moore, W.B., Xiao, H., Haeberlen, A., Phan, L.T.X., Sherr, M., Zhou, W.: Detecting covert timing channels with time-deterministic replay. In: Proceedings of the 11th USENIX Conference on Operating Systems Design and Implementation (OSDI 2014), pp. 541–554 (2014)
5. Gasior, W., Yang, L.: Network covert channels on the android platform. In: Proceedings of the Seventh Annual Workshop on Cyber Security and Information Intelligence Research (CSIIRW 2011), p. 61:1. ACM, New York (2011)
6. Gianvecchio, S., Wang, H.: An entropy-based approach to detecting covert timing channels. IEEE Trans. Dependable Secure Comput. **8**(6), 785–797 (2011)
7. Gianvecchio, S., Wang, H., Wijesekera, D., Jajodia, S.: Model-based covert timing channels: automated modeling and evasion. In: Lippmann, R., Kirda, E., Trachtenberg, A. (eds.) RAID 2008. LNCS, vol. 5230, pp. 211–230. Springer, Heidelberg (2008). doi:10.1007/978-3-540-87403-4_12
8. Giffin, J., Greenstadt, R., Litwack, P., Tibbetts, R.: Covert messaging through TCP timestamps. In: Dingledine, R., Syverson, P. (eds.) PET 2002. LNCS, vol. 2482, pp. 194–208. Springer, Heidelberg (2003). doi:10.1007/3-540-36467-6_15
9. Girling, C.G.: Covert channels in LAN's. IEEE Trans. Softw. Eng. **13**(2), 292–296 (1987)
10. Holloway, R., Beyah, R.: Covert DCF: a DCF-based covert timing channel in 802.11 networks. In: 2011 IEEE Eighth International Conference on Mobile Ad-Hoc and Sensor Systems, pp. 570–579 (2011)
11. Iglesias, F., Annessi, R., Zseby, T.: DAT detectors: uncovering TCP/IP covert channels by descriptive analytics. Secur. Commun. Netw. **9**(15), 3011–3029 (2016). sec.1531
12. Kamber, M., Winstone, L., Gong, W., Cheng, S., Han, J.: Generalization and decision tree induction: efficient classification in data mining. In: Proceedings Seventh International Workshop on Research Issues in Data Engineering. High Performance Database Management for Large-Scale Applications, pp. 111–120 (1997)
13. Kiyavash, N., Coleman, T.: Covert timing channels codes for communication over interactive traffic. In: IEEE International Conference on Acoustics, Speech, and Signal Processing, pp. 1485–1488 (2009)

14. Luo, X., Chan, E.W.W., Chang, R.K.C.: TCP covert timing channels: design and detection. In: IEEE International Conference on Dependable Systems and Networks With FTCS and DCC (DSN), pp. 420–429, June 2008

15. Mazurczyk, W., Szczypiorski, K.: Steganography of VoIP streams. In: Meersman, R., Tari, Z. (eds.) OTM 2008. LNCS, vol. 5332, pp. 1001–1018. Springer, Heidelberg (2008). doi:10.1007/978-3-540-88873-4_6

16. Padlipsky, M.A., Snow, D.W., Karger, P.A.: Limitations of end-to-end encryption in secure computer networks, eSD-TR-78-158 (1978)

17. Saeys, Y., Inza, I., Larrañaga, P.: A review of feature selection techniques in bioinformatics. Bioinformatics 23(19), 2507–2517 (2007)

18. Shah, G., Molina, A., Blaze, M.: Keyboards and covert channels. In: Proceedings of the 15th Conference on USENIX Security Symposium (USENIX-SS 2006), vol. 15. USENIX Association, Berkeley (2006)

19. Shen, J., Qing, S., Shen, Q., Li, L.: Optimization of covert channel identification. In: Third IEEE International Security in Storage Workshop (SISW 2005), pp. 13–95, December 2005

20. Shrestha, P.L., Hempel, M., Rezaei, F., Sharif, H.: A support vector machine-based framework for detection of covert timing channels. IEEE Trans. Dependable Secur. Comput. 13(2), 274–283 (2016)

21. Sohn, T., Seo, J.T., Moon, J.: A study on the covert channel detection of TCP/IP header using support vector machine. In: Qing, S., Gollmann, D., Zhou, J. (eds.) ICICS 2003. LNCS, vol. 2836, pp. 313–324. Springer, Heidelberg (2003). doi:10.1007/978-3-540-39927-8_29

22. TU Wien CN Group: Data Analysis and Algorithms (2017). https://www.cn.tuwien.ac.at/public/data.html

23. Walls, R.J., Kothari, K., Wright, M.: Liquid: a detection-resistant covert timing channel based on IPD shaping. Comput. Netw. 55(6), 1217–1228 (2011)

24. Wendzel, S., Zander, S., Fechner, B., Herdin, C.: Pattern-based survey and categorization of network covert channel techniques. ACM Comput. Surv. 47(3), 50:1–50:26 (2015)

25. Wray, J.C.: An analysis of covert timing channels. J. Comput. Secur. 1(3–4), 219–232 (1992)

26. Wu, J., Wang, Y., Ding, L., Liao, X.: Improving performance of network covert timing channel through Huffman coding. Math. Comput. Model. 55(1–2), 69–79 (2012). Advanced Theory and Practice for Cryptography and Future Security

27. Zander, S., Armitage, G., Branch, P.: An empirical evaluation of IP time to live covert channels. In: 2007 15th IEEE International Conference on Networks, pp. 42–47, November 2007

28. Zander, S., Armitage, G., Branch, P.: A survey of covert channels and countermeasures in computer network protocols. Commun. Surv. Tutor. 9(3), 44–57 (2007)

29. Zander, S., Armitage, G., Branch, P.: Stealthier inter-packet timing covert channels. In: Domingo-Pascual, J., Manzoni, P., Palazzo, S., Pont, A., Scoglio, C. (eds.) NETWORKING 2011. LNCS, vol. 6640, pp. 458–470. Springer, Heidelberg (2011). doi:10.1007/978-3-642-20757-0_36

30. Zhiyong, C., Yong, Z.: Entropy based taxonomy of network convert channels. In: 2009 2nd International Conference on Power Electronics and Intelligent Transportation System (PEITS), vol. 1, pp. 451–455, December 2009

31. Zi, X., Yao, L., Pan, L., Li, J.: Implementing a passive network covert timing channel. Comput. Secur. 29(6), 686–696 (2010)

Practical Estimation of Mutual Information on Non-Euclidean Spaces

Yoan Miche[1]([✉]), Ian Oliver[1], Wei Ren[1], Silke Holtmanns[1], Anton Akusok[3], and Amaury Lendasse[2]

[1] Nokia Bell Labs, Karakaari 13, 02760 Espoo, Finland
yoan.miche@nokia-bell-labs.com
[2] Department of Mechanical and Industrial Engineering
and the Iowa Informatics Initiative, The University of Iowa, Iowa City, USA
[3] Arcada University of Applied Sciences, Helsinki, Finland

Abstract. We propose, in this paper, to address the issue of measuring the impact of privacy and anonymization techniques, by measuring the data loss between "before" and "after". The proposed approach focuses therefore on data usability, more than in ensuring that the data is sufficiently anonymized. We use Mutual Information as the measure criterion for this approach, and detail how we propose to measure Mutual Information over non-Euclidean data, in practice, using two possible existing estimators. We test this approach using toy data to illustrate the effects of some well known anonymization techniques on the proposed measure.

1   Introduction

Legal and ethical data sharing and monetization is becoming a major topic and concern, for data holders. There is indeed a strong need to make use of all the Big Data accumulated by the hordes of devices that are becoming part of the Internet of Things (IoT) scene. One major difficulty holding back (some of) the parties in this data monetization and sharing scheme, is the ethical and legal problem related to the privacy of this collected data. Indeed, IoT devices are becoming more and more personal (even though smartphones are already holding on to very personal data), with wearables, medical-oriented devices, health and performance measuring devices... And while users often agree to the use of their collected data for further analysis by the service provider, data sharing to a third party is another type of problem. In this sense, data anonymisation in the broad sense is a rather hot topic, and of the utmost concern for such data sharing scenarios.

There exist many ways to obfuscate the data before data sharing, with the most extreme ones consisting in basically modifying the data so randomly and so much, that the end result becomes unusable. Encryption [9] (when properly carried out) would be one example of such data alteration. And while the promises of Homomorphic Encryption [7], for example, are appealing, the problem of the usability of the data by a third party remains the same: the data has already been

A. Holzinger et al. (Eds.): CD-MAKE 2017, LNCS 10410, pp. 123–136, 2017.
DOI: 10.1007/978-3-319-66808-6_9

so utterly modified by the encryption scheme, that the internal data structures are too altered to be used for even basic data mining.

Such approaches that obfuscate totally the data have several practical use cases; for example when storage is to be carried out by an untrusted third party. In this work, we focus on another type of use case: that of the need for usability of the data (in the eyes of a third party) while still carrying out some anonymization. The idea here, is to try and measure how much the data has been altered, in terms of its information content (and not in terms of the actual exact values contained in the data). We are thus looking for a measure that would allow for comparing usability to anonymization/privacy.

In this paper, we do not focus on the means of achieving privacy, or what tools can be used for anonymization, but on how to quantify objectively the information loss created by such techniques. Many techniques have already been proposed to alter the data so as to improve the anonymity levels in it: k-anonymity [8], l-diversity [4], differential privacy [2], as well as working towards ways to perform analysis on such modified or perturbed data [1,5]... We give a brief overview of some of these approaches in the next Sect. 2. One of the issues that we attempt to address in this paper, is the fact that they lack an objective criterion to establish how much the data has actually changed, after using such anonymization techniques. In Sect. 3, we introduce some of the notations for the following Sect. 4 about mutual information as a possible criterion for measuring the data loss. In this section, we detail our approach to estimate mutual information over any data set (including those with non-Euclidean data), and the computational details of how we propose to do it. We present the results of this approach over toy data sets in Sect. 5.

2   A Short Primer on Anonymization Techniques

We first propose in this section to illustrate the effect of some of the most common anonymization techniques, on a limited, traditional data set, depicted in Table 1. The presented anonymization techniques in the following are by no means an exhaustive account of all the possibilities for data anonymization, but probably represent some of the most widely used techniques, in practice.

Table 1. Example of health data records from a medical institution.

ID	Non-sensitive			Sensitive
	Zip code	Age	Nationality	Condition
01	13053	28	Russian	Heart disease
02	13068	29	American	Heart disease
03	13068	21	Japanese	Viral infection
04	13053	23	American	Viral infection
05	14853	50	Indian	Cancer

The example data in Table 1 depicts some medical records for a set of patients, possibly from a health care provider. The classification of the data attributes in "Sensitive" and "Non-Sensitive" categories is somewhat arbitrary in this case. The records from Table 1 show no obvious easily identifiable information when considering single fields. Nevertheless, relationships between the non-sensitive fields in this data can probably make it relatively easy to identify some individuals: within a zip code, the nationality and the age allow someone to restrict the set of possible individuals dramatically. The last individual in the table is even more striking as her age, nationality and zip code surely make her stand out of the rest.

2.1 k-anonymity

The term k-anonymity designates in general both the set of properties a data set has to satisfy to be k-anonymous, and the various techniques that can be used to achieve this property. In practice, a data set is said to be k-anonymous if the information for each individual record in the data set cannot be distinguished from at least $k-1$ other records from the very same data set. Two examples of techniques used to achieve k-anonymity are Suppression and Generalisation, and are described in the next two subsections.

Suppression. Suppression is obviously the crudest of the possible data alterations, as the data gets simply removed, either for a specific set of records in the data, or for a whole field of data. In the following example Table 2, the whole field of the Age of the records has been removed. This approach can obviously lead to strong data alteration, and thus disturb whatever process using the data afterwards. A more subtle solution is provided by Generalization, as follows.

Table 2. Effect of suppression (k-anonymity).

ID	Non-sensitive			Sensitive
	Zip code	Age	Nationality	Condition
01	13053	*	Russian	Heart disease
02	13068	*	American	Heart disease
03	13068	*	Japanese	Viral infection
04	13053	*	American	Viral infection
05	14853	*	Indian	Cancer

Generalization. The idea behind generalisation is to abstract the values in a certain field to higher level (more general) categories. In the example of the data from Table 1, this could mean replacing the last two digits from the Zip Code by zeros, for example, or abstracting the Nationality to "Asian, Caucasian,..."

Table 3. Effect of generalization (k-anonymity).

ID	Non-sensitive			Sensitive
	Zip code	Age	Nationality	Condition
01	13053	[20–30]	Russian	Heart disease
02	13068	[20–30]	American	Heart disease
03	13068	[20–30]	Japanese	Viral infection
04	13053	[20–30]	American	Viral infection
05	14853	[50–60]	Indian	Cancer

instead of country level specifics. In the following example Table 3, we generalised the age of the records to 10 years age ranges.

This approach asks the question of what is satisfying in terms of "granularity" of the abstraction? How much information is actually lost in generalising the data fields, and what is the best way to ensure k-anonymity: generalising several fields a little, or one field a lot?

2.2 Differential Privacy

Differential Privacy [2] aims at preserving higher level data statistical properties, typically by introducing controlled noise in the data fields. Without going into the details and the various versions of Differential Privacy [2], we focus in this work on the specific case of ε-differential privacy, in which the ε parameter basically acts as a control parameter for the trade-off between privacy and usability. More specifically, in the rest of the paper (and for the experiments section), we will use Laplace noise added to the data fields, with the ε parameter being the inverse of the Laplace distribution parameter λ.

In the following Sect. 3, we depart a little from the usual notations used in the data privacy literature, to present the mutual information estimators that we propose to use to measure the information loss created by the use of these anonymization techniques.

3 Notations

Let $\mathscr{X}_i = (\mathbb{X}_i, d_i)$ be a metric space on the set $\mathbb{X}_i$ with the distance function $d_i : \mathbb{X}_i \times \mathbb{X}_i \longrightarrow \mathbb{R}_+$. The $\mathscr{X}_i$ need not be Euclidean spaces, and in the cases discussed in the following sections, are not.

Let us then define by $\mathbf{X} = \left[\mathbf{x}^1, \ldots, \mathbf{x}^n\right]$ a $N \times n$ matrix, with each column vector $\mathbf{x}^i \in \mathbb{X}_i^{N \times 1}$. The $\mathbf{x}_i$ are thus discrete random variables representing a set of samples over the set of all the possible samples from the attribute represented here by $\mathbb{X}_i$. And $\mathbf{X}$ is a table over these attributes.

The fact that the $\mathscr{X}_i$ are not necessarily Euclidean spaces in this work poses the problem of the definition of the distance function associated, d_i. Indeed, most data mining and machine learning tools rely on the Euclidean distance and its properties; and even if the learning of the model does not require the use of Euclidean distances directly, the evaluation criterion typically relies on it, for example as a Mean Square Error for regression problems.

Similarly, as described in Sect. 4, information theory metrics estimators such as mutual information estimators typically rely on the construction of the set of nearest neighbours, and therefore also typically (although not necessarily) on the Euclidean distance.

3.1 Distances over Non-Euclidean Spaces

The argument for considering the use of distances over non-Euclidean spaces in this work, is that it is possible to tweak and modify such non-Euclidean distances so that their distribution and properties will be "close enough" to that of the original Euclidean distance.

More formally, let us assume that we have two metric spaces $\mathscr{X}_i = (\mathbb{X}_i, d_i)$ and $\mathscr{X}_j = (\mathbb{X}_j, d_j)$, with $\mathscr{X}_i$ the canonical d-dimensional Euclidean space (i.e. $\mathbb{X}_i = \mathbb{R}^d$ and d_i the Euclidean norm over it) and $\mathscr{X}_j$ a non-Euclidean metric space endowed with a non-Euclidean metric. Drawing uniformly samples from the set $\mathbb{X}_j$, we form $\mathbf{X}_j = \left[\mathbf{x}_j^1, \ldots, \mathbf{x}_j^n\right]$, a set of random variables, with $\mathbf{x}_j^l$ having values over $\mathbb{X}_j$. Denoting then by f_{d_j} the distribution of pairwise distances over all the samples in $\mathbf{X}_j$, we assume that it is possible to modify the non-Euclidean metric d_j such that

$$\lim_{n \to \infty} f_{d_j} = f_{d_i}, \tag{1}$$

where f_{d_i} is the distribution of the Euclidean distances d_i over the Euclidean space $\mathscr{X}_i$. The limit here is over n as the distribution f_{d_j} is considered to be estimated using a limited number n of random variables, and we are interested in the limit case where we can "afford" to draw as many random variables as possible to be as close to the Euclidean metric as possible. That is, that we can make sure that the non-Euclidean metric behaves over its non-Euclidean space, as would a Euclidean metric over a Euclidean space.

This assumption is "theoretically reasonable", as it comes down to being able to transform a distribution into another, given both. And while this may not be simple nor possible using linear transformation tools, most Machine Learning techniques are able to fit a continuous input to another different continuous output.

4 Mutual Information for Usability Quantification

4.1 Estimating Mutual Information

Using previous notations from Sect. 3, we use the definition of mutual information $I(\mathbf{x}_i, \mathbf{x}_j)$ between two discrete random variables $\mathbf{x}_i, \mathbf{x}_j$ as

$$I(\mathbf{x}_i, \mathbf{x}_j) = \sum_{x_i \in \mathbf{x}_i} \sum_{x_j \in \mathbf{x}_j} p(x_i, x_j) \log\left(\frac{p(x_i, x_j)}{p(x_i)p(x_j)}\right). \tag{2}$$

In practice, the marginals $p(x_i)$ and $p(x_j)$ as well as the joint $p(x_i, x_j)$ are often unknown, and we can then use estimators of the mutual information.

Most of the mutual information estimators (and most famously Kraskov's [3] and Pal's [6]) use the canonical distance defined in the metric space in which lies the data. Typically, this is defined and computable for a Euclidean space, with the traditional Euclidean distance used as the distance function.

In the following, we detail shortly the two mutual information estimators that are (arguably) the most used in practice. The goal of this description being to illustrate their dependency on the metric space's underlying distance functions. This is mainly to make the point that mutual information can thus be estimated using non-Euclidean distances over non-Euclidean spaces, given some precautions, as mentioned in the previous Sect. 3.1.

Kraskov's Estimator. In [3], Kraskov *et al.* propose a mutual information estimator (more precisely, two of them) relying on counts of nearest neighbours, as follows.

Kraskov's First Estimator The initial mutual information estimator $I^{(1)}$ between two random variables $\mathbf{x}_j^l$ and $\mathbf{x}_j^m$ is defined as

$$I^{(1)}(\mathbf{x}_j^l, \mathbf{x}_j^m) = \Psi(k) - <\Psi(\mathbf{n}_{\mathbf{x}_j^l} + 1) + \Psi(\mathbf{n}_{\mathbf{x}_j^m} + 1)> + \Psi(N), \qquad (3)$$

where Ψ is the digamma function, and the notation $<\cdot>$ denotes the average of the quantity between the brackets. In addition, the quantity $\mathbf{n}_{\mathbf{x}_j^l}$ (and defined in the same way, $\mathbf{n}_{\mathbf{x}_j^m}$) denotes the vector $\mathbf{n}_{\mathbf{x}_j^l} = \left[n_{\mathbf{x}_j^l}(1), \ldots, n_{\mathbf{x}_j^l}(N-1) \right]$ holding the counts of neighbours $n_{\mathbf{x}_j^l}(i)$ defined as

$$n_{\mathbf{x}_j^l}(i) = \mathrm{Card}\left(\{x_i \in \mathbf{x}_j^l : d_j(x_j - x_i) \leq \varepsilon(i)/2\}\right) \qquad (4)$$

where $\varepsilon(i)/2 = ||z_i - z_{k\mathrm{NN}(i)}||_{\max}$ is the distance between sample z_i and its k-th nearest neighbour in the joint space $\mathbf{z} = (\mathbf{x}_j^l, \mathbf{x}_j^m)$, and the distance $|| \cdot ||_{\max}$ defined as $||z_q - z_r||_{\max} = \max\left\{||x_j^l(q) - x_j^l(r)||, ||x_j^m(q) - x_j^m(r)||\right\}$, where $x_j^l(q)$ clunkily denotes the q-th sample from the random variable $\mathbf{x}_j^l$.

Kraskov's Second Estimator. The second mutual information estimator $I^{(2)}$ between two random variables $\mathbf{x}_j^l$ and $\mathbf{x}_j^m$ is defined as

$$I^{(2)}(\mathbf{x}_j^l, \mathbf{x}_j^m) = \Psi(k) - 1/k - <\Psi(\mathbf{n}_{\mathbf{x}_j^l}) + \Psi(\mathbf{n}_{\mathbf{x}_j^m})> + \Psi(N), \qquad (5)$$

with Ψ the digamma function, k the number of neighbours to use (to be decided by the user), and this time, $\mathbf{n}_{\mathbf{x}_j^l} = \left[n_{\mathbf{x}_j^l}(1), \ldots, n_{\mathbf{x}_j^l}(N-1) \right]$ is the vector holding counts of neighbours $n_{\mathbf{x}_j^l}(i)$ defined as

$$n_{\mathbf{x}_j^l}(i) = \mathrm{Card}\left(\left\{x_i \in \mathbf{x}_j^l : d_j(x_j - x_i) \leq \varepsilon_{\mathbf{x}_j^l}(i)/2\right\}\right) \qquad (6)$$

where $\varepsilon_{\mathbf{x}_j^l}(i)/2$ is the distance between sample z_i and its k-th nearest neighbour $z_{kNN(i)}$, both projected on the $\mathbf{x}_j^l$ space.

Basically, the calculation requires calculating the nearest neighbours of points in a joint space, and counting how many lie in a certain ball.

Note that while we have adapted the notations to our needs, here, the original article relies on the Euclidean distance, and not on arbitrary distances on non-Euclidean distances.

In the following, we illustrate the calculations of the mutual information by these two estimators, over simple non-Euclidean data, namely GPS traces of people.

5   Experimental Results

We take in the following experiments, a toy (synthetic) data set that has the same structure as internal data (which cannot be released), namely timestamped GPS locations. We generate five synthetic GPS traces for 5 individuals, as can be seen on Fig. 1. It is worth noting that some of the traces have similar routes, with identical start and end points, while others are totally different.

5.1   GPS Routes (Timestamped Data)

Assume we have a dataset $\boldsymbol{X} = [\boldsymbol{x}_1, ..., \boldsymbol{x}_N]^T$ to depict the trajectory of one specific person, where the attributes of each record $\boldsymbol{x}_i$ explain the location at the corresponding time t_i for this specific person. The locations are represented in GPS coordinates ($\boldsymbol{gps}$) with the form of latitudes ($\boldsymbol{lat}$) and longitudes ($\boldsymbol{lon}$). Each record $\boldsymbol{x}_i$ can then be described by: $\boldsymbol{x}_i = (\boldsymbol{gps}_i, \boldsymbol{t}_i) = ((\boldsymbol{lat}_i, \boldsymbol{lon}_i), \boldsymbol{t}_i)$. Hence, the mutual information of the dataset $\boldsymbol{I}(\boldsymbol{X})$ is in a $d \times d$ matrix (in this case $d = 2$: the number of attributes) with the elements holding the mutual information values of the pairwise attributes, illustrated by:

$$\boldsymbol{I}(\boldsymbol{X}) = \{I(\boldsymbol{x}^i, \boldsymbol{x}^j)\}_{1 \le i,j \le d}$$
$$= \begin{bmatrix} I(\boldsymbol{gps}, \boldsymbol{gps}) & I(\boldsymbol{gps}, t) \\ I(t, \boldsymbol{gps}) & I(t, t) \end{bmatrix}, \tag{7}$$

Note that the metric space of the GPS coordinates $\mathscr{X}^{(\boldsymbol{gps})} = (\mathbb{X}^{(\boldsymbol{gps})}, d^{(\boldsymbol{gps})})$ is a non-Euclidean space, because the distance of two GPS coordinates ($\boldsymbol{lat}, \boldsymbol{lon}$) is the shortest route between the two points on the Earth's surface, namely, a segment of a great circle. It is obviously not a Euclidean distance. Meanwhile, the metric space of time $\mathscr{X}^{(t)} = (\mathbb{X}^{(t)}, d^{(t)})$ is a Euclidean space with a typical Euclidean distance function.

We illustrate the mutual information matrices by introducing five experimental datasets, with each dataset recording the trajectory for one person. For each person, 100 timestamps and the corresponding $\boldsymbol{gps}$ locations are recorded, where the locations are measured at uniform sampling intervals. The trajectories in the datasets are shown in Fig. 1.

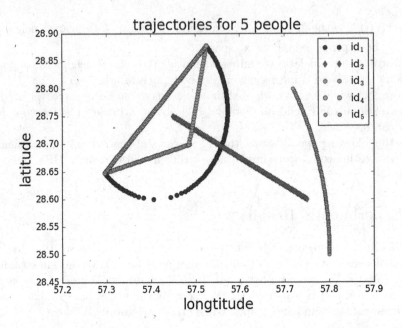

Fig. 1. Five trajectories from the five experimental datasets, respectively.

Table 4. Mutual information (MI) matrices of the five experimental datasets. $I^{(1)}$ and $I^{(2)}$ represent the MI calculated by the first and second *Kraskov* estimators.

	$\begin{bmatrix} I^{(1)}(gps, gps) & I^{(1)}(gps, t) \\ I^{(1)}(t, gps) & I^{(1)}(t, t) \end{bmatrix}$	$\begin{bmatrix} I^{(2)}(gps, gps) & I^{(2)}(gps, t) \\ I^{(2)}(t, gps) & I^{(2)}(t, t) \end{bmatrix}$
id_1	$\begin{bmatrix} 5.18 & 3.65 \\ 3.65 & 5.18 \end{bmatrix}$	$\begin{bmatrix} 4.18 & 3.20 \\ 3.20 & 4.18 \end{bmatrix}$
id_2	$\begin{bmatrix} 5.18 & 3.69 \\ 3.69 & 5.18 \end{bmatrix}$	$\begin{bmatrix} 4.18 & 2.65 \\ 2.65 & 4.18 \end{bmatrix}$
id_3	$\begin{bmatrix} 5.18 & 3.67 \\ 3.67 & 5.18 \end{bmatrix}$	$\begin{bmatrix} 4.18 & 2.74 \\ 2.74 & 4.18 \end{bmatrix}$
id_4	$\begin{bmatrix} 5.18 & 3.69 \\ 3.69 & 5.18 \end{bmatrix}$	$\begin{bmatrix} 4.18 & 2.60 \\ 2.60 & 4.18 \end{bmatrix}$
id_5	$\begin{bmatrix} 5.18 & 3.69 \\ 3.69 & 5.18 \end{bmatrix}$	$\begin{bmatrix} 4.18 & 2.93 \\ 2.93 & 4.18 \end{bmatrix}$

Table 4 shows the mutual information (MI) matrices of the five experimental *ids*, respectively. Here we use $I^{(1)}$ and $I^{(2)}$ to represent the values of MI calculated from the first and second *Kraskov* estimators, respectively. We can see that the MI element value of two identical attributes stays constant, regardless

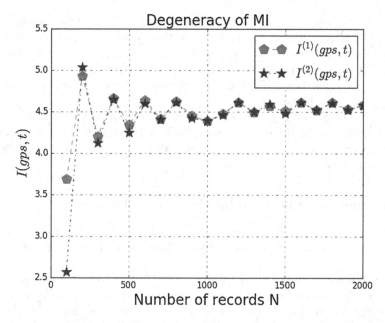

Fig. 2. Mutual information (MI) dependence on the number of samples in the dataset.

of the variables of the attribute itself: $I^{(1)}(gps, gps) = I^{(1)}(t, t) = 5.18$, and $I^{(2)}(gps, gps) = I^{(2)}(t, t) = 4.18$. Meanwhile, the MI matrices are symmetric with $I(gps, t) = I(t, gps)$ for both estimators, of course. The MI values of non-identical pairwise attributes (e.g., $I(gps, t)$) are found to be relatively smaller than those values of two identical attributes (e.g., $I(gps, gps)$), with the obvious reason that the two identical sets of variables are more mutually dependent than two different variables sets.

The values of $I(gps, t)$ are calculated to be in the ranges of $3.65 - 3.69$ and $2.60 - 3.20$ for $I^{(1)}$ and $I^{(2)}$, respectively, compared with the $I(gps, gps)$ values of 5.18 and 4.18 for the two estimators. We can see that $I^{(2)}$ is more sensitive than $I^{(1)}$ for ids with different trajectories, by giving disparate $I^{(2)}(gps, t)$ values. For example, the $I^{(2)}(gps, t)$ of id_1 with the value of 3.20 is larger than those for id_2, id_3, and id_4, with values around 2.7. This is mainly due to the relatively more peculiar trajectory of id_1.

5.2 Convergence of the MI Estimators

It is obvious that all the MI values calculated from $I^{(1)}$ are relatively larger than those from $I^{(2)}$. In principle, both estimators should give very similar results. The difference here is because the number of records with $N = 100$ in each dataset is so small that in the estimators $n_x(i)$ and $n_y(i)$ tend to be also very small with considerably large relative fluctuations. This will cause large statistical errors. We discuss here about the MI convergence with increasing numbers of records.

We take the trajectory of id_4 for example to explain the MI convergence. In the original dataset, there are 100 uniform timestamps and the corresponding 100 uniform locations. We increase the number of records N to 200, 300, 400, ..., 2000, by interpolating uniformly denser timestamps and locations into the trajectory. $I^{(1)}(\boldsymbol{gps}, t)$ and $I^{(2)}(\boldsymbol{gps}, t)$ is then calculated with the ratio of k/N kept to be 0.01 in the estimators.

The dependence of $I(\boldsymbol{gps}, t)$ values over number of record N is illustrated in Fig. 2. It can be seen that the discrepancy of $I^{(1)}$ and $I^{(2)}$ values is getting smaller with increasing N. When N is larger than 800, $I^{(1)}$ and $I^{(2)}$ converge to the values around 4.6.

5.3 k-anonymity Effects on the Trajectory Datasets

We have here used the Generalization approach from k-anonymity to modify the data set, and explore the influence of such changes on the mutual information values.

In the following Table 5, k-anonymity applied to the GPS field means that we have in practice rounded the GPS coordinates (lat and lon) by 2 digits, compared to the original precision; when applied to the time field, we have also rounded the time to 10 min intervals (instead of second precision).

Table 5. Effects of k-anonymity on mutual information (MI) matrices for the five experimental datasets.

$$\begin{bmatrix} I^{(1)}(\boldsymbol{gps}, \boldsymbol{gps}) & I^{(1)}(\boldsymbol{gps}, t) \\ I^{(1)}(t, \boldsymbol{gps}) & I^{(1)}(t, t) \end{bmatrix}$$

k-Anon	None (original)	GPS only	Time only	GPS and Time
id1	$\begin{bmatrix} 5.18 & 3.65 \\ 3.65 & 5.18 \end{bmatrix}$	$\begin{bmatrix} 5.18 & 3.70 \\ 3.70 & 5.18 \end{bmatrix}$	$\begin{bmatrix} 5.18 & 2.25 \\ 2.25 & 5.18 \end{bmatrix}$	$\begin{bmatrix} 5.18 & 3.35 \\ 3.35 & 5.18 \end{bmatrix}$
id2	$\begin{bmatrix} 5.18 & 3.69 \\ 3.69 & 5.18 \end{bmatrix}$	$\begin{bmatrix} 5.18 & 3.73 \\ 3.73 & 5.18 \end{bmatrix}$	$\begin{bmatrix} 5.18 & 2.25 \\ 2.25 & 5.18 \end{bmatrix}$	$\begin{bmatrix} 5.18 & 3.58 \\ 3.58 & 5.18 \end{bmatrix}$
id3	$\begin{bmatrix} 5.18 & 3.67 \\ 3.67 & 5.18 \end{bmatrix}$	$\begin{bmatrix} 5.18 & 3.79 \\ 3.79 & 5.18 \end{bmatrix}$	$\begin{bmatrix} 5.18 & 2.30 \\ 2.30 & 5.18 \end{bmatrix}$	$\begin{bmatrix} 5.18 & 3.58 \\ 3.58 & 5.18 \end{bmatrix}$
id4	$\begin{bmatrix} 5.18 & 3.69 \\ 3.69 & 5.18 \end{bmatrix}$	$\begin{bmatrix} 5.18 & 3.42 \\ 3.42 & 5.18 \end{bmatrix}$	$\begin{bmatrix} 5.18 & 2.23 \\ 2.23 & 5.18 \end{bmatrix}$	$\begin{bmatrix} 5.18 & 3.07 \\ 3.07 & 5.18 \end{bmatrix}$
id5	$\begin{bmatrix} 5.18 & 3.69 \\ 3.69 & 5.18 \end{bmatrix}$	$\begin{bmatrix} 5.18 & 3.64 \\ 3.64 & 5.18 \end{bmatrix}$	$\begin{bmatrix} 5.18 & 2.24 \\ 2.24 & 5.18 \end{bmatrix}$	$\begin{bmatrix} 5.18 & 3.48 \\ 3.48 & 5.18 \end{bmatrix}$

It should be noted that we only report the values for the first estimator, here. In practice, the changes in mutual information incurred by the chosen k-anonymity values on the GPS are relatively minimal, as can be seen in Table 5.

It is interesting to note that the changes on the time cause much more distortion in the data (in terms of the mutual information), possibly because the granularity of the generalization is higher for the time, given the "rounding" chosen. The most interesting feature is that by altering both GPS and time at the same time, the mutual information is higher than when time alone is affected. We explain this by the fact that when these two fields are changed in the same fashion at the same time, the disturbance to the relationship between them is less than when only changing the time. This change to both fields "preserves" some of the relationship better, it seems.

5.4   Differential Privacy Effects on the Trajectory Datasets

We have used ε-differential privacy to obfuscate the trajectory datasets by the Laplace mechanism. We define the privacy function to be a family set of $h = \{h^{(gps)}, h^{(t)}\}$, where $h^{(gps)}$, $h^{(t)}$ are the obfuscating functions to perturb the GPS field and time field, respectively.

Differential privacy was applied by adding controllable noise to the corresponding attribute in the dataset, which satisfies the Laplace distribution with mean μ and standard deviation b: $h^{(i)} = \text{diff}^{(i)}(\mu, b)$. Let ε be the differential privacy parameter, the standard deviation b of the Laplace noise can be then obtained by:

$$b = \frac{\Delta f}{\varepsilon}, \tag{8}$$

where Δf is the sensitivity of the attribute field.

In the following discussion, we used three family sets of privacy functions, which are:

$$
\begin{aligned}
h_1 &= \{\text{diff}^{(gps)}(\mu, b), & \emptyset^{(t)}\}; \\
h_2 &= \{\emptyset^{(gps)}, & \text{diff}^{(t)}(\mu, b)\}; \\
h_3 &= \{\text{diff}^{(gps)}(\mu, b), & \text{diff}^{(t)}(\mu, b)\},
\end{aligned}
\tag{9}
$$

where $\emptyset^{(i)}$ stands for taking no action to the attribute i. For example, h_1 means adding Laplace noise only to the GPS attribute, while the timestamps stay the same; h_2 means adding Laplace noise only to the timestamps attribute; h_3 means adding Laplace noises to both GPS and timestamps attributes.

Figure 3 shows the obtained pairwise MI values of $I(h^{(gps)}, h^{(t)})$, where the privacy function sets are applied to the GPS field and time fields with various privacy parameters ε from 0 to 20. We can see that $I(h^{(gps)}, h^{(t)})$ is monotonically decreasing when the privacy parameter ε decreases. When ε turns to close enough, but not equal, to 0, the MI values collapse at 0, where the fluctuations are the statistic errors caused by small number of sample N in the datasets. It can be well explained by the fact that with smaller values of ε, the amplitudes of the Laplace noise (calculated by Eq. 8) become larger, which distort the metric space or topology of the original datasets more extensively to higher levels with increasing privacy. In another word, we can say that small ε in differential privacy creates greatly anonymised datasets, and effectively alters the

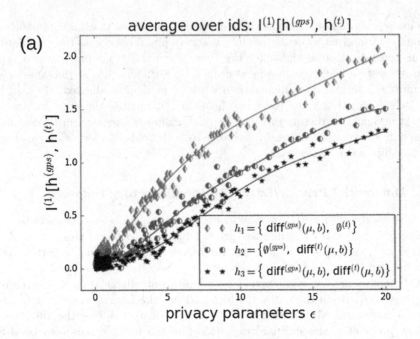

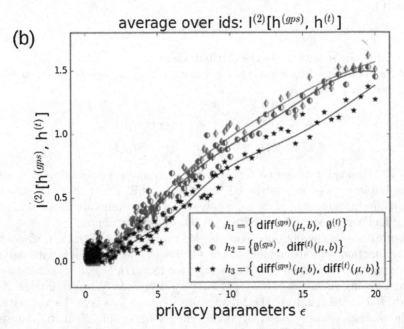

Fig. 3. Mutual information (MI) values of $I(h^{(gps)}, h^{(t)})$, with the GPS field and time field obfuscated by differential privacy technique with the privacy functions of $h^{(gps)}$ and $h^{(t)}$, respectively. The MI values are obtained by taking the average of $I(h^{(gps)}, h^{(t)})$ values from the 5 trajectories. The discrete markers are the obtained averaged MI values, while the corresponding solid lines are the fitted functions with machine learning technique. (a) and (b) are the MI values calculated by the first and second *Kraskov* estimators, respectively.

metric space with big distortion in terms of the mutual information between the data fields (GPS, time), while the information contents extracted from the anonymised datasets will reduce as a trade-off of increasing privacy. The linkability between the attributes is thus weakened to prevent re-identification of the individuals. Hence the pairwise MI values are decreased.

The efficiencies of altering the MI values by the privacy functions h_1, h_2, and h_3 can be compared in Fig. 3. Both estimators indicate that when applying differential privacy technique on GPS field (h_1) and time field (h_2) separately at the same privacy parameters ε, the time field is more sensitive to reduce the MI values, compared to the GPS field. Moreover, differential privacy applied on both GPS and time (h_3) fields at the same time is the most efficient data anonymization function (in terms of affecting the data relationships regarding mutual information).

As we have discussed before, small MI values stand for high distorsions of the data anonymization, at the possible cost of unusable data, while large MI values imply small alteration of the dataset topology, with a potentially high re-identifiability risk. Therefore, we want to find an acceptable range of MI values, where the dataset is sufficiently anonymized to ensure as low as possible risk of re-identification, while the amount of information in the distorted data is still sufficiently usable for future data analysis (in terms of relationships between data fields). Our goal is to control and quantify this distortion, by restricting the privacy parameters in the anonymization functions to specific, acceptable ranges, or by conveying restrictions over the obfuscation functions, also in a controllable manner.

6 Conclusion

In this paper, we have proposed an applied information theoretic approach to measure the impact of privacy techniques such as k-anonymity and differential privacy, for example. We examine, by this approach, the disturbances in the relationships between the different columns ("fields") of the data, thus focusing on a data usability aspect, rather than actually measuring privacy. We propose to do this on any data that can be taken over a metric space, i.e. for which a distance between elements is the sole practical need. We develop an approach to estimate mutual information between such data types, using two well known estimators, and demonstrate their behaviour over simple experimental tests. We finally investigate the effects of k-anonymity (specifically, generalisation) and differential privacy over timestamped GPS traces, and illustrate the effects of these widely used privacy techniques over the information content and the relationships contained in the data. In effect, the results obtained are as expected, except possibly for the case where the generalisation in k-anonymity is performed over both fields at the same time, and leads to some preservation of the data structure and relationships. Future work will include other data types and other mutual information estimators to verify the results observed in this work.

References

1. Domingo-Ferrer, J., Rebollo-Monedero, D.: Measuring risk and utility of anonymized data using information theory. In: Proceedings of the 2009 EDBT/ICDT Workshops (EDBT/ICDT 2009), pp. 126–130. ACM, New York (2009)
2. Dwork, C.: Differential privacy: a survey of results. In: Agrawal, M., Du, D., Duan, Z., Li, A. (eds.) TAMC 2008. LNCS, vol. 4978, pp. 1–19. Springer, Heidelberg (2008). doi:10.1007/978-3-540-79228-4_1
3. Kraskov, A., Stögbauer, H., Grassberger, P.: Estimating mutual information. Phys. Rev. E **69**, 066138 (2004)
4. Li, N., Li, T.: t-closeness: privacy beyond κ-anonymity and ℓ-diversity. In: Proceedings of IEEE 23rd International Conference on Data Engineering (ICDE 2007) (2007)
5. Malle, B., Kieseberg, P., Weippl, E., Holzinger, A.: The right to be forgotten: towards machine learning on perturbed knowledge bases. In: Buccafurri, F., Holzinger, A., Kieseberg, P., Tjoa, A.M., Weippl, E. (eds.) CD-ARES 2016. LNCS, vol. 9817, pp. 251–266. Springer, Cham (2016). doi:10.1007/978-3-319-45507-5_17
6. Pál, D., Póczos, B., Szepesvári, C.: Estimation of rényi entropy and mutual information based on generalized nearest-neighbor graphs. In: Lafferty, J.D., Williams, C.K.I., Shawe-Taylor, J., Zemel, R.S., Culotta, A. (eds.) Advances in Neural Information Processing Systems, vol. 23, pp. 1849–1857. Curran Associates Inc. (2010)
7. Samanthula, B.K., Howser, G., Elmehdwi, Y., Madria, S.: An efficient and secure data sharing framework using homomorphic encryption in the cloud. In: Proceedings of the 1st International Workshop on Cloud Intelligence (Cloud-I 2012), pp. 8:1–8:8. ACM, New York (2012)
8. Sweeney, L.: κ-anonymity: a model for protecting privacy. Int. J. Uncertain. Fuzziness Knowl. Based Syst. **10**(5), 557–570 (2002)
9. Wei, J., Liu, W., Hu, X.: Secure data sharing in cloud computing using revocable-storage identity-based encryption. IEEE Trans. Cloud Comput. **PP**(99), 1 (2016)

IntelliAV: Toward the Feasibility of Building Intelligent Anti-malware on Android Devices

Mansour Ahmadi[✉], Angelo Sotgiu, and Giorgio Giacinto

University of Cagliari, Cagliari, Italy
mansour.ahmadi@diee.unica.it

Abstract. Android is targeted the most by malware coders as the number of Android users is increasing. Although there are many Android anti-malware solutions available in the market, almost all of them are based on malware signatures, and more advanced solutions based on machine learning techniques are not deemed to be practical for the limited computational resources of mobile devices. In this paper we aim to show not only that the computational resources of consumer mobile devices allow deploying an efficient anti-malware solution based on machine learning techniques, but also that such a tool provides an effective defense against novel malware, for which signatures are not yet available. To this end, we first propose the extraction of a set of lightweight yet effective features from Android applications. Then, we embed these features in a vector space, and use a pre-trained machine learning model on the device for detecting malicious applications. We show that without resorting to any signatures, and relying only on a training phase involving a reasonable set of samples, the proposed system outperforms many commercial anti-malware products, as well as providing slightly better performances than the most effective commercial products.

Keywords: Android · Malware detection · Machine learning · On-device · TensorFlow · Mobile security · Classification

1 Introduction

Nowadays, mobile devices are ubiquitous tools for everyday life. Among them, Android devices dominated the global smartphone market, with nearly 90% of the market share in the second quarter of 2016 [25]. The majority of the security issues affecting Android systems can be attributed to third party applications (app) rather than to the Android OS itself. Based on F-secure reports on mobile threats [35], researchers found 277 new malware families, among which 275 specifically targeting Android devices. Also other recent reports clearly show that the malware infection rate of Android mobile devices is soaring. In particular, a report from McAfee [30] reported a significant growth of mobile malware in the wild. We believe that this huge amount of mobile malware needs to be timely detected, possibly by smart tools running on the device, because it has

A. Holzinger et al. (Eds.): CD-MAKE 2017, LNCS 10410, pp. 137–154, 2017.
DOI: 10.1007/978-3-319-66808-6_10

been shown that malware can bypass offline security checks, and live in the wild for a while. As a matter of fact, to the best of our knowledge, even the most recent versions of Android anti-malware products are still not intelligent enough to catch most of the novel malware.

The success of machine learning approaches for malware detection and classification [5,8,26,36,41], as well as the advance in machine learning software for the execution in mobile environments, motivated us to empower Android devices with a machine-learning anti-malware engine. Although modern mobile devices come to the market with a huge amount of computational power, the development of any Android anti-malware product should consider its efficiency on the device to avoid battery drain, in particular when machine learning techniques are employed, as they are known to be computational demanding. On the other hand, we observe that an intelligent Android anti-malware product doesn't need to be unnecessarily complex, as it has been shown that Android malware executes simpler tasks than the desktop counterparts [7]. All the aforementioned reasons motivate the proposal for a machine learning solution to be deployed on mobile devices to detect potential malicious software.

1.1   On-Device Advanced Security

Although there are many offline systems proposed for mobile malware detection, mostly based on machine learning approaches (see Sect. 5), there are many reasons for a user to have an intelligent security tool capable of identifying potential malware on the device.

(*i*) The Google Play store is not totally free of malware. There has been many reports that have shown that malware could pass the Google security checks, and remain accessible to users for sometime on the Play store until someone flags it as inappropriate. For instance, the Check Point security firm reported a zero-day mobile ransomware found in Google Play in January 2017, which was dubbed as a *Charger* application, and was downloaded by more than a million users [31]. Another report from the same vendor cites the case of new variants of the famous Android malware family HummingBad [33]. We vet these samples in Sect. 3.2.

(*ii*) Third-party app stores are popular among mobile users, because they usually offer applications at great discounts. Moreover, the Google Play store has restricted access in some countries, so people have to download their required applications from third-party app stores. Nevertheless, security checks on the third-party stores are not as effective as those available on the Google Play store. Therefore, third-party markets are a good source of propagation for mobile malware. Many malware samples have been found on these stores during the past years, that were downloaded by millions of users. In addition, quite often users can be dodged by fake tempting titles like free games when browsing the web, so that applications are downloaded and installed directly on devices from untrusted websites. Another source of infection is phishing SMS messages that contain links to malicious applications. Recent reports by Lookout and Google [24,27] show how a targeted attack malware, namely *Pegasus*, which is suspected to infect devices via a phishing attack, could remain undetected for a few years. We vet these samples in Sect. 3.2.

(*iii*) One of the main concerns for any 'computing' device in the industry, is to make sure that the device a user buys is free of malware. Mobile devices make no exception, and securing the 'supply chain' is paramount difficult, for the number of people and companies involved in the supply chain of the components. There is a recent report that shows how some malware were added to Android devices somewhere along the supply chain, before the user received the phone [32]. We vet these samples in Sect. 3.2.

(*iv*) To the best of our knowledge, almost all of the Android anti-malware products are mostly signature-based, which lets both malware variants of known families, and zero-day threats to devices. There are claims by a few Android anti-malware vendors that they use machine learning approaches, even if no detail is available on the mechanisms that are actually implemented on the device. We analyze this issue in more details in Sect. 3.2.

All of the above observations show that an anti-malware solution based on machine-learning approaches, either completely, or as a complement to signatures, can reduce the vulnerability of Android devices against novel malware.

1.2   Contribution

Accordingly, in this paper we introduce IntelliAV[1], which is a practical intelligent anti-malware solution for Android devices based on the open-source and multi-platform TensorFlow library. It is worth to mention that this paper does not aim to propose yet another learning-based system for Android malware detection, but by leveraging on the existing literature, and on previous works by the authors, we would like to test the feasibility of having an on-device intelligent anti-malware tool to tackle the deficiencies of existing Android anti-malware products, mainly based on pattern matching techniques. To the best of our knowledge, the performances of learning-based malware detection systems for Android have been only tested off-device, i.e., with computational power and memory space well beyond the capabilities of mobile devices. More specifically, the two main contributions of IntelliAV are as follows:

(i) We propose a machine-learning model based on lightweight and effective features extracted on a substantial set of applications. The model is carefully constructed to be both effective and efficient by wisely selecting the features, the model, and by tuning the parameters as well as being precisely validated to be practical for the capabilities of Android devices.

(ii) We show how the proposed model can be embedded in the IntelliAV application, and easily deployed on Android devices to detect new and unseen malware. Performance of IntelliAV has been evaluated by cross-validation, and achieved 92% detection rate that is comparable to other off-device learning-based Android malware detection relying on a relatively small set of

---

[1] http://www.intelliav.com.

features. Moreover, `IntelliAV` has been tested on a set of unseen malware, and achieved 72% detection rate that is higher than the top 5 commercial Android anti-malware products.

The rest of the paper is organized as follows: First, we reveal the detail of `IntelliAV` by motivating the choice of features and the procedure followed to construct the model (Sect. 2). We then present the experimental setup and results (Sect. 3). After that, we briefly mention the limitations of IntelliAV (Sect. 4) and review the related works on Android malware detection (Sect. 5). Finally, we conclude our paper discussing future directions of `IntelliAV` (Sect. 6).

2   System Design

The architecture of the proposed `IntelliAV` system is depicted in Fig. 1, and its design consists of two main phases, namely offline training the model, and then its operation on the device to detect potential malware samples. As a first phase, a classification model is built offline, by resorting to a conventional computing environment. It is not necessary to perform the training phase on the device, because it has to be performed on a substantial set of samples whenever needed to take into account the evolution of malware. The number of times the model needs to be updated should be quite small, as reports showed that just the 4% of the total number of Android malware is actually new malware [10]. To perform the training phase we gathered a relatively large number of applications (Sect. 3.1). Then, a carefully selected set of characteristics (features) is extracted from the applications to learn a discriminant function allowing the distinction between malicious and benign behaviors (Sect. 2.1). Next, the extracted features are passed to the model construction step in which a classification function is learnt by associating each feature to the type of applications it has been extracted

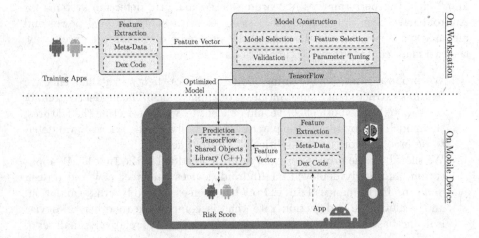

Fig. 1. Overview of `IntelliAV`.

from, i.e., malware or goodware (Sect. 2.2). Finally, as the second phase, the model is embedded in the `IntelliAV` Android application that will provide a risk score for each application on the device (Sect. 2.3).

2.1 Feature Extraction

The feature extraction step is the core phase for any learning-based system. Various kinds of features have been proposed for Android malware detection by the security community, such as permissions, APIs, API dependencies, Intents, statistical features, etc. (see Sect. 5 for a detailed discussion on the issue of feature extraction for Android malware detection). However, some sets of features related to basic Android behaviors, like permissions, APIs, and Intents, usually allow achieving reasonable detection results, with the aim to alert for the presence of probably harmful applications [8,36]. Extracting this set of features is also feasible on mobile devices because they do not need deep static analysis, thus requiring a limited computational effort. Therefore, with the aim of extracting a set of efficient and effective features for `IntelliAV`, we resorted to the following four sets of features: permissions, Intent Filters, statistical features based on the 'manifest' of Android applications, and the APIs, which are extracted from the dex code. Therefore, to construct the feature vector, we considered all the permissions and intent-filters that are used by the samples included in the training set. In addition, four statistical features from application's components such as the total number of activities, services, broadcast receivers, and content providers are added to the feature vector as they can reveal the amount of abilities each application has. For instance, the number of activities in many malware categories is usually fewer than the number of activities available in benign applications, except for the case of malware that is built by repackaging benign applications. Moreover, we manually selected a set of 179 APIs as features and included in the feature vector. The selected APIs are those that reveal some particular characteristics of application that are known to be peculiar to either goodware or malware. For instance, the `invoke` API from the `java.lang.reflect.Method` class shows whether an application uses reflection or not. Note that permissions and APIs are coded as binary features, which means that their value is either one or zero depending on the feature being or not present in the application. By contrast, intent-filters are integer-valued features, as they represent the number of times an intent-filters is declared in the manifest. Considering this count for intent-filter features makes them more meaningful rather than simply considering their presence or not in the application. Similarly, the application's components are represented as integer valued features, as we count the number of components for each different type (e.g., activities, services, etc.). On the other hand, if we considered the number of permissions, we would have ended up with useless information, as each permission needs to be declared just once in the `manifest`. The same reasoning motivates the use of binary feature to represent API usage. The main reason is that although it is possible to get the count of the usage of an API in an application, the procedure would increase the processing time without producing more useful information, so that we ignored it. In total, the feature

Table 1. Features used in `IntelliAV`.

Category	Number of features	Type
Meta-data		
Permissions	322	Binary
Intent Filters	503	Count
Statistical	4	Count
Dex code		
APIs	171	Binary

vector contains 3955 features. To avoid overfitting, and make `IntelliAV` faster on the mobile device, we decided to reduce the number of feature by selecting the 1000 meaningful features thorough a feature selection procedure (see Sect. 2.2). The final set consists of 322 features related to permissions, 503 features related to Intent filters, 4 statistical features from components (e.g., count of activities), and 171 features related to API usage (see Table 1).

2.2 Model Construction

To discriminate malware from benign applications, we need to rely on binary classification algorithms. Over the past years, a large number of classification techniques have been proposed by the scientific community, and the choice of the most appropriate classifier for a given task is often guided by previous experience in different domains, as well as by trial-and-error procedures. However, among all of the existing classifiers, Random Forest classifier [14] have shown high performances in a variety of tasks [19]. Random Forests algorithm is an ensemble learning method in which a number of decision trees are constructed at training time by randomly selecting the features used by each decision tree, and it outputs the class of an instance at testing time based on the collective decision of the ensemble. As far as the Random forest model is an ensemble classifier, it often achieves better results than a single classifier. The main reason of achieving good results by Random Forests is that ensemble methods reduce the variance in performances of a number of decision trees, which in turn are complex models with low bias. So, the final model exhibits low bias, and low variance, which makes the model more robust against both the *underfitting* and *overfitting* problems [13].

To be able to train our model offline, as well as to test it on Android devices, we built `IntelliAV` on top of TensorFlow [2]. More specifically, we employ an implementation of Random Forests in TensorFlow, called TensorForest [16]. TensorFlow is an open source library for machine learning, which was released by Google in November 2015. To the best of our knowledge, `IntelliAV` is the first anti-malware tool that has proposed employing TensorFlow. The TensorFlow model is highly portable as it supports the vast majority of platforms such as Linux, Mac OS, Windows, and mobile computing platforms including Android and iOS. TensorFlow computations are expressed as data flow graphs. Nodes in the graph represent mathematical operations, while the graph edges represent the multidimensional data arrays (tensors) communicating between them.

As mentioned in the previous subsection, to simplify the learning task and reduce the risk of the so-called *overfitting* problem, i.e., to avoid that the model fits the training set but exhibits a low generalization capability with respect to novel unknown samples, we exploited feature selection that reduced the feature set size by removing irrelevant and noisy features. In particular, as done in [4], we computed the so-called *mean decrease impurity* score for each feature, and retained those features which have been assigned the highest scores. Note that the mean decrease impurity technique is often referred to as the Gini impurity, or information gain criterion.

2.3   On-Device Testing

As we mentioned before, TensorFlow eases the task of using machine learning models on mobile devices. So, we embedded in `IntelliAV` the trained model obtained according to the procedure described in Sect. 2.2. The size of the TensorFlow models depends on the complexity of the model. For instance, if the number of trees in TensorForest increases, consequently the size of the model increases as well. The size of `IntelliAV` model that we obtained according to the above procedure and that we transferred to the device, is about 14.1 MB. Having said that, when it is embedded into the apk, the model is compressed and the total size of the model becomes just 3.3 MB. Whenever an application needs to be tested, first, `IntelliAV` extracts the features from the application on the device, then it loads the model, and finally it feeds the model by the extracted features to get the application's risk score. The model provides a likelihood value between 0 and 1, denoting the degree of maliciousness of the application, that we scale to a percentage that we called *risk score*, to make it more understandable for the end user. We empirically provide the following guideline for interpreting the risk score. If the risk score is lower than 40%, the risk is low and we suggest to consider the application as being benign. If the risk score is between 40% and 50%, then the application should be removed if the user isn't sure about the trustworthiness of the application. Finally, the application has to be removed if the risk score is higher than 50%. These thresholds have been set after testing the system on a set containing different applications. We deployed `IntelliAV` so that two main abilities are provided, as shown in Fig. 2. `IntelliAV` can scan all of the installed applications on the device, and verify their risk scores (Quick Scan). In addition, when a user downloads an apk, it can be analyzed by `IntelliAV` before installation to check the related risk score, and take the appropriate decision (Custom Scan). To access the contents of an application's package on the external storage, `IntelliAV` needs the `READ_EXTERNAL_STORAGE` permission. To access the contents of the packages of installed applications, `IntelliAV` needs to read `base.apk` in a sub-directory with a name corresponding to the package name, which is located in */data/app/* directory. As far as the permission of `base.apk` file is `-rw-r--r--`, which means every user can read the content of

(a) Scan installed applications   (b) Scan an APK

Fig. 2. IntelliAV abilities.

this file, IntelliAV doesn't need neither any permission, nor a rooted device to evaluate the installed applications.

3   Experimental Analysis

In this section, we address the following research questions:

- Is IntelliAV able to detect new and unseen malware (Sect. 3.2)?
- Are the performances of IntelliAV comparable to the ones of popular mobile anti-malware products, although IntelliAV is completely based on machine learning techniques (Sect. 3.2)?
- Which is the overhead of IntelliAV on real devices (Sect. 3.3)?

Before addressing these questions, we discuss the data used, and the experimental settings of our evaluation (Sect. 3.1).

3.1   Experimental Setup

To evaluate IntelliAV, we have collected 19,722 applications, divided into 10,058 benign and 9,664 malicious applications from VirusTotal [39]. When gathering malicious applications, we considered their diversity, by including samples belonging to different categories, such as Adware, Ransomware [6,28], GCM malware [3], etc. All of the gathered samples have been first seen by VirusTotal between January 2011 and December 2016. The whole process of feature extraction and model construction was carried out on a laptop with a 2 GHz quad-core processor and 8 GB of memory. Two metrics that are used for evaluating the performance of our approach are the False Positive Rate (FPR) and the True Positive Rate (TPR). FPR is the percentage of goodware samples misclassified as badware, while TPR is the fraction of correctly-detected badware samples (also known as detection rate). A Receiver-Operating-Characteristic (ROC) curve reports TPR against FPR for all possible model's decision thresholds.

3.2 Results

To better understand the effectiveness of `IntelliAV`, we evaluate it in following scenarios.

Cross Validation. One might fit a model on the training set very well, so that the model will perfectly classify all of the samples that are used during the training phase. However, this might not provide the model with the generalization capability, and that's why we evaluated the model by a cross-validation procedure to find the best tuned parameters to be used for constructing the final model as a trade-off between correct detection and generalization capability. Consequently, we evaluated `IntelliAV` on the set of applications described in Sect. 3.1 through a 5-fold cross validation, to provide statistically-sound results. In this validation technique, samples are divided into 5 groups, called folds, with almost equal sizes. The prediction model is built using 4 folds, and then it is tested on the final remaining fold. The procedure is repeated 5 times on different folds to be sure that each data point is evaluated exactly once. We repeated the procedure by running the Random Forest algorithm multiple times to obtain the most appropriate parameters. The ROC of the best fitted model is shown in Fig. 3. The values of FPR and TPR are respectively 4.2% and 92.5% which is quite acceptable although the set of considered features is relatively small, namely 1000 features.

Evaluation on the Training Set. To verify the effectiveness of the tuned parameters based on the cross-validation procedure explained in Sect. 3.2, we tested the model on all the samples used for training. Table 2 shows the results on the training set. It shows that `IntelliAV` misclassified just a few training samples. This shows how the model is carefully fitted on the training set, so that is able to correctly classify almost all of the training samples with very high accuracy, while it avoids being overfitted, and thus can detect unseen malware with a high accuracy as well (see the following).

Evaluation on New Malware. We then tested the system on a set made up of 2311 malware samples, and 2898 benign applications, that have been first seen by VirusTotal between January and March of 2017. We considered an application

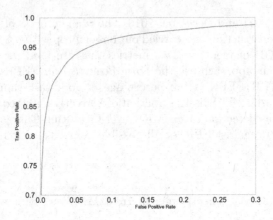

Fig. 3. ROC curve of TensorForest (5-fold cross validation). FPR and TPR are respectively 4.2% and 92.5%.

Table 2. Training on the set of samples explained in Sect. 3.1 and testing on the same set. GT refers to the Ground-truth of samples.

Train	Test		
#Samples	GT (#Samples)	Classified as	
		Malicious	Benign
19,722	Malicious (9,664)	9,640 (TPR = 99.75%)	24
	Benign (10,058)	7 (FPR = 0.07%)	10,051

as being malicious when it was labeled as malware by at least 5 of the tools used by VirusTotal. This set of test samples contains randomly selected applications that were newer than the samples in the training set, and thus they were not part of the training set.

Test results are shown in Table 3. The detection rate on the test set is 71.96%, which is quite good if compared with the performances of other Android anti-malware solutions that are available in the market, as shown in Sect. 3.2. Moreover, the false positive rate is around 7.52%, which is acceptable if we consider that an individual user typically installs a few dozen applications, and thus it might receive a false alert from time to time. This casual alert allows the user that the application has some characteristics similar to badware, and so it can be used only if the source is trusted. It is also worth noting that our classification of false positives is related to the classification provided by VirusTotal at the time of writing. It is not unlikely that some of these applications might turn out to be classified as malware by other anti-malware tools in the near future, as we have already noticed during the experiments. However, due to the small time frame, we haven't the possibility to collect enough examples to provide reliable statistics, as the samples used for the test phase are quite recent. We expect in a future work to show how many applications were correctly predicted as being

Table 3. Training on the set of samples described in Sect. 3.1, and testing on new samples in 2017. GT refers to the Ground-truth of samples.

Train	Test		
#Samples	GT (#Samples)	Classified as	
		Malicious	Benign
19,722	Malicious (2311)	1,663 (TPR = 71.96%)	648
	Benign (2898)	218 (FPR = 7.52%)	2,680

malicious before their signatures were created. However, our experience suggests that even if the application is benign but labeled as being potentially risky by IntelliAV, then the user might look for less risky alternatives applications in Google Play [37]. In fact, we believe that it is better that people is aware of some applications that might be potentially harmful, even if it turns out not to be so, rather than missing some real threats.

Challenging Modern AV Vendors. Based on the recent reports by Virustotal [39], there is an increase in the number of anti-malware developers that resort to machine learning approaches for malware detection. However, the main focus of these products appears to be on desktop malware, especially Windows PE malware. Based on the available public information, there are just a few evidences of two anti-malware developers that use machine learning approaches for Android malware detection, namely Symantec [18] and TrustLook [38]. Their products are installed by more than 10 million users. While it is not clear to us how these products use machine learning, we considered them as two candidates for comparison with IntelliAV. To provide a sound comparison, in addition to the Symantec and Trustlook products, we selected three other Android anti-malware products, i.e., AVG, Avast, and Qihoo 360, that are the most popular among Android users as they have been installed more than 100 million times.[2] We compared the performances of IntelliAV on the test dataset (see Sect. 3.2) with the ones attained by these five popular Android anti-malware As shown in Fig. 4, IntelliAV performs slightly better than two of the products used for comparison, while it outperforms the other three. As we gathered the label assigned by anti-malware products to the test samples at most two months after they are first seen in VirusTotal, the comparison could be more interesting if we had the label given to samples at the time they are first seen in the wild. As an additional check, we performed a comparison in detection performance by considering a set of very recent malware reported by four vendors, namely Check Point, Fortinet, Lookout, and Google (see Table 4). The good performances of IntelliAV compared to the ones of other products, shows that the selected lightweight features and training procedure allows attaining very good performances, especially if we consider that 21 of the considered samples were first seen before 2017, so it is

---

[2] http://www.androidrank.org/.

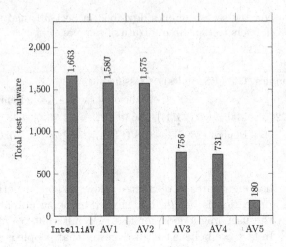

Fig. 4. Comparison between the detection rate of IntelliAV with top five Android anti-malware. We didn't put the name of vendors as we don't aim to rank other anti-malware products.

expected that they can be detected by anti-malware tools either by signatures, or by the generalization capability provided by their machine learning engines. If we have a close look at the two misclassified samples by `IntelliAV` (Table 4), we can see that the associated risk scores are quite close to the decision threshold that we set at training time. The main reasons for the misclassification of these two samples can be related to the use of the `runtime.exec` API to run some shell commands, and to the presence of native-code that is used to hide some of their malicious behaviors.

3.3 `IntelliAV` Overhead on Device

To better understand the efficiency of `IntelliAV`, we show the time consumption for feature extraction as well as classification of some medium/large-sized applications on three devices with different technical specifications. The three mobile devices used for the reported experiments are a Samsung Galaxy S6 Edge (released in April, 2015), a Huawei P8 Lite (released in May, 2015), and an LG D280 L65 (released in June, 2014), which respectively have 3 GB, 2 GB, and 1 GB of RAM. In addition, we computed the time required on the Android Emulator that is dispatched along with Android Studio. The time is simply computed by specifying a timer before starting the feature extraction procedure, that stops when the features from both the manifest and the dex code are extracted. For classification, the reported time refers to the interval between the feature vector is passed to the model, to the production of the risk score. The time required to load the model is negligible, and so we are not reporting it for the sake of clarity. As shown in Table 5, the time required to analyze even large applications is less than 10 s, which makes `IntelliAV` practical and reasonable as the number of

Table 4. Point to point comparison of `IntelliAV` and three anti-malware vendors on some recent and well-known malware reported by Check Point, Fortinet, Lookout, and Google from January to April of 2017. These samples were evaluated on an Android emulator. The `time` column refers to the required time for performing both feature extraction and classification on the emulator.

#	MD5	Size	Unseen	time(s)	Risk Score	AV5	AV1	AV3	VT 1st check
			IntelliAV			2017 check			
colspan across Reported malware by Checkpoint [32, 31, 33]									
1	60806c69e0f4643609dcdf127c8e7ef5	66 KB	✓	0.38	83% (✓)	(✓)	(✓)	(✓)	2016-01 (02/56)
2	fcbb243294bb87b039f113352a8db158	12.4 MB	✓	0.40	37% (✗)	(✗)	(✓)	(✗)	2016-03 (19/55)
3	4e91ff9ac7e3e349b5b9fe36fb505cb4	48 KB	✓	0.37	93% (✓)	(✓)	(✓)	(✓)	2016-03 (13/57)
4	944850ee0b7fc774c055a2233478bb0f	842 KB	✓	0.51	98% (✓)	(✗)	(✗)	(✗)	2014-02 (00/48)
5	629da296cba945662e436bbe10a5cdaa	3.7 MB	✓	0.69	92% (✓)	(✓)	(✓)	(✗)	2014-07 (13/51)
6	1aac52b7d55f4c1c03c85ed067bf69d9	3.5 MB	✓	0.75	94% (✓)	(✓)	(✓)	(✓)	2013-11 (23/47)
7	379ec59048488fdb74376c4ffa00d1be	2.2 MB	✓	0.57	79% (✓)	(✓)	(✓)	(✓)	2015-09 (26/56)
8	d5f5480a7b29ffd51c718b63d1ffa165	9.1 MB	✓	0.82	89% (✓)	(✗)	(✓)	(✗)	2015-12 (03/55)
9	4d904a24f8f4c52726eb340b329731dd	13.2 MB	✓	0.95	72% (✓)	(✗)	(✓)	(✗)	2014-08 (11/51)
10	59b62f8bc982b31d5e0411c74dbe0897	2.5 MB	✓	0.45	83% (✓)	(✓)	(✓)	(✓)	2016-01 (31/55)
11	9ed38abb335f0101f55ad20bde8468dc	8.1 MB	✓	0.77	67% (✓)	(✗)	(✓)	(✗)	2016-02 (16/55)
12	4a3a7b03c0d0460ed8c5beff5c20683c	575 KB	✓	0.42	68% (✓)	(✓)	(✓)	(✓)	2017-03 (00/55)
13	660638f5212ef61891090200c354a6d5	32.7 MB	✓	1.13	96% (✓)	(✓)	(✓)	(✗)	2016-07 (13/55)
14	f48122e9f4333ba3bb77fac869043420	349 KB	✓	0.40	81% (✓)	(✓)	(✓)	(✗)	2015-09 (04/57)
15	0e987ba8da76f93e8e541150d08e2045	12.8 MB	✓	0.98	88% (✓)	(✗)	(✓)	(✗)	2017-03 (07/60)
16	51c328fccf1a8b4925054136ccdb1cda	874 KB	✓	0.44	83% (✓)	(✗)	(✗)	(✓)	2014-08 (05/53)
17	3f188b9aa8f739ee0ed572992a21b118	1.57 MB	✓	0.48	89% (✓)	(✓)	(✓)	(✓)	2014-04 (24/51)
18	7fff1e78089eb387b6adfa595385b2c9	13.4 MB	✓	0.52	63% (✓)	(✓)	(✓)	(✓)	2015-03 (02/57)
19	2b83bd1d97eb911e9d53765edb5ea79e	2.3 MB	✓	0.43	77% (✓)	(✗)	(✗)	(✓)	2017-01 (16/58)
20	48ff097022ea7886b53f80edf2972033	1.3 MB	✓	0.47	63% (✓)	(✗)	(✗)	(✓)	2017-03 (28/59)
21	a3836485ecac78f576e1753269350824	14.6 MB	✓	0.84	38% (✗)	(✗)	(✗)	(✗)	2016-12 (14/57)
22	a4e75471dbf0bb0d3ec26d854cb7fe12	14.1 MB	✓	0.72	62% (✓)	(✗)	(✗)	(✓)	2016-12 (10/56)
23	7253e0a13d2d1db1547e9984a4ce7abd	1.3 MB	✓	0.57	63% (✓)	(✗)	(✗)	(✓)	2017-03 (26/59)
colspan across Reported malware by Fortinet [22, 23, 20, 21]									
24	193058ae838161ee4735a9172ebc25ec	1.4 MB	✓	0.56	89% (✓)	(✗)	(✗)	(✗)	2017-01 (05/24)
25	f479f2a29354a8b889cb529a2ee2c1b4	1.1 MB	✓	0.35	61% (✓)	(✗)	(✗)	(✓)	2017-03 (12/59)
26	cad94ac28640c771b1d2de5e786dc352	776 KB	✓	0.37	96% (✓)	(✗)	(✓)	(✓)	2016-11 (20/56)
27	40507254b8156de817f02c0ed111e99f	0.2 MB	✓	0.37	83% (✓)	(✓)	(✓)	(✓)	2016-11 (08/57)
colspan across Reported malware by Lookout and Google [27, 24]									
28	cc9517aafb58279091ac17533293edc1	57 KB	✓	0.63	89% (✓)	(✗)	(✗)	(✗)	2016-02 (00/53)
29	7c3ad8fec33465fed6563bbfabb5b13d	252 KB	✓	0.37	82% (✓)	(✗)	(✗)	(✓)	2017-04 (03/60)
30	3a69bfbe5bc83c4df938177e05cd7c7c	19 KB	✓	0.36	81% (✓)	(✗)	(✗)	(✗)	2017-04 (01/60)

$$\frac{28}{30} \; \odot \; \Big| \; \frac{12}{30} \quad \frac{19}{30} \quad \frac{16}{30} \; \Big|$$

installed applications on each device is not too large. The classification part is performed in native code, that provides a fast execution. As expected, it can be noted that the largest fraction of the time required by `IntelliAV` is spent for feature extraction, especially for the extraction of the API features. This figure is even worse in the case an application is made up of multiple dex files, because the extraction of API features is much slower. For example, the Uber app is made up of 10 dex files, so that searching for a specific API requires much more time compared to applications having just one dex file.

Table 5. Overhead of `IntelliAV` on different devices for very large applications. F.E. refers to feature extraction time and C. refers to classification time. The number in parenthesis shows the RAM size of the device.

App	APK size (MB)	Galaxy S6 Edge Marshmallow (3 GB)		Huawei P8 Lite Lollipop (2 GB)		LG D280 L65 KitKat (1 GB)		Emulator Marshmallow (1.5 GB)	
		F.E. (s)	C. (s)	F.E. (s)	C. (s)	F.E. (s)	C. (s)	F.E. (s)	C. (s)
Google Trips	8.19	0.67	0.003	0.82	0.005	3.86	0.012	0.43	0.001
LinkedIn Pulse	12.9	1.28	0.003	1.14	0.005	4.40	0.012	0.55	0.001
Stack Exchange	8.15	1.27	0.004	1.27	0.006	5.13	0.014	0.60	0.001
Telegram	12.41	1.36	0.005	1.74	0.007	5.52	0.016	0.69	0.002
WhatsApp	27.97	2.29	0.006	3.22	0.008	12.91	0.018	1.10	0.002
SoundCloud	33.14	2.67	0.006	2.84	0.008	11.83	0.018	1.14	0.002
Spotify	34.65	2.51	0.006	3.03	0.008	13.67	0.018	1.22	0.002
Twitter	31.77	4.53	0.004	5.95	0.006	24.46	0.016	2.26	0.002
LinkedIn	40.39	4.67	0.004	4.69	0.006	16.73	0.016	2.40	0.001
Airbnb	54.34	8.24	0.006	8.79	0.008	35.71	0.018	4.23	0.002
Messenger	59.43	5.85	0.011	7.94	0.013	19.13	0.028	3.35	0.004
Uber	37.26	6.66	0.004	7.64	0.006	43.88	0.016	4.29	0.002
Average	30.05	3.50	0.005	4.08	0.007	16.43	0.016	1.86	0.002

4   Limitations

As far as `IntelliAV` is based on static analysis, it inherits some of the well-known limitations of static analysis approaches. For instance, we didn't address reflection and dynamic code loading techniques that are used to hide the malicious code. Moreover, in the proposed implementation, `IntelliAV` doesn't handle those malware samples that use JavaScript to perform an attack. However, the most common evasion techniques are based on obfuscation of names, and the use of downloaders that download the malicious payload at run-time. The reported test results show that `IntelliAV` is robust against these common obfuscation techniques as it doesn't rely on features extracted from strings or names of classes or methods. In addition, as far as `IntelliAV` runs on the device, it can track all downloaded and installed apps, scanning them on the fly. Consequently, it can be more robust compared to off-device systems. In addition, we are aware that the system can be a victim of evasion techniques against the learning approach, such as mimicry attacks that let an attacker inject some data to the app so that its features resembles the ones of benign apps [12]. Consequently, more methodological and experimental analysis will be needed to make a quantitative evaluation of the robustness of `IntelliAV` in an adversarial environment, to provide the system with the required hardening. Nonetheless, we believe that the good performances of the proposed system is a good starting point for further development. Moreover, employing the multiple classifier system approach, considering a larger number of semantic features, as well as performing a fine grained classifier parameter tuning, can provide a degree of robustness against adversarial attacks against the machine learning engine.

5   Related Works

At present, a large number of papers addressed the topic of detecting Android malware by proposing different systems. The proposed approaches can be divided into two main categories, namely offline malware detection, and on-device malware detection. While a complete overview is outside of the scope of this paper, and we suggest the interested reader to resort to one of the good survey that have been recently published (e.g., the recent taxonomy proposed in [34]), we provide here some of the more closely related papers that rely on static analysis technique. We omit reviewing the malware classification systems based on dynamic analysis [5,15,17] as they have their own benefits and pitfalls. Moreover, as we are dealing with an on-device tool, it is not officially possible that a process access system calls of other process without root privileges, which makes the dynamic analysis approaches almost impractical on the end user device.

Offline Malware Detection. Usually, offline testing has no hard computational constraints, thanks to the availability of computational power compared to the one available on mobile devices, thus allowing for sophisticated application analysis. Hence, a number of approaches have been proposed to construct complex models capable of detecting malware with a very high accuracy. Some of the prominent approaches that focus on building a model and offline testing of Android applications by static analysis techniques are briefly summarized. Mud-Flow [11], AppAudit [40], and DroidSIFT [42] rely on information flow analysis [9], while DroidMiner [41], and MaMaDroid [29] use API sequences to detect malware. The use of complex features such as information flows and API sequences, makes these approach more difficult to be carried out on the device. Lighter approaches have been proposed, such as Drebin [8], DroidAPIMiner [1], and DroidSieve [36] that make use of meta-data as well as syntactic features, and that allow for their porting to on-device applications.

On-Device Malware Detection. Based on the best of our knowledge, there are a few approaches in the research community that used machine learning for on-device malware detection, and none of them is publicly available for performance comparison. One that of the most cited research works on this topic is Drebin, and while the paper shows some screenshots of the UI, the application itself is not available. Among the commercial Android anti-malware tools, two of them claim to use machine learning techniques, as evaluated and reported in Sect. 3.2, but the real use of machine learning by these tools is blurred. Finally, Qualcomm recently announced the development of a machine learning tool for on-device mobile phone security, but the details of the system, as well as its performances are not available [26].

As an overall comparison with the previous approaches, we believe that IntelliAV provides a first practical example of an on-device anti-malware solution for Android systems, completely based on machine learning techniques, that can move a step toward having an advanced security tool on mobile devices.

6   Conclusions and Future Work

In this paper, we introduced a practical learning-based anti-malware tool for Android systems on top of TensorFlow, in which both the efficiency and the effectiveness are considered. We showed that through the careful selection of a set of lightweight features, and a solid training phase comprising both a robust classification model, and a representative set of training samples, an efficient and effective tool can be deployed on Android mobile device. Our tool will be freely available so that it can help the end user to provide easy protection on the device, as well as allowing researchers to better explore the idea of having intelligent security systems on mobile devices. As a future plan, we aim to address the limitations of IntelliAV, to improve its robustness against attacks on the machine learning engine, while keeping the efficiency intact.

Acknowledgement. We appreciate VirusTotal's collaboration for providing us the access to a large set of Android applications.

References

1. Aafer, Y., Du, W., Yin, H.: DroidAPIMiner: mining API-level features for robust malware detection in android. In: Zia, T., Zomaya, A., Varadharajan, V., Mao, M. (eds.) SecureComm 2013. LNICSSITE, vol. 127, pp. 86–103. Springer, Cham (2013). doi:10.1007/978-3-319-04283-1_6
2. Abadi, M., Barham, P., Chen, J., Chen, Z., Davis, A., Dean, J., Devin, M., Ghemawat, S., Irving, G., Isard, M., Kudlur, M., Levenberg, J., Monga, R., Moore, S., Murray, D.G., Steiner, B., Tucker, P., Vasudevan, V., Warden, P., Wicke, M., Yu, Y., Zheng, X.: Tensorflow: a system for large-scale machine learning. In: OSDI, pp. 265–283. USENIX Association (2016)
3. Ahmadi, M., Biggio, B., Arzt, S., Ariu, D., Giacinto, G.: Detecting misuse of google cloud messaging in android badware. In: SPSM, pp. 103–112 (2016)
4. Ahmadi, M., Ulyanov, D., Semenov, S., Trofimov, M., Giacinto, G.: Novel feature extraction, selection and fusion for effective malware family classification. In: CODASPY, pp. 183–194 (2016)
5. Amos, B., Turner, H., White, J.: Applying machine learning classifiers to dynamic android malware detection at scale. In: 2013 9th International Wireless Communications and Mobile Computing Conference (IWCMC), pp. 1666–1671, July 2013
6. Andronio, N., Zanero, S., Maggi, F.: HELDROID: dissecting and detecting mobile ransomware. In: Bos, H., Monrose, F., Blanc, G. (eds.) RAID 2015. LNCS, vol. 9404, pp. 382–404. Springer, Cham (2015). doi:10.1007/978-3-319-26362-5_18
7. Aresu, M., Ariu, D., Ahmadi, M., Maiorca, D., Giacinto, G.: Clustering android malware families by http traffic. In: MALWARE, pp. 128–135 (2015)

8. Arp, D., Spreitzenbarth, M., Hubner, M., Gascon, H., Rieck, K.: Drebin: effective and explainable detection of android malware in your pocket. In: NDSS (2014)
9. Arzt, S., Rasthofer, S., Fritz, C., Bodden, E., Bartel, A., Klein, J., Le Traon, Y., Octeau, D., McDaniel, P.: Flowdroid: precise context, flow, field, object-sensitive and lifecycle-aware taint analysis for android apps. In: Proceedings of the 35th ACM SIGPLAN Conference on Programming Language Design and Implementation, PLDI 2014, NY, USA, pp. 259–269. ACM, New York (2014)
10. AV-TEST: Security report 2015/16 (2017). https://goo.gl/FepOGQ
11. Avdiienko, V., Kuznetsov, K., Gorla, A., Zeller, A., Arzt, S., Rasthofer, S., Bodden, E.: Mining apps for abnormal usage of sensitive data. In: ICSE, pp. 426–436 (2015)
12. Biggio, B., Corona, I., Maiorca, D., Nelson, B., Šrndić, N., Laskov, P., Giacinto, G., Roli, F.: Evasion attacks against machine learning at test time, pp. 387–402 (2013)
13. Bishop, C.: Pattern Recognition and Machine Learning. Information Science and Statistics, 1st edn. Springer, New York (2006)
14. Breiman, L.: Random forests. Mach. Learn. **45**(1), 5–32 (2001)
15. Burguera, I., Zurutuza, U., Nadjm-Tehrani, S.: Crowdroid: behavior-based malware detection system for android. In: Proceedings of the 1st ACM Workshop on Security and Privacy in Smartphones and Mobile Devices, SPSM 2011, NY, USA, pp. 15–26. ACM, New York (2011)
16. Colthurst, T., Sculley, D., Hendry, G., Nado, Z.: Tensorforest: scalable random forests on tensorflow. In: Machine Learning Systems Workshop at NIPS (2016)
17. Dash, S.K., Suarez-Tangil, G., Khan, S., Tam, K., Ahmadi, M., Kinder, J., Cavallaro, L.: Droidscribe: classifying android malware based on runtime behavior. In: 2016 IEEE Security and Privacy Workshops (SPW), pp. 252–261, May 2016
18. eweek: symantec adds deep learning to anti-malware tools to detect zero-days, January 2016. http://www.eweek.com/security/symantec-adds-deep-learning-to-anti-malware-tools-to-detect
19. Fernández-Delgado, M., Cernadas, E., Barro, S., Amorim, D.: Do we need hundreds of classifiers to solve real world classification problems? J. Mach. Learn. Res. **15**(1), 3133–3181 (2014)
20. Fortinet: Android locker malware uses google cloud messaging service, January 2017. https://blog.fortinet.com/2017/01/16/android-locker-malware-uses-google-cloud-messaging-service
21. Fortinet: deep analysis of android rootnik malware using advanced anti-debug and anti-hook, January 2017. https://goo.gl/dq5w8R
22. Fortinet: teardown of a recent variant of android/ztorg (part 1), March 2017. https://blog.fortinet.com/2017/03/15/teardown-of-a-recent-variant-of-android-ztorg-part-1
23. Fortinet: teardown of android/ztorg (part 2), March 2017. http://blog.fortinet.com/2017/03/08/teardown-of-android-ztorg-part-2
24. Google: An investigation of chrysaor malware on android, April 2017. https://android-developers.googleblog.com/2017/04/an-investigation-of-chrysaor-malware-on.html
25. IDC: smartphone OS market share, q2 2016 (2016). http://www.idc.com/promo/smartphone-market-share/os
26. Islam, N., Das, S., Chen, Y.: On-device mobile phone security exploits machine learning. IEEE Pervasive Comput. **16**(2), 92–96 (2017)
27. Lookout: pegasus for android, April 2017. https://info.lookout.com/rs/051-ESQ-475/images/lookout-pegasus-android-technical-analysis.pdf

28. Maiorca, D., Mercaldo, F., Giacinto, G., Visaggio, A., Martinelli, F.: R-packdroid: API package-based characterization and detection of mobile ransomware. In: ACM Symposium on Applied Computing (2017)
29. Mariconti, E., Onwuzurike, L., Andriotis, P., De Cristofaro, E., Ross, G., Stringhini, G.: MaMaDroid: detecting android malware by building markov chains of behavioral models. In: ISOC Network and Distributed Systems Security Symposiym (NDSS), San Diego, CA (2017)
30. McAfee: mobile threat report (2016). https://www.mcafee.com/us/resources/reports/rp-mobile-threat-report-2016.pdf
31. Check point: charger malware calls and raises the risk on google play. http://blog.checkpoint.com/2017/01/24/charger-malware/
32. Check point: preinstalled malware targeting mobile users. http://blog.checkpoint.com/2017/03/10/preinstalled-malware-targeting-mobile-users/
33. Check point: whale of a tale: hummingbad returns. http://blog.checkpoint.com/2017/01/23/hummingbad-returns/
34. Sadeghi, A., Bagheri, H., Garcia, J., Malek, S.: A taxonomy and qualitative comparison of program analysis techniques for security assessment of android software. IEEE Trans. Softw. Eng. **PP**(99), 1 (2016)
35. f secure: mobile threat report q1 2014 (2014). https://www.f-secure.com/documents/996508/1030743/Mobile_Threat_Report_Q1_2014.pdf
36. Suarez-Tangil, G., Dash, S.K., Ahmadi, M., Kinder, J., Giacinto, G., Cavallaro, L.: Droidsieve: fast and accurate classification of obfuscated android malware. In: Proceedings of the Seventh ACM on Conference on Data and Application Security and Privacy (CODASPY 2017), pp. 309–320 (2017)
37. Taylor, V.F., Martinovic, I.: Securank: starving permission-hungry apps using contextual permission analysis. In: Proceedings of the 6th Workshop on Security and Privacy in Smartphones and Mobile Devices (SPSM 2016), NY, USA, pp. 43–52. ACM, New York (2016)
38. Trustlook: trustlook AI, March 2017. https://www.trustlook.com/
39. VirusTotal: virustotal blog, March 2017. http://blog.virustotal.com/2017_03_01_archive.html
40. Xia, M., Gong, L., Lyu, Y., Qi, Z., Liu, X.: Effective real-time android application auditing. In: IEEE Symposium on Security and Privacy, pp. 899–914. IEEE Computer Society (2015)
41. Yang, C., Xu, Z., Gu, G., Yegneswaran, V., Porras, P.: DroidMiner: automated mining and characterization of fine-grained malicious behaviors in android applications. In: Kutyłowski, M., Vaidya, J. (eds.) ESORICS 2014. LNCS, vol. 8712, pp. 163–182. Springer, Cham (2014). doi:10.1007/978-3-319-11203-9_10
42. Zhang, M., Duan, Y., Yin, H., Zhao, Z.: Semantics-aware android malware classification using weighted contextual API dependency graphs. In: CCS, New York, NY, USA, pp. 1105–1116 (2014)

DO NOT DISTURB? Classifier Behavior on Perturbed Datasets

Bernd Malle[1,2], Peter Kieseberg[1,2], and Andreas Holzinger[1(✉)]

[1] Holzinger Group HCI-KDD, Institute for Medical Informatics,
Statistics and Documentation, Medical University Graz, Graz, Austria
{b.malle,a.holzinger}@hci-kdd.org
[2] SBA Research gGmbH, Favoritenstrae 16, 1040 Wien, Austria
PKieseberg@sba-research.org

Abstract. Exponential trends in data generation are presenting today's organizations, economies and governments with challenges never encountered before, especially in the field of privacy and data security. One crucial trade-off regulators are facing regards the simultaneous need for publishing personal information for the sake of statistical analysis and Machine Learning in order to increase quality levels in areas like medical services, while at the same time protecting the identity of individuals. A key European measure will be the introduction of the General Data Protection Regulation (GDPR) in 2018, giving customers the 'right to be forgotten', i.e. having their data deleted on request. As this could lead to a competitive disadvantage for European companies, it is important to understand which effects deletion of significant data points has on the performance of ML techniques. In a previous paper we introduced a series of experiments applying different algorithms to a binary classification problem under anonymization as well as perturbation. In this paper we extend those experiments by multi-class classification and introduce outlier-removal as an additional scenario. While the results of our previous work were mostly in-line with our expectations, our current experiments revealed unexpected behavior over a range of different scenarios. A surprising conclusion of those experiments is the fact that classification on an anonymized dataset with outliers removed in beforehand can almost compete with classification on the original, un-anonymized dataset. This could soon lead to competitive Machine Learning pipelines on anonymized datasets for real-world usage in the marketplace.

Keywords: Machine learning · Knowledge bases · Right to be forgotten · Perturbation · K-anonymity · SaNGreeA · Information loss · Cost weighing vector · Multi-class classification · Outlier analysis · Variance-sensitive analysis

© IFIP International Federation for Information Processing 2017
Published by Springer International Publishing AG 2017. All Rights Reserved
A. Holzinger et al. (Eds.): CD-MAKE 2017, LNCS 10410, pp. 155–173, 2017.
DOI: 10.1007/978-3-319-66808-6_11

1   Introduction and Related Work

In today's data-driven industries which increasingly form the backbone of the 21st century's economy, personal information is no longer only stored by private companies, public service organizations or health providers. They also constitute a vital building-block for business intelligence and as a decision-making basis for improving services or public investments in measures for disease or natural disaster prevention. Therefore lies a crucial advantage in the publication, linkage, and systematic analysis of data sets from heterogeneous sources via statistics as well as Machine Learning. Any kind of institution which fails or is forbidden to engage in such activities, will in time face serious disadvantages on the marketplace or a lack in service quality compared to entities able to do so.

One specific challenge for data processing entities is increasingly imposed on them by the law. Under the new European General Data Protection Regulations (*GDPR*) taking effect on June 1st, 2018, customers are given a *right-to-be-forgotten*, meaning that an organization is obligated to remove a customer's personal data upon request. For many organizations, this would incur serious additional investments and costs from their IT infrastructure, as even backup- or statistical systems must be connected, lest no 'forgotten' data will reappear. Nevertheless, the law will allow data analysis on anonymized datasets (for which a right-to-be-forgotten makes no sense from a technical point of view), so that organizations will soon be faced with the question: Do we learn on original data & bear all costs of the impeding bureaucracy, or shall we analyze anonymized datasets and risk significantly lower insights.

This brings us to the field of Privacy aware machine learning (PAML) [6], enabled and fostered by concepts like *k-anonymity* [20], in which a record is released only if it is indistinguishable from at least $k - 1$ other entities in the dataset. However, due to many personal records being high-dimensional in nature and k-anonymity being highly dependent on spatial locality (density) in order to effectively implement the technique in a statistically robust way, it might be difficult to anonymize data without suffering an intolerable amount of information loss [1]. Moreover, automatic dimensionality reduction might be helpful to preserve variance, but extracting the meaning, and therefore relevance, of arbitrary features would assist in making sense of the data with respect to a specific application domain [10].

Moreover, the original privacy requirement of *k-anonymity* [22] has over time been refined by concepts like *l-diversity* [16] (in which every equivalence group must contain at least l diverse sensitive values from the original dataset), *t-closeness* [15] (which prescribes that the local distribution over sensitive values within an equivalence group must not differ from it's global distribution by more than a threshold *t*) as well as *delta-presence* [19] (which links the quality of anonymization to the risk posed by inadequate anonymization). Additionally, there is a whole discipline of measures summarized as *differential privacy* [7], which deals with methods of securely releasing sensitive information upon database queries by injecting controlled noise into responses.

As far as PAML is concerned, a comparison of different Machine Learning algorithms on anonymized datasets was already conducted in 2014 [24] by applying 6 different algorithms on 3 datasets, with very diverse results per algorithm. The main weakness of this paper is its usage of extremely differently-sized datasets which does not easily allow comparison; moreover they only used one very low privacy setting of $k = 2$, preventing the authors from examining more interesting behavior as information content degrades further; this is a main point of our work.

The authors of [17] propose a scheme for controlling over-generalization of less identity-vulnerable QIs in diverse classes by determining the importance of QIs via Random Forest pre-computations as well as computing sensitive attribute diversity via the Simpson index [21]. Their resulting adaptive anonymization algorithm was compared to Mondrian [13] as well as IACk [14] and shows improvements w.r.t information loss as well as coverage (the number of descendant leaf nodes of generalized values in the taxonomy). Accuracy measured on classification tree, random forest and SVM shows equal or better performance when applied to a dataset anonymized by their proposed solution; it is interesting to note that their performance on large factors of k not only remains stable, but in some cases increases with k, the same behavior we also observed in some of our experiments.

A recent paper [12] proposes the introduction of an additional requirement for anonymization on top of k-anonymity called h-ceiling, which simply restricts generalizations within an equivalence class to a certain level below suppression. In the case on an equivalence class being able to satisfy h-ceiling but not k-anonymity (their method applies full-domain generalization), counterfeit records are inserted into the respective group; each insertion is also collected in a journal which is eventually published with the anonymized data. Their approach unsurprisingly yields lower reconstruction error and information loss as well as more fine-grained query results due to less generalization. However, their experiments mostly fix $k = 5$ and therefore simply try to reduce information loss due to anonymization, but do not try to examine ML performance over a wider range of k factors; moreover, there seems to be some inconsistency in their predictions.

Finally, we should also reference our previous work on this topic [18], in which we conducted a comparison study of binary classification performance on perturbed (selective deletion) vs. wholesale anonymized data. Our experiments showed that perturbation was still significantly less damaging to Machine Learning performance than even slight anonymization; that state of our previous research marks the connecting point to this paper.

2 K-Anonymity and Information Loss

While there are several data-structures which can contain and convey personal information we might want to protect (free text, audio, images, graph structures etc.) we are focusing our work on tabular data, since most unstructured documents of sensitive nature today can be mapped to tabular data and since delicate information is most easily extracted from those. Figure 1 illustrates the original tabular concept of three different categories of data we will encounter in such tables:

- **Identifiers** directly reveal the identity of a person without having further analysis of the data. Examples are first and last names, email address or social security number (SSN). As personal identifiers are hard to generalized (see Fig. 3) in a meaningful way (truncating an email address to 'host' would not yield much usable information), those columns are usually removed. The figure displays this column in a red background color.
- **Sensitive data,** or 'payload', is crucial information for statisticians or researchers and can therefore not be erased or perturbed; such data usually remains untarnished within the released dataset. The table shows one column in green background color representing such data.
- **Quasi identifiers (QI's),** colored in the table with an orange background, do not directly identify a person (age=35), but can be used in combination to restrict possibilities to such a degree that a specific identity follows logically. For instance, [23] mentioned that 87% of U.S. citizens in 2002 could be re-identified by just using the 3 attributes *zip code, gender* and *date of birth*. On the other hand, this information might hold significant information for the purpose of research (e.g. zip code could be of high value in a study on disease spread). Therefore we generalize this kind of information, which means to lower its level of granularity. As an example, one could generalize grades from A+ to B- into A's and B's and then further up to encompass 'all' (also denoted as '*'), as shown in Fig. 3.

Name	Age	Zip	Gender	Disease
Alex	25	41076	Male	Allergies
...	...	...	...	...

Fig. 1. The three types of data considered in (k-)anonymization

As described in [5], k-anonymization requires a data release to contain at least $k - 1$ duplicate entries for every occurring combination of attributes. One can imagine this as a clustering problem with each cluster's (also called *equivalence class*) quasi-identifier state being identical for every data point it contains. One can achieve this via suppression and generalization, where by suppression we mean simple deletion, whereas generalization refers to a decrease in a value's granularity. As an example, in Fig. 2, an input dataset has been transformed through k-anonymization into a clustered set with each cluster being at least of $size = 3$; thus the data is said to be $3 - anonymized$.

Generalization works through a concept called *generalization hierarchies/taxonomies*, which run from leaf nodes denoting particular values ('France') via internal nodes ('Western Europe') to their most general root ('all

Node	Name	Age	Zip	Gender	Disease
X1	Alex	25	41076	Male	Allergies
X2	Bob	25	41075	Male	Allergies
X3	Charlie	27	41076	Male	Allergies
X4	Dave	32	41099	Male	Diabetes
X5	Eva	27	41074	Female	Flu
X6	Dana	36	41099	Female	Gastritis
X7	George	30	41099	Male	Brain Tumor
X8	Lucas	28	41099	Male	Lung Cancer
X9	Laura	33	41075	Female	Alzheimer

Node	Age	Zip	Gender	Disease
X1	25-27	4107*	Male	Allergies
X2	25-27	4107*	Male	Allergies
X3	25-27	4107*	Male	Allergies
X4	30-36	41099	*	Diabetes
X5	27-33	410**	*	Flu
X6	30-36	41099	*	Gastritis
X7	30-36	41099	*	Brain Tumor
X8	27-33	410**	*	Lung Cancer
X9	27-33	410**	*	Alzheimer

Fig. 2. Tabular anonymization: input table and anonymization result

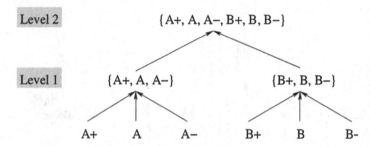

Figure 1: A possible generalization hierarchy for the attribute "Quality".

Fig. 3. Example of a typical generalization hierarchy taken from [2]

countries' or '*'). Such a hierarchy is depicted in Fig. 3. In generalizing the original input value, one traverses the tree from a leaf node upwards until a certain condition is met. In the case of k-anonymity, we satisfy this condition when we can construct an equivalence group with all quasi-identifiers being duplicates of one another.

As each level of generalization invokes an increasing loss of specificity, we do not want to construct our clusters inefficiently, but minimize a dataset's overall information loss [2]. This makes k-anonymization an NP-hard problem due to an exponential number of possible data-row combinations one can examine.

3 Experiments

The following sections will describe our series of experiments in detail, encompassing the dataset used, the algorithms chosen for classification as well as a description of the overall process employed to obtain our results.

3.1 Data

As input data we chose the training set of the adults dataset from the UCI Machine Learning repository which was generated from US census data and

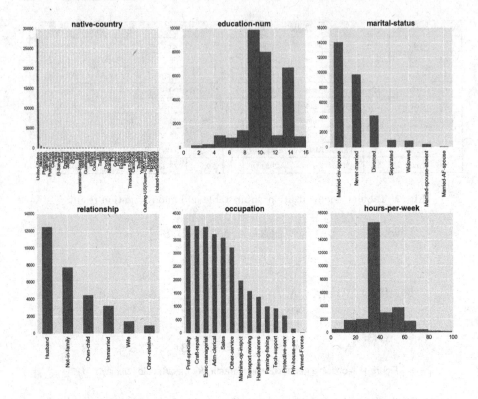

Fig. 4. Initial distribution of six selected data columns of the adult dataset.

contains approximately 32,000 entries (30162 after deleting rows with incomplete information). All but one columns were considered for experimentation, the remaining representing duplicate information (education => education_num). Figure 4 shows the attribute value distribution of 6 arbitrarily selected columns of the original (un-anonymized) dataset.

Amongst these distribution, two clearly stand out: *native-country* as well as *hours-per-week*, which are both dominated by a single attribute value (*United-States* and *40*, respectively). In order to demonstrate the effect of anonymization on attribute value distributions, Fig. 5 shows the same attribute distributions under anonymization by a factor of $k = 19$. Although the dominance of the *United-States* was successfully "broken" by this method, in several instances the *generalized-to-all*-value (*) now skews the data set even more. In addition to the incurred information loss this might be another reason for degraded classifier performance on such data.

3.2   Anonymization Algorithm

We implemented our own version of a greedy clustering algorithm called SaN-GreeA (Social network greedy clustering, [4]) in JavaScript mainly for three

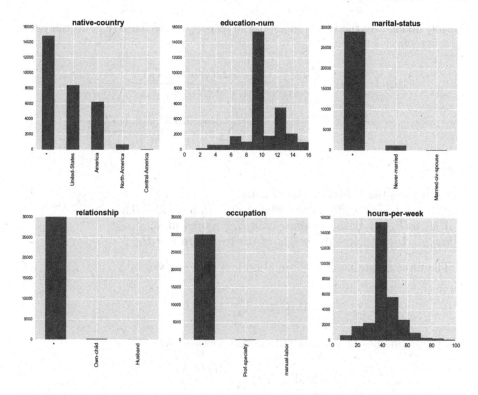

Fig. 5. Anonymized distribution of six selected data columns of the adult dataset, anonymization factor $k = 19$, with equal weight for each attribute.

reasons: (1) apart from 'normal' tabular anonymization tt has a network anonymization component based on stochastic reconstruction error, so it is possible for us to use this algorithm in later works regarding the impact of anonymization on graph algorithms; (2) we wanted a simple conceptual model so we could interact with the algorithm and thus conduct interactive Machine Learning experiments in the future (those experiments are well under way at the time of this writing); (3) we wanted an algorithm capable of running in the browser so we could run our experiments online especially w.r.t. (2). The main downside of this choice is the reduced algorithmic performance of $O(n^2)$ as well as a further slow-down for JS vs. native code of a factor of about 3–4. In the future, we will strive to implement faster algorithms which nevertheless retain properties suitable for our needs, narrowing down the simplicity - performance trade-off.

As mentioned, SaNGreeA consists of two strategies for tabular as well as network anonymization, with two respective metrics for information loss. The *Generalization Information Loss* or *GIL* consists of a categorical as well as a continuous part, with the former measuring the distance of a level-of-generalization from it's original leaf node in the generalization hierarchy (taxonomy), while the latter measures the range of a continuous-valued generalization (e.g. age cohort

[35–40]) divided by the whole range of the respective attribute (e.g. overall age-range [17–90]).

$$\text{GIL}(cl) = |cl| \cdot \left(\sum_{j=1}^{s} \frac{size(gen(cl)[N_j])}{size(min_{x \epsilon N}(X[N_j]), max_{x \epsilon N}(X[N_j]))} \right.$$

$$\left. + \sum_{j=1}^{t} \frac{height(\Lambda(gen(cl)[C_j]))}{height(H_{C_j})} \right)$$

where:

- $|cl|$ denotes the cluster cl's cardinality;
- $size([i1, i2])$ is the size of the interval $[i1, i2]$, i.e., $(i2 - i1)$;
- $\Lambda(w), w \epsilon H_{C_j}$ is the sub-hierarchy of H_{C_j} rooted in w;
- $height(H_{C_j})$ denotes the height of the tree hierarchy H_{C_j};

The total generalization information loss is then given by:

$$\text{GIL}(G, S) = \sum_{j=1}^{v} \text{GIL}(cl_j)$$

And the normalized generalization information loss by:

$$\text{NGIL}(G, S) = \frac{\text{GIL}(G, S)}{n \cdot (s + t)}$$

As for the networking-part of this algorithm, it introduces a measure called *structural information loss* (SIL). The SIL is composed of two different components, which represent statistical errors of (1) intra-cluster as well as (2) inter-cluster reconstruction.

For the exact mathematical definitions of SIL & NSIL the reader is kindly referred to the original paper. Because the structural information loss cannot be computed exactly before the assembly of all clusters is completed, the exact computations were replaced by the following distance measures:

Distance between two nodes:

$$\text{dist}(X^i, X^j) = \frac{|\{l|l = 1..n \land l \neq i, j; b_l^i \neq b_l^j|}{n - 2}$$

Distance between a node and a cluster:

$$\text{dist}(X, cl) = \frac{\sum_{X^j \epsilon cl} \text{dist}(X, X^j)}{|cl|}$$

Since SaNGreeA follows the greedy-clustering paradigm, it runs in quadratic time w.r.t. the input size in number of nodes. This worked well within milliseconds for a problem size of a few hundred nodes, but took up to 60 min on the whole adult training dataset. Finally, as stated above, we chose SaNGreeA for its intuitive simplicity and graph anonymization capabilities, the latter of which are serving us well in a different branch of our ongoing research efforts; for the experiments in this paper, we restricted ourselves to the tabular anonymization capabilities of the algorithm.

3.3 Dataset Creation

To examine the effect of perturbation, anonymization, outlier-removal as well as outlier-removal+anonymization on classifier performance, we designed the following processing pipeline:

1. Taking the original (preprocessed) dataset as input, we transformed its attributes to boolean values, so instead of *native-country* $->$ *United-States* we considered *United-States* $->$ *yes/no.*
2. We ran 4 different classifiers on the resulting data and computed their respective F1 score. The 4 classifiers used were *gradient boosting* representing the boosting paradigm, *random forest* representing the bagging technique, *logistic regression* as a representative of categorical prediction via optimization of a coefficient vector, as well as *linear SVC* representing Support Vector Machines constructing hyperplanes in sufficiently high-dimensional spaces.
3. For our perturbation experiments, we extracted the most/least significant attribute values according to the logit coefficients as depicted in Fig. 6. For each of these attribute values, we subsequently deleted a specific percentage $p \in \{0.2, 0.4, 0.6, 0.8, 1.0\}]$ of data rows containing that value, resulting in a series of new datasets of reduced size.
4. In order to measure the effects of k-anonymization on classifier performance, we applied SaNGreeA's GIL component to generate datasets with a k-factor of $k \in \{3, 7, 11, 15, 19, 23, 27, 31, 35, 100\}$. Furthermore, we used each of these settings with 3 different weight vectors: (1) equal weights for all attributes, (2) age information preferred ($\omega(age) = 0.88$, $\omega(other\_attributes) = 0.01$) and (3) race information preferred ($\omega(race) = 0.88$, $\omega(other\_attributes) = 0.01$).
5. The outlier-removal datasets were created by executing scikit-learn's Isolation-Forest in order to identify and remove outliers in a range of 5%–95% (stepsize: 5%) from the original dataset. This resulted in 18 new datasets for analysis.
6. Finally, in order to analyze classifier performance on an outlier/anonymization combination, we repeated the procedure described for anonymization on a surrogate dataset that had 30% of its outliers removed in beforehand.

4   Results and Discussion

4.1   Perturbed Datasets - Selective Deletion

In order to be able to compare the impact of selectively deleting the most/least important attribute values (in fact, the whole data points containing those values) on different classifiers, we chose to select these values via examining the logit

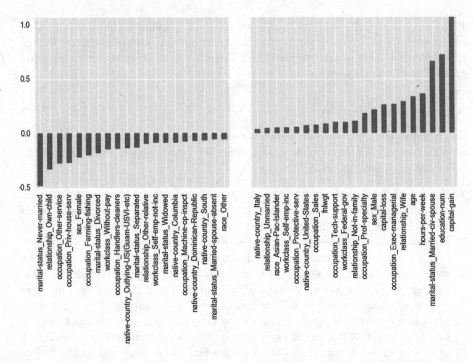

Fig. 6. Attribute values within the adult dataset which contribute highest/lowest certainty to the classification of income (truncated at 1.0). The rightmost columns represent information which enable a classifier to discern most clearly between classes, while the leftmost columns (depending on their actual score) could even confuse the algorithm. We chose this example because income is a binary decision, so the values don't change per category to predict.

coefficients produced during logistic regression. Although this possibly entails non-erasure of the values specifically significant for each classifier, we chose algorithmic comparison as the more insightful criterion; the implicit assumption that the same attribute values would influence all classifiers approximately equally was largely confirmed by our results.

In contrast to binary classification, determining the 'right' values to delete for a multi-class problem is not always possible: Values contributing highly to the decision boundary for one class might be less significant in the case of another - accordingly one would expect inconclusive behavior in the case of a target for which the highest/lowest log coefficients do not line up over class boundaries.

For each of the targets 'marital-status' and 'education-num' we measured those interesting coefficients in the hope of improving/degrading algorithmic performance; that means deletion of highest logit's is supposed to remove certainty from an algorithm and decreasing performance, while deletion of lowest logit's is supposed to remove uncertainty, thus improving performance. Our analysis showed that while 'marital-status' had mainly the same most/least significant

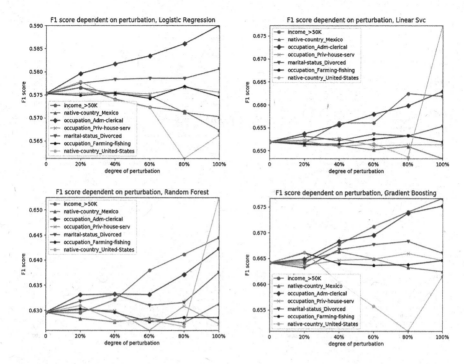

Fig. 7. Multi-class classification on target *education-num* under perturbation by selective deletion of the most/least contributing attribute values. Since different values are significant for deciding on different classes of education level, progressive deletion of this data results in indeterminate behavior.

logit's across all classes, the attribute values for 'education-num' were rather diverse in this area.

In the latter case this lead to erratic behavior of the resulting performance curves, as can be seen in (Fig. 7). It is interesting to note that 'income_ >50 k' obviously held much larger significance for Logistic Regression than for the other classifiers, as their results showed f1 score improvement with this particular value eviscerating.

In the case of 'marital-status' almost the same attribute values were rated as most/least significant across all classes - this results in very clear outputs with the erasure of highly important values decreasing performance drastically while deletion of confusing values leading to a significant increase in classifier performance (Fig. 8). While it is not surprising that relationship information shows high correlation with marital status, the opposite effects of *sex_Female* and *sex_Male* stand out as a slight curiosity - being a woman in this dataset seems to point less distinctly to a specific marital status than being a man.

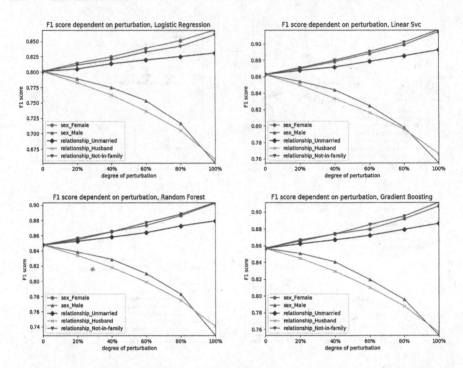

Fig. 8. Multi-class classification on target *marital-status* under perturbation by selective deletion of the most/least contributing attribute values. Since the same values are significant for deciding different classes of marital status, progressive deletion leads to orderly increase/decrease of ML performance.

4.2   Anonymized Datasets

Analogous to our previous work [18] we performed anonymization on the adult dataset for a range of values of k, but this time extending the range to $k \in \{3, 7, 11, 15, 19, 23, 27, 31, 35, 100\}$ for a broader observational basis of algorithmic behavior, especially towards higher values of k, as already conducted by other researchers [12,17]. As we set out to examine multi-class classification performance, we chose the 'marital-status' and 'education-num' columns of the adult dataset as targets, treating income as an independent input feature. For 'marital-status' we left the 7 categorical values in the original dataset unchanged, whereas we clustered the 16 continuous 'education-num' levels into the 4 groups 'elementary school', 'high school including graduate', 'college up to Bachelors' as well as 'advanced studies'.

Our observation generally show the same type of behavior than in our previous experiments on target *income*, with one notable exception: The Random Forest classifier shows a sharp drop in algorithmic performance when operating on the very skewed 'age' and 'race' feature vectors, only to recover its discriminative power and increase in performance up to a k of 100. We also note a somewhat similar behavior for Logistic Regression, albeit not as distinctly. A possible

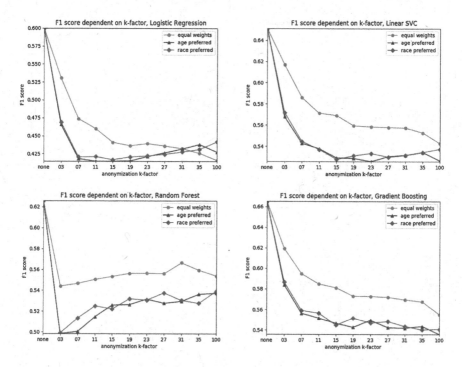

Fig. 9. Multi-class classification on target *education-num* on the adult dataset under several degrees of k-anonymization.

explanation for this behavior could lie in the *bagging*-nature of Random Forest, meaning that the algorithm bootstraps by randomly sampling data-points from the overall population into possibly overlapping bags of 'local' data. As larger swaths of the input data become more and more equal with increasing levels of k, this would lead to less local over-fitting, thus making the job easier for a global averaging-strategy to filter out variance and improve generalization ability. However, if this was true, the maximum performance should not be recorded on the original (un-anonymized) dataset, thus we are currently at a loss of an adequate explanation for this specific case.

Classifier performance on target *marital-status* displayed the same basic behavior as above, including the mysterious conduct of the Random Forest in case of our age- and race-vectors. Moreover, the classification results are generally better than for *education-num*, which is probably caused by our somewhat arbitrary clustering of education levels during pre-processing. All in all, the pure anonymization-related results were almost in line with our expectations; in addition, our previous assessment that implementation of the 'right-to-be-forgotten' for individual users is preferable to wholesale anonymization, has not changed for the multi-class case.

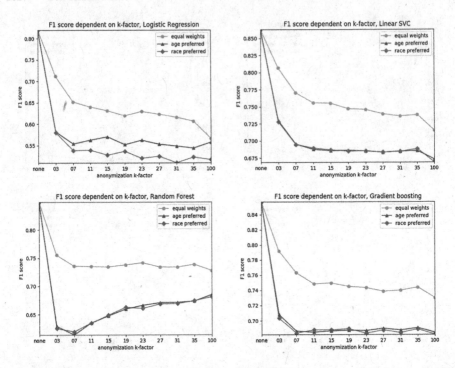

Fig. 10. Multi-class classification on target *marital-status* on the adult dataset under several degrees of k-anonymization.

4.3 "Outliers" Removed

One question we didn't tackle in our previous work was the one of outlier removal; this is relevant due to the fact that e.g. people showing abnormal behavior could be supposed to exercise their 'right-to-be-forgotten' more frequently, especially in a social network scenario. For our experiments we chose the original adult dataset's income target, especially since we could thus directly compare the results with those of our previous work [18]. We used scikit-learn's Isolation-Forest classifier to identify outliers according to a given *contamination* level and performed an initial round of removing outliers in a range of 0.5%–5%. Since ML performance decreased only marginally under those settings and we thus assumed that the dataset had been curated in such a way as to exclude significant outliers, we pivoted to a much broader investigation of examining classifier performance on a dataset with increasingly eviscerating variance. Thus we repeated the same procedure for "outlier" levels of 5%–95%, gradually diminishing the dataset's size from over 30 k to about 1.5 k data points. In order to account for that dramatic reduction, we compared classifier behavior with a control instance of the adult dataset with the same levels of truncation, but under random deletion of data points, thus not targeting variance in the control set (Fig. 9).

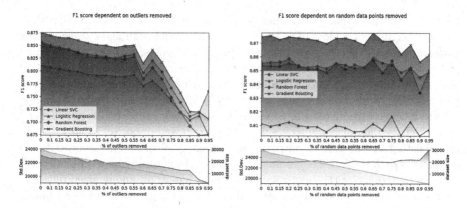

Fig. 11. Binary classification on target income based on a dataset with different degrees of outliers removed (=variance loss) vs. the same degree of data randomly deleted.

The results are shown in Fig. 11 and exhibit similar behavior to the removal of most-significant attribute values in our previous work: While performance only decreases slightly for deletion levels under 55%, we see a dramatic drop over the second half of the range. The obvious explanation for this behavior lie in the fact that more homogeneous clusters of data make it harder for any algorithm to construct a decision boundary - though it is noteworthy that this applies to all 4 classifiers the same despite their fundamentally different approaches. Lastly, the comparison set shows no significant increase/decrease of performance over the whole range of data deletion, supporting our conclusion that decreasing data set size was not the dominating influence for the observed algorithmic behavior (Fig. 10).

4.4   Anonymization on Outliers Removed

One problem with outliers during anonymization is that it forces the algorithm to over-generalize attribute values; this can either happen towards the end-stages of a greedy-clustering procedure like SaNGreeA (in which case the damage might be limited to the outliers themselves), but could also influence a full-domain generalizing algorithm during determination of a whole column's suitable generalization level (in which case the whole dataset would suffer significantly higher information loss). This fact in combination with our previously described results based on outlier removal gave rise to an interesting possibility: what if we *combined* outlier removal with anonymization? On the one hand classifier performance degrades with loss of variance, but for the very same reason information loss during anonymization might be limited to much more sufferable levels.

This led to our last round of experiments in which we took the adult dataset with 30% outliers removed and conducted k-anonymization as described in the respective earlier section (for time- and comparison reasons only on marital-status), the results of which can be seen in Fig. 12. We were astonished to observe that - for the most part - classifiers performed better under this setting than under anonymization alone. For logistic regression, although age & race vectors performed worse then their anonymized-only counterparts, performance for equal weights was better for $k < 11$. With Random Forest, all vectors performed better than their anonymization-only counterparts, with $k = 3$ only 2% below original performance. With Linear SVC, age & race performed worse at the beginning ónly to recover with increasing performance towards $k = 100$, whereas the equal vector behaved about equal to it's non-outlier-removed opposite. Finally, Gradient Boosting in this setting outperforms it's anonymization-only competitor in all settings with it's $k = 3$ equal weight vector performance lying within only half a percentage point of the performance on the original, un-anonymized dataset.

As a side-note, we observe that under these settings, SVC starts to mimic Random Forest's behavior of an initial collapse in performance for the age- and range-vectors with a subsequent recovery towards higher levels of k. We do not yet have an adequate explanation for this and will investigate deeper in our future efforts.

Those amazing results raise a few burning questions: (1) Can we repeat that performance on real-world data? (2) Could we combine this technique with interactive Machine Learning/Anonymization which yield better weight vectors? (3) Do those advantages only hold for a toy algorithm or will they persist under more

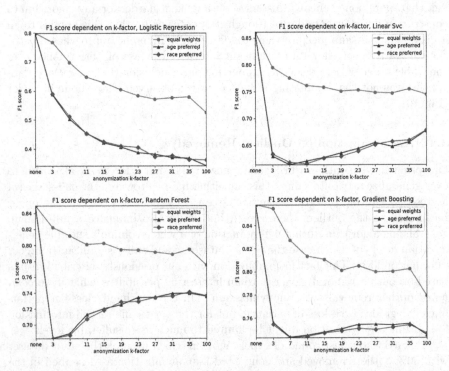

Fig. 12. Multi-class classification on target marital status based on a dataset with 30% outliers removed AND under different degrees of k-anonymization.

sophisticated Anonymization pipelines? (4) Can we further enhance those results by mixing synthetic data into the dataset? (5) Will better feature engineering compensate for our original drop in performance and thus moot our insight? and (6) can we apply this conclusion to other data structures like social networks? These points shall now briefly be discussed before concluding the paper.

5   Open Problems/Future Challenges

1. **Real world data.** Despite the convenient availability of well-curated datasets with many thousands of data rows, actual industry datasets are usually orders of magnitudes larger. This has consequences for their internal data topology and thus the performance of ML algorithms; e.g. [3] observe that variance error can be expected to decrease as training set size increases (though this might have nothing to do with variance in the dataset itself).

2. **Interactive machine learning.** We have demonstrated experiments with different weight vectors in our approach regarding anonymization. However, data utility is highly subjective w.r.t. the specific area of application; therefore choosing the importance of attributes with regard to the particular environment is best done by a human. The problem of (k-)anonymization thus lends itself to interactive Machine Learning (iML) with a human-in-the-loop approach [8,9,11]. We have implemented software for iML Anonymization and are currently collecting test results which will soon be ready for publication.

3. **Real world algorithms.** While we only anonymizing our datasets via simple k-anonymization through greedy clustering, there are much more sophisticated algorithms available, capable of fine-tuning generalization levels to the specific data topology of an input set in order to minimize information loss. It remains to be seen if such algorithms can still profit from removal of outliers as a pre-processing step.

4. **Synthetic datasets.** In recent years it has become common to augment (small) datasets via synthetically generated, additional data-points [25]. By controlling the data generation process, one would be able to also control variance-injection into a dataset. Therefore, instead of outlier-removal, one could enrich a dataset by introducing lower-variance data points before anonymization.

5. **Better feature engineering.** For our experiments, we considered practically all columns of the adult dataset, although some exhibited much higher variance than others. It is therefore conceivable that by careful feature engineering the basis for anonymization could be sufficiently improved, rendering outlier-removal unnecessary.

6. **Graph structure anonymization.** This includes questions of measuring structural outliers in a graph (maybe via centrality- or component-based analysis?) as well as outlier removal (do they have to be deleted or will randomly adding edges to such nodes suffice?). Our team is currently devising experiments in this direction, but our efforts are still in the early stages.

6 Conclusion

In this paper we continued our initial experiments on the effects of anonymization and perturbation of knowledge bases on classifier performance and expanded our efforts to multi-class classification, outlier-removal as well as a combined outlier/anonymization approach. Our results show that selective deletion of significant attribute values is preferable to general anonymization, insofar a dataset's topology allows for such conduct. We have furthermore seen that reducing variance in a dataset prevents algorithms of different breeds alike from finding efficient discriminators between classes, leading to a significant degradation of machine learning performance. Finally, we were astonished to observe that combining outlier-removal with anonymization can - under circumstances - yield almost as good a performance as classification on the original, un-anonymized dataset itself. We believe that this insight, in combination with work on interactive Anonymization we are currently conducting, state-of-the art anonymization techniques (we were using a rather simple algorithm for this paper), as well as the introduction of synthetic data, will enable us to soon propose competitive Machine Learning pipelines for real-world usage to counterbalance any regulatory disadvantage European companies are currently facing on the marketplace.

References

1. Aggarwal, C.C.: On k-anonymity and the curse of dimensionality. In: Proceedings of the 31st International Conference on Very Large Data Bases VLDB, pp. 901–909 (2005)
2. Aggarwal, G., Feder, T., Kenthapadi, K., Motwani, R., Panigrahy, R., Thomas, D., Zhu, A.: Approximation algorithms for k-anonymity. J. Priv. Technol. (JOPT) (2005)
3. Brain, D., Webb, G.: On the effect of data set size on bias and variance in classification learning. In: Proceedings of the Fourth Australian Knowledge Acquisition Workshop, pp. 117–128. University of New South Wales (1999)
4. Campan, A., Truta, T.M.: Data and structural k-anonymity in social networks. In: Bonchi, F., Ferrari, E., Jiang, W., Malin, B. (eds.) PInKDD 2008. LNCS, vol. 5456, pp. 33–54. Springer, Heidelberg (2009). doi:10.1007/978-3-642-01718-6_4
5. Ciriani, V., De Capitani di Vimercati, S., Foresti, S., Samarati, P.: κ-anonymity. In: Yu, T., Jajodia, S. (eds.) Secure Data Management in Decentralized Systems. Advances in Information Security, vol. 33, pp. 323–353. Springer, Boston (2007)
6. Duchi, J.C., Jordan, M.I., Wainwright, M.J.: Privacy aware learning. J. ACM (JACM) **61**(6), 38 (2014)
7. Dwork, C.: Differential privacy: a survey of results. In: Agrawal, M., Du, D., Duan, Z., Li, A. (eds.) TAMC 2008. LNCS, vol. 4978, pp. 1–19. Springer, Heidelberg (2008). doi:10.1007/978-3-540-79228-4_1
8. Holzinger, A., Plass, M., Holzinger, K., Crişan, G.C., Pintea, C.-M., Palade, V.: Towards interactive machine learning (iML): applying ant colony algorithms to solve the traveling salesman problem with the human-in-the-loop approach. In: Buccafurri, F., Holzinger, A., Kieseberg, P., Tjoa, A.M., Weippl, E. (eds.) CD-ARES 2016. LNCS, vol. 9817, pp. 81–95. Springer, Cham (2016). doi:10.1007/978-3-319-45507-5_6

9. Holzinger, A.: Interactive machine learning for health informatics: when do we need the human-in-the-loop? Brain Inform. (BRIN) **3**(2), 119–131 (2016). Springer

10. Holzinger, A.: Introduction to machine learning & knowledge extraction (make). Mach. Learn. Knowl. Extract. **1**(1), 1–20 (2017)

11. Kieseberg, P., Malle, B., Frhwirt, P., Weippl, E., Holzinger, A.: A tamper-proof audit and control system for the doctor in the loop. Brain Inform. **3**(4), 269–279 (2016)

12. Lee, H., Kim, S., Kim, J.W., Chung, Y.D.: Utility-preserving anonymization for health data publishing. BMC Med. Inform. Decis. Making **17**(1), 104 (2017)

13. LeFevre, K., DeWitt, D.J., Ramakrishnan, R.: Mondrian multidimensional k-anonymity. In: Proceedings of the 22nd International Conference on Data Engineering (ICDE 2006), p. 25. IEEE (2006)

14. Li, J., Liu, J., Baig, M., Wong, R.C.-W.: Information based data anonymization for classification utility. Data Knowl. Eng. **70**(12), 1030–1045 (2011)

15. Li, N., Li, T., Venkatasubramanian, S.: t-closeness: privacy beyond k-anonymity and l-diversity. In: IEEE 23rd International Conference on Data Engineering (ICDE 2007), pp. 106–115. IEEE (2007)

16. Machanavajjhala, A., Kifer, D., Gehrke, J., Venkitasubramaniam, M.: l-diversity: privacy beyond k-anonymity. ACM Trans. Knowl. Disc. Data (TKDD) **1**(1), 1–52 (2007)

17. Majeed, A., Ullah, F., Lee, S.: Vulnerability-and diversity-aware anonymization of personally identifiable information for improving user privacy and utility of publishing data. Sensors **17**(5), 1–23 (2017)

18. Malle, B., Kieseberg, P., Weippl, E., Holzinger, A.: The right to be forgotten: towards machine learning on perturbed knowledge bases. In: Buccafurri, F., Holzinger, A., Kieseberg, P., Tjoa, A.M., Weippl, E. (eds.) CD-ARES 2016. LNCS, vol. 9817, pp. 251–266. Springer, Cham (2016). doi:10.1007/978-3-319-45507-5_17

19. Nergiz, M.E., Clifton, C.: Delta-presence without complete world knowledge. IEEE Trans. Knowl. Data Eng. **22**(6), 868–883 (2010)

20. Samarati, P.: Protecting respondents identities in microdata release. IEEE Trans. Knowl. Data Eng. **13**(6), 1010–1027 (2001)

21. Simpson, E.H.: Measurement of diversity. Nature **163**, 688 (1949)

22. Sweeney, L.: Achieving k-anonymity privacy protection using generalization and suppression. Int. J. Uncertaint. Fuzziness Knowl. Based Syst. **10**(5), 571–588 (2002)

23. Sweeney, L.: k-anonymity: a model for protecting privacy. Int. J. Uncertaint. Fuzziness Knowl. Based Syst. **10**(05), 557–570 (2002)

24. Wimmer, H., Powell, L.: A comparison of the effects of K-anonymity on machine learning algorithms, pp. 1–9 (2014)

25. Wong, S.C., Gatt, A., Stamatescu, V., McDonnell, M.D.: Understanding data augmentation for classification: when to warp? In: 2016 International Conference on Digital Image Computing: Techniques and Applications (DICTA), pp. 1–6. IEEE (2016)

A Short-Term Forecast Approach
of Public Buildings' Power Demands
upon Multi-source Data

Shubing Shan[1,2(✉)] and Buyang Cao[1,2]

[1] School of Software Engineering, Tongji University, 200092 Shanghai, China
1410786@tongji.edu.cn
[2] China Intelligent Urbanization Co-Creation Center,
Tongji University, 200092 Shanghai, China

Abstract. Due to the significant increase of the global electricity demand and the rising number of urban population, the electric consumption in a city has attracted more attentions. Given the fact that public buildings occupy a large proportion of the electric consumption, the accurate prediction of electric consumptions for them is crucial to the rational electricity allocation and supply. This paper studies the possibility of utilizing urban multi-source data such as POI, pedestrian volume etc. to predict buildings' electric consumptions. Among the multiple datasets, the key influencing factors are extracted to forecast the buildings' electric power demands by the given probabilistic graphical algorithm named EMG. Our methodology is applied to display the relationships between the factors and forecast the daily electric power demands of nine public buildings including hotels, shopping malls, and office buildings in city of Hangzhou, China over the period of a month. The computational experiments are conducted and the result favors our approach.

Keywords: Electricity demand · Short-term forecast · Multi–source data · Grey relational analysis · Probabilistic graph

1 Introduction

With the population growth and economic development, the global electric consumption is increasing yearly. In the past decades, the proportion of the world's urban population has been rising and the per capita electric consumption has gradually increased. The electric power demand in a city is undergoing drastic changing. According to the latest statistics released by the World Bank in 2016 [1], the global per capita electric consumption rose to 3104.7 kWh (kilowatt hour) in 2013 up from 2027.4 kWh in 2006 and the percentage of the world's urban population increased by 3.9% from 2006 to 2014. As the result, the urban electric consumption will rise sharply worldwide. Meanwhile, the urban public buildings have always been one of major electric consumption groups around the world [2, 3]. The topic of building energy demand-side is the focus of researches today because an accurate prediction of demand is very important for every country to work out the reasonable plan of energy production and reduce carbon emissions [4–6]. It also plays a vital role in rationally

A. Holzinger et al. (Eds.): CD-MAKE 2017, LNCS 10410, pp. 174–188, 2017.
DOI: 10.1007/978-3-319-66808-6_12

allocating a city's electricity, avoiding peak-hour power shortage, saving public funds, reducing economic risks, and reducing environmental pollution caused by excessive electricity generation [7, 8].

In the past researchers paid close attentions mainly to the influences of four factors including meteorological factors, building attributes, time series, and occupancy rates. Among them meteorological data, building attribute data and time series data can be more easily obtained, but the occupancy is difficult to obtain accurately. There are two possible ways to obtain building occupancy data including manual counting and automatic sensing. The former method is not only time-consuming but also cannot be conducted in real time. Thus, the occupancy data obtained is usually a macroscopic statistical data by such as the annual average occupancy. The automatic sensing way is to install a sensing device and a data collecting system in the building records real-time building occupancy. But this method requires expensive hardware and software investment, which makes it difficult to be applied extensively. It inspires us to invent a way to capture the occupancy upon other data. From the practice, we know the occupancy of a building is influenced by regional functions and regional vitality [9–11]. Therefore, we try to acquire the occupancy rate of a building through the urban multi-source data such as POI and pedestrian volume data in the surrounding area of the building to support the forecast of building electric consumption. Furthermore, few scholars have studied the relationships between factors such as weather and time series and their impacts on the occupancy of a building. We use the probability graph model to represent the relationships between various influence factors and electric consumptions and an approximate inference algorithm to predict public buildings' electric consumptions.

This paper has the following contributions:

(1) It studies the relationships between urban multi-source data with electric consumptions to predict building electric consumptions.
(2) It applies the probability graph model to study and express the relationships between various factors, and an approximate inference algorithm known as EMG is proposed to predict building electric consumptions.
(3) We evaluate the proposed approaches using the real data from nine public buildings in city of Hangzhou, China. In our computational experiments, the MAPE is used for the quality criterion. A comparative analysis is performed by using the regression analysis. The result indicates that our approach has a better accuracy.

This paper is organized as follows. Related work is presented in Sect. 2. Section 3 gives the methodology including grey correlation analysis and probability graph algorithm. Section 4 is the case study and results. Several tests and statistical analysis are provided in Sect. 5. The paper is concluded with some remarks.

2   Related Work

In the past researchers have been continuously exploring four approaches to forecast buildings' energy consumptions including meteorological, architectural attributes, occupancy, and time series predictions. Some studies explore the impact of meteorological factors on building energy consumption. Zheng et al. study the effects of hour of day and outside air temperature on hot water energy consumption by a data driven method [12]. Yang et al. investigate some variables such as time of day and outdoor air dry-bulb temperature, and apply artificial neural network to make a short-term electric consumption prediction for commercial buildings [13]. Nelson et al. conduct the research on the influence of meteorological factor on residential buildings' energy and use a quadratic regression analysis approach to predict the demand of buildings' energy [14]. Ambera et al. investigate the influence of five important factors (temperature, solar radiation, relative humidity, wind speed, and weekday index) on administration buildings' energy. They use a multiple regression model and a genetic programming model to forecast daily electricity consumption [15]. James et al. look into the impact of climate change on peak and annual building energy consumption [16].

Many scholars pay closer attention to the effect of architectural attributes on the electric consumption. Lu use a physical–statistical approach which includes physical model and the statistical time series model to predict the energy consumption of buildings. The physical model simulates the basic energy consumption of different buildings and the statistical time series model reflects the heterogeneity of various buildings [17]. Akin makes a short-term prediction of electric demand through the detailed data and information of the house [18]. Cara et al. develop the auto-regressive models with building specific inputs for forecasting power demands [19]. Kristopher et al. carry out a study that utilizes statistical learning methods to predict the future monthly energy consumptions for single-family detached homes using building attributes and monthly climate data [20].

Researchers also try to utilize occupancy and time series factors to predict the building energy consumptions. Ferlito et al. use the building properties, occupancy rate and weather to predict buildings' energy consumption by Artificial Neural Network method [21]. Sandels et al. explore the influence of weather, occupancy, and temporal factors on electricity consumptions of a Swedish office building [22]. Kim et al. study the influence of building occupancy and construction area allocation on building electric consumption, and uses the linear equation method to predict the electric consumption of buildings [23]. López-Rodríguez et al. conclude that building electricity demand is highly correlated with occupancy time in buildings, and build an occupancy statistical model for creating active occupancy with the aim to predict electricity consumptions [24]. Kavousian studies the structural and behavioral determinants of residential electricity consumption. This study shows that electric consumption is not significantly related to income level, home ownership, or building age [25].

3 Methodology

3.1 Grey Correlation Analysis

The grey relational analysis has been widely studied and applied since its birth [26, 27]. It determines the degree of association upon the similarity of the curves represented by the two series. The grey correlation degree is used to represent the degree of association.

The grey correlation degree is computed as follows:

Step 1: Set a data column (*reference column*) of the historical electric consumptions as shown in (1). Let m be the number of records for one of the underlying six buildings' electric consumptions during 92 days.

$$X_0' = (x_0(1), x_0(2), \ldots, x_0(m))^T, \quad m \le 92 \tag{1}$$

Step 2: The reference column together with the comparing columns form a matrix A. We apply a normalization process to all data in the matrix for the analysis accuracy. The normalized data matrix B is shown (2). The n is number of factors. The first column is normalized reference column and others are normalized comparing columns. The normalization process utilizes the Initiative Value method (3) where X_i' (1) is the value of first row of matrix A.

$$(X_0, X_1, \ldots, X_n) = \begin{pmatrix} x_0(1) & \cdots & x_n(1) \\ \vdots & \ddots & \vdots \\ x_0(m) & \cdots & x_n(m) \end{pmatrix} \tag{2}$$

$$xi(k) = \frac{x'i(k)}{x'i(1)} \quad i = 0, 1, \ldots, n; \ k = 1, 2, \ldots, m \tag{3}$$

Step 3: We compute one by one the absolute difference between the elements in normalized comparing and reference ones. Correlation coefficients between normalized comparing and normalized reference columns are calculated. In formula (4), ρ is the distinguishing coefficient that takes values in the range (0, 1). The smaller the ρ value is, the greater the difference between correlation coefficients is. It may be adjusted based on the practical needs of the system.

$$\xi_i(k) = \frac{(minimink|x0(k) - xi(k)| + \rho maximaxk|x0(k) - xi(k)|)}{(|x0(k) - xi(k)| + maximaxk|x0(k) - xi(k)|)} \quad k = 1, \ldots, m \tag{4}$$

Step 4: Using the outcome obtained in step 3, the mean value of correlation coefficients for each *comparing column* can be calculated upon (5) respectively. The purpose of this is to acquire the correlation between every pair of comparing column and reference column and yield the grey correlation degree. The larger the value, the greater the influence of the comparing column.

$$r_{0i} = \frac{1}{m \sum_{k=1}^{m} \xi_i(k)} \tag{5}$$

3.2   Probability Graph Model

There are three steps to construct a probabilistic graphical model: structure learning, parameter learning, and inference.

- Structure learning

The obtained data may be incomplete, so we use the SEM (Structural Expectation-Maximization) algorithm [28] to learn structure. It is adopted in the structure learning based on an incomplete data set. Figure 1 shows the Pseudo code of the algorithm.

```
SEM (
G⁰, // Initial network structure
Θ⁰,⁰, // Initial parameter value
D, // Missing dataset
R // Optimization of the number of parameters between the two structural optimization
    )
1  For t=0,..., until convergence
2  For r=0 to R-1
3    Θᵗ,ʳ⁺¹← Expectation-Maximization(Gᵗ, Θt,r ,D)
4  Θᵗ=Θᵗ,ᴿ
5  L←All of the Gᵗ to do a plus side, edge reduction or edge of the candidate model structure
6  Gᵗ⁺¹←arg max Score(G|Dt,Θᵗ)
7  Θᵗ⁺¹,⁰←Estimate Gᵗ⁺¹ parameter values
8  If (Score(Gᵗ⁺¹,Θᵗ⁺¹,0|D)≤Score(Gᵗ, Θᵗ|D))
9     Return (Gᵗ, Θᵗ)
10 Return(Gᵗ⁺¹,Θᵗ⁺¹)
```

Fig. 1. The pseudo code of SEM algorithm

- Parameter learning and inference

In the Probabilistic Graphical model, EM (Expectation-Maximization) algorithm is an approximate learning and inference algorithm [29], which can resolve the incomplete graph problem. The Gibbs algorithm [30] is data sampling algorithm upon the Monte Carlo method to reduce the amount of data and speed up the calculation. Here we propose a hybrid algorithm, EMG algorithm, which utilizes the advantages of both algorithms.

The pseudo code of the EMG algorithm is shown in Fig. 2. The algorithm includes three parts, the first is to generate a sample data set for each entity variable by the Gibbs algorithm. The distribution of the sample data set is similar to the real data set. Second, it obtains the current parameters of each entity from the sample dataset, and uses the current parameters and graph structure to compute the expected value of each entity variable. Finally, it recalculates the parameters of each entity by the expected value of it. It iterates until the estimated parameter reaches the local optimum or reaches the specified number of iterations.

- The sample dataset

The approximate inference algorithm based on Gibbs sampling is one of the simplest and the most popular methods of data sampling. It uses each node as a variable to conduct a random sampling, and then assigns an initial value to each variable to get an initial state. It computes each node's conditional probability to achieve a new value and

```
// Dataset generation algorithm based on Gibbs-sample
Procedure Gibbs-Sample (
    X // The set of variables that need to be sampled
    Φ //Define Factor Sets of P_Φ
    P (0) (X) //Initial State Distribution
    T //Sampling Times
    D. // Sample dataset
    G, // Bayesian network structure
    θ. // Bayesian network parameters
    θ⁰. // Bayesian network initial parameters
)
//Producing a sample x (0) from the distribution P (0) (X)
1 For t=1,...,T
2     X(t)←x(t-1)
3       For each Xi ∈X
4         Sampled xi(t) From P_Φ(Xi|xi)
5         Replace Xi in x(t)
6 Return x(0),...,x(T)
7 Return D={ x(0),..., x(T)}
//EM parameter learning algorithm
    // E-step
8 For each i=1, ..., n // Initialize the data structure
9 For each xi,μi ∈ Val (Xi , PaG_xi)
10 M̄xi|μi ← 0
11 For each m=1,..., M
        // The data model D [m] is used to carry out the reasoning operation on the network
        structure and //the current parameters
12 Run inference on (G, θ) using evidence D[m]
13 For each i = 1,..., n
14     For each xi, μi ∈ Val (Xi, PaG_xi)
15      M̄ xi|μi ← M̄ xi|μi + p(xi,μi|D[m])
16 Return {M̄ xi|μi:∀i = 1,...,n,∀xi,μi ∈Val (Xi, PaG_xi)
    // M-step
17 For each t=0, 1,..., until convergence
18 {M̄'xi|μi} ←Compute-ESS (G, θ', D)
19 For each i=1,...n
20    For each xi,μi ∈Val(Xi, PaG_xi)
21 θ^(t+1)_xi|μi←M̄'xi|μi/M̄'μi
22 Return θ'
```

Fig. 2. The pseudo code of EMG algorithm

state based on the Markov Cover. The above steps repeat until the number of samples reaches a given threshold and the sample data set is obtained.

- Parameter learning

The weights of each entity in the graph are obtained by the parameter learning of the EMG algorithm. Its parameter learning is similar to the EM parameter learning algorithm.

E-Step. It uses the graph structure and the current parameters to calculate the expected value of missing variables.

M-Step. In the M-step by scanning the inferred results from the E-step, the algorithm recalculates the new maximum parameter distribution and replaces the old parameters with new ones. It repeats until the parameters converge, and we have learned the unknown parameters.

- Inference

In the E-step (Line 12–16) of EMG algorithm, we call exact inference method, i.e., use the simple Bayesian rule, to compute the values of the hidden entity nodes, for each instance of the observed data. This is actually an inference process.

4   Case Study and Result

This paper uses the nine public buildings in Hangzhou, China for the case study. Among them there are shopping malls, hotels and office buildings to illustrate the (predicting) methodology. The paper explores the correlations between buildings' electric consumptions and influencing factors including: architectural property, weather, air quality, population and POI data. All the different sorts of data obtained will be further processed.

4.1   Data Preparation

- The architectural property data

In spite of different functions and structures, the buildings possess some common attributes or properties. The property data collected includes building age, number of stories (including ground and underground), and total area (m^2) as well as window/wall ratio.

- Historical Electric Consumption Data

The historical data of daily electric consumption is acquired for these public buildings from January 1, 2015 to January 31, 2016. The daily electric consumptions spanned from 0:00 a.m. to 23:59:59 p.m. The electricity unit is KWH (kilowatt hour). In order to verify the prediction, this paper divides the data set into two subsets: data for May, June and July used as the training sets while data for August used as the testing one to validate the model.

- Weather and Air Quality Data

The weather data collected contains the daily average temperature and humidity from January 1, 2015 to November 31, in City of Hangzhou, China. The temperature unit is degree centigrade, and the humidity unit is percentage.

- POI Data

POI data contains a number of specific functional facilities such as restaurants, bus stops, etc. The dataset has the name, address, coordinate and other attributes of the functional properties. In our paper six functional facilities (POI) within 200 meters around concerned buildings are included. The six types of POI are office buildings, shopping malls, restaurants, hotels, metro stations and bus stations. The number of bus stations is calculated according to distinguish bus routes. For example, bus line 12 and bus line 39 stop at the same station A then the number of stops at A will be counted as two.

- Pedestrian Volume Data

We collect pedestrian volume data within 50 meters around the building from January 1, 2015 to November 31, 2015.

Due to the widespread use of mobile phones, the number of mobile phone users can accurately reflect the changes in pedestrian volume.

- Occupancy Data

We collect the average statistical data for each month in 2015. Occupancy data is the ratio of average number of people in a building to the total building accommodation capacity

- Time series Data

We divide the year into four quarters and use the vector to represent it. For example, the first quarter can be expressed as 1, 0, 0, 0.

4.2 Influence Factors

4.2.1 Scatter Diagram

The following scatting diagrams disclose that the correlation of the occupancy between with pedestrian volume and number of POI.

Figure 3 is the scatter diagram of the three hotel buildings. Figure 4 is the scatter diagram of the three office buildings. Figure 5 is the scatter diagram of the three shopping buildings. The occupancy rate of various public buildings is highly correlated with number of POI and pedestrian volume. Therefore, number of POI and occupancy rate are the impact factors of building electric consumption.

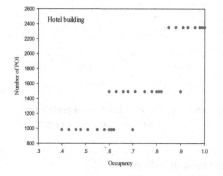

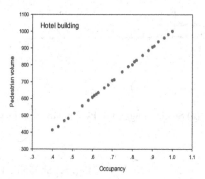

(a) Scatter diagram of POI and average occupancy

(b) Scatter diagram of pedestrian volume and occupancy

Fig. 3. Hotel building scatter diagram

4.2.2 Remove Noisy Factors

Although the relationships between factors and electric consumptions can be represented by scatterplots, to accurately analyze the correlations between factors and public buildings' electric consumptions we use the gray relational analysis method introduced in Sect. 3.1 to remove the noise factors.

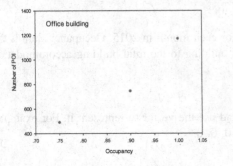

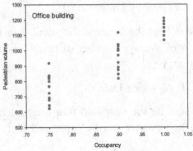

(a) Scatter diagram of POI and average Occupancy   (b) Scatter diagram of pedestrian volume and occupancy

Fig. 4. Office building Scatter diagram

(a) Scatter diagram of POI and average Occupancy   (b) Scatter diagram of pedestrian volume and Occupancy

Fig. 5. Shopping building scatter diagram

As shown in Table 1, we extracted potential fifteen factors from the prepared multi-source data in Sect. 4.1. The Grey Correlation analysis is used to determine whether all fifteen factors (X1,..., X15) listed in Table 1 have significant impacts on the underlying public buildings' electric consumptions.

The grey theory [33] has the advantage of using less data while producing higher accuracy. It has been widely studied and applied since its birth.

The grey correlation degrees between potential 15 factors and buildings' electric consumptions are shown in Table 2. According to the grey theory, the correlation degree above 0.5 (the threshold value) will be treated as key influence factors.

As shown in Table 2, it is interesting to see the correlations of influence factors vary significantly with building types. For instance, Pedestrian volume has the greatest impact on the electricity consumption of a shopping building, while its impact on an office building's one is minimal. The more pedestrians in a shopping building the more

Table 1. Fifteen factors

Daily electricity consumption	Age of building	No. of stories	Total area	Window-wall Ratio	Daily average temperature	Daily average humidity	Time series
X0'	X1	X2	X3	X4	X5	X6	X7
Pedestrian Volume	No. of office buildings	No. of malls	No. of restaurants	No. of hotels	No. of metro stations	No. of bus stations	Total No. of POI
X8	X9	X10	X11	X12	X13	X14	X15

Table 2. Analysis Result by Grey Theory

Factor	Correlation degree (Hotel building)	Correlation degree (Office building)	Correlation degree (Shopping building)
Age of building, x1	0.49	0.37	0.41
No. of stories, x2	0.43	0.62	0.33
Total area, x3	0.77	0.81	0.79
Window-wall Ratio, x4	0.57	0.55	0.43
Daily average temperature, x5	0.71	0.66	0.59
Daily average humidity, x6	0.49	0.38	0.31
Time series, x7	0.68	0.72	0.61
Pedestrian Volume, x8	0.58	0.48	0.71
No. of office buildings, x9	0.44	0.48	0.37
No. of shopping malls, x10	0.48	0.39	0.31
No. of restaurants, x11	0.59	0.66	0.69
No. of hotels, x12	0.48	0.41	0.37
No. of metro stations, x13	0.36	0.39	0.41
No. of bus stations, x14	0.67	0.70	0.69
Total No. of POI, x15	0.65	0.69	0.70

consumptions in that building. Nevertheless, during the normal working hours the number of staff members in an office building is relatively stable.

4.3 Prediction

Section 4.2 explores the key factors that influence public buildings' electric consumptions. The prediction of electric consumption is realized via probabilistic graphical model for the sake of sorting out the interrelations between the factors and their influences on the buildings' electric consumption. According to the modeling method given in Sect. 3.2, we construct the corresponding probability graph models for various public buildings. Figure 6 shows the probabilistic graphical model for three kinds of public buildings.

Based on the obtained probabilistic graph models, the parameter learning, and inference algorithms described in Sect. 3.2, we are able to predict the electricity consumption of nine public buildings for a given month. Our results are compared and analyzed based on the outcomes yielded by another classic forecasting algorithm: multivariable linear regression model. The prediction results are depicted in Fig. 7.

In Fig. 7, the consumption patterns predicted by our approach look similar to the actual electric consumptions. It is hard to tell the best forecasting model by visualization. In order to quantify the qualities further, we apply MAPE (Mean Absolute Percentage Error) to evaluate the algorithm.

5 Error Analysis and Discussion

The mean absolute percentage error (MAPE) indicates the prediction accuracy of a forecasting method. Generally, a lower MAPE interprets better prediction accuracy.

Table 3 summarizes the results yielded by our approach and other benchmarked approaches.

The average prediction error of our approach is 6.98%. The predictions' errors of other four methods are 7.86%, 7.69%, 8.29% and 14.99%, respectively. However, the error of five methods is within the recommended ASHRAE limits—30% for predictions [31]. TC method: total consumption forecast using the proposed ANN and only using total consumption data. EUs method: total consumption forecast using the proposed method and obtaining the prediction as the aggregation of the different EUs [32]. The urban multi-source based methods proposed in this paper produces the predictions with better accuracy while the datasets needed for the model are relatively easy to access. It is expected that in real applications, our approach would be easier to be deployed.

In addition, our approach extracts crucial factors from total fifteen potential ones and uses grey correlation analysis to conduct predictions. This indicates that reducing unimportant factors mitigates some noisy influence due to loosely-related factors and produces a better prediction accuracy. Using different critical influence factors, we have constructed the special probability graph models for various public buildings to help improving the prediction accuracy. Our approach uses the probabilistic graphical algorithm (EMG) is the combination of the Expectation-Maximization and Gibbs

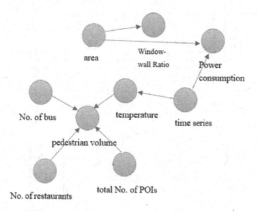

(a) PGM structure of Hotel building

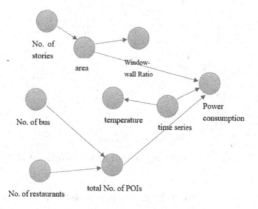

(b) PGM structure of Office building

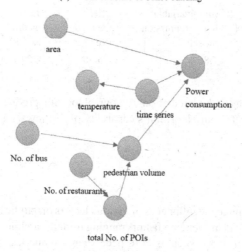

(C) PGM structure of Shopping building

Fig. 6. Probabilistic Graphical models for various public buildings

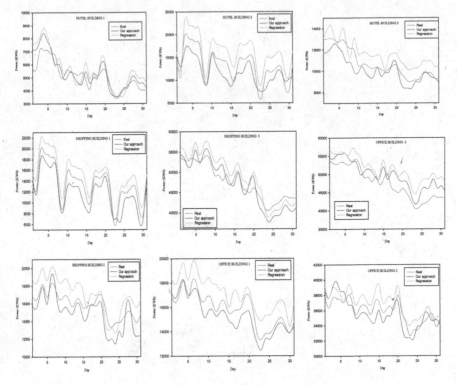

Fig. 7. Forecast results of six buildings by different algorithm

Table 3. Experiment Results

Average Error difference	Methods				
	Our approach	(multivariable linear regression model)	(EUs method) Ref 32	TC method Ref 32	(Heuristic Method) Ref 32
MAPE (%)	6.98%	7.86%	7.69%	8.29%	14.99%

methods. On the average, the predictions of our algorithm produce less error other methods that demonstrates our algorithm's capability of dealing with different types of public buildings.

6   Conclusion

In this paper, we investigate the influences of various factors on public buildings' electric consumptions. The critical influencing factors ranging from the architectural properties to some spatiotemporal attributes such as POI, pedestrian volume, etc. are collected and studied. This research reveals the profound influence of spatiotemporal data on electric consumptions from a new perspective. Furthermore, integrating various influencing factors in our approach is unique and more efficient comparing to other methods. However, there are some issues to be addressed in the future research. For example, the dataset is still not big enough in terms of time span due to data acquisition restrictions and costs. The number of investigated buildings is relatively small. We will explore more how different forecasting algorithms fare as more data (longer time span, more public buildings, etc.) being collected and provide better insights in selecting suitable prediction methods under different circumstances for urban electric power demands.

Acknowledgements. This work was supported by CIUC and TJAD [grant number CIUC20150011] and National Natural Science Foundation of China [grant number 61271351].

References

1. The World Bank: Indicators. http://data.worldbank.org/indicator. Accessed 06 Apr 2017
2. Ahmad, A.S., Hassan, M.Y., Abdullah, M.P., Rahman, H.A., Hussin, F., Abdullah, H., Saidur, R.: A review on applications of ANN and SVM for building electrical energy consumption forecasting. Renew. Sustain. Energy Rev. **33**, 102–109 (2014)
3. Santamouris, M., Cartalisb, C., Synnefab, A., Kolokotsa, D.: On the impact of urban heat island and global warming on the power demand and electricity consumption of buildings—a review. Energy Buil. **98**, 119–124 (2015)
4. Jorn, K.G., Milan, P., Raúl, A.: Estimation and analysis of building energy demand and supply costs. Energy Procedia **83**, 216–225 (2015)
5. Moulay Larbi, C., Medjdoub, B., Michael, W., Raid, S.: Energy planning and forecasting approaches for supporting physical improvement strategies in the building sector: a review. Renew. Sustain. Energy Rev. **64**, 761–776 (2016)
6. Afees, A.S., Taofeek, O.A.: Modeling energy demand: Some emerging issues. Renew. Sustain. Energy Rev. **54**, 1470–1480 (2016)
7. Radu, P., Vahid, R.D., Jacques, M.: Hourly prediction of a building's electricity consumption using case-based reasoning, artificial neural networks and principal component analysis. Energy Buil. **92**, 10–18 (2015)
8. Fabiano Castro, T., Reinaldo Castro, S., Fernando Luiz Cyrino, O., Jose Francisco Moreira, P.: Long term electricity consumption forecast in Brazil: a fuzzy logic approach. Socio-Econ. Plann. Sci. **54**, 18–27 (2016)
9. Yamauchi, T., Michinori, K., Tomoko, K.: Development of quantitative evaluation method regarding value and environmental impact of cities. Fujitsu Sci. Tech. J. **50**, 112–120 (2014)
10. Liang, H., Yu, Z., Duncan, Y., Jingbo, S., Lei, Z.: Detecting urban black holes based on human mobility data. In: Proceedings of the 23rd SIGSPATIAL International Conference on Advances in Geographic Information Systems, pp. 1–10. ACM, Bellevue (2015)
11. Jing, Y., Yu, Z., Xing, X.: Discovering regions of different functions in a city using human mobility and POIs. In: KDD 2012 Proceedings of the 18th ACM SIGKDD International Conference on Knowledge Discovery and Data Mining, pp. 186–194. ACM, New York (2012)
12. Zheng, O.N., Charles, O.N.: Development of a probabilistic graphical model for predicting building energy performance. Appl. Energy **164**, 650–658 (2016)
13. Young Tae, C., Raya, H., Youngdeok, H., Young, M.L.: Artificial neural network model for forecasting sub-hourly electricity usage in commercial buildings. Energy Build. **111**, 184–194 (2016)

14. Nelson, F., Rafe Biswas, M.A.: Regression analysis for prediction of residential energy consumption. Renew. Sustain. Energy Rev. **47**, 332–343 (2015)
15. Ambera, K.P., Aslamb, M.W., Hussainc, S.K.: Electricity consumption forecasting models for administration buildings of the UK higher education sector. Energy Build. **90**, 127–136 (2015)
16. James, A.D., Willy, J.G., John, H.H., Daniel, C.S., Michael, J.S., Trenton, C.P., Maoyi, H., Ying, L., Jennie, S.R.: Impacts of climate change on energy consumption and peak demand in buildings: a detailed regional approach. Energy **79**, 20–32 (2015)
17. Xiaoshu, L., Tao, L., Charles, J.K., Martti, 'V.: Modeling and forecasting energy consumption for heterogeneous buildings using a physical–statistical approach. Appl. Energy **144**, 261–275 (2015)
18. Akin, T., Borhan, M.S.: Short-term residential electric load forecast-ing: a compressive spatio-temporal approach. Energy Build. **111**, 380–392 (2016)
19. Cara, R.T., Rakesh, P.: Building-level power demand forecasting framework using building specific inputs: development and applications. Appl. Energy **147**, 466–477 (2015)
20. Kristopher, T.W., Juan, D.G.: Predicting future monthly residential energy consumption using building characteristics and climate data: a statistical learning approach. Energy Build. **128**, 1–11 (2016)
21. Ferlito, S., Mauro, A.G., Graditi, S., De Vito, M., Salvato, A., Buonanno, G., Di, F.: Predictive models for building's energy consumption: an Artificial Neural Network (ANN) approach. In: XVIII AISEM Annual Conference, pp. 1–4, IEEE, Trento (2015)
22. Sandels, C., Widén, J., Nordström, L., Andersson, E.: Day-ahead predictions of electricity consumption in a Swedish office building from weather, occupancy, and temporal data. Energy Build. **108**, 279–290 (2015)
23. Yang-Seon, K., Jelena, S.: Impact of occupancy rates on the building electricity consumption in commercial buildings. Energy Build. **138**, 591–600 (2017)
24. López-Rodríguez, M.A., Santiago, I., Trillo-Montero, D., Torriti, J., Moreno-Munoz, A.: Analysis and modeling of active occupancy of the residential sector in Spain: an indicator of residential electricity consumption. Energy Policy **62**, 742–751 (2013)
25. Amir, K., Ram, R., Martin, F.: Determinants of residential electricity consumption: using smart meter data to examine the effect of climate, building characteristics, appliance stock, and occupants' behavior. Energy **55**, 184–194 (2013)
26. Zhifeng, Z., Chenxi, Y., Wenyang, C., Chenyang, Y.: Short-term photovoltaic power generation forecasting based on multivariable grey theory model with parameter optimiza-tion. In: Mathematical Problems in Engineering, pp. 1–9 (2017)
27. Ju-Long, D.: Control problems of grey systems. Syst. Control Lett. **5**, 288–294 (1982)
28. Koller, D.: Probabilistic Graphical Models: Principles and Techniques. The MIT Press, Cambridge (2009)
29. McLachlan, G., Krishnan, T.: The EM Algorithm and Extensions, 2nd edn. Wiley-Interscience press, New York (2008)
30. William, M.D.: A theoretical and practical implementation tutorial on topic modeling and gibbs sampling. In: Proceedings of the 49th Annual Meeting of the Association for Computational Linguistics: Human Language Technologies, pp. 642–647. Springer, Oregon (2011)
31. ASHRAE: ASHRAE Guideline 14: Measurement of Energy and Demand Savings, ASHRAE, Atlanta (2002)
32. Guillermo, E., Carlos, Á., Carlos, R., Manuel, A.: New artificial neural network prediction method for electrical consumption forecasting based on building end-uses. Energy Build. **43**, 3112–3119 (2011)

MAKE VIS

On the Challenges and Opportunities in Visualization for Machine Learning and Knowledge Extraction: A Research Agenda

Cagatay Turkay[1][✉], Robert Laramee[2], and Andreas Holzinger[3]

[1] GiCentre, Department of Computer Science, City, University of London, London, UK
`Cagatay.Turkay.1@city.ac.uk`
[2] Department of Computer Science, University of Swansea, Swansea, UK
`r.s.laramee@swansea.ac.uk`
[3] Holzinger Group, HCI-KDD, Institute for Medical Informatics/Statistics, Medical University Graz, Graz, Austria
`andreas.holzinger@hci-kdd.org`

Abstract. We describe a selection of challenges at the intersection of machine learning and data visualization and outline a subjective research agenda based on professional and personal experience. The unprecedented increase in the amount, variety and the value of data has been significantly transforming the way that scientific research is carried out and businesses operate. Within data science, which has emerged as a practice to enable this data-intensive innovation by gathering together and advancing the knowledge from fields such as statistics, machine learning, knowledge extraction, data management, and visualization, visualization plays a unique and maybe *the* ultimate role as an approach to facilitate the human and computer cooperation, and to particularly enable the analysis of diverse and heterogeneous data using complex computational methods where algorithmic results are challenging to interpret and operationalize. Whilst algorithm development is surely at the center of the whole pipeline in disciplines such as Machine Learning and Knowledge Discovery, it is visualization which ultimately makes the results accessible to the end user. Visualization thus can be seen as a mapping from arbitrarily high-dimensional abstract spaces to the lower dimensions and plays a central and critical role in interacting with machine learning algorithms, and particularly in interactive machine learning (iML) with including the human-in-the-loop. The central goal of the CD-MAKE VIS workshop is to spark discussions at this intersection of visualization, machine learning and knowledge discovery and bring together experts from these disciplines. This paper discusses a perspective on the challenges and opportunities in this integration of these discipline and presents a number of directions and strategies for further research.

Keywords: Visualization · Machine learning · Knowledge extraction

© IFIP International Federation for Information Processing 2017
Published by Springer International Publishing AG 2017. All Rights Reserved
A. Holzinger et al. (Eds.): CD-MAKE 2017, LNCS 10410, pp. 191–198, 2017.
DOI: 10.1007/978-3-319-66808-6_13

1   Introduction

The unprecedented increase in the amount, variety and the value of data has been significantly transforming the way that scientific research is carried out and businesses operate. Knowledge generated from data drives innovation in almost all application domains, including health, transport, cyber security, manufacturing, digital services, and also scientific domains such as biology, medicine, environmental and physical sciences, the humanities and social sciences to name a few [1]. The archived data, however, is becoming increasingly complex and heterogeneous, and making sense of such data collections is becoming increasingly challenging.

Algorithmic approaches are increasingly providing effective solutions to problems that are related to well-defined tasks such as classification or predictive modelling based on trend analysis to name a few [2]. However, there are several other problems where the objectives are much less well-defined – often leading to partial or uncertain computational results that require manual interventions from analysts to be useful, or to results that are so complex that interpretation is a barrier against their effective use. The field of visualization, and in particular visual analytics, is a discipline that is motivated by these complex problems that require a concerted effort from computational methods and the human analyst to be addressed [3]. Expert users have the domain knowledge to steer algorithmic power to where it is needed the most [4], and offer the capability and creativity to fine-tune computational results and turn them into *data-informed decisions* [5]. As a growing field, there are already several effective examples where the combination of visualisation and machine learning are being developed to offer novel solutions for data-intensive problems [1].

Visualization of machine learning results will become even more important in the future as with new European regulations, there emerges a need of interpretability of machine learning outcomes, which poses enormous challenges on the visualization, because machine learning techniques for data analysis can be basically seen as a problem of pattern recognition, and there is a (not so little) gap between data modeling and knowledge extraction. Machine learning models may be described in diverse ways, but to consider that some knowledge has been achieved from their description, cognitive factors of the users have to be considered. Even worse, such models can be useless unless they *can be* interpreted, and the process of human interpretation follows rules that go well beyond technical understanding. Consequently, interpretability is a paramount quality that machine learning methods should aim to achieve if they are to be applied for solving practical problems of our daily life [6].

In this position statement, we stress the importance of this merger between these two fields and present a mini-research agenda to spark and inform the discussions at the 2017 CD-MAKE VIS workshop. We present here a non-comprehensive but a representative sample of recent work, discuss opportunities in further research, and challenges in bringing these domains together.

2   A Few Examples of Visualization and Machine Learning Integration

Visualization is an important method of transforming the symbolic into the geometric, offers opportunities for discovering knowledge in data and fosters insight into data [7]. There are several examples for the importance of visualization in health, e.g. Otasek et al. [8] present work on Visual Data Mining (VDM), which is supported by interactive and scalable network visualization and analysis. Otasek et al. emphasize that knowledge discovery within complex data sets involves many workflows, including accurately representing many formats of source data, merging heterogeneous and distributed data sources, complex database searching, integrating results from multiple computational and mathematical analyses, and effectively visualizing properties and results. Mueller et al. [9] demonstrate the successful application of data Glyphs in a disease analyser for the analysis of big medical data sets with automatic validation of the data mapping, selection of subgroups within histograms and a visual comparison of the value distributions.

A good example for the catenation of visualization with ML is clustering: Clustering is a descriptive task to identify homogeneous groups of data objects based on the dimensions (i.e. values of the attributes). Clustering methods are often subject to other systems, for example to reduce the possibility of recommender systems (e.g. Tag-recommender on Youtube videos [10]); for example clustering of large high-dimensional gene expression data sets has widespread application in -omics [11]. Unfortunately, the underlying structure of these natural data sets is often fuzzy, and the computational identification of data clusters generally requires (human) expert knowledge about cluster number and geometry.

The high-dimensionality of data is a huge problem in health informatics - but in many other domains - and the curse of dimensionality is a critical factor for clustering: With increasing dimensionality the volume of the space increases so fast that the available data becomes sparse, hence it becomes impossible to find reliable clusters; also the concept of distance becomes less precise as the number of dimensions grows, since the distance between any two points in a given data set converges; moreover, different clusters might be found in different sub spaces, so a global filtering of attributes is also not sufficient. Given that large number of attributes, it is likely that some attributes are correlated, therefore clusters might exist in arbitrarily oriented affinity sub spaces. Moreover, high-dimensional data likely includes *irrelevant* features, which may obscure to find the relevant ones, thus increases the danger of modeling artifacts - issues which are simply not true. The problem is that we are confronted with subjective similarity functions; there are a lot of examples of subjective grouping in our daily life (e.g. cars are perceived differently).

Subspace clustering problems are hard, because for the grouping very different characteristics can be used: highly subjective and context specific. What is recognized as comfort for end-users of individual systems, can be applied in scientific research for the interactive exploration of high-dimensional data sets [12]. Consequently, iML-approaches can be beneficial to support finding solutions in hard biomedical problems [13].

Humans are good in comparison for the determination of similarities and dissimilarities - described by nonlinear multidimensional scaling (MDS) models [14]. MDS models represent similarity relations between entities as a geometric model that consists of a set of points within a metric space. The output of an MDS routine is a geometric model of the data, with each object of the data set represented as a point in n-dimensional space. In such operations, the human intervention can help in generating semantically relevant projections or in curating new "bespoke" projection axes [15].

A relatively new technique in that respect is "t-SNE" [16] that visualizes high-dimensional data by giving each data point a location in a two or three-dimensional map. t-SNE was tested with many different data sets and showed much better results than e.g. Isomap [17] or Locally Linear Embedding [18].

Visualizing properties of t-SNE is discussed by Martin Wattenberg and Fernanda Viegas in their recent keynote talk at the EuroVis 2017 Conference in Baracelone, Spain, "Visualization: The Secret Weapon of Machine Learning." See Fig. 1.

Fig. 1. The Keynote Talk delivered by Martin Wattenberg and Fernanda Viegas at the EuroVis Conference in 2017, Barcelona, Spain. This excellent and informative talk is archived and can be viewed at the following url: https://youtu.be/E70lG9-HGEM

The above discussion only scratches the surface in this multidisciplinary research area, for more comprehensive selection of work, good starting points are review papers by Endert et al. [1] and Sacha et al. [19].

3   Challenges and Opportunities for Research

In this section we identify a short list of potential future research directions that can build on a synergy between these disciplines.

Comprehensive analysis of several disjoint data sources: With the advent of new data generation and collection mechanisms, analysts have now the chance to work with not only a single data set but with several data sets coming from diverse channels with different characteristics [20]. In addition to data that is available within their own organisations, they also have access to extremely rich, open data repositories that can add significant value to their analyses. Analysts are often advised to be to be "magnetic" towards new data sources in their everyday practices and integrate a large variety of information sources to generate valuable insight [21]. Analysts will benefit significantly from models that can learn from multiple data sources, however, existing tools are often developed to work with a single, well-defined data source. Making sense of such diverse information sources that are not even physically linked requires methods where "semantic" links between the data sources are built exploratively and visualization can play an important role to facilitate such cross-dataset analysis.

Developing balanced interaction models for human-machine collaboration: Interactive data analysis solutions rely on the effective elicitation of expert knowledge in steering the computational methods whilst dealing with ill-defined problems. However, interaction is a costly operation and experts are often in need of approaches that provide them reliable solutions quickly and accurately [22]. In order to develop effective human-in-the-loop systems [23], there is a need to strike the right balance between computation and human initiative. Certain, often well-defined, tasks are better suited for computation and tasks can be broken down into smaller sub-tasks where little user intervention is needed and user's role is then to harmonize the various observations made through these sub-components. Such an approach can make these systems more effective and utilizes expert's knowledge for tasks where it matters the most. Designing such systems, however, requires an in-depth understanding of tasks, and rigorous user testing.

"Learning" the user: An area where machine learning models can enhance interactive data analysis is through methods that are trained on user interaction data. Users interact with interactive systems in distinctive ways and often the successful execution of an analysis session depends on the accurate identification of *user intent* [1]. Algorithms can be trained on user activity logs to understand the user better and can offer "personalized" analytical recommendations to improve the data analysis process.

Visual storytelling for enhanced interpretation and algorithmic transparency: An emerging trend in visualization is the use of storytelling techniques to communicate concepts effectively [24]. As algorithms get more and more complex and tend to carry black-box characteristics, interpreting an algorithmic outcome is increasingly gaining importance. Recent examples by the Google Big Picture team[1] or promising innovative publications such as Distill.pub[2] are demonstrating how an effective use of visualization can help unravel algorithms and make them more accessible for wider audiences and also help in educational purposes. However, examples so far are often designed case-by-case basis and further research is needed to develop guidelines, best-practices and a systematic characterization of the role and scope of visualization and interaction.

The list above highlights some of the emerging and core opportunities for joint research projects, however, the field is open for innovation and it is expected to evidence the emergence of new ideas and topics as the discipline matures.

4   A Potential Road-Map for Bridging the Communities

Visualization and machine learning communities are currently disjoint communities with limited overlap between the researchers actively contributing to both domains.

There are several recent initiatives, including the yearly CD-MAKE conference, or the MAKE-Journal [25] that aims to bring the two communities closer. The recently organized Dagstuhl events on *"Bridging Information Visualization with Machine Learning"* [26,27] are solid efforts to bring together researchers work on joint projects. There is now a machine learning tutorial at EuroVis[3] conference, however, more presence from the visualization domain within Machine Learning events, such as NIPS[4], ICML[5], or KDD[6] is needed to transfer state-of-the-art research in visualization over to the Machine Learning domain and vice versa. How important this is can be inferred by a recent discussion during the Google's Vision 2016 talks[7], where Google's director of product, Aparna Chennapragada emphasized that *"the UI must be proportional to AI"* .

5   Conclusion

This position paper discussed some of the emerging trends, opportunities, and challenges in the merger of visualization, machine learning and knowledge discovery domains. As evidenced by the increasing activities and recent publications in the area, there is great potential for impactful future research that is likely to transform the ways that data-intensive solutions and services are designed and

---

[1] https://research.google.com/bigpicture/.
[2] http://distill.pub/.
[3] http://mlvis2017.hiit.fi/.
[4] https://nips.cc/.
[5] https://2017.icml.cc/.
[6] http://www.kdd.org/.
[7] https://www.youtube.com/watch?v=Rnm83GqgqPE.

developed. We identify a number of challenges to spark further discussions and research, however, the presented list is far from being comprehensive and reflects a biased overview of the authors. This multidisciplinary research field is open to several other novel problems and developments that can significantly contribute to the societal and academic impact of the existing research carried out in both domains. As it stands now, the biggest barrier to such multidisciplinary research is the limited number of joint venues to *bridge* the two communities and a limited interest in both communities. There is, however, increasing awareness and appreciation of the ongoing research in both fields and it is highly likely that this merger of visualization and machine learning will be attracting further attention.

References

1. Endert, A., Ribarsky, W., Turkay, C., William Wong, B.W., Nabney, I., Blanco, I.D., Rossi, F.: The state of the art in integrating machine learning into visual analytics. Comput. Graph. Forum (2017). http://onlinelibrary.wiley.com/doi/10.1111/cgf.13092/full

2. Marsland, S.: Machine Learning: An Algorithmic Perspective. CRC Press, Boca Raton (2015)

3. Keim, D.A., Mansmann, F., Schneidewind, J., Thomas, J., Ziegler, H.: Visual analytics: scope and challenges. In: Simoff, S.J., Böhlen, M.H., Mazeika, A. (eds.) Visual Data Mining. LNCS, vol. 4404, pp. 76–90. Springer, Heidelberg (2008). doi:10.1007/978-3-540-71080-6_6

4. Williams, M., Munzner, T.: Steerable, progressive multidimensional scaling. In: IEEE Symposium on Information Visualization, INFOVIS 2004, pp. 57–64. IEEE (2004)

5. Turkay, C., Slingsby, A., Lahtinen, K., Butt, S., Dykes, J.: Supporting theoretically-grounded model building in the social sciences through interactive visualisation. Neurocomputing (2017). http://www.sciencedirect.com/science/article/pii/S0925231217307610

6. Vellido, A., Martín-Guerrero, J.D., Lisboa, P.J.: Making machine learning models interpretable. In: ESANN - European Symposium on Artificial Neural Network. vol 12. pp.163–172 (2012)

7. Ward, M., Grinstein, G., Keim, D.: Interactive Data Visualization: Foundations, Techniques, and Applications. AK Peters, Ltd, Massachusetts (2010)

8. Holzinger, A., Jurisica, I.: Knowledge discovery and data mining in biomedical informatics: the future is in integrative, interactive machine learning solutions. In: Holzinger, A., Jurisica, I. (eds.) Interactive Knowledge Discovery and Data Mining in Biomedical Informatics. LNCS, vol. 8401, pp. 1–18. Springer, Heidelberg (2014). doi:10.1007/978-3-662-43968-5_1

9. Mueller, H., Reihs, R., Zatloukal, K., Holzinger, A.: Analysis of biomedical data with multilevel glyphs. BMC Bioinform. **15**, S5 (2014)

10. Toderici, G., Aradhye, H., Paşca, M., Sbaiz, L., Yagnik, J.: Finding meaning on youtube: tag recommendation and category discovery. In: IEEE Conference on Computer Vision and Pattern Recognition (CVPR 2010), pp. 3447–3454. IEEE (2010)

11. Sturm, W., Schreck, T., Holzinger, A., Ullrich, T.: Discovering medical knowledge using visual analytics - a survey on methods for systems biology and omics data. In Bühler, K., Linsen, L., John, N.W. (eds.): Eurographics Workshop on Visual Computing for Biology and Medicine, Eurographics EG, pp. 71–81 (2015)

12. Müller, E., Assent, I., Krieger, R., Jansen, T., Seidl, T.: Morpheus: interactive exploration of subspace clustering. In: Proceedings of the 14th ACM SIGKDD International Conference on Knowledge Discovery and Data Mining KDD 2008, ACM, pp. 1089–1092 (2008)

13. Hund, M., Sturm, W., Schreck, T., Ullrich, T., Keim, D., Majnaric, L., Holzinger, A.: Analysis of patient groups and immunization results based on subspace clustering. In: Guo, Y., Friston, K., Aldo, F., Hill, S., Peng, H. (eds.) BIH 2015. LNCS, vol. 9250, pp. 358–368. Springer, Cham (2015). doi:10.1007/978-3-319-23344-4_35

14. Shepard, R.N.: The analysis of proximities: Multidimensional scaling with an unknown distance function. Psychometrika **27**, 125–140 (1962)

15. Kim, H., Choo, J., Park, H., Endert, A.: Interaxis: steering scatterplot axes via observation-level interaction. IEEE Trans. Vis. Comput. Graph. **22**, 131–140 (2016)

16. Maaten, L.v.d., Hinton, G.: Visualizing data using t-sne. J. Mach. Learn. Res. **9**, 2579–2605 (2008)

17. Tenenbaum, J.B., de Silva, V., Langford, J.C.: A global geometric framework for nonlinear dimensionality reduction. Science **290**, 2319–2323 (2000)

18. Roweis, S.T., Saul, L.K.: Nonlinear dimensionality reduction by locally linear embedding. Science **290**, 2323–2326 (2000)

19. Sacha, D., Zhang, L., Sedlmair, M., Lee, J.A., Peltonen, J., Weiskopf, D., North, S.C., Keim, D.A.: Visual interaction with dimensionality reduction: A structured literature analysis. IEEE Trans. Vis. Comput. Graph. **23**, 241–250 (2017)

20. Kehrer, J., Hauser, H.: Visualization and visual analysis of multifaceted scientific data: A survey. IEEE Trans. Vis. Comput. Graph. **19**, 495–513 (2013)

21. Cohen, J., Dolan, B., Dunlap, M., Hellerstein, J.M., Welton, C.: Mad skills: new analysis practices for big data. Proc. VLDB Endowment **2**, 1481–1492 (2009)

22. Yi, J.S., ah Kang, Y., Stasko, J.: Toward a deeper understanding of the role of interaction in information visualization. IEEE Trans. Vis. Comput. Graph. **13**, 1224–1231 (2007)

23. Holzinger, A.: Interactive machine learning for health informatics: when do we need the human-in-the-loop? Springer Brain Inform. (BRIN) **3**, 119–131 (2016)

24. Kosara, R., Mackinlay, J.: Storytelling: the next step for visualization. Computer **46**, 44–50 (2013)

25. Holzinger, A.: Introduction to machine learning & knowledge extraction (make). Mach. Learn. Knowl. Extr. **1**, 1–20 (2017)

26. Keim, D.A., Rossi, F., Seidl, T., Verleysen, M., Wrobel, S.: Information visualization, visual data mining and machine learning (Dagstuhl Seminar 12081). Dagstuhl Rep. **2**, 58–83 (2012)

27. Keim, D.A., Munzner, T., Rossi, F., Verleysen, M.: Bridging information visualization with machine learning (Dagstuhl Seminar 15101). Dagstuhl Rep. **5**, 1–27 (2015)

Quantitative Externalization of Visual Data Analysis Results Using Local Regression Models

Krešimir Matković[1(✉)], Hrvoje Abraham[2], Mario Jelović[2], and Helwig Hauser[3]

[1] VRVis Research Center, Vienna, Austria
`Matkovic@VRVis.at`
[2] AVL-AST d.o.o., Zagreb, Croatia
`{Hrvoje.Abraham,Mario.Jelovic}@AVL.com`
[3] University of Bergen, Bergen, Norway
`Helwig.Hauser@UiB.no`

Abstract. Both interactive visualization and computational analysis methods are useful for data studies and an integration of both approaches is promising to successfully combine the benefits of both methodologies. In interactive data exploration and analysis workflows, we need successful means to quantitatively externalize results from data studies, amounting to a particular challenge for the usually qualitative visual data analysis. In this paper, we propose a hybrid approach in order to quantitatively externalize valuable findings from interactive visual data exploration and analysis, based on local linear regression models. The models are built on user-selected subsets of the data, and we provide a way of keeping track of these models and comparing them. As an additional benefit, we also provide the user with the numeric model coefficients. Once the models are available, they can be used in subsequent steps of the workflow. A model-based optimization can then be performed, for example, or more complex models can be reconstructed using an inversion of the local models. We study two datasets to exemplify the proposed approach, a meteorological data set for illustration purposes and a simulation ensemble from the automotive industry as an actual case study.

Keywords: Interactive visual data exploration and analysis · Local regression models · Externalization of analysis results

1 Introduction

In the currently evolving information age, both data exploration and analysis become increasingly important for a large variety of applications and both interactive visualization as well as computational methods (from statistics, machine learning, etc.) establish themselves as indispensable approaches to access valuable information in large and complex datasets. With interactive visualization, the analyst is included in the knowledge crystallization loop and thus also open-ended and ill-defined exploration and analysis questions can be investigated,

A. Holzinger et al. (Eds.): CD-MAKE 2017, LNCS 10410, pp. 199–218, 2017.
DOI: 10.1007/978-3-319-66808-6_14

often also on the basis of data with certain deficiencies (noise, errors, etc.). With computational data analysis, exact quantitative results can be achieved, based on advanced and fast algorithms that also often are completely automated. In visual analytics, one key question is whether we can successfully combine both approaches to integrate the mutual advantages in hybrid solutions, based both on interactive visualization and on computational data analysis.

One special challenge with interactive visual data exploration and analysis is the question of how to effectively and efficiently externalize valuable findings such that following steps in an application workflow can successfully build on them. Only very few works in visualization research [17,27,32] have so far focused on this question and suggested selected solutions. In particular the quantitative externalization of findings from qualitative interactive visual data analysis is genuinely difficult, while many workflows clearly would benefit from solutions that could pass on results in quantitative form—think, for example, of an analyst, who studies some relevant data curves in a graph view and wishes to use their inclination (quantitatively) in a subsequent work process.

In this paper, we now propose a new solution for quantitatively externalizing findings from interactive visual data exploration and analysis. We describe a method that enables the analyst to interactively measure certain data relations in a visualization. This is realized by locally modeling selected data relations of interest with a linear data model and then externalizing the model parameters from this process. For several reasons, most importantly including their stability properties and their simplicity, we focus on linear local models in this work— clearly, many other, non-linear models could be considered for this purpose, as well. While linear models often are too simple for global data approximations, they often provide good results locally. In order to fit the linear models locally to selected data, we use several different regression methods, depending on which of these methods achieves the best results. We present our solution in the context of a system with coordinated multiple views that enables such an externalization through interactive means.

In our solution, we assume the user to be involved in an iterative, interactive data exploration and analysis process. During the visual data drill-down, the user instantiates locally a linear modeling process of selected subsets of data. The corresponding model parameters are then returned back to the user in a quantitative form. Models and data are also shown together in the visualization. In this way, the user can easily interpret the findings, and, since the modeling results are available explicitly, rank the findings in order to choose those to use subsequently.

Already in 1965, John Tukey pointed out that combining the power of a graphical presentation with automatic computer analysis would enable more successful solutions [31]. Later, Anscombe [1] illustrated how important it is to also see the data, in addition to considering statistical measures. Nonetheless, a recent study by Kandogan et al. [11] explains that still data analysts do not regularly use visualization due to a lack of means to quantify analysis results.

The main contribution of this paper is thus not a new visual metaphor—we use standard views. Instead, we integrate solutions from machine learning into visualization (modeling by regression) in order to quantitatively externalize valuable findings from interactive data studies. We also suggest to keep track of the computed models and we provide a fast and intuitive way to instantiate new models in the visualization. This way, a powerful combination of automatic and interactive data analysis is realized, combining valuable advantages from both approaches, i.e., the quantitative results from regression modeling, and the user-steered local modeling from the visualization. The quantitative externalization of otherwise qualitative results makes them easier to describe and rank, while the visualization is useful to spot and understand shortcomings and imprecisions of the automatically fitted models.

In this paper, we focus on complex data, which, in addition to scalar independent and dependent data, also contains families of curves, i.e., time-dependent attributes. We deploy a coordinated multiple views system, which supports on-the-fly data derivation and aggregation as an important basis for our approach. The interactive approach makes modeling very quick and efficient and also easier accessible for domain experts, who are not experts in machine learning or statistics. In the following, we first introduce the new approach along with a relatively simple meteorology example (for illustration purposes), before we then evaluate it informally based on an application case in the automotive industry.

2   Related Work

Our research is related to several fields. Interactive visual analysis (IVA) facilitates knowledge discovery in complex datasets by utilizing a tight feedback loop of computation, visualization and user interaction [13,14,29]. IVA provides an interactive and iterative data exploration and analysis framework, where the user guides the analysis [26], supported by a variety of computational analysis tools. The interactive visual analysis exploits human vision, experience, and intuition in order to analyze complex data. Tam et al. identify the potential of so called "soft knowledge", which is only available in human-centric approaches [28], including the ability to consider consequences of a decision and to infer associations from common sense.

The interactive exploration process is mostly qualitative. Recent research, however, focuses increasingly on quantitative aspects. Radoš et al. [24] structure the brushing space and enhance linked views using descriptive statistics. Kehrer et al. [12] integrate statistical aggregates along selected, independent data dimensions in a framework of coordinated, multiple views. Brushing particular statistics, the analyst can investigate data characteristics such as trends and outliers. Haslett et al. [6] introduce the ability to show the average of the points that are currently selected by the brush.

Lampe and Hauser [17] support the explanation of data by rapidly drafting, fitting and quantifying model prototypes in visualization space. Their method is related to the statistical concept of de-trending, where data that behaves according to a model is de-emphasized, leaving only the residuals (potentially outliers and/or other model flaws) for further inspection. Piringer et al. [23] introduce a system for the visual evaluation of regression models for simulation data. They focus on the evaluation of the provided models, while we focus on the description of data relations by means of local regression models. We exploit on-the-fly data aggregation as described by Konyha et al. [15].

Shao et al. [25] present new research on combing regression modeling and interactive visual analysis. They build models based on selected subsets of data, as we do here, but they depict them on-the-fly during interaction. Neither do they provide a system for any house-keeping of models, or for the comparison of models. They also do only depict modeling results visually, while we provide models coefficients as well as quality-of-fit indicators.

In this work, we focus on an engineering example, while complex data is also common in other domains. Holzinger [7] introduces a concept of interactive machine learning for complex medical data, where a human-in-the-loop approach is deployed. The approach has been evaluated as a proof-of-concept study [8] and as a means to analyze patient groups based on high-dimensional information per patient [10].

In this paper, we make use of the common least squares, the Lasso, and the Huber regression models, described, for example, in standard literature on regression modeling [4].

3   Data Description and Problem Statement

In this paper, we focus on complex data in the form of records that contain different types of attributes. In contrast to the conventional approach, where attributes are scalar values (numerical or categorical), we also address complex attributes, i.e., curves (time-dependent attributes). Such a data organization is more natural for many cases in science and engineering.

We illustrate our approach based on a simple data set describing meteorological stations in the United States [21]. Global summaries per month are used, containing the statistics of 55 climatological variables. Each record corresponds to a single station with the following scalar attributes: longitude, latitude, elevation, state, and station name. Further, we also study two curve attributes: the mean temperatures per month throughout the year and the according mean precipitation values. Figure 1 illustrates the data. Figure 2 shows all stations as points in a scatterplot and temperature and precipitation curves in two curve views. The curve view depicts all curves plotted over each other. A density mapping is deployed and areas where curves are more dense can be seen, accordingly.

We differentiate independent from dependent attributes and some of our dependent attributes are curves. In our data model, the independent part of a data point is described as $\mathbf{x} = (x_1, \ldots, x_m)^\top$, i.e., a point in $\mathbb{R}^m$, and the corresponding dependent output part $\mathbf{y} = (y_1, \ldots, y_n)^\top$, i.e., a point in $\mathbb{R}^n$, where m can be seen as the number of control parameters and n as the number of outputs. This assumes that there is a function $\mathbf{S}$ that maps inputs to outputs.

This function can be a numerical simulation or a measurement method:

$$\mathbf{y} = \mathbf{S}(\mathbf{x}) \tag{1}$$

In the case of an ensemble of simulations or measurements, we then have a set of pairs: $E = \{(\mathbf{x}_j, \mathbf{y}_j)\}$. As indicated above, any y_i can also be a curve $y_i(t)$, given at a particular sequence of t-values.

Interactive visual analysis is a proven method for analyzing such data. However, if we want to quantify and compare results, we have to deploy quantitative analysis. If we, for example, assume that there is a correlation between the maximum yearly temperatures and the latitude of the weather station, we easily can show a corresponding scatterplot and see if there is such a relation. Figure 3 shows such a scatterplot. But how can we communicate our findings? And moreover, once we can quantify it, how can we compare it with other findings?

We thus propose to locally fit linear regression models for user-selected subsets of data, and then to return the model values to the user. This way, the findings are quantified and externalized. Accordingly, they can be also compared, the best ones can be identified and then used in subsequent tasks. In fact, there are many relevant application scenarios, where a model of the data (or a data subset) is needed. If a process has to be optimized, for example, a regression model can be very useful. Further, if we want to reconstruct our simulation or measurement, i.e., find inputs which correspond to a desired output, a corresponding linear model can easily be inverted and we thus can easily derive target input values. All these operations assume a model which is a good representation of the data (globally and/or locally). Our approach makes such analysis tasks possible, combining the best from interactive and from automatic data analysis.

ID	Latitude	Longitude	Elevation	State	station Name	Temp (t)	Prec (t)
11084	31.0581	-87.0547	25.9	AL	REWTON 3 SSE	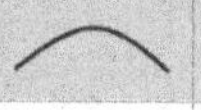	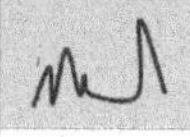
12813	30.5467	-87.8808	7	AL	AIRHOPE 2 NE		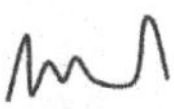
13160	32.8347	-88.1342	38.1	AL	AINESVILLE LOCK	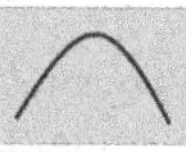	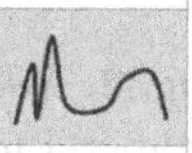
...	...	...	...	...	...	...	...

Fig. 1. Structure of complex data, including also curves as attributes. Temperatures and precipitation values are stored as functions of time. The curves in the table are only symbolic, the actual curves have different shapes.

4 Interactive Regression Modeling

We deploy linear regression models to quantify local analysis results. In order to build a regression model we first extract scalar aggregates from the curve

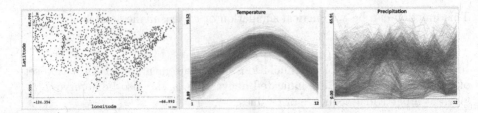

Fig. 2. A visualization of the illustrative, meteorological data. The scatterplot on the left mimics a map of the weather stations in the United States. The curve views show the monthly mean temperatures and precipitation values for each station. The temperature curves are quite similar in their shape (cold winters, warm summers), while the precipitation curves exhibit more variation

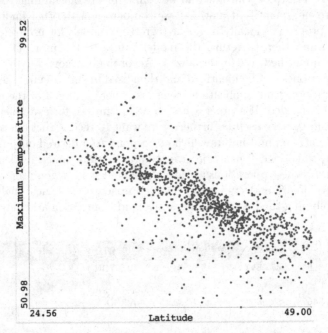

Fig. 3. A scatterplot showing the relation between latitude and the maximum monthly temperature value, i.e., the maximum of the temperature curves shown in Fig. 2. As expected, southern stations have higher temperatures.

attributes. The attributes of interest strongly depend on the analyst's tasks. Accordingly, there isn't any predefined set of attributes which would be valid for all data sets and all cases, but the interactive, on-demand derivation of such aggregates proves useful instead [15].

In the following, we first summarize the models we use and then we illustrate the main idea using the meteorological data set and simple scalar aggregates. A more complex case which includes complex aggregates is described in the case study section.

4.1   Linear Regression Models

The most standard linear regression model that we use is the common least squares method, as proposed already by Legendre in 1805 [18] as well as by Gauss in 1809 [5]. Both applied it to astronomical observations in order to determine the orbits of planets around the Sun.

The objective function for a dataset with N M-dimensional inputs x_{ij}, output vector y_i and the regression coefficients vector $\mathbf{w} = (w_0, w_1, \ldots, w_M)^\top$ is

$$F_{LS}(\mathbf{w}) = RSS(\mathbf{w}) = \sum_{i=1}^{N} \left(y_i - w_0 - \sum_{j=1}^{M} w_j x_{ij} \right)^2. \tag{2}$$

This objective function is also known as the Residual Sum of Squares or just as $RSS(\mathbf{w})$.

Lasso regression, being in principle very similar to the least squares method, adds an additional constraint to the minimization of the objective function in order to limit the extent of the fitting coefficients:

$$F_{Lasso}(\mathbf{w}) = RSS(\mathbf{w}), \ \sum_{j=1}^{M} |w_j| \le t. \tag{3}$$

It was named and analyzed in detail by Tibshirani in 1996 [30], after Breiman's influential paper in 1995 [2], introducing the *nonnegative garrote* method, and Frank and Friedman's 1993 paper [3], where the same constraint is considered as one form of the *generalized ridge penalty*, but without any analysis and results.

The Lasso-regularization is controlled via tuning parameter t and for a sufficiently large t the method is equivalent to the least squares approach. Generally, Lasso regression ensures a more stable result for some classes of base functions, such as polynomials, and it can be also used for feature selection as it tends to reduce the regression coefficients of less important inputs to zero (or close to 0). For this reason it is often used in the analysis of multidimensional data, machine learning, etc.

Another interesting property is that it also can be used to determine minimal models when the number of regression parameters is greater than the number of input cases, e.g., fitting a 10th degree polynomial to just 6 data points, a case in which the least squares method would just return one of many non-unique solutions (or none at all). It is important to notice, however, that the method is not scale-invariant, so the data has to be normalized in a certain way (*standardized*) to get useful results.

Huber regression follows a similar approach, but divides the residuals

$$r_i = y_i - w_0 - \sum_{j=1}^{M} w_j x_{ij} \tag{4}$$

into two classes: *small* and *big* residuals. For some given parameter δ, a quadratic function is used for *small* residuals ($|r_<|/\sigma \le \delta$), and linear absolute values for *big* residuals ($|r_>|/\sigma > \delta$), where σ is determined during the minimization together with the regression coefficients w_j:

$$F_{Huber}(\mathbf{w}, \sigma) = \sum \left(\left(\frac{r_\le}{\sigma} \right)^2 + \left| \frac{r_>}{\sigma} \right| \right). \tag{5}$$

This approach was introduced by Huber in 1964 [9] and it ensures that a small number of outliers does not have a big influence on the result (as they would if the quadratic form would be used for them, as well). Due to the reduced sensitivity to outliers, Huber regression belongs to the important class of *robust regressors*.

The fitting score of a regression model is measured by the determination coefficient R^2, defined as

$$R^2 = 1 - \frac{u}{v}, \quad u = \sum_{i=1}^{N}(y_i - z_i)^2, \quad v = \sum_{i=1}^{N}(y_i - \overline{y})^2 \tag{6}$$

where y_i, $\overline{y}$, and z_i are the dataset outputs, the mean of the outputs, and the model-predicted values, respectively. The highest possible score is 1. When the model returns just the output mean $\overline{y}$, the score is 0; and bad models get (arbitrarily) negative scores.

4.2   Interactive Modeling

It is essential to enable the user to interactively select scalar aggregates during the analysis. In our solution, it is anytime possible to compute new aggregates and to thereby extend the data table by additional synthetic data attributes. Often, it is not fully clear in the first place which aggregates indeed are most useful and all scalar aggregates that we describe in this paper were computed on the fly during the data exploration and analysis. This solution brings important flexibility and reduces the pressure on the analyst to define all necessary aggregates in advance. In the following, we illustrate our main idea by selecting three basic aggregates, i.e., the minimum, the maximum, and the mean of the temperature and of the precipitation curves. Accordingly, our data table then has six additional scalar columns.

A reasonably compact regression model, which successfully captures all data relations for all weather stations across the entire United States, relating longitudes and latitudes (as independent attributes) and the six scaler aggregates of the temperatures and the precipitation values (as dependent data), would be very challenging to construct (if possible at all). Also, one needs to assume that there are important additional factors with an influence on the temperature and precipitation values (like elevation, etc.). Accordingly, we simply dismiss the idea of creating a global model, in particular it is clear that we cannot expect to find a useful linear global model. Instead, we focus on local modeling of selected data subsets, providing also the possibility to select which regression model to select. In a regression model specification dialog we set independent and dependent variables (see Fig. 4), and three different models are computed automatically.

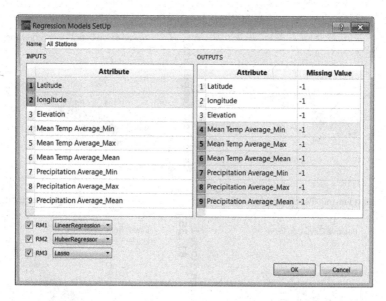

Fig. 4. A model is created for all data or for a subset which is specified by means of brushing. The user enters the name of the subset (*All Stations* here), and specifies which attributes are considered as independent (*Latitude and Longitude* here), and which are dependent. Further, the user can select up to three models to be built.

Regression Models												Output 0			Output 1	
New Model	Name	Model	Input Columns	Output Columns and QoF												
Clear Tables			1	2	14		15	16	17	18	19	1	2	Intercept	1	2
	All Stations	Linear			0.719		0.565	0.782	0.671	0.35	0.544	86.8	-1.88	-0.172	102	-0.8
		Huber			0.679		0.556	0.777	0.669	0.334	0.508	103	-2.06	-0.0642	100	-0.8
		Lasso			0.719		0.564	0.781	0.671	0.35	0.544	85.8	-1.83	-0.164	101	-0.8

Fig. 5. A part of the user interface which shows the regression models' parameters. For each output column the overall quality of fit measure—fitting score R^2—is depicted. Further, for each output column (dialog is cropped in this figure) the values of the coefficients of the models are shown. This way, the user can compare multiple models. This output is then the starting point for any subsequent use of the models.

The results of the computation are depicted in two ways. On the one hand they are shown in a table and on the other hand they can be also visualized. The table specifies the model name, input parameters, and output parameters. Further, we show the fitting score R^2 for each output parameter, and the intercept and linear coefficients for each of input parameters and for every output parameter fit (see Fig. 5). In contrast to some interactive applications, which do not offer a way to keep the data about the models, we keep the table as long as it is not explicitly deleted. By doing so, we make it possible for the user to compare different models, and to chose the best one for subsequent processing.

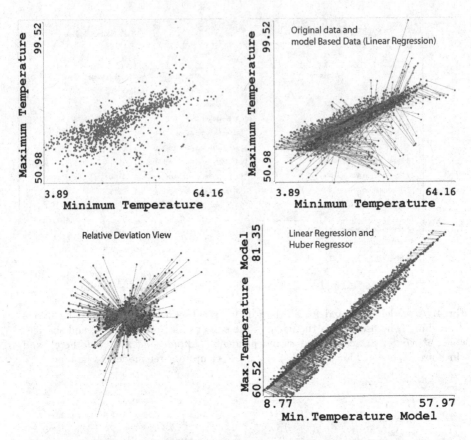

Fig. 6. Visualization for model evaluation. The scatterplot in the top left corner shows the minimum and the maximum temperatures for all stations. The top right view shows the same data in blue, and the vales computed using the linear regression in orange. Corresponding points are connected to visualize deviations. The bottom left view shows relative deviations only (imagine all blue points at the origin). The bottom right view compares two models, here linear regression and a Huber model. (Color figure online)

In particular, the findings are also externalized in this way. The different models are computed using different subsets of data, and different modeling methods.

The quality-of-fit measure alone is often not sufficient to evaluate the models. It gives a good hint on model precision, but visualization can revel much more insight here. This is especially true for Huber and other robust regression models as the influence of outliers and the definition of *good* and *bad* heavily depend on the dataset structure and the context.

In order to visualize the results, we use a modified scatterplot which shows original data points and the corresponding points, computed using a model, at the same time. The points' color differ, and we also show thin connecting lines between corresponding points. If the analyst is interested in relative error values, both for visualization and for interaction, we also can show relative deviations by placing all original points in the origin. In addition, the same technique can be used to compare different regression models with each other. Figure 6 shows different visualizations of the computed models. The top-left scatterplot shows the original data (minimum vs. maximum temperatures of all meteorological stations also shown in Fig. 2). The top-right scatterplot shows the same data in blue and temperatures as computed using a linear regression model in orange. In an ideal case the points would perfectly coincide. In our case, however, large deviations are visible as expected. The view in the bottom-left shows relative deviations only—all blue points are aligned in the origin, and the orange points show the relative deviation for each station—we can see certain directions of particularly large errors. The bottom-right figure depicts how a Huber regression model (blue points) differs from linear regression (orange points). The data shown in the table in Fig. 5 represent the same models. Obviously, there are multiple ways to visualize model accuracy. After long discussions with a domain expert, and after considering several options, we agreed to use these modified scatterplots. On the one hand, our users are used to scatterplots, and on the other hand, we are also able to meet main requirements posed by the domain, i.e., to show how models differ from original data, to see the error characteristics, and to visually compare different model results. We plan to extend the number of compared items to more then two in the future, expecting that we would need a more formal evaluation of such a design then, also.

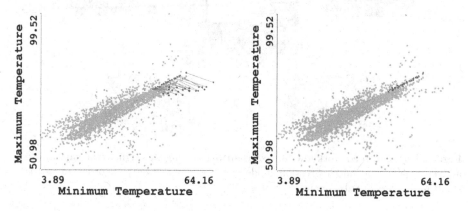

Fig. 7. Original points (in blue) and fitted points (in orange) for all Florida stations. The scatterplot on the left shows the points fitted using a global regression model, and the scatterplot on the right shows the points fitted using the model created for the Florida stations only. The local model, as expected, provides a much better fit. (Color figure online)

Instead of aiming at a global model for all the data, we focus on modeling parts of the data with local models (and considering a collection of them instead of one global model). In a way, this is related to piece-wise modeling, as for example with splines. One important aspect of our solution is the interactive instantiation and placement of local models. The user simply brushes a subset of data points in a view, activates the modeling dialog, and the models are computed and integrated, accordingly.

Figure 7, for example, shows all meteorological stations in Florida. The left scatterplot shows the model computed for all points—only the Florida stations are highlighted. The right scatterplot shows a linear regression model which is computed for the stations in Florida only. As weather characteristics are comparably similar across the state, the local regression model represents the data much better. Now that we have a well-fitted model for Florida, we could easily use it to estimate temperatures or precipitation values in other locations in Florida, or we could invert it, and find locations for desired temperatures and precipitation values. Note that we do all modeling using the scalar aggregates of the temperature and the precipitation curves. Clearly, we can also show the original curves in order to check the models in more detail.

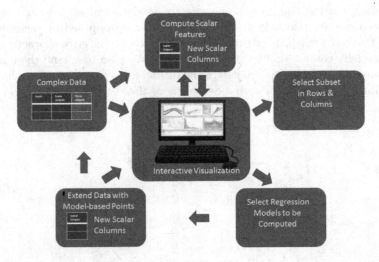

Fig. 8. The suggested workflow for externalizing findings. A tight interplay of interactive visualization and regression model building is necessary in order to use the resulting models in subsequent processes.

This simple example illustrates the suggested workflow for interactive local modeling of complex data, also illustrated in Fig. 8, that unfolds as an iterative and interactive visual analytics process, where the user can initiate a computation of new features whenever needed, and the computation of new regression models for selected subsets of data at any time. The visualization, depicted in the center of the diagram, is an essential part, and it is used as the control mechanism for all analysis steps—all steps are initiated from the visualization, and all results are then visible to the user in return. Importantly, this workflow now includes that valuable findings are explicitly described in terms of the

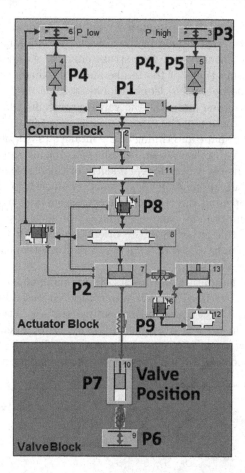

Fig. 9. The simulation model for the computation of the simulation ensemble. The control parameters are shown in red next to the corresponding elements. The output values are indicated in blue. (Color figure online)

parameters (coefficients) of all computed models. The visualization also provides essential means to compare and evaluate the individual models.

Along with our research, we implemented this new workflow in ComVis [19], a visual analytics system based on coordinated multiple views. Regression modeling is realized on the basis of scikit-learn [22], a Python library for machine learning by calling the respective methods in scikit-learn package from ComVis.

5   Case Study

In the following, we present a case study from the automotive simulation domain. We used our new interactive local modeling solution to analyze a Variable Valve

Actuation (VVA) system for an automotive combustion engine. Optimizing VVA solutions is an active research field in the automotive industry and it is closely related to the development of new four-stroke engines. A precise control of the opening and the closing times of the intake and the exhaust valves is essential for an optimal engine operation. Conventional systems use a camshaft, where carefully placed cams open and close the valves at specific times, dependent on the mechanical construction of the cams. Variable valve actuation makes it then possible to change the shape and timing of the intake and exhaust profiles. In our case, we deal with a hydraulic system, i.e., an electronically controlled hydraulic mechanism that opens the valves independently of the crankshaft rotation.

Understanding and tuning of VVA systems is essential for automotive engineers. The valves' opening directly influences combustion, and therefore, also emission and consumption. A complete analysis of such a system is certainly beyond the scope of this paper. Still, we briefly present our joint evaluation in context of this case study, based on expertise in automotive engineering as well as in interactive visualization.

We study simulation data that consists of nine independent parameters and two dependent curve-attributes and it was computed based on the simulation model shown in Fig. 9. The independent parameters are: actuator volume size ($P1$), actuator piston area ($P2$), inflow pressure ($P3$), opening/closing time ($P4$), maximum flow area ($P5$), cylinder pressure ($P6$), valve mass ($P7$), port cut discharge coefficient ($P8$), and damper discharge coefficient ($P9$).

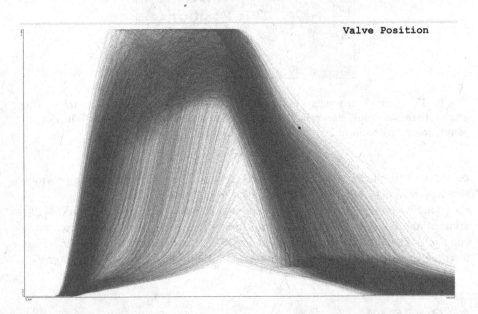

Fig. 10. Almost 5000 curves are shown from the simulation ensemble. Each curve shows the valve position for one hundred degrees of crankshaft revolution. The valve position is only one of many attributes in the dataset.

We computed simulation output for 4993 combinations of the control parameters. Here we focus on the valve position curves which describe the valve position relative to the closed state as a function of the crankshaft angle (see Fig. 10). The valve opens when the curve rises and it closes when the curve declines; at the zero value of y-axis the valve is completely closed.

We see a great amount of variation in the curves' shapes with some rising steeply, some finishing early, and some not opening much at all. We needed a set of suitable scalar aggregates that describe these curves sufficiently well so that we could derive appropriate regression models for the data. Eventually, an important related task is optimization, for example supported by interactive ensemble steering [20]. In our case, we first aimed at extracting valuable findings, based on a visual analysis session of a user with automotive engineering expertise (supported by a visualization expert).

In order to properly capture the valve behavior, we decided to derive the following scalar aggregates during the analysis:

- *area under the curve*: quantity of mixture that enters/exits the cylinder
- *time of maximum opening*: time span during which the valve is open more than 98% of its maximum
- *time of opening*: first time when the valve opening is greater than 0
- *average opening of the value*: corresponds to the mean flow resistance
- *average valve opening velocity*: the average opening velocity from the start of the opening until 98% of the maximum is reached
- *velocity and acceleration at maximal opening*: corresponds to the force and moment when the valve hits its maximal opening
- *average valve closing velocity*: this velocity is computed for two ranges, i.e., one steeper and one less steep part of the curve
- *velocity and acceleration at closing*: corresponds to the force and moment when the valve closes again

Based on this derivation, the data set is extended by ten additional attributes. We select all data and compute regression models. As expected, we cannot capture all relevant relations between the inputs and the outputs by one global, linear model. Figure 11 shows a selection of deviation plots for a global model and we see overly large deviations, making it immediately clear that a more detailed approach is needed.

During the exploratory process, the analyst drills down into the data, and focuses on selected subsets. It is straight-forward to select relevant subsets of the data in the visualization (like in Fig. 10, using a line brush [16] that extends over a subset of the shown curves). In our case, we started with selecting the curves that rise quickly, stay open for a long time, and then close smoothly (see Fig. 12, on the left). New models were then created for these curves. In the visualization, it becomes clear that the deviations are much more moderate, indicating more useful models. Figure 12 (on the right) shows some of the deviation plots (the images are cropped, but drawn using the same scale as in Fig. 11). The derived

Fig. 11. A selection of deviation plots for a global model, showing that a more detailed analysis is needed.

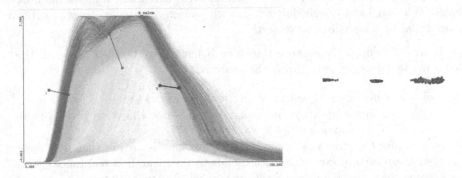

Fig. 12. After an interactive visual drill-down procedure, the expert focuses on a subset of desired curve shapes—fast opening and large integral value. New models are computed using only this subset of the data. The deviation plots on the right show that the according models are much more precise. Explicit model coefficients are also available, and remain visible during the entire analysis session.

(local) models are precise enough to be used in optimization or ensemble steering, but the corresponding parameter space domain has to be considered, of course.

Once satisfied with the local models (according to the visualization of all deviations), the analyst checks the regression models coefficients, and the findings can be described quantitatively. Figure 13 shows such a case. The analyst saw (in a scatterplot) that the opening velocity (slope of the curves when they rise) clearly depends on the P5 input parameter. He then decided to compute an according model. A quick model check (Fig. 13 on the right) showed that the deviations were smaller for the medium values of the opening velocities. The details view then revealed:

$$velocity_{opening} = 0.0435 \cdot P5 + 0.0523 \tag{7}$$

Computing the same regression model, only taking medium velocity into account results in the following equation:

$$velocity_{opening} = 0.0246 \cdot P5 + 0.0881 \tag{8}$$

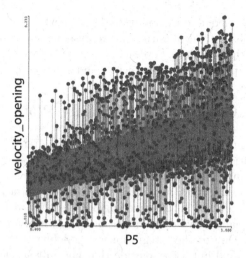

Fig. 13. A linear dependency between parameter P5 and the opening velocity is assumed after seeing this image. The model fits medium velocity values relatively good. Accordingly, the analyst computes another model, and results are indeed a bit better.

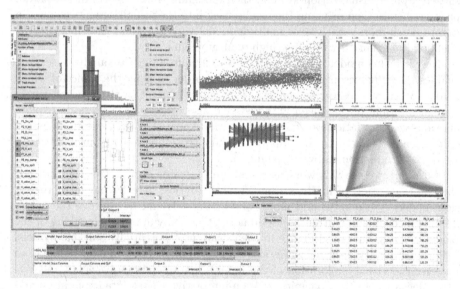

Fig. 14. A screenshot of an analysis session. Many views are used simultaneously, and the expert seamlessly switches between automatic and interactive analysis in an iterative interactive loop.

As a result, the analyst gained a quantitative understanding of how the average opening velocity depends on the P5 parameter in the middle opening velocity range. Finding an inverse function is then trivial, so parameter estimation for any desired velocities can be easily made.

The process continued, and the analyst selected new subsets. Figure 14 shows a screenshot of one display taken during the analysis session. Ideally, the analysis is conducted on multiple displays. Several different views are used simultaneously in a continuous interplay between interactive and automatic methods.

6   Discussion, Conclusion, and Future Work

The quantification and externalization of findings is often essential for a successful data exploration and analysis and in this paper we show how local linear regression models can be used for this purpose. The resulting models are easy to comprehend and easy to invert, for example, during optimization. Our informal evaluation in the domain of automotive engineering showed that model reconstruction and the quantitative communication of findings are two very important analysis tasks. Due to the integration of modeling with visualization, we achieve a valuable mixed-initiative solution that not only accelerates the process of modeling, but also provides valuable means to model evaluation and comparison. Compared to a less integrated approach, e.g., when first exporting data subsets from a visualization system, then modeling these subsets in a separate package, before then bringing the results back into the visualization, we now can iterate much more swiftly over multiple model variations and thus increase the likelihood of eventually deriving high-quality results.

Keeping the model data available throughout an entire analysis session, enables the comparison of different models in order to defer the choice of which model to use in subsequent analysis steps up to a point in the process, where enough information has been gathered. We also observe that users do explore and analyze the data more freely, when they know that previous findings are still available (related to the important undo/redo functionality in most state-of-the-art production software products).

All in all, we see this work as a first step towards even better solutions for the externalization of findings from visual analytics, here by means of regression models. We plan to add more complex models and to improve the model keeping mechanism. Currently, we do not support any automatic ranking of the models, or any kind of guidance in the selection of potentially suitable models. Additional quality-of-fit measures also may be implemented. Further, we plan to improve the visual exploration of the models' parameters (coefficients, quality-of-fit measures, etc.), also capitalizing on interactive visual data exploration and analysis, all in the same framework. Also the integration of other, non-linear models is relatively straight-forward, even though an according solution—while certainly more powerful—is likely to become more complex, also. An even better evaluation and a more thorough case study is also subject of future work.

Acknowledgements. The VRVis Forschungs-GmbH is funded by COMET, Competence Centers for Excellent Technologies (854174), by BMVIT, BMWFW, Styria, Styrian Business Promotion Agency, SFG, and Vienna Business Agency. The COMET Programme is managed by FFG.

References

1. Anscombe, F.J.: Graphs in statistical analysis. Am. Stat. **27**(1), 17–21 (1973)
2. Breiman, L.: Better subset regression using the nonnegative garrote. Technometrics **37**(4), 373–384 (1995). http://dx.doi.org/10.2307/1269730
3. Frank, I.E., Friedman, J.H.: A statistical view of some chemometrics regression tools. Technometrics **35**(2), 109–135 (1993). http://www.jstor.org/stable/1269656
4. Freedman, D.: Statistical Models: Theory and Practice. Cambridge University Press, Cambridge (2005)
5. Gauss, C.: Theoria motus corporum coelestium in sectionibus conicis solem ambientium. sumtibus F. Perthes et I. H. Besser (1809)
6. Haslett, J., Bradley, R., Craig, P., Unwin, A., Wills, G.: Dynamic graphics for exploring spatial data with application to locating global and local anomalies. Am. Stat. **45**(3), 234–242 (1991). http://www.jstor.org/stable/2684298
7. Holzinger, A.: Interactive machine learning for health informatics: when do we need the human-in-the-loop? Brain Inform. **3**(2), 119–131 (2016)
8. Holzinger, A., Plass, M., Holzinger, K., Crişan, G.C., Pintea, C.-M., Palade, V.: Towards interactive machine learning (iML): applying ant colony algorithms to solve the traveling salesman problem with the human-in-the-loop approach. In: Buccafurri, F., Holzinger, A., Kieseberg, P., Tjoa, A.M., Weippl, E. (eds.) CD-ARES 2016. LNCS, vol. 9817, pp. 81–95. Springer, Cham (2016). doi:10.1007/978-3-319-45507-5_6
9. Huber, P.J.: Robust estimation of a location parameter. Ann. Math. Stat. **35**(1), 73–101 (1964). http://dx.doi.org/10.1214/aoms/1177703732
10. Hund, M., Böhm, D., Sturm, W., Sedlmair, M., Schreck, T., Ullrich, T., Keim, D.A., Majnaric, L., Holzinger, A.: Visual analytics for concept exploration in subspaces of patient groups. Brain Inform. **3**(4), 233–247 (2016)
11. Kandogan, E., Balakrishnan, A., Haber, E., Pierce, J.: From data to insight: work practices of analysts in the enterprise. IEEE Comput. Graph. Appl. **34**(5), 42–50 (2014)
12. Kehrer, J., Filzmoser, P., Hauser, H.: Brushing moments in interactive visual analysis. In: Proceedings of the 12th Eurographics/IEEE - VGTC Conference on Visualization, EuroVis 2010, pp. 813–822. Eurographics Association, Aire-la-Ville, Switzerland (2010)
13. Keim, D., Andrienko, G., Fekete, J.-D., Görg, C., Kohlhammer, J., Melançon, G.: Visual analytics: definition, process, and challenges. In: Kerren, A., Stasko, J.T., Fekete, J.-D., North, C. (eds.) Information Visualization. LNCS, vol. 4950, pp. 154–175. Springer, Heidelberg (2008). doi:10.1007/978-3-540-70956-5_7
14. Keim, D.A., Kohlhammer, J., Ellis, G., Mansmann, F.: Mastering the Information Age - Solving Problems with Visual Analytics. Eurographics Association (2010). http://books.google.hr/books?id=vdv5wZM8ioIC
15. Konyha, Z., Lež, A., Matković, K., Jelović, M., Hauser, H.: Interactive visual analysis of families of curves using data aggregation and derivation. In: Proceedings of the 12th International Conference on Knowledge Management and Knowledge Technologies, i-KNOW 2012, pp. 24:1–24:8. ACM, New York (2012)
16. Konyha, Z., Matković, K., Gračanin, D., Jelović, M., Hauser, H.: Interactive visual analysis of families of function graphs. IEEE Trans. Vis. Comput. Graph. **12**(6), 1373–1385 (2006)
17. Lampe, O.D., Hauser, H.: Model building in visualization space. In: Proceedings of Sigrad 2011 (2011)

18. Legendre, A.: Nouvelles méthodes pour la détermination des orbites des comètes. Méthode pour déterminer la longueur exacte du quart du méridien, F. Didot (1805)

19. Matković, K., Freiler, W., Gracanin, D., Hauser, H.: Comvis: a coordinated multiple views system for prototyping new visualization technology. In: 2008 12th International Conference Information Visualisation, pp. 215–220, July 2008

20. Matković, K., Gračanin, D., Splechtna, R., Jelović, M., Stehno, B., Hauser, H., Purgathofer, W.: Visual analytics for complex engineering systems: hybrid visual steering of simulation ensembles. IEEE Trans. Vis. Comput. Graph. **20**(12), 1803–1812 (2014)

21. National Oceanic and Atmospheric Administration: Climate data online (2017). https://www.ncdc.noaa.gov/cdo-web/datasets/. Accessed 19 June 2017

22. Pedregosa, F., Varoquaux, G., Gramfort, A., Michel, V., Thirion, B., Grisel, O., Blondel, M., Prettenhofer, P., Weiss, R., Dubourg, V., Vanderplas, J., Passos, A., Cournapeau, D., Brucher, M., Perrot, M., Duchesnay, E.: Scikit-learn: machine learning in python. J. Mach. Learn. Res. **12**, 2825–2830 (2011)

23. Piringer, H., Berger, W., Krasser, J.: HyperMoVal: interactive visual validation of regression models for real-time simulation. Comput. Graph. Forum **29**, 983–992 (2010)

24. Radoš, S., Splechtna, R., Matković, K., Đuras, M., Gröller, E., Hauser, H.: Towards quantitative visual analytics with structured brushing and linked statistics. Comput. Graph. Forum **35**(3), 251–260 (2016). http://dx.doi.org/10.1111/cgf.12901

25. Shao, L., Mahajan, A., Schreck, T., Lehmann, D.J.: Interactive regression lens for exploring scatter plots. In: Computer Graphics Forum (Proceedings of EuroVis) (2017, to appear)

26. Shneiderman, B.: Inventing discovery tools: combining information visualization with data mining. Inform. Vis. **1**(1), 5–12 (2002)

27. Shrinivasan, Y.B., van Wijk, J.J.: Supporting exploration awareness in information visualization. IEEE Comput. Graph. Appl. **29**(5), 34–43 (2009)

28. Tam, G.K.L., Kothari, V., Chen, M.: An analysis of machine-and human-analytics in classification. IEEE Trans. Vis. Comput. Graph **23**(1), 71–80 (2016)

29. Thomas, J.J., Cook, K.A.: A visual analytics agenda. IEEE Comput. Graph. Appl. **26**(1), 10–13 (2006)

30. Tibshirani, R.: Regression shrinkage and selection via the lasso. J. Roy. Stat. Soc. Ser. B (Methodological) **58**(1), 267–288 (1996). http://www.jstor.org/stable/2346178

31. Tukey, J.: The technical tools of statistics. Am. Stat. **19**, 23–28 (1965)

32. Yang, D., Xie, Z., Rundensteiner, E.A., Ward, M.O.: Managing discoveries in the visual analytics process. SIGKDD Explor. Newsl. **9**(2), 22–29 (2007). http://doi.acm.org/10.1145/1345448.1345453

Analysis of Online User Behaviour for Art and Culture Events

Behnam Rahdari, Tahereh Arabghalizi, and Marco Brambilla(⊠)

Politecnico di Milano, Via Ponzio, 34/5, 20133 Milano, Italy
{behnam.rahdari,tahereh.arabghalizi}@mail.polimi.it,
marco.brambilla@polimi.it

Abstract. Nowadays people share everything on online social networks, from daily life stories to the latest local and global news and events. Many researchers have exploited this as a source for understanding the user behaviour and profile in various settings. In this paper, we address the specific problem of user behavioural profiling in the context of cultural and artistic events. We propose a specific analysis pipeline that aims at examining the profile of online users, based on the textual content they published online. The pipeline covers the following aspects: data extraction and enrichment, topic modeling, user clustering, and prediction of interest. We show our approach at work for the monitoring of participation to a large-scale artistic installation that collected more than 1.5 million visitors in just two weeks (namely *The Floating Piers*, by *Christo and Jeanne-Claude*). We report our findings and discuss the pros and cons of the work.

Keywords: Social media · Big data · Behaviour analysis · Data mining

1 Introduction

1.1 Context

Today social networks are the most popular communication channels for users looking to share their experiences and interests. They host considerable amounts of user-generated materials for a wide variety of real-world events of different type and scale [2]. Social media has a significant impact in our daily lives. People share their opinions, stories, news, and broadcast events using social media. Monitoring and analyzing this rich and continuous flow of user-generated content can provide valuable information, enabling individuals and organizations to acquire insightful knowledge [8].

 ̄Due to the immediacy and rapidity of social media, news events are often reported and spread on Twitter, Instagram, or Facebook ahead of traditional news media [15]. With the fast growth of social media, Twitter has become one of the most popular platforms for people to post short messages. Events like breaking news can easily draw people's attention and spread rapidly on Twitter.

A. Holzinger et al. (Eds.): CD-MAKE 2017, LNCS 10410, pp. 219–236, 2017.
DOI: 10.1007/978-3-319-66808-6_15

Therefore, the popularity and significance of an event can be measured by the volume of tweets covering the event. Furthermore, the relevant tweets are also indicators of opinions and reactions to events [6].

Obtaining demographic information about social media users, their interests and their behaviour is the main concern of *user profiling*, which in turn can be used to understand more about users and improve their satisfaction [16].

Various research works that have been conducted in user profiling, for instance in the field of recommender systems. However, the number of studies and analyses on the impact of cultural and art events in social media is rather limited, and focused on English-only content, while overlooking the other languages. Considering this, we propose a **domain-specific approach to profile social media users engaged in a cultural or art event**, regardless of their language and their location.

1.2   Problem Statement

In this study, we intend to respond the following questions:

- What are the **topics of interest of the social media users** who published their experiences or opinions about a cultural or artistic event?
- What **demographic features** can be revealed about these users?
- What is the **predicted level of engagement and areas of interest** of perspective users approaching the event?

To tackle the above questions, we suggest an approach that addresses two core aspects:

1. **User profiling:** the process of extracting user features, raising the level of abstraction of the discussed concepts, and deriving the topics of interest. The interest domains and behaviour of social media users who share their opinions about a cultural or artistic event.
2. **User interest prediction:** the anticipation of whether a social media user will be attracted by the current or similar event in the (near) future and, if yes, with what kind of interest and background.

1.3   Proposed Solution

The first step of our approach is to collect the required data about an event from social media. After cleaning and transforming this collected data to a proper format, we define some steps to perform data analysis in different levels. The first step of analysis is to extract the main topics from the provided dataset by using topic modeling techniques. After that, we perform different clustering algorithms on the outputs of topic modeling and then employ cluster validation techniques to evaluate the obtained results. Ultimately, using the outcomes of data analysis, we can employ a classification method to anticipate the interest areas of the future users in similar events.

Notice therefore that in our specific setting we cluster users by topics of interest, and not merely based on lexical similarity based on used words.

1.4   Structure of the Paper

The paper is organized as follows: Sect. 2 discusses the related work; Sect. 3 describes our approach, with practical implementation details reported in Sect. 4; Sect. 5 presents the case study and Sect. 6 reports the outcomes of the analysis. Finally, Sect. 7 concludes and outlines the future work.

2   Related Work

Knowledge Discovery in Databases (KDD) is the nontrivial process of identifying valid, novel, potentially useful, and ultimately understandable patterns in the data. The KDD process involves using the database along with any required selection, preprocessing, subsampling, and transformations; applying data-mining methods (algorithms) to enumerate patterns from it; and evaluating the products of data mining to identify the subset of the enumerated patterns that are deemed useful for increasing knowledge [9].

Past works have found that content extracted from social media is a meaningful reflection of the human behind the social network account posting that content. Works like [26,28] mainly focus on clustering web users, while studies such as [1,10,22] specifically address clustering of people in social networks based on textual and non-textual features. There are also several works that address user profiling in online social networks. For instance, in [3] the authors propose a method to select experts within the population of social networks, according to the information about their social activities.

Other works [18,21] focus on event analysis in social media. The former analyzes the resulted heterogeneous network, and use it in order to cluster posts by different topics and events; while the latter performs analysis and comparison of temporal events, rankings of sightseeing places in a city, and study mobility of people using geo-tagged photos. Some works [11] leverage Twitter lists to extract the topics that users talk about and [25] introduces validation methods to evaluate clustering results. All these works have delivered new solutions to social media analysis field and investigated the problems of profiling users and analyzing events by employing different data mining approaches.

In comparison to the mentioned studies, our research proposes a complex approach that aims clustering social media users based on their topic of interest, extracted from their distinct features. We design a specific analysis pipeline for art events and we show it at work on real case studies.

3   Approach

The approach presented in this paper defines a specific KDD process that comprises some data enrichment and preprocessing steps, followed by data mining phases which lead to significant knowledge extraction results in our scenarios. We propose the pipeline reported in Fig. 1: first we extract all the required data from the social media platforms; in the next phase, we transform and enrich the data to proper formats for the subsequent analysis and then store it; and finally, data analysis techniques are applied on the clean, enriched and preprocessed data. The next sections describe each phase of the process in detail.

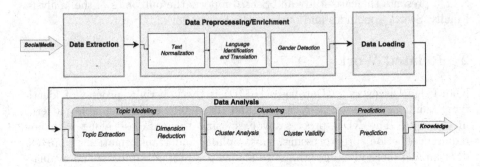

Fig. 1. Content analysis pipeline for art and culture events

3.1   Data Extraction

In this phase raw data is extracted by addressing the social network API with the appropriate query, which is able to extract information on the event of interest. We concentrate on Twitter as a good representative of social content in the context of live events and participation. Therefore, we exploit the Twitter API for data extraction [24].

3.2   Data Preprocessing

Since the collected raw data is incomplete and inconsistent, as described next, we need to apply preprocessing techniques to prepare an appropriate dataset which can be used for next analyses and experiments. The preprocessing phase consists of three main steps to be followed:

- **Text Normalization:** Textual properties (especially in social media) include a great deal of non-standard characters, punctuation, symbols, stop words, etc. that must be omitted for making the data clean and standard. Furthermore, it is essential to reduce derived words to their word stem or root form.
- **Language Identification and Translation:** Unsurprisingly, social media users do not always tweet in English, so having text in different languages are not unexpected. The majority of research works only focus on English contents, and thus the importance of language as a demographic feature is overlooked. Hence, with the aim of making data more coherent and unambiguous, and for expanding the coverage of the approach to world-wide scenarios, we apply language detection and translation into English, for homogenisation.
- **Gender Detection:** Twitter does not provide users' gender in their objects. Since we consider this a crucial demographic feature, we enrich the data with gender information.

Table 1. Data schema

Entity	Attribute	Description
Tweet	Id	The representation of the unique identifier for this tweet
	Username	The user who posted this tweet
	Text	The actual UTF-8 text of the status update
	Date	Date and time when this tweet was created
	Retweets	Number of times this tweet has been retweeted
	Favorites	Indicates how many times this tweet has been liked
	Mentions	The users who are mentioned in this tweet
	Hashtags	Represents hashtags which have been parsed out of this tweet text
	Geo	Represents the geographic location of this tweet
User	Id	The representation of the unique identifier for this user
	Username	The unique name of this user
	Full name	The name of this user, as they've defined it
	Tweets	The user's most recent (20) tweets
	Follower count	The number of followers this user currently has
	Following count	The number of users this user is following
	Status count	The number of tweets issued by this user
	Listed count	The number of public lists that this user is a member of
	Favorite count	The number of tweets this user has favorited
	Bio	The user-defined UTF-8 string describing their account
	Hashtags	The hashtags included in this user's most recent (20) tweets
	Mentions	The users who are mentioned in this user's most recent (20) tweets
	Location	The user-defined location for their profile
	Language	The user's self-declared user interface language
	Gender	Represents gender of user (added after data preprocessing)
	Lists	Names of the lists that user is member of

- **Data Loading:** In this phase the clean and enriched data is stored in appropriate format for large scale analysis (CSV file).

3.3 Data Analysis Overview

In order to avoid manual tagging of data, which would be costly and not scalable across multiple experiment or usage scenarios, we opt for unsupervised techniques, namely clustering and topic modeling.

Since we want to profile users based on the texts they share on Twitter, first we need to create a Document-Term Matrix (DTM) which discovers the importance (frequency) of terms that occur in a collection of documents. It is noteworthy that, from now on, our "document" of interest is the social network user. Therefore, in practice a document corresponds to each user's textual feature, namely: personal *biography*, *hashtags* used in the tweets, text of the *tweets* posted, and *Twitter lists* the user belongs to (see Table 1). Therefore, each entry of DTM contains the frequency of each term occurred in each document.

As one can easily understand, this matrix is very big and extremely sparse. With the objective to get a more high-level and understandable sense of the documents, we apply topic extraction by means of Latent Dirichlet Allocation (LDA) on the matrix. The output of LDA is also a matrix that assigns a probability to each pair of document and extracted topic: in practice, we obtain a probability of a document (i.e., user) to be interested in a given topic. We then use this LDA output for clustering users.

We also define a prediction phase, where we use a classification method (specifically, Decision Trees), to create a model that can anticipate whether a newcomer user might be interested in the event, and can predict the topic(s) of interest for that user.

3.4   Topic Modeling

Topic models can help to organize and offer insights to understand large collections of unstructured text bodies [20]. They allow the probabilistic modeling of term frequency occurrences in documents. The fitted model can be used to estimate the similarity between documents as well as between a set of specified keywords using an additional layer of latent variables which are referred to as topics [14]. The input data for topic models is a document-term matrix (DTM). The rows in this matrix correspond to the documents and the columns to the terms. The entry m_{ij} indicates how often the jth term occurred in the ith document.

In this study, topic modeling phase consists of two steps:

- **Topic Extraction:** to discover the abstract topics that occur in the collection of our documents, we apply a topic model such as *Latent Dirichlet Allocation (LDA)* which benefits from Gibbs sampling algorithm [12]. For fitting the LDA model to a given document-term matrix, the number of topics needs to be fixed a-priori. Because the number of topics is in general not known, models with several different numbers of topics are fitted and the optimal number is determined in a data-driven way [14]. Maximum values of Deveaud et al. (2014) method and minimum values of Cao et al. (2009) estimation are considered optimal and are used in this study to identify the number of topics in LDA. The output of this model is a *topic probability matrix* that contains the probability of each topic associated to each document. In practice, this tells us the probability that a given user is interested in a given topic.

- **Dimension Reduction:** Since the extracted topics from LDA are possibly correlated, it is suggested to employ *Principal Component Analysis (PCA)* to convert them to a set of values of linearly uncorrelated topics. This transformation of data to a lower dimensional feature space not only reduces the time and storage required but also makes the data visualization and interpretation easier.

3.5 Clustering

Clustering aims to organize a collection of data items into clusters, such that items within a cluster are more "similar" to each other than they are to items in the other clusters [13]. In this work, this phase of the pipeline is divided into two steps:

- **Cluster Analysis:** In order to profile social media users based on the texts they share about a specific event, different cluster algorithms namely *K-means, Hierarchical,* and *DBSCAN* are used and compared, in order to select the best option in our specific setting.
- **Cluster Validity:** When cluster analysis was performed, it's crucial to evaluate how good the resulting clusters are. The evaluation indices, that are applied to judge various aspects of cluster validity are traditionally classified into three types: unsupervised (internal), supervised (external), and relative [23].

In this study, *Silhouette Coefficient* and *Dunn's Index* as internal indices and *Entropy* as an external criterion are selected in order to evaluate and compare the different aspects of clustering results.

3.6 Prediction of User Interest

In order to guide event planning professionals to market, plan and implement their events more effectively, we propose to predict the category or the interest area of potential new users who might be involved in the similar cultural or art events in the future. Accordingly, beside the outlined unsupervised techniques that were employed to profile users, we opt for a supervised learning algorithm namely *decision tree*, which builds a classification model, for prediction of new users' interests, based on the user categories that we obtained from clustering. Decision tree learning is a typical inductive algorithm based on instance, which focus on classification rules displaying as decision trees inferred from a group of disorder and irregular instance [5].

To build the decision tree, first our dataset should be divided into training and test sets, with training set used to build the model and test set used to validate it. Since our target is to predict the interest domain of new users in terms of *user category*, the tree will be fed with the training dataset in which the category of users has been attached to and used as the target feature.

In addition, the input variables comprise several features of the user, namely: the topic probabilities defined for each textual features of the user (coming from the *topic probabilities matrix* generated by the LDA analysis), namely the biography, hashtags, tweets and lists; gender, language, number of followings and followers and number of tweets. Consequently, the decision tree generates a set of prediction rules that determine new users' interest areas, regarding a cultural or art event, based on the values of the features.

4   Implementation

In the preprocessing phase, we use the Yandex API [27] for language identification and translation of stems into English, and the NamSor API [19] for gender detection. In the preliminary phases we store the data in a relational database for fast sequential preprocessing, and then we generate CSV files to be fed to the analysis phases.

All analyses, statistics, evaluations and results representations are done in R, a flexible statistical programming language and environment that is open source and freely available for all mainstream operating systems [17].[1]

5   Case Study

For sixteen days, from June 18 through July 3 2016, Lake Iseo in Italy was reimagined by the world-renowned artists Christo and Jeanne-Claude.[2] More than 100,000 square meters of shimmering yellow fabric, carried by a modular floating dock system of 220,000 high-density polyethylene cubes, undulated with the movement of the waves as The Floating Piers rose just above the surface of the water. Visitors were able to experience the work of art by walking on it from Sulzano to Monte Isola and to the island of San Paolo, which was framed by The Floating Piers [4] (see Fig. 2[3]). More than 1.5 million people visited the installation in those 2 weeks.

We use this artistic event as a use case for our method. We extracted the social media content relevant to the event and we applied the analysis pipeline over it. The datasets were obtained from Twitter, during a time period from June 10th to July 30th 2016 and contain 14,062 tweets and 23,916 users. Figure 3 represents the total number of tweets, retweets, favorites and engaged users (per day), one week before the event starts until the end of July. As one can see, users tend to

---

[1] We use `tm` package for all the text-mining methods for importing data, corpus handling, preprocessing and creation of document-term matrices; `topicmodels` package for LDA; `cluster`, `fpc`, `dbscan` and `NbClust` for clustering and cluster validation; `ggplot2`, `rgl`, `ggmap`, `wordcloud` and `RColorBrewer` packages for interactive graphics; `rpart`, `rpart.plot` and `party` packages for decision tree modeling and prediction.

[2] http://christojeanneclaude.net/projects/the-floating-piers.

[3] Photo Credits: Harald Bischoff, *Christo's "The Floating Piers", lake of Iseo, Italy 2016*. License: Creative Commons Attribution-Share Alike 3.0 Unported.

Fig. 2. The Floating Piers by Christo and Jeanne-Claude

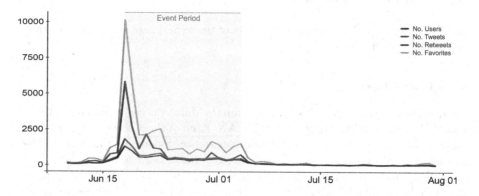

Fig. 3. Tweets, retweets, favorites and users timeline

tweet about the installation at the early days of the event while the engagement of the users dramatically decreases afterwards.

According to the statistics, unlike Instagram users, most Twitter users are not willing to specify the location of their published tweets. Therefore, we also extracted Instagram posts (30,256 posts and 94,666 users) related to the event during the same time span and displayed the density of these posts on geographical plots in Fig. 4.

As one can see the density of posts has a direct relationship with their locality which means most Instagram posts have been published near the main venue of the event.

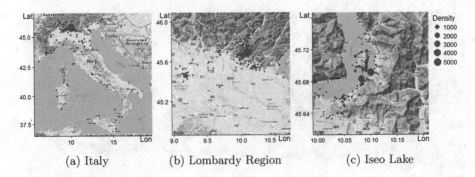

(a) Italy   (b) Lombardy Region   (c) Iseo Lake

Fig. 4. Density of Instagram posts in different coordinates

6   Results and Discussion

In this section, the most significant results of the experiment over the case study are shown and discussed.

6.1   User Clustering

As discussed earlier, we apply and compare different clustering algorithms, namely K-means, Hierarchical and DBSCAN. Each of them is separately applied on our data collections. Each collection consists of documents that correspond to each textual property of users including bio, hashtags, tweets and lists.

Subsequently, to achieve the most accurate results, different cluster validity measures are employed. Among the existing validation metrics, Silhouette width, Dunn index and Entropy are selected to evaluate the clustering results. Silhouette width and Dunn index combine measures of compactness and separation of the clusters. Thus, algorithms that produce clusters with high Dunn index and high Silhouette width are more desirable. On the other hand, Entropy is a metric that is a measure of the amount of disorder in a vector. So, smaller values of entropy indicate less disorder in a clustering, which means a better clustering [7].

Table 2 represents these measures values for each algorithm that was applied on each feature collection. It should be noted that, the number of clusters in each experiment is either determined by the clustering algorithm itself like DBSCAN or calculated through different methods like Elbow for K-means. According to this table, Hierarchical clustering (with three clusters) can be considered as the best algorithm which has produced more pleasant results compared to the other two. Furthermore, among all four examined textual features, users' biography (Bio) performs best. Consequently, as table suggests (bold numbers), from now on we only focus on hierarchical clustering performed on users' biography.

Table 2. Evaluation of clustering results

Algorithms	Indices	Features			
		Bio	Hashtags	Tweets	Lists
K-Means	No. Clusters	3	3	4	3
	Silhouette	0.457	0.427	0.425	0.535
	Dunn	0.047	0.003	0.001	0.001
	Entropy	1.070	0.799	0.725	0.736
DBSCAN	No. Clusters	5	4	5	5
	Silhouette	0.051	0.329	0.106	0.270
	Dunn	0.020	0.008	0.001	0.001
	Entropy	1.207	0.053	0.716	0.394
Hierarchical	No. Clusters	3	3	3	3
	Silhouette	**0.595**	0.520	0.506	0.331
	Dunn	**0.050**	0.006	0.001	0.001
	Entropy	**0.015**	0.377	0.725	0.905

6.2   Applying Topic Modeling

As mentioned earlier, in this study, the input data for clustering models is a topic probability matrix that contains the probability of each topic associated to each document (user). This matrix is generated after applying LDA on document-term matrix, in which each row is a user' biography and each column is a term. As indicated in Sect. 3.4, Deveaud et al. (2014) and Cao et al. (2009) can help to determine the number of topics before LDA is applied. Accordingly, the optimum values of these metrics offer 6 as the number of topics for LDA. Having all required parameters set, LDA is applied and returns the topic probability matrix along with the top terms of each extracted topic which are presented in a word network in Fig. 5.

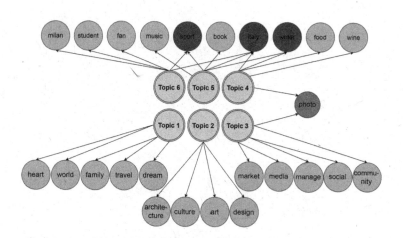

Fig. 5. Word network representation of top terms in each topic

By investigating through these terms, it seems that the extracted topics are correlated and need to be transformed to a lower-dimensional set, supplied by PCA procedure. The result of applying PCA on topics is represented in Table 3.

Table 3. PCA quantitative results

	Topic.1	Topic.2	Topic.3	Topic.4	Topic.5	Topic.6
Standard deviation	1.1188726	1.0683576	0.7789327	0.7789327	0.44049766	1.290478e-07
Proportion of variance	0.4172919	0.3804627	0.2022454	0.1022776	0.03880764	2.775558e-15
Cumulative proportion	**0.4172919**	**0.7977546**	**1.0000000**	1.000000e+00	1.000000e+00	1.000000e+00

As the table suggests, we only consider the first three principal components (topics) where cumulative proportion passes 95% threshold. Consequently, in clustering phase, we will perform the hierarchical algorithm on topic probability matrix, exploiting only these three PCA-selected topics.

6.3   Cluster Hierarchy

As indicated in previous sections, hierarchical algorithm returns more acceptable results. This algorithm's output is a dendrogram which is illustrated in Fig. 6.

Unlike K-means algorithm, hierarchical algorithm does not require the optimal number of clusters to be defined at the beginning. In this clustering algorithm clusters are defined by cutting branches off the dendrogram. To determine the cutting section, various methods can be used. We used a convention which represents that a dendrogram can be cut where the difference is most significant.

To extract better insights over the situation, we report in Fig. 6 the three main clusters drawn in different colors. Each leaf in this tree represents a Twitter user engaged in the Floating Piers event through tweeting, retweeting or liking a post. According to this result, it can be concluded that nearly 60% of users

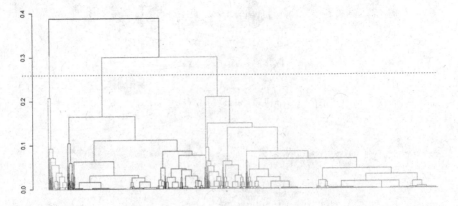

Fig. 6. Dendrogram representation of Twitter users (Color figure online)

lies in first cluster (green), over 35% in second (blue) and the rest (about 5%) in the third cluster (red).

6.4   Cluster Labeling/User Profiling

Having all the user objects in each cluster, we are able to label the obtained clusters or in other words to identify the categories of users. The five most frequent words, that users published about the event, along with the frequency of each word are indicated in Table 4. In this table, Cluster 1 refers to the biggest cluster (green), Cluster 2 refers to the second biggest cluster (blue) and Cluster 3 refers to the smallest cluster (red). It can be seen that the most frequent words in each cluster convey specific meanings. People in first cluster mostly talk about "Travel" introducing themselves in their Twitter bio. People in second cluster are "Art" lovers and people in third cluster state their positions as "Technology" fans and social media marketing addicted. Henceforth, we call the users in first, second and third cluster Travel Lovers, Art Lovers and Tech Lovers respectively.

Table 4. The five most frequent words and their frequency in each cluster

Cluster 1 (Travel)		Cluster 2 (Art)		Cluster 3 (Tech)	
Word	Freq.	Word	Freq.	Word	Freq.
Travel	1070	Art	962	Social	677
Italian	832	Design	811	Market	641
Passion	797	Culture	749	Media	618
Lover	632	Photograph	598	Manag	502
Food	614	Artist	537	Founder	435

To depict a weighted list of the words that are used in users' bio in each cluster, we employ word networks and word clouds, which are visual representations of textual data. The word networks and word clouds related to users' bio in each cluster are illustrated in Figs. 7 and 8 respectively.

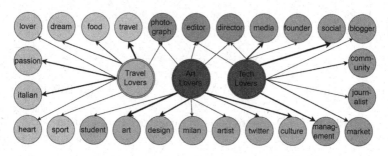

Fig. 7. Word network representation of top terms in each cluster - the thickness of the connections is proportional to the frequency of words in clusters

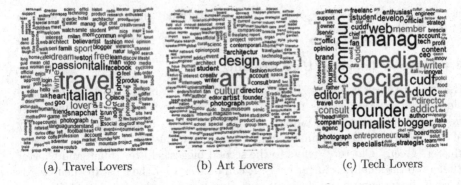

(a) Travel Lovers   (b) Art Lovers   (c) Tech Lovers

Fig. 8. Word cloud for each cluster

6.5   Demographic Analysis - Language

We can use demographic features like language and gender which help to compare users in three clusters. As Fig. 9 shows Italian is the most common language of users in three clusters while second place belongs to English, followed by the sum of all the other languages (French, Dutch, etc.). As one can see, the flows of languages follow the flow of tweets in all three clusters and have a peak on the opening day of the event. The bias towards Italian is particularly evident in the travel lovers cluster, while it's less strong in the art lovers. This suggests that travelers visiting the event are mostly Italians, while people coming from abroad are not generic tourists, but more specifically art lovers, which come on purpose for the event.

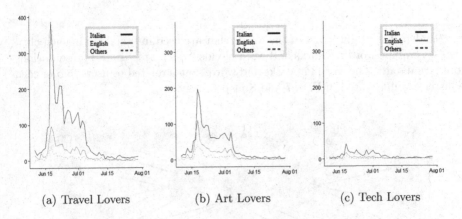

(a) Travel Lovers   (b) Art Lovers   (c) Tech Lovers

Fig. 9. Time series of posts by language for each cluster

6.6 Demographic Analysis - Gender

Figure 10 demonstrates that the number of males who got involved in the Floating Piers overweighs the number of females but the difference is not substantial and can be overlooked. In addition, since Travel lovers are the highest majority, the number of males and females are the highest in this category. The presence of males is slightly higher in art lovers.

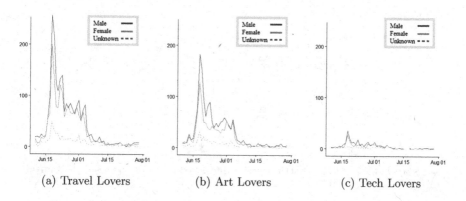

(a) Travel Lovers   (b) Art Lovers   (c) Tech Lovers

Fig. 10. Time series of posts by gender for each cluster

6.7 Prediction of Interests of New Users

As mentioned in Sect. 3.6, we suggested to employ decision tree to predict the possible interests of the potential future users, based on the categories that were acquired from clustering the current users. There are two competing concerns: with less training data, our parameter estimates have greater variance. With less testing data, our performance statistic will have greater variance. Thus, we divide our dataset into training and testing sets with the ratio of 80:20, such that neither variance is too high. Figure 11 can give an intuition of how the decision tree creates the prediction rules.

In addition, the extracted rules from the tree are formulated as follows:

```
- Rule 1: if (0.36 < Bio_score < 0.37 OR Bio_score < 0.35) then new
               user is interested in event and is a Travel Lover

- Rule 2: if (0.35 < Bio_score < 0.36 AND Status_count > 14.5) OR
               (Bio_score > 0.37 AND language != Italian) then new user
                        is interested in event and is an Art Lover

- Rule 3: if (Bio_score > 0.37 AND Language = Italian) then new user
                        is interested in event and is a Tech Lover

- Otherwise: then new user is NOT interested in event
```

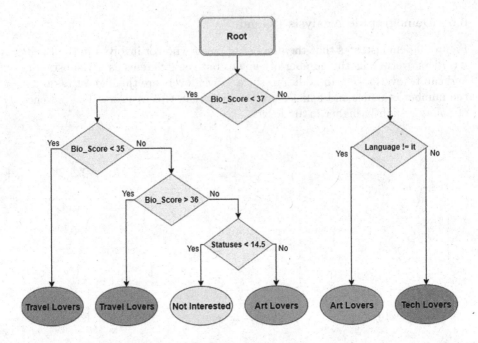

Fig. 11. The decision tree representation

where the only relevant features identified by the decision tree are: the Bio_score, representing the topic probability for the biography feature; the Status_count, representing the total number of tweets of the user; and the Language.

In order to evaluate the decision tree, we use the test dataset that determines an accuracy of 62%. Now for new users, we can simply use the above rules and specify their categories (Travel, Art or Tech) or identify them as "not interested" in a similar event in the future.

Notice that the power of the solution, considering the obtained rules, is that of being able of classifying a user as interested and as engaged in travel, art or technology essentially looking at its biography.

7   Conclusion and Future Work

In this study, we proposed a complex approach that addresses user profiling and user interest prediction regarding arts and cultural events on social media. This approach is equipped with a preprocessing step that enriches user data in terms of language and gender. The outcomes of this research can help event organizers to decide what categories of users they are dealing with and have a clear understanding about the characteristics of users who are more likely to be attracted by the similar events in the future.

We used "The Floating Piers" event as a case study to show how the proposed approach works with the real life scenarios. We clustered users based on their interests in three main categories and then described and compared the behavior and properties of users in each cluster. In addition, using decision tree modeling resulted in a set of rules that predicts the interest domain of future users.

However, since the current study merely addresses the text content that users share on social media, it can go further with considering other types of media namely photo in other social network platforms such as Instagram, Facebook, Google+, Flickr, Foursquare, etc. that might result in a clearer and wider picture of the characteristics and behaviour of users with respect to cultural and artistic events. Last but not least, applying other techniques like semantic analysis, image processing and network analysis can also help us to improve the accuracy and coverage of the results.

References

1. Arabghalizi, T., Rahdari, B.: Event-based user profiling in social media using data mining approaches. Master's thesis, Politecnico di Milano, April 2017
2. Becker, H., Naaman, M., Gravano, L.: Learning similarity metrics for event identification in social media. In: Proceedings of the Third ACM International Conference on Web Search and Data Mining, WSDM 2010, pp. 291–300. ACM, New York (2010). http://doi.acm.org/10.1145/1718487.1718524
3. Bozzon, A., Brambilla, M., Ceri, S., Silvestri, M., Vesci, G.: Choosing the right crowd: expert finding in social networks. In: Joint 2013 EDBT/ICDT Conferences, EDBT 2013 Proceedings, Genoa, Italy, 18–22 March 2013, pp. 637–648 (2013). http://doi.acm.org/10.1145/2452376.2452451
4. Christo: The floating piers (2016). http://christojeanneclaude.net/projects/the-floating-piers
5. Dai, Q.Y., Zhang, C.P., Wu, H.: Research of decision tree classification algorithm in data mining. Int. J. Database Theory Appl. **9**, 1–8 (2016)
6. Diao, Q.: Event identification and analysis on Twitter. Ph.D. thesis, Singapore Management University (2015)
7. Dziopa, T.: Clustering validity indices evaluation with regard to semantic homogeneity. In: Position Papers of the 2016 Federated Conference on Computer Science and Information Systems, FedCSIS 2016, Gdańsk, Poland, 11–14 September 2016, pp. 3–9 (2016). https://doi.org/10.15439/2016F371
8. Farzindar, A., Wael, K.: A survey of techniques for event detection in twitter. Comput. Intell. **31**(1), 132–164 (2015). http://dx.doi.org/10.1111/coin.12017
9. Fayyad, U.M., Piatetsky-Shapiro, G., Smyth, P.: From data mining to knowledge discovery: an overview. In: Advances in Knowledge Discovery and Data Mining, pp. 1–34. American Association for Artificial Intelligence, Menlo Park, CA, USA (1996). http://dl.acm.org/citation.cfm?id=257938.257942
10. Friedemann, V.: Clustering a Customer Base Using Twitter Data. Technical report, stanford university department of computer science, October 2015

11. Ghosh, S., Sharma, N., Benevenuto, F., Ganguly, N., Gummadi, K.: Cognos: crowd-sourcing search for topic experts in microblogs. In: Proceedings of the 35th International ACM SIGIR Conference on Research and Development in Information Retrieval, SIGIR 2012, pp. 575–590. ACM, New York (2012). http://doi.acm.org/10.1145/2348283.2348361

12. Griffiths, T.: Gibbs sampling in the generative model of latent dirichlet allocation. Technical report (2002)

13. Grira, N., Crucianu, M., Boujemaa, N.: Unsupervised and semi-supervised clustering: a brief survey. In: 'A Review of Machine Learning Techniques for Processing Multimedia Content', Report of the MUSCLE European Network of Excellence (FP6) (2004)

14. Grun, B., Hornik, K.: Topicmodels: an r package for fitting topic models. J. Stat. Softw. **40**(13), 1–30 (2011)

15. Hu, Y.: Event Analytics on Social Media: Challenges and Solutions. Ph.D. thesis, Arizona State University (2014)

16. Kanoje, S., Girase, S., Mukhopadhyay, D.: User profiling trends, techniques and applications. Int. J. Adv. Found. Res. Comput. (IJAFRC) **1**, 119–125 (2014)

17. Kelley, K., Lai, K., Wu, P.J.: Using r for data analysis: a best practice for research. In: Osborne, J. (ed.) Best Practices in Quantitative Methods. SAGE publishing (2008)

18. Kisilevich, S., Krstajic, M., Keim, D., Andrienko, N., Andrienko, G.: Event-based analysis of people's activities and behavior using flickr and panoramio geotagged photo collections. In: 2010 14th International Conference Information Visualisation, pp. 289–296, July 2010

19. NamSorSAS: Namsor api. http://www.namsor.com

20. Patil, M., Kankal, S.: Topic digging over asynchronous text sequences. Int. J. Eng. Comput. Sci. **5**, 19548–19551 (2016)

21. Prangnawarat, N., Hulpus, I., Hayes, C.: Event analysis in social media using clustering of heterogeneous information networks. In: The Twenty-Eighth International Flairs Conference (2015)

22. Singh, K., Shakya, H.K., Biswas, B.: Clustering of people in social network based on textual similarity. Perspect. Sci. **8**, 570–573 (2016). http://www.sciencedirect.com/science/article/pii/S2213020916301628, recent Trends in Engineering and Material Sciences

23. Tan, P.N., Steinbach, M., Kumar, V.: Cluster analysis: basic concepts and algorithms. In: Introduction to Data Mining, 1st edn. Addison-Wesley Longman Publishing Co., Inc. (2005)

24. Twitter: Api overview (2017). https://dev.twitter.com/overview/api

25. Van Craenendonck, T., Blockeel, H.: Using internal validity measures to compare clustering algorithms. In: Benelearn 2015 Poster presentations (online), pp. 1–8 (2015)

26. Xiao, J., Zhang, Y., Jia, X., Li, T.: Measuring similarity of interests for clustering web-users. In: Proceedings of the 12th Australasian Database Conference, ADC 2001, pp. 107–114. IEEE Computer Society, Washington, DC (2001). http://dl.acm.org/citation.cfm?id=545538.545551

27. Yandex: Translate api (2014–2017). https://tech.yandex.com/translate

28. Zhou, G., Ding, H., Zhou, G., Zhang, W.: A user clustering algorithm considering user's interest-offset. In: International Conference on Cyberspace Technology (CCT 2013), pp. 62–67, November 2013

On Joint Representation Learning of Network Structure and Document Content

Jörg Schlötterer[(✉)], Christin Seifert, and Michael Granitzer

University of Passau, Innstraße 33, 94032 Passau, Germany
{joerg.schloetterer,christin.seifert,michael.granitzer}@uni-passau.de
http://www.uni-passau.de

Abstract. Inspired by the advancements of representation learning for natural language processing, learning continuous feature representations of nodes in networks has recently gained attention. Similar to word embeddings, node embeddings have been shown to capture certain semantics of the network structure. Combining both research directions into a joint representation learning of network structure and document content seems a promising direction to increase the quality of the learned representations. However, research is typically focused on either word or network embeddings and few approaches that learn a joint representation have been proposed. We present an overview of that field, starting at word representations, moving over document and network node representations to joint representations. We make the connections between the different models explicit and introduce a novel model for learning a joint representation. We present different methods for the novel model and compare the presented approaches in an evaluation. This paper explains how the different models recently proposed in the literature relate to each other and compares their performance.

Keywords: Representation learning · Network embeddings · Document embeddings

1 Introduction

Recently, there has been an uptake of the representation learning methods from the domain of natural language processing to network structures. Network representation learning addresses the sparsity issue commonly faced by machine learning applications in networks by representing nodes in a unified low-dimensional space. These node representations have been shown to retain certain properties of the network structure, such as homophily or structural equivalence [3]. However, in most networks additional information beyond the network structure is associated with a vertex, such as textual content or meta data. Consider for example a paper citation network as depicted in Fig. 1. In this network, the additional information associated with a node is textual information, i.e., the document content. Even further, each node is a vertex in the graph and a document at once.

© IFIP International Federation for Information Processing 2017
Published by Springer International Publishing AG 2017. All Rights Reserved
A. Holzinger et al. (Eds.): CD-MAKE 2017, LNCS 10410, pp. 237–251, 2017.
DOI: 10.1007/978-3-319-66808-6_16

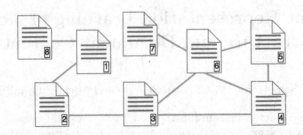

Fig. 1. Paper citation network with textual information (document content) and link information (citations) (Color figure online)

Both types, the network node and the document, can be represented as real-valued vectors with fixed length, so called embeddings. These embeddings can then be utilized as input features for subsequent tasks like node classification or link prediction see e.g. [3,11]. The goal of node (or document) classification in the citation network is to assign a particular category to a document (node), in order to organize a document collection. Link prediction in the context of a paper citation network refers to identifying relevant papers, which have not been cited in the paper at hand. Reasons for relevant papers not being cited are for example space constraints or authors publishing at the same time and hence not knowing about each others work.

For the citation network in Fig. 1, embeddings can be obtained by different means: Based on the textual document content, embeddings can be obtained via the Paragraph Vector (PV) [7] approach. An alternative way is to use the network or link information, for example with Spectral Clustering [12]. In this paper, we focus on node embeddings, like Deepwalk [9], LINE [11] or Node2Vec [3], that build on the representation learning techniques from the natural language processing domain. Only few approaches have been proposed that combine both modalities, link and text information. To the best of our knowledge, TADW [13] and Paper2Vec [2] are the only methods that combine both modalities using representation learning.

In this paper, we first provide background information about word and document embeddings and their adaption to graph structures. From this, we derive a novel baseline approach for a joint embedding of textual content and network structure. The assumption for the joint embeddings is that they retain information from both modalities (textual content and network structure). We assume these joint embeddings to be richer in expressiveness than representations trained on either text or network alone and hence provide a higher quality representation for subsequent tasks like node classification or link prediction. Then we review related work and present an evaluation of the different approaches (text only, graph only and combined). We conclude with an outlook on future work.

2   Background

In this section, we present models that use shallow neural networks to create the vector representations. We start with word embeddings, followed by their extension to document embeddings and their adaptation to graph structures. The common principle for all these models is the distributional hypothesis "you shall know a word by the company it keeps" [1], which states that words in similar contexts tend to have similar meanings [4]. That is, similar words (or nodes) tend to appear in similar word (node) neighborhoods.

2.1   Word Embeddings

The approach to compute continuous vector representations of words proposed by Mikolov et al. [7] became famous as Word2Vec. A sliding window is moved across a sentence, in order to define the context for a word. This process is illustrated in Fig. 2. The words, considered as context are defined by the window size, which is the maximum distance between the word under consideration and a context word. In our example, the window size is 2, i.e., 2 words to the left of $w(t)$, the word under consideration, and 2 words to the right are considered as context: The context words for *fox* are *quick, brown, jumped, over*.

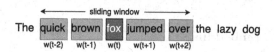

Fig. 2. Illustration of word embedding sliding window with window size 2

Mikolov et al. proposed two model architectures to compute the embeddings: The continuous bag-of-words (CBOW) model, illustrated in Fig. 3a and the continuous skip-gram (SG) model, illustrated in Fig. 3b. While CBOW tries to predict a word, given the context, SG tries to predict the context, given a word. Both models use a three-layer neural network, with linear activation in the hidden layer and a softmax in the output layer. The input in the SG model is a one-hot-coding and similarly in the CBOW model, a k-hot-coding activating the k inputs of the words in context. The output of the hidden layer in the CBOW model are the averaged weights between the activated inputs and the hidden layer. That is, only the weights of the k activated inputs are considered. Similarly, in the SG model, only the weights from the input word are considered. No averaging is needed in this case and hence, the output of the hidden layer is just a copy of the weights between the active input and the hidden layer. Furthermore, the SG model is trained by pairs of word and context word. The training pairs within the context window of our example from Fig. 2 are: (fox, quick), (fox, brown), (fox, jumped) and (fox, over). As an optimization step, Mikolov et al. suggest to give less weight to more distant context words, since

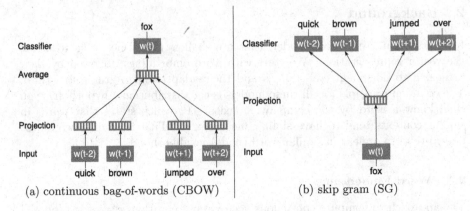

Fig. 3. Illustration of the two model architectures of Word2Vec (CBOW and SG) with the sliding window context from the example sentence in Fig. 2. The projection corresponds to the weights between input and hidden layer, i.e., the word embeddings.

more distant words are usually less related to the current word. This is achieved by not always sampling pairs from the complete window, but sampling the pairs from a randomly smaller window. The final embedding vector of a word is given by the weights between its corresponding input neuron and the hidden layer.

2.2   Document Embeddings

With Paragraph Vector [5], Quoc and Mikolov extended the Word2Vec approach to sentences and documents (also known as Doc2Vec). Therefore, they extended the two architectures presented in the previous section with an additional paragraph identifier, yielding the distributed memory (PV-DM) model, illustrated in Fig. 4a and the distributed bag-of-words (PV-DBOW) model, illustrated in Fig. 4b.

While PV-DM extends the CBOW model, PV-DBOW corresponds to the SG model. In PV-DM, a sliding window is moved across the paragraph (or document), similar to sliding a window across the sentences in Word2Vec. In contrast to Word2Vec, an additional paragraph identifier is added to the context. This paragraph identifier can be thought of as another word, which acts as a memory that remembers what is missing from the current context – or the topic of the paragraph. Therefore, it got named distributed memory. PV-DBOW uses the paragraph identifier to predict the context words. Here, context words are the words contained in the paragraph. The model is trained by pairs of (<paragraph_id>, <word in paragraph>). In the figure, we illustrated only four context words, i.e., four training pairs. Of course, during training, all of the words in a paragraph are to be considered.

It is to note that the paragraph identifier is just a symbolic token, which carries no semantic meaning in itself. However, the embedding of this identifier, i.e. the weights between the corresponding input neuron and the hidden layer

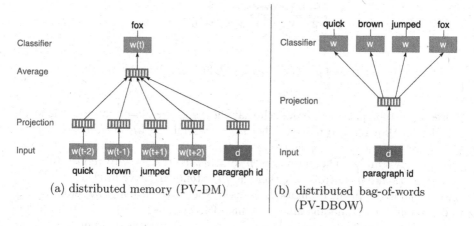

(a) distributed memory (PV-DM)

(b) distributed bag-of-words (PV-DBOW)

Fig. 4. Illustration of the two model architectures (PV-DM and PV-DBOW) of paragraph vector (Doc2Vec). The left part (PV-DM) shows the sliding window context from Fig. 2. PV-DBOW (right part) does not use a sliding window, instead all words from the sentence are considered as context.

(indicated as "projection" in the figure), does: After training the neural network, documents with similar content should have a similar representation in the embedding space, i.e., their weight vectors (projections) should be similar.

2.3 Graph Embeddings

With Deepwalk [9], Perozzi et al. adapt the Word2Vec approach for learning vector representations of vertices in a network. Therefore, they sample random walks for each node in the network and apply the skip gram (SG) model on the sampled walks. Those random walks can be thought of as the equivalent of sentences in the Word2Vec approach, with nodes resembling words. Accordingly, a sliding window is moved across the sampled walks to define the context. The analogies between nodes as words and walks as sentences apply only on the conceptual level. The actual input to the Deepwalk algorithm is in fact a graph. In our case, it is a citation network, as illustrated in Fig. 1, in which nodes correspond to papers and edges are given by the citations.

The sliding window across a walk is illustrated in Fig. 5. The figure is the graph equivalent to Fig. 2, the sliding window across a sentence. The random walk was sampled from the graph in Fig. 1. Perozzie et al. applied the SG model to train the vector representations, i.e., the current node predicts the nodes in the context. Alternatively, the CBOW model can also be applied to train the vectors, i.e., the nodes in the context predict the current node. We refer to the skip gram (SG) model on graphs as DW-SG and to the continuous bag-of-words (CBOW) model on graphs as DW-CBOW.

With Node2Vec [3] an extension to Deepwalk has been proposed, that allows to guide the walks in their exploration of the network. That is, the sampling

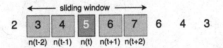

Fig. 5. Illustration of graph embedding sliding window with window size 2

procedure can be parametrized, such that the walks are biased towards the local neighborhood or tend to move further away (resembling breadth-first or depth-first search in the most extreme cases). The parameters, introduced to guide the walk are p and q. The parameter p controls the tendency to re-visit already visited nodes and q controls, whether the walk tends to move further away from the original node. In the evaluation, we used Node2Vec with a parameter setting that resembles the random walk sampling of Deepwalk ($p = 1, q = 1$). We refer to it as N2V. Typically, the SG model is used to train vector representations of nodes and we are also using that model, that is, we use N2V and N2V-SG synonymously.

3   Combining Link and Text Information

In this section, we present a novel model to learn combined embeddings for documents/nodes, fusing link and text information. We first show, how the Paragraph Vector approach (PV-DM and PV-DBOW as presented in Sect. 2.2 *document embeddings*) can be adapted to graph structures and then, how it can be extended to include textual information.

3.1   Paragraph Vector on Graphs

In Deepwalk, the Word2Vec approach is adapted to learn node representations. As a pre-requisite for our model, we show how the Paragraph Vector approach can also be adapted to represent nodes. Therefore, we assign the start node of each random walk as the paragraph identifier and treat the rest of the walk as paragraph content. That means, we sample a sub-graph around the starting node and learn an embedding vector for this sub-graph. If the walk length is chosen equal or larger than the network diameter, the random walks may cover the whole network. That is, the sampled sub-graph may not be a real sub-graph, but contain all nodes from the original graph.

On graphs, PV-DBOW is similar to DW-SG, if the walk length of PV-DBOW equals the window size of DW-SG. In this case, both models have the same context radius. In PV-DBOW, the walk length defines the maximum distance between the start node and nodes on the sampled walks. The random walks cannot contain nodes, that are further away from the start node than the walk length. Similarly, in DW-SG, the window size defines the maximum distance between the node under consideration and nodes to be considered as context. As those are sampled with random walks without jump probabilities, nodes that require more steps than the window size to be reached, are outside the context. It is to note, that while Deepwalk also has the walk length parameter, this parameter can be chosen to be larger, as the context radius is constrained afterwards by the window size.

3.2   Fusing Link and Text Information

We now have means to apply the Paragraph Vector model on both modalities, text and link information. This leads us to a combined model, by simply sharing the paragraph identifier between the text and the graph model. This is possible, as the paragraph identifier is just a symbolic identifier of the document or sub-graph respectively. We illustrate the combined model in Fig. 6. The illustrated model corresponds to the PV-DM approach, hence we refer to this architecture as text graph distributed memory (TG-DM). The left part of the figure is completely equivalent to PV-DM applied to textual content (cf. Fig. 4a), while the right part is equivalent to PV-DM for a sampled sub-graph (i.e. the set of walks with the same start node). These two models are combined via the shared weights of the paragraph identifier. This paragraph identifier is just a symbolic identifier, hence the "2" can be thought of as a document id and at the same time as a node id.

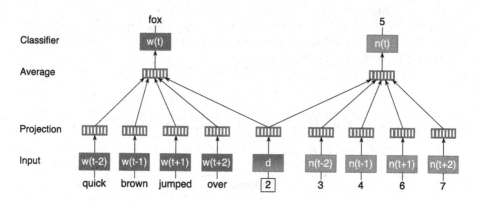

Fig. 6. Illustration of text graph distributed memory (TG-DM) model. The paragraph vector d is shared between the text (left part) and the network model (right part), acting as distributed memory for both of them at the same time.

The combination of text and link information with the PV-DBOW approach is achieved in the exact same fashion, by sharing the paragraph identifier. Hence we refer to the combination via PV-DBOW as text graph distributed bag-of-words (TG-DBOW). The term *words* in this case also includes network nodes, because walks are considered as sentences in a document. We investigated different methods to train the TG-DBOW model, namely: TG-MIX, TG-SPLIT and TG-SUM, which we present in the following.

TG-DBOW uses the skip gram architecture and hence, the training consists of a paragraph identifier and context words and nodes. The simplest method is then to use the architecture of PV-DBOW and treat the context nodes from the sampled random walks as words in the document. Again, the paragraph identifier is just a symbolic token, hence we can use the same identifier for the node and document. We call this method TG-MIX, which is depicted in Fig. 7:

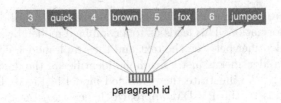

Fig. 7. TG-MIX

Another way to learn a combined embedding via TG-DBOW is to separate the output layers for nodes and words. We call this approach TG-SPLIT, depicted in Fig. 8. In this case, we alternate between showing the network paragraph identifier and context word pairs, and paragraph identifier and context node pairs. While the weights for the paragraph identifier are shared, the prediction of a context word or node is separated by using two separate softmax layers. These separate softmax layers are indicated with the two separate error measures E_1 and E_2 in the figure.

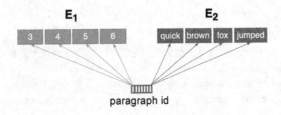

Fig. 8. TG-SPLIT

The third method, which we call TG-SUM, is depicted in Fig. 9. Here, we train the network by providing triples of paragraph identifier, context word and context node. That is, for a given paragraph identifier, the network simultaneously has to predict the context word and the context node. In contrast to TG-SPLIT, where in each alternating step the error to be propagated back is either E_1 or E_2, the error in TG-SUM is the sum of both errors $(E_1 + E_2)$ in every step. In preliminary experiments, TG-SPLIT outperformed TG-MIX and TG-SUM, hence we included only TG-SPLIT in the evaluation.

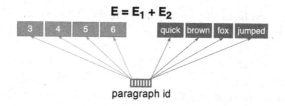

Fig. 9. TG-SUM

4   Related Work

In this section, we present two closely related approaches: TADW - Text Associated Deepwalk [13] and Paper2Vec [2]. To the best of our knowledge, these are the only two approaches that build upon the representation learning techniques from the natural language processing domain and combine text and link information into a single embedding.

4.1   Paper2Vec

With Paper2Vec, Ganguly and Pudi [2] do not propose a completely new model, but rather combine and extend existing models in a clever way. Paper2Vec is modeled around a citation network, i.e., the data for this approach needs to have at least a similar structure (documents with textual content, that are connected via links). Their contribution to improve the learned representations is two-fold: First, they enrich the citation graph with artificial edges, based on the similarity of documents and second, they initialize the node embeddings with the paragraph vector representations obtained from the documents.

The intuition behind the enrichment of the citation graph with artificial edges is that those are links, which should actually be there, but are omitted because of the following potential reasons: Authors may not be fully aware of all the current work in the field and hence, might miss to cite some papers. Also, space constraints limit the amount of citable papers and trivially, two papers might appear at the same time and therefore the authors may not know about each others work. Adding artificial edges between similar documents can then be considered as adding the missing links. To this end, the authors first compute an embedding for each paper with the PV-DM approach. Then, they add artificial links between each document and its k nearest neighbors, based on their similarity in the document embedding space.

To create the final embeddings, Paper2Vec applies the Deepwalk algorithm on the enriched graph that contains both, the original and artificial edges. Instead of randomly initializing the vector representations of the nodes in this graph, the authors initialize them with the document embeddings learned in the previous step. This raises the interesting question, whether this initialization avoids start configurations, that would result in a local optimum or whether the initialization preserves information from the document content, that cannot be learned via the network structure.

4.2 TADW

As a first important step of the TADW approach, Yang et al. [13] showed that Deepwalk factorizes a matrix of transition probabilities, similar to Word2Vec factorizing a matrix of co-occurrences. More precisely, each entry in the matrix that gets factorized with Deepwalk is the logarithm of the average probability that vertex v_i randomly walks to vertex v_j in a fixed number of steps. Similarly, depending on the network architecture, an entry in the matrix that gets factorized by Word2Vec is the logarithm of the weighted co-occurrence between a (word, context word)-pair [8] or the Shifted Positive Pointwise Mutual Information (SPMI) of the pair [6]. The matrix factorization of Deepwalk is illustrated in Fig. 10. The vertex representation of Deepwalk, i.e., the node embeddings, is given by the matrix W. The second step of TADW is then to incorporate text information. Instead of factorizing M into a product of two matrices, TADW factorizes M into a product of three matrices, where the third factor is a matrix of text features. This process is illustrated in Fig. 11. The text feature matrix T is a low-dimensional representation of the tf-idf matrix of the document contents, obtained via singular value decomposition. The matrices W and H are obtained by alternately optimizing them. The final vector representation is obtained by concatenating W and $H \times T$, resulting in a 2d-dimensional embedding.

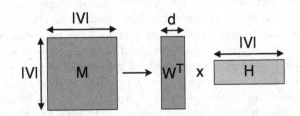

Fig. 10. Matrix factorization of Deepwalk.

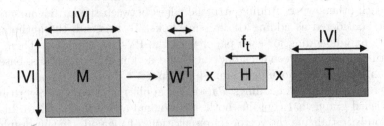

Fig. 11. Matrix factorization of Text Associated Deepwalk (TADW).

5 Evaluation

We evaluated[1] the aforementioned models on a node classification task on the CORA-ML dataset[2]. This dataset contains 2708 scientific publications from the machine learning domain. Each paper is assigned to one of seven classes (e.g. neural networks or reinforcement learning). The citation network of these publications consists of 5429 links. Each document in the dataset is described as a binary vector of 1433 dimensions, indicating the presence of the corresponding word. The document contents are short texts, generated from title, containing 18 words on average. On this dataset, node classification is equivalent to document classification. A label is assigned to a node or document respectively, while both represent the same thing (a document is at the same time a node in the citation network).

For a quick reference, we list the evaluated approaches again with a short description. The text-only models are colored green, the network-only models orange and the joint models blue.

PV-DBOW. The distributed bag-of-words model of paragraph vector [5]. Document embeddings are trained by predicting the context, i.e., the words in the corresponding document.

PV-DM. The distributed memory model of paragraph vector [5]. Predicts a word from the context words together with a paragraph identifier. The paragraph identifier acts as a memory for the context and is the document embedding.

DW-SG. Deepwalk with the skip gram model [9]. Node embeddings are trained by predicting the context, i.e., the neighboring nodes on a sampled random walk.

N2V. According to the authors, with parameters ($p = 1$, $q = 1$), N2V resembles DeepWalk [3]. We used it as an alternative to DW-SG in the evaluation.

CC. Naive baseline concatenation of document (PV-DBOW) and node embeddings (N2V).

TG-DM The paragraph vector model with distributed memory combining link and text information.

TG-SPLIT. The paragraph vector model with the skip-gram split approach, i.e. two separate output layers in the corresponding neural network.

P2V. The Paper2Vec approach, adding artificial links and initializing node with document embeddings [2].

TADW. Text associated deepwalk, factorizing the matrix of transition probabilities into three matrices [13].

We learned the vector representations on the whole dataset. Then we trained a support vector machine (SVM) on different portions of the data to predict the class in a supervised fashion, with the vector representations as input features.

---

[1] evaluation scripts are available at https://github.com/schloett/tg-split.
[2] http://www.cs.umd.edu/~sen/lbc-proj/LBC.html.

We opted for an SVM as it was also used in the related work for the node classification task [2,13]. The training portions were varied in 10% steps from 10% to 90%. We averaged the accuracy over 20 random splits for each percentage. An overview with the average accuracy across all training portions is given in Table 1. We were not able to run the Matlab implementation of TADW, due to issues with the mex-file, therefore, we had to exclude TADW from this comparison. The detailed results with averaged accuracy over the random splits for every percentage is given in Table 2. We explored different hyper-parameter settings with Bayesian Optimization [10], but did not find a major improvement. Therefore, we decided to stick to similar parameters as reported in the related work. We set the dimension of all the trained vector representations to 100. For the models including network information, we sampled 10 walks with a length of 40 for each node. We chose a window size of 5 and for models with negative sampling, we set the amount of samples to 10. As TG-SPLIT performed better than TG-SUM and TG-MIX in preliminary experiments, we only included TG-SPLIT in the evaluation.

Table 1. Results overview, with averaged accuracy over all training portions.

Text-only		Network-only	Joint				
PV-DM	PV-DBOW	N2V	CC	TG-DM	TG-SPLIT	P2V
53.5	65.4	83.4	84.8	54.7	83.1	78.7

Beyond the results from our evaluation, the detailed Table 2 contains the results reported in the original papers of TADW and Paper2Vec for comparison. The column "source" indicates the paper, from which the results were copied and the corresponding rows are colored with a light gray background. Both papers reported accuracy scores only up to a training percentage of 50%. It is to note, that the document contents used for evaluation in Paper2Vec differ from the original CORA-ML dataset. In Paper2Vec, the authors used the full text of the documents, while the original dataset contains less information (18 words per document on average). This explains the rather large difference in the text-only baselines[3] and also has an influence on the other methods, that take the document content into account. Hence the results are not directly comparable. Further, the evaluation was carried out on random splits of the data (20 splits in our experiments, 10 splits in Paper2Vec and TADW). The actual splits are of course not the same, but the differences in the averaged results are less significant than the aforementioned differences in the data.

As can be seen from the table, the approach for combining link and text information presented in Sect. 3 does not outperform the naive baseline of concatenating node and document embeddings. Also, its performance is close to the

---

[3] Even though the tf-idf dimensions are the same (1433) they contain different information. For tf-idf in Paper2Vec, the authors "kept the maximum features (sorted by df value) as 1433".

Table 2. Detailed results, with averaged accuracy over random splits for every training percentage. Light gray rows indicate results reported in the paper corresponding to source. The use of full text documents in the evaluation data is indicated by *. Text-only approaches are colored green (upper part), network-only are colored orange (middle part) and combined approaches are colored blue (lower part) and further separated by two lines.

source	model (dimensions)	SVM training ratio								
		10%	20%	30%	40%	50%	60%	70%	80%	90%
	PV-DM (100)	43.3	48.9	51.8	53.7	54.9	56.2	56.7	57.7	58.3
	PV-DBOW (100)	57.9	62.3	64.4	65.7	66.7	67.2	67.7	68.3	68.6
p2v*	PV-DM (100)	76.8	81.1	82.8	83.5	84.4	n.a.	n.a.	n.a.	n.a.
	tf-idf (1433)	37.9	47.8	55.6	61.6	65.2	68.4	70.7	72.0	73.4
p2v*	tf-idf (1433)	78.5	82.8	84.7	86.0	86.9	n.a.	n.a.	n.a.	n.a.
tadw	tf-idf (200)	58.3	67.4	71.1	73.3	74.0	n.a.	n.a.	n.a.	n.a.
	N2V (100)	77.2	80.7	82.5	83.6	84.5	84.8	85.3	85.8	85.9
tadw	DW-SG (100)	76.4	78.0	79.5	80.5	81.0	n.a.	n.a.	n.a.	n.a.
p2v*	DW-SG (100)	76.0	80.7	82.7	84.3	85.3	n.a.	n.a.	n.a.	n.a.
	P2V (100)	75.3	77.1	78.2	78.8	79.3	79.8	80.0	80.2	79.9
p2v*	P2V (100)	83.4	86.5	87.5	88.3	88.9	n.a.	n.a.	n.a.	n.a.
	TG-DM (100)	43.5	48.3	51.8	54.1	56.1	57.7	59.1	60.5	61.5
	TG-SPLIT (100)	73.4	79.7	82.3	83.9	84.9	85.5	85.9	86.1	86.3
	CC (200)	78.4	82.0	83.7	84.9	85.8	86.4	86.8	87.3	87.6
p2v*	CC (200)	80.6	83.8	85.1	86.4	87.1	n.a.	n.a.	n.a.	n.a.
tadw	CC (300)	76.5	80.4	82.3	83.3	84.1	n.a.	n.a.	n.a.	n.a.
p2v*	TADW (160)	82.4	85.0	85.6	86.0	86.7	n.a.	n.a.	n.a.	n.a.
tadw	TADW (200)	82.4	85.0	85.6	86.0	86.7	n.a.	n.a.	n.a.	n.a.

performance of node embeddings alone and inferior to TADW. With our model showing no improvement over the concatenated baseline, we assume that it is not able of making use of text information to complement link information and vice versa: Intuitively, we aim for similar embeddings of papers that have either similar content, similar citations or both. That is, papers with similar content should have a similar representation in the embedding space, regardless of their link structure (accordingly for papers with similar citations). This similarity criterion does not seem to be reflected in the embeddings, potentially because the optimization objective during learning the embeddings is to predict the context (or to predict from the context), not the class label.

We were not able to reproduce the high accuracy reported by Paper2Vec, which we account in particular to the differences in the dataset used for evaluation: Paper2Vec used the full text of the document, while the documents in the original CORA-ML dataset, which we used are short texts (18 words on average). Also, we may not have found the optimal set of hyper-parameters for the P2V approach. The accuracies of P2V are even lower than N2V. This may be caused by the lower quality document embeddings (cf. PV-DM vs. p2v* PV-DM), as those are used to add artificial links to the graph. It seems that more noisy links are added, lowering the performance of the node embeddings trained on the enriched network.

Summarizing the results, the novel baseline TG-SPLIT does not improve over the naive baseline of simply concatenating the node and document embeddings. In fact, its performance is comparable to the network-only model N2V. This indicates that the joint representation TG-SPLIT cannot make use of the mutual benefit, that we expected from incorporating network structure and document content.

6   Summary and Future Work

In this paper, we presented an overview on representation learning for combined network and text information, based on recent representation learning models from the natural language domain. Therefore, we gave a summary of the most prominent word embedding model and its extension to documents. We also summarized approaches, that adapt the word embeddings for network learning. We showed how document embeddings can be adapted to graph structures and introduced a novel baseline for a combined learning. We evaluated the presented models on a paper citation network. Results show, that the introduced baseline TG-SPLIT does not improve over the naive baseline of concatenating node and document embeddings and is comparable to the network-only model N2V. That is, TG-SPLIT does not seem to be able to connect network structure to document content for a mutual benefit.

In future work, we aim to investigate the question raised in Sect. 4.1 on whether the initialization of node embeddings with document embeddings avoids local optima or transfers information from the document content to the node representation (or whether it is a combination of both and how the influence of each is). We further aim to investigate other neural network architectures for the combined learning, in order to find a bridge between the text and the link information, similarly to TADW.

References

1. Firth, J.R.: A synopsis of linguistic theory 1930–55. In: Studies in Linguistic Analysis (Special Volume of the Philological Society), vol. 1952–1959, pp. 1–32. The Philological Society, Oxford (1957)
2. Ganguly, S., Pudi, V.: Paper2vec: combining graph and text information for scientific paper representation. In: Jose, J.M., Hauff, C., Altıngovde, I.S., Song, D., Albakour, D., Watt, S., Tait, J. (eds.) ECIR 2017. LNCS, vol. 10193, pp. 383–395. Springer, Cham (2017). doi:10.1007/978-3-319-56608-5_30

3. Grover, A., Leskovec, J.: Node2vec: scalable feature learning for networks. In: Proceedings of the 22nd ACM SIGKDD International Conference on Knowledge Discovery and Data Mining, KDD 2016, NY, USA, pp. 855–864. ACM, New York (2016)

4. Harris, Z.: Distributional structure. Word **10**(23), 146–162 (1954)

5. Le, Q., Mikolov, T.: Distributed representations of sentences and documents. In: Proceedings of the 31st International Conference on Machine Learning, PMLR, Bejing, China, 22–24 June 2014, pp. 1188–1196 (2014)

6. Levy, O., Goldberg, Y.: Neural word embedding as implicit matrix factorization. In: Proceedings of the 27th International Conference on Neural Information Processing Systems, NIPS 2014, pp. 2177–2185. MIT Press, Cambridge (2014)

7. Mikolov, T., Sutskever, I., Chen, K., Corrado, G., Dean, J.: Distributed representations of words and phrases and their compositionality. In: Proceedings of the 26th International Conference on Neural Information Processing Systems, NIPS 2013, pp. 3111–3119. Curran Associates Inc., USA (2013)

8. Pennington, J., Socher, R., Manning, C.D.: Glove: global vectors for word representation. In: Empirical Methods in Natural Language Processing (EMNLP), pp. 1532–1543 (2014)

9. Perozzi, B., Al-Rfou, R., Skiena, S.: Deepwalk: online learning of social representations. In: Proceedings of the 20th ACM SIGKDD International Conference on Knowledge Discovery and Data Mining, KDD 2014, NY, USA, pp. 701–710. ACM, New York (2014)

10. Snoek, J., Larochelle, H., Adams, R.P.: Practical bayesian optimization of machine learning algorithms. In: Proceedings of the 25th International Conference on Neural Information Processing Systems, NIPS 2012, pp. 2951–2959. Curran Associates Inc., USA (2012)

11. Tang, J., Qu, M., Wang, M., Zhang, M., Yan, J., Mei, Q.: Line: large-scale information network embedding. In: Proceedings of the 24th International Conference on World Wide Web, WWW 2015, pp. 1067–1077. International World Wide Web Conferences Steering Committee, Republic and Canton of Geneva, Switzerland (2015)

12. Tang, L., Liu, H.: Leveraging social media networks for classification. Data Min. Knowl. Discov. **23**(3), 447–478 (2011)

13. Yang, C., Liu, Z., Zhao, D., Sun, M., Chang, E.Y.: Network representation learning with rich text information. In: Proceedings of the 24th International Conference on Artificial Intelligence, IJCAI 2015, pp. 2111–2117. AAAI Press (2015)

MAKE AAL

Ambient Assisted Living Technologies from the Perspectives of Older People and Professionals

Deepika Singh[1]([⊠]), Johannes Kropf[1], Sten Hanke[1], and Andreas Holzinger[2]

[1] AIT Austrian Institute of Technology, Wiener Neustadt, Austria
`deepika.singh@ait.ac.at`
[2] Holzinger Group, HCI-KDD, Institute for Medical Informatics/Statistics,
Medical University Graz, Graz, Austria

Abstract. Ambient Assisted Living (AAL) and Ambient Intelligence technologies are providing support to older people in living an independent and confident life by developing innovative ICT-based products, services, and systems. Despite significant advancement in AAL technologies and smart systems, they have still not found the way into the nursing home of the older people. The reasons are manifold. On one hand, the development of such systems lack in addressing the requirements of the older people and caregivers of the organization and the other is the unwillingness of the older people to make use of assistive systems. A qualitative study was performed at a nursing home to understand the needs and requirements of the residents and caregivers and their perspectives about the existing AAL technologies.

Keywords: Smart homes · Ambient assisted living · Independent living · Ageing · Quality of life

1 Introduction

The aging population is the one of the major concerns of the world due to its direct socioeconomic implications. According to the United Nations' report, the number of people aged 65 years and above is expected to grow from 901 million in 2015 to 1.4 billion in 2030 [1,2]. According to the European population projections, it is expected that by 2040, one third of the elderly population will be aged 80 years and above. This demographic changes in the population is due to declines in fertility rate, continuous increases in the life expectancy and the retirement of the baby-boom generation [1,3].

Over aging leads to many problems ranging from basic functional disabilities to severe health problems e.g. osteoarthritis, diabetes, depression, chronic obstructive pulmonary diseases and dementia. In addition to the medical problems, the fact of being dependent on family members and/or care providers for their daily activities, cause embarrassment, social inactivity and poor nutrition etc.

A. Holzinger et al. (Eds.): CD-MAKE 2017, LNCS 10410, pp. 255–266, 2017.
DOI: 10.1007/978-3-319-66808-6_17

For long-term care and continuous assessment of physical and mental health in the older people there has been an increasing demand of nursing homes in the last decade [4,5]. However, this does not solve their problems completely; thus technology is the tool which can provide them an independent and happier life and at the same time accurate and timely personal care by the nursing home staff.

To overcome some of the mentioned problems, there has been a rapid development in ambient assisted living technologies (AAL) in Europe [6]. Different AAL solutions towards home monitoring, fall detection, social interaction have been developed using machine learning techniques. Technologies such as smart homes, assistive robots, mobile and wearable sensors have gained a lot of attention, but there are still many challenges that need to be addressed [7]. The concept of the smart home is a promising and cost-effective way of improving home care for the older people and the disabled in a non-obtrusive way, allowing greater independence, maintaining good health and preventing social isolation. There have been major advancements in the area of smart homes research that is enriching the home environment with technology (e.g., sensors and interconnected devices in a network) [8]. The most popular smart home projects are MavHome (Managing an Adaptive Versatile Home) [9], GatorTech [10], CASAS smart home [11], EasyLiving project [12] etc. The design of smart home depends on user requirement and living lifestyle of the resident; several approaches are proposed to identify activities of daily living of the resident of the home [13]. Although, the detection of a specific activity depends on the selection of appropriate set of sensors, data processing techniques and effective algorithms to understand daily lifestyle and human behavior [13,14]. The development of such systems lack in addressing the requirements of the older people and caregivers of the organization. One possibility to overcome this issue is proposed by applying extreme usability methods [15]. Additionally, various machine learning approaches have been used to develop an intelligent system for activity recognition; most common methods are Naive Bayes [16], Hidden Markov Model [17], and Conditional Random Field [18] classifiers. Despite the number of machine learning approaches, the accuracy of activity recognition is still not robust and unable to deal with uncertainty. There exist lot of challenges that need to be addressed in implementing effective solutions for older people [19].

To develop adaptable smart home technologies according to the specific needs of the older residents, their suggestions and inputs are much needed. A number of studies have been carried out where older people are participating in providing suggestions and opinions about the technologies [20]. Residents and family members indicated that they feel safe and had an overall positive attitude towards devices and installation of sensors [21] knowing that someone is monitoring them for their wellbeing [22]. The parameters of quality of life are usually evaluated by the older people on the basis of social contacts, dependency, health, material circumstances and social comparisons [23]. Certainly, AAL solutions and assistive technologies have a positive impact on different dimensions of health and quality of life. The needs and problems of older people can be addressed by applying appropriate solutions which influence the physical, mental and social dimensions of quality of life [24]. Nevertheless, the most important aspect is the acceptance of technology/devices by the older people and professionals [25].

Within the framework of this study, we wanted to know the different perspectives of the older people and care giving professionals of a particular nursing home. From the older people point of view we were interested in the following things: (i) how comfortable they are with the existing technologies (sensors, cameras, robots); any (ii) specific need they would require assistance or (iii) activities which they could imagine to be monitored; (iv) their problems and fears. From the caregiver point of view we were interested in the following: which data/information would be useful for them to provide accurate and timely attention to the patients. The study is aimed to understand the needs better so that more useful AAL solutions can be developed considering the inputs from the residents and caregivers.

2   Methodology

2.1   Planning

The research activity was planned at Zuyderland nursing home situated in Sittard-Geleen (The Netherlands) for 4 weeks. This nursing home is a part of Zuyderland Medical and Health care Group in the province of Limburg, Netherlands. The nursing home has a total of 273 residents and it is divided into small scale living apartments (48 residents), elderly care apartments (100 residents) and 3 apartments blocks for independent living (125 residents). The residents from the elderly care apartments and independent living apartment were contacted to participate in the study.

The research activities to be performed were divided for each week such that in the first week we collected information about the facilities which are provided to the patients in the hospital and the nursing home. The interviews with the residents and professionals of the hospital and the nursing home were conducted in the second week. The next two weeks were spent on transcribing the answers of the interview questions and analysis of the data obtained from the interviews. The aim of the study was to acquire knowledge about the daily living lifestyle of the old people and to investigate the needs, problems they face. In addition, it was also beneficial to know from the opinions of residents and caring staff about various existing ICT solutions and ambient assisted technologies including Smart Care Home. The caregivers had prior knowledge of existing AAL technologies from former research projects.

2.2   Focus Group and Sampling

Care professionals and residents of the nursing home were contacted to ask for the participation in the study. The aim was to enroll large number of people who can best discuss and share their experiences. The residents for the study were chosen by the nursing home's caring staff since they were knowing their exact medical conditions. For example, this activity should not to disturb any of the medical routines of residents, therefore, the residents suffering from severe chronic diseases (such as cancer and last stage heart diseases), and those with pacemakers and other required monitoring electronic devices such as ECG, pulse oximetry etc. have been excluded from the study. The focus group of the study was composed of residents and professionals as specified below:

1. Residents from the independent living apartments
2. Residents from elderly care apartments
3. Professionals include Physiotherapist, Occupational therapist and Dietician
4. Caring staff of the nursing home
5. Innovation and development experts

The total sample size was consisting of seven residents ($n = 7$) and six professionals ($n = 6$). The characteristics of all the 13 participants interviewed are shown in Tables 1 and 2. We have assigned code to each participant such that "R" and "P" denote resident and professional respectively. The average age of the residents was 80 years and the average experience of the professional in dealing with problems of older people was 17 years.

Table 1. Demographics of the residents

ID	Age (years)	Gender	Work Status
R1	90	Male	All of them were retired
R2	82	Male	
R3	80	Female	
R4	74	Female	
R5	65	Male	
R6	86	Female	
R7	81	Female	

Table 2. Details of professionals

ID	Age (years)	Gender	Specialization	Experience with elderly(in years)
P1	53	Female	Dietician	20
P2	39	Male	Physiotherapist	16
P3	33	Female	Occupational therapist	11
P4	37	Male	Caregiver	21
P5	39	Male	Innovation expert	17
P6	40	Male	Innovation expert	18

2.3   Data Collection

The interview questions for the residents were finalized after having discussions with care home professionals ranging from nurses (who are in direct contact with the residents) to the innovation experts and vice-versa. The inputs from them were well addressed in the final questionnaires in both the cases. As already stated, the final aim of the interviews was to answer the following questions:

- What are the problems faced by the elderly in performing the daily living activities?
- How smart care homes can contribute to the needs and requirements of the elderly and caregivers?
- An opinion about existing AAL technologies and how it can be improved?

In the beginning of the interview, the objective of the study were explained to the participants and they were told that they can leave or interrupt the interview whenever they feel any discomfort and/or unwillingness to answer. Since the interview were conducted in an informal way of talking, the timing was varied from 25 to 60 min. Consents were taken for audio recording the sessions so as not to miss any important points and actual responses can be quoted. All the participants agreed to audio record the interviews and the data collected were transcribed verbatim for the accuracy immediately after the interview.

The questions were framed in the simplest way for sake of clarity; they were also allowed to seek any sort of clarification needed. In order to make the residents comfortable, the interviewer started with an informal conversation, e.g.

Q: What are your hobbies?

Q: What do you like to do in your free time inside the home?

And the interview progressed in a manner of fluent conversation. However, the framed questions were asked clearly in the running conversation to be consistent with the responses so that it may not lead to any ambiguity in comparison.

The interviews with the residents were performed in two groups, one group was the residents from independent living apartments (R1–R4) and other group was of residents from the elderly care apartments (R5–R7). Interviews with professionals and caregivers were conducted on one-to-one basis.

2.4   Ethics

The research was conducted with the prior permission and after the approval from the hospital and care organization authorities. To ensure confidentiality, an agreement was signed by the researcher with the organization. Full anonymity was promised to all the participants.

2.5   Data Analysis

The transcribed data was matched with the audio taped version to remove any discrepancies. Data analysis was performed using qualitative content analysis approach [26, 27]. Analysis process includes various steps:

- Organizing and collection of data;
- repeated reading of the data;
- look for meaningful data and labeling it into codes;
- grouping the codes in subcategories;
- grouping subcategories into categories to generate themes.

To ensure the rigor in this study following criteria have been fulfilled: (i) getting familiar with the residents to form trusting relationships, verifying responses with the participants (credibility); (ii) selection of the participants (dependability); (iii) using extracts from the interviews to support findings (transferability); (iv) and establishing an audit trail (confirmability) [28].

3   Findings and Discussions

With consideration to the care needs, we decided to perform a thematic analysis focusing on different important aspects of healthy living; three themes were identified: *daily living, social engagement and technology*. The themes have different categories and subcategories, as shown in Table 3. We have also included some quotes from residents and professionals in the discussion section to highlight the exact needs without generalization.

Table 3. Care needs of the elderly

Themes	Categories	Subcategories
Daily Living	Problems and needs	Eating
		Cooking
		Grooming
		Housekeeping
		Bathroom usage
	Psychological care	Privacy
		Safety
Social Engagement	Participation in social activities	Social events in elderly home
		Special events
		Visit with family members
	Physical activities	Exercise
		Indoor activities
		Outdoor activities
Technology	Adaptability with technology	Devices
		Robots
		Security cameras

3.1 Daily Living

In our study we observed the daily living lifestyle of the residents in the nursing home. All the residents have their own private apartments in assistive environment with 24 × 7 availability of the caring staff.

The residents have different problems and needs which are mainly defined by their health conditions. The residents suffering from some physical disabilities, mild chronic diseases and fractures, find difficulty in performing most of their daily activities (such as going to toilet, showering, walking or moving inside their apartment, eating), therefore, they seek more assistance from caregivers. The caregivers help the residents in order to follow their daily routine.

P3: "I watch them and analyze that they find difficulties in moving or walking, I look for possibilities so that person can move in their room and actively participate in the environment either with care or some aids."

P3: "The first thing which the patients want to do without any assistance is going to the toilet; as dependence on care givers brings the sense of embarrassment among the patients."

The older people sometimes do not express their urges out of embarrassment which causes poor nutrition and imbalance diet.

R6: "I cannot pick something from refrigerator, or from table because I cannot move. Every time I have to ring and call the nurse"

P1: "I met a patient who told me that I eat less, because I have call somebody to get me something to eat and drink"

In some cases, they need assistance even for small things such as picking up bottle for drinking, cloths from the wardrobe etc.

P2: "Residents also need assistance in household activities like closing the door, curtains, turning off the TV and all these activities takes lot of time of the nurses"

From the interview we found out the major factors which affect the patients physiologically are: feeling of embarrassment; helplessness and loneliness; depression and lack of motivation.

R5: "My hobbies are painting but I do not have motivation of doing it"

One of main challenges for the caregivers is monitoring the resident who do not interact with anyone and keep themselves inside the apartment. In that case, the caregivers cannot track the patients daily activities and prescribed dietary plan. In addition, they sometimes lie and even refuse to take any help by the caregivers.

P1: "A patient answered when offered help: Oh No, I dont need anything. Dont do that, dont make anything for me"

3.2 Social Engagement and Physical Activities

Engagement of the residents in social and physical activities depends on the personal choices, interests and their health conditions. From the interviews, we analyzed that most of the residents participate in the social activities organized within the nursing home but only very few of them go out for some physical activity, walking or swimming. They like to go out only with family member and on some special occasions. This unwillingness could be due the fear of fall, fear of exhaustion and thus always need a companion with them.

There are few challenges with the residents suffering from severe chronic disease, disabilities; such residents do not like to participate mainly due to the feeling of helplessness and embarrassment. The other major factor which cause less physical activity and less exercise is due to the pain.

P2: "Pain has a strong influence on daily living and most important domain where we can act as physical therapist. Would be good if I know in which activities and movement patients suffers pain"

The residents participate in the exercise sessions and trainer motivates them to continue with their exercise. But sometimes exercise during the sessions is not just enough and they are advised to follow a routine. However, it is very difficult to know from the older people that whether they are exercising in their homes or not?

P2: "I do not know whether the patient exercise in their own home or not"

The less physical activity also causes poor nutrition; as the patients do not consume food and/or liquid if they remain inactive for a longer duration.

From the perspective of professionals, quality of life can be improved by motivating and engaging older people in different social activities of their interest which keep them physically active, thus decrease depression and feeling of loneliness.

3.3   Technology

The adaptability with technology is one the most important point to be considered while designing a smart home. It does not solve the purpose if a highly sophisticated device is provided but they do not feel comfortable in using it. We found out from the responses of the older people that they find the technology beneficial and useful especially from the safety point of view; but they have their preferences and restrictions.

P2: "When residents see everybody is using it then they use it"

Table 4. Technology

ID	Smart phone	Tablet	Laptop/Computer
R1	No	Yes	No
R2	No	Yes	Yes
R3	No	Yes	No
R4	Yes	Yes	No
R5	Yes	Yes	Yes
R6	No	Yes	No
R7	No	No	Yes

Table 4 highlights the comfort levels of the older people in using various devices among smart phone, tablet and laptop/computer. As it is clear from the table, among all the devices, majority of the residents find tablet more comfortable in using than smart phones and computer.

In the study, we also inquired from the residents whether they are comfortable with robots and they like to see robots assisting them in daily activities in their home. Most of them disagreed with having robots inside their apartments. Residents pointed out that they are more comfortable in using tablets and agreed in using wearable devices but do not want big robots around them.

R4: "No! I do not want robot inside my apartment"
R1: "I cannot cuddle it and they do not give hugs"

In concern with the home security, we asked whether they like to put cameras outside their apartment door to see who visited them, in their absence. The residents strictly denied that they do not want to put camera inside and outside their apartment.

R2: "If someone wants to meet me, he/she can come again"

From the perspective of the older people and professionals, a personalized intelligent assistive technologies will be desirable which can provide independence, ensure safety, and should be adaptable according to needs of the residents.

3.4   Suggestions/Recommendations

As one of the main motives of the study was to seek suggestions from the residents and professionals for making the nursing home smart.

P1: "when I know how active the patient is, it would be nice for me to know how much energy he/she spent per day and will help me in making diet plan and improve accordingly. Now it is always guess and I have to ask patient every time"

P1: "Would be good if there is some system which help in cooking and preparing the meals. In kitchen, if stove get automatically turned off when not in use"

In general, from the caregivers perspective, some family members of the residents want to keep a track of their health status and daily updates from the nursing home. A system or application which sends out daily notifications to family members and notify them in case any emergency, would be really desirable.

P4: "Would be good to have system for caregiver and resident in the apartment which controls the lighting, door open/close, curtains open/close and inside temperature level"

P3: "If I could know information about small activities from smart home like whether patient is going to bathroom by their own, getting meal or drinks from the kitchen, would be very helpful"

R3: "It would be good if I know my sleeping patterns and activity level inside my home, so I can show that data to my doctor"

From the perspective of the residents safety is the major concern. In the nursing home, residents have a personal alarm system, which they find very useful and beneficial. They use it for calling the caregiver in case of any assistance required and emergency inside the home. However, the residents recommended that such kind of system would be really useful, if they could use it when they are out. In that case, they would feel safer in going out alone, which enhances physical activeness and social involvement.

4   Conclusion

The findings of our study provide insights into the problems and needs of the residents of the nursing home. It also highlights the challenges faced by the caregivers during monitoring of the older people. Suggestions and recommendations have been pointed out from both the sides aiming at an independent and confident life of the residents. We summarize them as follows:

Although, the needs and problems are varied according to the individuals needs. The residents from the independent living apartments *(R1–R4)* do not really want home automation as they can perform basic daily activities. They think it can make them less physically active. On the other hand residents from the elderly care apartments *(R5–R7)* get regular assistance by the caregivers and there is evident need of a smart care home to reduce less personal assistance in basic household activities such as lock/unlock doors, opening/closing window shields, lights controlling etc. However, all the residents agreed to have a system which could monitor their physical activities. Such system would be really useful for the caregivers in order to know the activity level of the residents and deviations from the normal behavior. From patients and caregivers point of view, information about the following would be really useful: walking patterns, sleep analysis, real time location, fall detection and physical activity level.

All the participants agreed that assistive technologies and AAL solutions can have beneficial effects on quality of life and health. Majority of the residents feel comfortable in using tablet over smart phone and laptop. Big robots and cameras are not preferred by the residents; but they are open for wearable devices. On contrary, the professionals find robots a valuable contributions in smart care homes.

Based on the findings of this study it is recommended that a personalized smart home solution which can monitor daily living activities would be really useful for such nursing homes and even for private homes where old people live alone. Such system should be capable of detecting the users activity level and thus sends out recommendations to perform some physical activity when the user is inactive for a while. It can also notify the care staff and/or family members about the abnormalities.

Acknowledgement. This work has been funded by the European Union Horizon2020 MSCA ITN ACROSSING project (GA no. 616757). The authors would like to thank all the participants for their contributions; Esther Veraa, Cindy Wings, Maarten Coolen from Zuyderland, Sittard-Geleen, Netherlands for their valuable inputs and immense support.

References

1. DESA: United nations department of economic and social affairs/population division: world population ageing 2015 (2015)
2. Kleinberger, T., Becker, M., Ras, E., Holzinger, A., Müller, P.: Ambient intelligence in assisted living: enable elderly people to handle future interfaces. In: Stephanidis, C. (ed.) UAHCI 2007. LNCS, vol. 4555, pp. 103–112. Springer, Heidelberg (2007). doi:10.1007/978-3-540-73281-5_11
3. Molinuevo, D.: Services for older people in Europe, October 2008
4. Bettio, F., Verashchagina, A.: Long-term care for the elderly. Provisions and providers in 33 European countries, November 2010
5. Ribbe, M.W., Ljunggren, G., Steel, K., Topinkova, E., Hawes, C., Ikegami, N., Henrard, J.C.: Nursing homes in 10 nations: a comparison between countries and settings. Age Ageing **26**(suppl 2), 3–12 (1997)
6. Blackman, S., Matlo, C., Bobrovitskiy, C., Waldoch, A., Fang, M.L., Jackson, P., Mihailidis, A., Nygård, L., Astell, A., Sixsmith, A.: Ambient assisted living technologies for aging well: a scoping review. J. Intell. Syst. **25**(1), 55–69 (2016)
7. Rashidi, P., Mihailidis, A.: A survey on ambient-assisted living tools for older adults. IEEE J. Biomed. Health Inform. **17**(3), 579–590 (2013)
8. Chan, M., Campo, E., Estève, D., Fourniols, J.Y.: Smart homes current features and future perspectives. Maturitas **64**(2), 90–97 (2009)
9. Das, S.K., Cook, D.J., Battacharya, A., Heierman, E.O., Lin, T.Y.: The role of prediction algorithms in the mavhome smart home architecture. IEEE Wirel. Commun. **9**(6), 77–84 (2002)
10. Helal, S., Mann, W., El-Zabadani, H., King, J., Kaddoura, Y., Jansen, E.: The gator tech smart house: A programmable pervasive space. Computer **38**(3), 50–60 (2005)
11. Rashidi, P., Cook, D.J.: Keeping the intelligent environment resident in the loop (2008)
12. Krumm, J., Harris, S., Meyers, B., Brumitt, B., Hale, M., Shafer, S.: Multi-camera multi-person tracking for easyliving. In: Third IEEE International Workshop on Visual Surveillance, Proceedings, pp. 3–10. IEEE (2000)
13. Skubic, M., Alexander, G., Popescu, M., Rantz, M., Keller, J.: A smart home application to eldercare: current status and lessons learned. Technol. Health Care **17**(3), 183–201 (2009)
14. Ni, Q., García Hernando, A.B., de la Cruz, I.P.: The elderlys independent living in smart homes: a characterization of activities and sensing infrastructure survey to facilitate services development. Sensors **15**(5), 11312–11362 (2015)
15. Holzinger, A., Errath, M., Searle, G., Thurnher, B., Slany, W.: From extreme programming and usability engineering to extreme usability in software engineering education (xp+ue/spl rarr/xu). In: 29th Annual International Computer Software and Applications Conference, COMPSAC 2005, vol. 2, pp. 169–172. IEEE (2005)

16. Tapia, E.M., Intille, S.S., Larson, K.: Activity recognition in the home using simple and ubiquitous sensors. In: Ferscha, A., Mattern, F. (eds.) Pervasive 2004. LNCS, vol. 3001, pp. 158–175. Springer, Heidelberg (2004). doi:10.1007/978-3-540-24646-6_10

17. Nguyen, N.T., Phung, D.Q., Venkatesh, S., Bui, H.: Learning and detecting activities from movement trajectories using the hierarchical hidden Markov model. In: IEEE Computer Society Conference on Computer Vision and Pattern Recognition, CVPR 2005, vol. 2, pp. 955–960. IEEE (2005)

18. Nazerfard, E., Das, B., Holder, L.B., Cook, D.J.: Conditional random fields for activity recognition in smart environments. In: Proceedings of the 1st ACM International Health Informatics Symposium, pp. 282–286. ACM (2010)

19. Sun, H., De Florio, V., Gui, N., Blondia, C.: Promises and challenges of ambient assisted living systems. In: Sixth International Conference on Information Technology: New Generations, ITNG 2009, pp. 1201–1207. IEEE (2009)

20. Dongen, J.J.J., Habets, I.G.J., Beurskens, A., Bokhoven, M.A.: Successful participation of patients in interprofessional team meetings: a qualitative study. Health Expectations (2016)

21. Demiris, G., Rantz, M.J., Aud, M.A., Marek, K.D., Tyrer, H.W., Skubic, M., Hussam, A.A.: Older adults' attitudes towards and perceptions of smart home-technologies: a pilot study. Med. Inform. Internet Med. 29(2), 87–94 (2004)

22. Alam, M.R., Reaz, M.B.I., Ali, M.A.M.: A review of smart homes past, present, and future. IEEE Trans. Syst. Man Cybern. Part C (Appl. Rev.) 42(6), 1190–1203 (2012)

23. Netuveli, G., Blane, D.: Quality of life in older ages. Br. Med. Bull. 85(1), 113–126 (2008)

24. Siegel, C., Hochgatterer, A., Dorner, T.E.: Contributions of ambient assisted living for health and quality of life in the elderly and care services-a qualitative analysis from the experts perspective of care service professionals. BMC Geriatrics 14(1), 112 (2014)

25. Holzinger, A., Schaupp, K., Eder-Halbedl, W.: An investigation on acceptance of ubiquitous devices for the elderly in a Geriatric Hospital environment: using the example of person tracking. In: Miesenberger, K., Klaus, J., Zagler, W., Karshmer, A. (eds.) ICCHP 2008. LNCS, vol. 5105, pp. 22–29. Springer, Heidelberg (2008). doi:10.1007/978-3-540-70540-6_3

26. Elo, S., Kyngäs, H.: The qualitative content analysis process. J. Adv. Nurs. 62(1), 107–115 (2008)

27. Miles, M.B., Huberman, A.M.: Qualitative Data Analysis: An Expanded Sourcebook. Sage, Thousand Oaks (1994)

28. Krefting, L.: Rigor in qualitative research: the assessment of trustworthiness. Am. J. Occup. Ther. 45(3), 214–222 (1991)

Human Activity Recognition
Using Recurrent Neural Networks

Deepika Singh[1]([✉]), Erinc Merdivan[1]([✉]), Ismini Psychoula[2], Johannes Kropf[1],
Sten Hanke[1], Matthieu Geist[3], and Andreas Holzinger[4]

[1] AIT Austrian Institute of Technology, Wiener Neustadt, Austria
{deepika.singh,erinc.merdivan}@ait.ac.at
[2] School of Computer Science and Informatics, De Montfort University, Leicester, UK
[3] CentraleSupelec, Châtenay-Malabry, France
[4] Holzinger Group, HCI-KDD, Institute for Medical Informatics/Statistics,
Medical University Graz, Graz, Austria

Abstract. Human activity recognition using smart home sensors is one
of the bases of ubiquitous computing in smart environments and a topic
undergoing intense research in the field of ambient assisted living. The
increasingly large amount of data sets calls for machine learning methods.
In this paper, we introduce a deep learning model that learns to classify
human activities without using any prior knowledge. For this purpose,
a Long Short Term Memory (LSTM) Recurrent Neural Network was
applied to three real world smart home datasets. The results of these
experiments show that the proposed approach outperforms the existing
ones in terms of accuracy and performance.

Keywords: Machine learning · Deep learning · Human activity recognition · Sensors · Ambient assisted living · LSTM

1 Introduction

Human Activity recognition has been an active research area in the last decades
due to its applicability in different domains and the increasing need for home
automation and convenience services for the elderly [1]. Among them, activity
recognition in Smart Homes with the use of simple and ubiquitous sensors, has
gained a lot of attention in the field of ambient intelligence and assisted living
technologies for enhancing the quality of life of the residents within the home
environment [2].

The goal of activity recognition is to identify and detect simple and complex
activities in real world settings using sensor data. It is a challenging task, as the
data generated from the sensors are sometimes ambiguous with respect to the
activity taking place. This causes ambiguity in the interpretation of activities.
Sometimes the data obtained can be noisy as well. Noise in the data can be
caused by humans or due to error in the network system which fails to give

A. Holzinger et al. (Eds.): CD-MAKE 2017, LNCS 10410, pp. 267–274, 2017.
DOI: 10.1007/978-3-319-66808-6_18

correct sensor readings. Such real-world settings are full of uncertainties and calls for methods to learn from data, to extract knowledge and helps in making decisions. Moreover, the inverse probability allows to infer unknowns and to make predictions [3].

Consequently, many different probabilistic, but also non-probabilistic models, have been proposed for human activity recognition. Patterns corresponding to the activities are detected using sensors such as accelerometers, gyroscopes or passive infrared sensors, *etc.*, either using feature extraction on sliding window followed by classification [4] or with Hidden Markov Modeling (HMM) [5].

In recent years, there has been a growing interest in deep learning techniques. Deep learning is a general term for neural network methods which are based on learning representations from raw data and contain more than one hidden layer. The network learns many layers of non-linear information processing for feature extraction and transformation. Each successive layer uses the output from the previous layer as input. Deep learning techniques have already outperformed other machine learning algorithms in applications such as computer vision [6], audio [7] and speech recognition [8].

In this paper, we introduce a recurrent neural network model for human activity recognition. The classification of the human activities such as cooking, bathing, and sleeping is performed using the Long Short-Term Memory classifier (LSTM) on publicly available Benchmark datasets [9]. An evaluation of the results has been performed by comparing with the standardized machine learning algorithms such as Naive Bayes, HMM, Hidden Semi-Markov Model (HSMM) and Conditional Random Fields (CRF).

The paper is organized as follows. Section 2 presents an overview of activity recognition models and related work in machine learning techniques. Section 3 introduces Long Short-Term Memory (LSTM) recurrent neural networks. Section 4 describes the datasets that were used and explains the results in comparison to different well-known algorithms. Finally, Sect. 5 discusses the outcomes of the experiments and suggestions for future work.

2   Related Work

In previous research, activity recognition models have been classified into data-driven and knowledge-driven approaches. The data-driven approaches are capable of handling uncertainties and temporal information [10] but require large datasets for training and learning. Unfortunately, the availability of large real world datasets is a major challenge in the field of ambient assisted living. The knowledge-driven techniques are used in predictions and follow a description-based approach to model the relationships between sensor data and activities. These approaches are easy to understand and use but they cannot handle uncertainty and temporal information [11].

Various approaches have been explored for activity recognition, among them the majority of the techniques focuses on classification algorithms such as Naive Bayes (NB) [12], Decision Trees [13], HMM [5], CRF [14], Nearest Neighbor (NN) [15], Support Vector Machines (SVM) [16] and different boosting techniques.

A simple probabilistic classifier in machine learning is the Naive Bayes classifier which yields good accuracy with large amounts of sample data but does not model any temporal information. The HMM, HSMM, and CRF are the most popular approaches for including such temporal information. However, these approaches sometimes discard pattern sequences that convey information through the length of intervals between events. This motivates the study of recurrent neural networks (RNN) which promises the recognition of patterns that are defined by temporal distance [17].

LSTM is a recurrent neural network architecture that is designed to model temporal sequences and learn long-term dependency problems. The network is well suited for language modeling tasks; it has been shown that the network in combination with clustering techniques increases the training and testing time of the model [18] and outperforms the large scale acoustic model in speech recognition systems [19].

3   LSTM Model

LSTM is a recurrent neural network architecture that was proposed in [20]. Another version without a forget gate was later proposed in [21] and extended in [22]. LSTM has been developed in order to deal with gradient decay or gradient blow-up problems and can be seen as a deep neural network architecture when unrolled in time. The LSTM layer's main component is a unit called memory block. An LSTM block has three gates which are input, output and forget gates. These gates can be seen as write, read and reset operations for the cells. An LSTM cell state is the key component which carries the information between each LSTM block. Modifications to the cell state are controlled with the three gates described above. An LSTM single cell, as well as how each gate is connected to each other and the cell state itself, can be seen in Fig. 1.

Each gate and cell state are governed by multiplicative equations that are given by:

$$i_t = \sigma(W_{xi}x_t + W_{hi}h_{t-1} + W_{ci}c_{t-1} + b_i),$$
$$f_t = \sigma(W_{xf}x_t + W_{hf}h_{t-1} + W_{cf}c_{t-1} + b_f),$$
$$o_t = \sigma(W_{xo}x_t + W_{ho}h_{t-1} + W_{co}c_t + b_o),$$
$$c_t = f_t c_{t-1} + i_t \tanh(W_{xc}x_t + W_{hc}h_{t-1} + b_c),$$
$$h_t = o_t \tanh c_t,$$

with W being the weight matrix and x is the input, σ being the sigmoid and tanh is the hyperbolic tangent activation function. The terms i, f and o are named after their corresponding gates and c represents the memory cell [23].

By unrolling LSTM single cells in time we construct an LSTM layer where h_t is the hidden state and y_t is the output at time t as shown in Fig. 2.

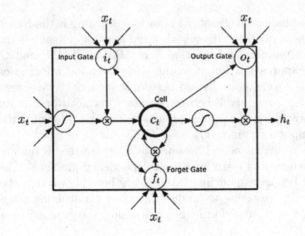

Fig. 1. LSTM single cell image [23].

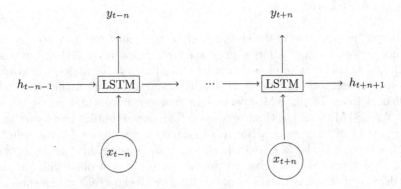

Fig. 2. Illustrations of an LSTM network with x being the binary vector for sensor input and y being the activity label prediction of the LSTM network.

4   Experiments

4.1   Dataset

Publicly available and annotated sensor datasets have been used to evaluate the performance of the proposed approach [9]. In this dataset, there are three houses with different settings to collect sensory data. The three different houses were all occupied by a single user named A, B, and C respectively. Each user recorded and annotated their daily activities. Different number of binary sensors were deployed in each house such as passive infrared (PIR) motion detectors to detect motion in a specific area, pressure sensors on couches and beds to identify the user's presence, reed switches on cupboards and doors to measure open or close status, and float sensors in the bathroom to measure toilet being flushed or not. The data were annotated using two approaches: (1) keeping a diary in

Table 1. Details of the datasets.

	House A	House B	House C
Age	26	28	57
Gender	Male	Male	Male
Setting	Apartment	Apartment	House
Rooms	3	2	6
Duration	25days	14days	19days
Sensors	14	23	21
Activities	10	13	16
Annotation	Bluetooth	Diary	Bluetooth

which the activities were logged by hand and (2) with the use of a blue tooth headset along with a speech recognition software. A total of three datasets were collected from the three different houses. Details about the datasets are shown in Table 1 where each column shows the details of the house with the information of the user living in it, the sensors placed in the house and the number of activity labels that were used.

The data used in the experiments have different representation forms. The first form is raw sensor data, which are the data received directly from the sensor. The second form is last-fired sensor data which are the data received from the sensor that was fired last. The last firing sensor gives continuously 1 and changes to 0 when another sensor changes its state. For each house, we left one day out of the data to be used later for the testing phase and used the rest of the data for training. We repeated this for every day and for each house. Separate models are trained for each house since the number of sensors varies, and a different user resides in each house. Sensors are recorded at one-minute intervals for 24 h, which totals in 1440 length input for each day.

4.2   Results

The results presented in Table 2 show the performance of the LSTM model on raw sensor data in comparison with the results of NB, HMM, HSMM and CRF [9]. Table 3 shows the results of the LSTM model on last-fired sensor data again in comparison with the results of NB, HMM, HSMM and CRF. For the LSTM model, a time slice of (70) with hidden state size (300) are used. For the optimization of the network, Adam is used with a learning rate of 0.0004 [24] and Tensorflow was used to implement the LSTM network. The training took place on a Titan X GPU and the time required to train one day for one house is approximately 30 min, but training times differ amongst the houses. Since different houses have different days we calculated the average accuracy amongst all days. The training is performed using a single GPU but the trained models can be used for inference without losing performance when there is no GPU.

Table 2. Results of raw sensor data

Model	House A	House B	House C
Naive Bayes	77.1 ± 20.8	80.4 ± 18.0	46.5 ± 22.6
HMM	59.1 ± 28.7	63.2 ± 24.7	26.5 ± 22.7
HSMM	59.5 ± 29.0	63.8 ± 24.2	31.2 ± 24.6
CRF	89.8 ± 8.5	78.0 ± 25.9	46.3 ± 25.5
LSTM(Ours)	**89.8 ± 8.2**	**85.7 ± 14.3**	**64.22 ± 21.9**

Table 2 shows the results of different models on raw data from three different houses. The LSTM model has the best performance for all three data sets. In House B and House C, LSTM improves the best result significantly especially on House C where the improvement is approximately 40%.

Table 3. Results of last-fired sensor data

Model	House A	House B	House C
Naive Bayes	95.3 ± 2.8	86.2 ± 13.8	87.0 ± 12.2
HMM	89.5 ± 8.4	48.4 ± 26.0	83.9 ± 13.9
HSMM	91.0 ± 7.2	67.1 ± 24.8	84.5 ± 13.2
CRF	**96.4 ± 2.4**	**89.2 ± 13.9**	**89.7 ± 8.4**
LSTM	95.3 ± 2.0	88.5 ± 12.6	85.9 ± 10.6

Table 3 shows the results on last fired data from three different houses using the same models as in Table 2. The LSTM model did not improve the results in this section but it matched the best performance for two data sets with a slight drop in House C.

5   Discussion

The results presented in this paper show that the deep learning based approaches for activity recognition from raw sensory inputs can lead to significant improvement in performance, increased accuracy, and better results. As shown in Sect. 4.2 our LSTM based activity predictor matched or outperformed existing probabilistic models such as Naive Bayes, HMM, HSMM and CRF on raw input and in one case improved the best result by 40%. Predicting on raw input also reduces the human efforts required on data preprocessing and handcrafting features which can be very time consuming when it comes to an AAL (Ambient Assisted Living) environment.

6   Future Work

Our future work will focus on reducing the variance on our predictions and early stopping criteria while training on different days. The LSTM model has different hyperparameters which affect the performance of the model significantly. Different optimization and hyperparameter search techniques could be investigated in the future. Since the LSTM model has proven to be superior on raw data it would be interesting to also apply other deep learning models. One problem is that deep learning badly captures model uncertainty. Bayesian models offer a framework to reason about model uncertainty. Recently, Yarin and Ghahramani (2016) [25] developed a theoretical framework casting dropout training in deep neural networks as approximate Bayesian inference in deep Gaussian processes. This mitigates the problem of representing uncertainty in deep learning without sacrificing either computational complexity or test accuracy.

Acknowledgement. This work has been funded by the European Union Horizon2020 MSCA ITN ACROSSING project (GA no. 616757). The authors would like to thank the members of the project's consortium for their valuable inputs.

References

1. Roecker, C., Ziefle, M., Holzinger, A.: Social inclusion in ambient assisted living environments: home automation and convenience services for elderly users. In: Proceedings of the International Conference on Artificial Intelligence (ICAI 2011), pp. 55–59. CSERA Press, New York (2011)
2. Chen, L., Hoey, J., Nugent, C.D., Cook, D.J., Yu, Z.: Sensor-based activity recognition. IEEE Trans. Syst. Man Cybern., Part C (Applications and Reviews) **42**, 790–808 (2012)
3. Holzinger, A.: Introduction to machine learning and knowledge extraction (MAKE). Mach. Learn. Knowl. Extr. **1**, 1–20 (2017)
4. Roggen, D., Cuspinera, L.P., Pombo, G., Ali, F., Nguyen-Dinh, L.-V.: Limited-Memory Warping LCSS for real-time low-power pattern recognition in wireless nodes. In: Abdelzaher, T., Pereira, N., Tovar, E. (eds.) EWSN 2015. LNCS, vol. 8965, pp. 151–167. Springer, Cham (2015). doi:10.1007/978-3-319-15582-1_10
5. Duong, T.V., Bui, H.H., Phung, D.Q., Venkatesh, S.: Activity recognition and abnormality detection with the switching hidden semi-markov model. In: IEEE Computer Society Conference on Computer Vision and Pattern Recognition, CVPR 2005, vol. 1, pp. 838–845. IEEE (2005)
6. Lee, H., Grosse, R., Ranganath, R., Ng, A.Y.: Convolutional deep belief networks for scalable unsupervised learning of hierarchical representations. In: Proceedings of the 26th Annual International Conference on Machine Learning, pp. 609–616. ACM (2009)
7. Lee, H., Pham, P., Largman, Y., Ng, A.Y.: Unsupervised feature learning for audio classification using convolutional deep belief networks. In: Advances in Neural Information Processing Systems, pp. 1096–1104 (2009)
8. Hinton, G., Deng, L., Yu, D., Dahl, G.E., Mohamed, A.R., Jaitly, N., Senior, A., Vanhoucke, V., Nguyen, P., Sainath, T.N., et al.: Deep neural networks for acoustic modeling in speech recognition: The shared views of four research groups. IEEE Sig. Process. Mag. **29**, 82–97 (2012)

9. Kasteren, T.L., Englebienne, G., Kröse, B.J.: Human activity recognition from wireless sensor network data: Benchmark and software. In: Chen, L. (ed.) Activity Recognition in Pervasive Intelligent Environments, pp. 165–186. Atlantis Press, Amsterdam (2011)

10. Yuen, J., Torralba, A.: A data-driven approach for event prediction. In: Daniilidis, K., Maragos, P., Paragios, N. (eds.) ECCV 2010. LNCS, vol. 6312, pp. 707–720. Springer, Heidelberg (2010). doi:10.1007/978-3-642-15552-9_51

11. Ye, J., Stevenson, G., Dobson, S.: Kcar: a knowledge-driven approach for concurrent activity recognition. Pervasive Mob. Comput. **19**, 47–70 (2015)

12. Tapia, E.M., Intille, S.S., Larson, K.: Activity recognition in the home using simple and ubiquitous sensors. In: Ferscha, A., Mattern, F. (eds.) Pervasive 2004. LNCS, vol. 3001, pp. 158–175. Springer, Heidelberg (2004). doi:10.1007/978-3-540-24646-6_10

13. Bao, L., Intille, S.S.: Activity recognition from user-annotated acceleration data. In: Ferscha, A., Mattern, F. (eds.) Pervasive 2004. LNCS, vol. 3001, pp. 1–17. Springer, Heidelberg (2004). doi:10.1007/978-3-540-24646-6_1

14. Van Kasteren, T., Noulas, A., Englebienne, G., Kröse, B.: Accurate activity recognition in a home setting. In: Proceedings of the 10th International Conference on Ubiquitous Computing, pp. 1–9. ACM (2008)

15. Wu, W., Dasgupta, S., Ramirez, E.E., Peterson, C., Norman, G.J.: Classification accuracies of physical activities using smartphone motion sensors. J. Med. Internet Res. **14**, e130 (2012)

16. Zhu, Y., Nayak, N.M., Roy-Chowdhury, A.K.: Context-aware activity recognition and anomaly detection in video. IEEE J. Sel. Top. Sig. Proces. **7**, 91–101 (2013)

17. Ribbe, M.W., Ljunggren, G., Steel, K., Topinkova, E., Hawes, C., Ikegami, N., Henrard, J.C., JÓNnson, P.V.: Nursing homes in 10 nations: a comparison between countries and settings. Age Ageing **26**, 3–12 (1997)

18. Sundermeyer, M., Schlüter, R., Ney, H.: Lstm neural networks for language modeling. In: Interspeech, pp. 194–197 (2012)

19. Sak, H., Senior, A., Beaufays, F.: Long short-term memory recurrent neural network architectures for large scale acoustic modeling. In: Fifteenth Annual Conference of the International Speech Communication Association (2014)

20. Hochreiter, S., Schmidhuber, J.: Long short-term memory. Neural Comput. **9**, 1735–1780 (1997)

21. Gers, F.A., Schmidhuber, J., Cummins, F.: Learning to forget: continual prediction with lstm. Neural Comput. **12**, 2451–2471 (2000)

22. Gers, F.A., Schraudolph, N.N., Schmidhuber, J.: Learning precise timing with lstm recurrent networks. J. Mach. Learn. Res. **3**, 115–143 (2002)

23. Zhang, S., Zheng, D., Hu, X., Yang, M.: Bidirectional long short-term memory networks for relation classification. In: PACLIC (2015)

24. Kingma, D., Ba, J.: Adam: A method for stochastic optimization. arXiv preprint arXiv:1412.6980 (2014)

25. Gal, Y., Ghahramani, Z.: Dropout as a bayesian approximation: representing model uncertainty in deep learning. In: Balcan, M.F., Weinberger, K.Q. (eds.) Proceedings of The 33rd International Conference on Machine Learning (ICML), vol. 48, pp. 1050–1059. PMLR (2016)

Modeling Golf Player Skill
Using Machine Learning

Rikard König[1](✉), Ulf Johansson[1], Maria Riveiro[2],
and Peter Brattberg[1]

[1] University of Borås, Borås, Sweden
{rikard.konig,ulf.johansson,peter.brattberg}@hb.se
[2] University of Skövde, Skövde, Sweden
maria.riveiro@his.se

Abstract. In this study we apply machine learning techniques to Modeling Golf Player Skill using a dataset consisting of 277 golfers. The dataset includes 28 quantitative metrics, related to the club head at impact and ball flight, captured using a Doppler-radar. For modeling, cost-sensitive decision trees and random forest are used to discern between less skilled players and very good ones, i.e., Hackers and Pros. The results show that both random forest and decision trees achieve high predictive accuracy, with regards to true positive rate, accuracy and area under the ROC-curve. A detailed interpretation of the decision trees shows that they concur with modern swing theory, e.g., consistency is very important, while face angle, club path and dynamic loft are the most important evaluated swing factors, when discerning between Hackers and Pros. Most of the Hackers could be identified by a rather large deviation in one of these values compared to the Pros. Hackers, which had less variation in these aspects of the swing, could instead be identified by a steeper swing plane and a lower club speed. The importance of the swing plane is an interesting finding, since it was not expected and is not easy to explain.

Keywords: Classification · Decision trees · Machine learning · Golf · Swing analysis

1 Introduction

Golf is a major sport that is today played by over 60 million people all over the [1]. The golf swing of a pro may look simple, but it is a combination of several complex biomechanical motions that need to be performed at high speeds with high accuracy. Hence, both pros and amateurs spend considerable time on perfecting their swings. However, due to the very complex chain of movements, the help of a teaching professional is most often needed to identify problems in a swing.

Golf instructors require a deep theoretical knowledge about golf swings and a lot of first hand teaching experience to be able to teach at a high level. Naturally, finding the problem with a swing is a crucial skill that must be mastered. Since the golf swing is such a complex movement and since the club head moves at great speeds, golf swing analysis has long been an art requiring very sharp eyes. When determining the effectiveness of a swing, many teaching professionals often start by observing the ball flight and thereafter the club and body motion [2].

Lately, new technology, such as the TrackMan Launch Monitor Radar (TM) [3], has made it possible to measure numerous characteristics of the golf swing quantitatively. TM units use a Doppler-radar to register information about the club head at the point of impact with the ball and the trajectory of the ball. In total, TM delivers 28 metrics, where eight are related to the club head and twenty are related to the ball flight.

Of course, technology like TM is a great tool for teaching professionals when analyzing swings. However, in practice, due to the complexity of the swing and the many metrics, teachers often focus on only a few parameters they consider the most important ones. In essence, the TM solves the problem of characterizing a swing quantitatively, but does not help to identify good and bad aspects of a particular swing.

Naturally, many previous studies have focused on analyzing the swing quantitatively using high speed video, e.g. see [4, 5]. However, due to the tedious manual labor related to video analysis, these and similar studies have only used a small number of players (20–45). A small number of example swings in combination with several metrics make an analysis of the interaction between different swing variables difficult. Hence, these and similar studies have been restricted to an analysis of single variables using statistical techniques.

By using a TM-unit, it is, however, feasible to collect quantitative data from a larger number of golfers, since all metrics are calculated automatically. More data enables the use of more powerful techniques, like machine learning, for modeling golf player skill. In this study, we evaluate whether it is possible to discern a good swing from a bad one by only using data from the club head at impact and from ball flight.

2 Background

Golf is a game in which the player aims to hit the ball from the tee to a hole in as few strokes as possible. A golf course normally consists of 18 holes, where each hole is designed to be played with a certain number of strokes. The number of intended strokes is called the *par* of the hole and ranges from 3–5 strokes. A golf course also has a par, calculated as the sum of the par of each hole, which is normally 72 strokes.

Golf has a handicap system which is designed to let golfers with different levels of skill compete against each other. There are several different handicap systems of which the EGA [6] and USGA are dominant. The EGA system is predominant in Europe and the USGA in the USA. In essence, a handicap system lets players deduct strokes according to their handicap (hcp). A hcp lies in the range of 36 to −4 (called +4). One simple way of calculating the final score using a hcp is to subtract the player hcp from the total number of strokes. When golfers play better than their hcp, e.g., the score minus the hcp is lower than the course par, their hcp is reduced a fraction and if they play worse it is increased. Hence, a player's hcp is supposed to be an estimation of that golfer's current skill level, where a better player has a lower hcp.

Broadie in [7], sorted golf shots on a course into four different categories:

- *Long game* - shots longer than 100 yards.
- *Short game* - shots shorter than 100 yards, not including sand shots.
- *Sand game* - shots from bunker no longer than 50 yards.
- *Putting* - shots on the green.

To become a skilled player, all of these shots must be mastered, but according to Brodie, the long game is the most important one for amateur players' hcp.

The long game consists of shots from the tee and longer shots on the course. Tee shots can be hit with the driver, which is designed to hit the longest shots, or iron clubs, which are designed for different specific distances. Shots from the fairway are most often done using iron clubs.

Swings can be described in numerous ways using different terms; however, in this study, the terminology of the TM software is used consistently for simplicity. In total, Trackman delivers eight metrics related to the club head (CLUB):

- *ClubSpeed* - Speed of the club head at the instant prior to impact.
- *AttackAngle* - Vertical movement of the club through impact.
- *ClubPath* - Horizontal movement of the club through impact. (+) = inside-out, (−) = outside-in.
- *SwingPlane* - Bottom half of the swing plane relative to the ground.
- *SwingDirection* - Bottom half of the swing plane relative to the target line.
- *DynLoft* - Orientation of the club face, relative to the plumb line, at point of impact (POI).
- *FaceAngle* - Orientation of the club face, relative to the target line, at POI. (+) = open face, i.e., for a right-handed golfer to the right of the target line (−) = closed face.
- *FaceToPath* - Orientation of the club face, relative to the club path, at POI. (+) = open path, i.e., for a right-handed golfer to the right of the club path (−) = closed path.

In addition to these CLUB-related metrics, TM also registers twenty metrics related to the ball flight (BALL):

- *BallSpeed,BallSpeedC* - Ball speed the instant after impact, speed at landing.
- *SmashFactor* - Ball speed/club head speed at the instant after POI.
- *LaunchAngle* - Launch angle, relative horizon, immediately after impact.
- *LaunchDirection* - Starting direction, relative to the target line, of the ball immediately after impact. (+) = right, (−) = left.
- *SpinRate* - Ball rotation per minute the instant after impact.
- *SpinAxis* - Tilt of spin axis. (+) = fade/slice, (−) = draw/hook.
- *VertAngleC* - Ball landing angle, relative to the ground at zero elevation.
- *Height, DistHeight, SideHeight* - Maximum height of shot at apex, distance to apex, apex distance from the target line.
- *LengthC, LengthT* - Length of shot, C = calculated carry at zero elevation, T = calculated total including bounce and roll at zero elevation.

- *SideC, SideT* - Distance from the target line, C = at landing, T = calculated total including bounce and roll. (+) = right, (−) = left.

Access to launch monitors producing quantitative data, and a consensus about impacting variables, have allowed a revision of swing theory. Most importantly, improved analysis has produced a fundamental change in the understanding of the ball flight. Traditionally, the club path was believed to determine the starting direction and the face angle (opening or closing the club head) to be responsible for the curvature of the shot. Modern golf theory, however, has established that it is in fact mainly the face angle that determines the starting direction [8]. Using Trackman terminology, the CLUB parameters, *FaceAngle* and *ClubPath* are the most important factors responsible for the starting direction of the ball, where *FaceAngle* is credited for 85% of the direction [8]. Similarly, the curvature of the shot is a direct function of the difference between the ClubPath and the FaceAngle (*FaceToPath*), where a negative value represents a right-to-left movement, i.e., a draw for a right-handed golfer. Naturally, the aim in most cases, is to produce a fairly straight shot down the target line, which is achieved with a *ClubPath* and *FaceAngle* of approximately zero. The *LaunchAngle* of the ball is dependent on the *DynamicLoft* which, in turn, is related to the *AttackAngle*; a higher *DynamicLoft* will produce higher shots.

Golf theory maintains that the swings for iron clubs and those for the driver differ slightly; first, the driver is designed for longer shots and is hence longer than iron clubs, which results in higher *ClubSpeeds*. Secondly, when hitting with the driver, the ball is placed towards the front facing leg, instead of in the middle, as done with iron clubs. This is done to hit the ball on the way up of the swing, i.e., with a positive *AttackAngle*, thus decreasing the *DynLoft* and thereby producing a longer shot due to a lower *SpinRate*. Shots with iron clubs are instead hit on the way down in the swing with a negative *AttackAngle*, in order to produce spin and thereby better control the length and direction of the shot.

3 Related Work

Golf is a sport that many people are passionate about and, hence, much research regarding all aspects of the game has been carried out. However, not as much work based on quantitative data has been carried out, since the necessary technology has only become available in recent years. The following section presents a selection of some recent relevant studies where quantitative data was analyzed and related to players' skill.

In [4] Fradkin Sherman and Finch performed a quantitative study of how the *ClubSpeed* correlated with player hcp. Here, *ClubSpeed* speed was measured using high speed video and averaged over the strokes. Data was collected from forty-five male Australian golfers with hcps in the range of 2–27. The results show a very strong correlation (0.95) between hcp and club head speed.

Sweeny et al. performed another quantitative study in [5] and noted that even if many coaching and biomechanical texts describe how the kinematics of the club head at impact lead to distance and accuracy, there is limited quantitative evidence for these claims. Hence, an opto-reflective system was used to analyze the swings with the driver of 21 male golfers. Using the kinematics of the club at impact, i.e. *ClubSpeed*, orientation path and centeredness, five kinematics of early ball flight, i.e., *BallSpeed*, *LaunchAngle*, *LaunchDirection*, *SpinRate* and *SpinAxis*, were modeled. Experiments show that these club kinematics could explain a significant part of the early ball flight, i.e., R^2 values between 0.71–0.82 were achieved.

In [9] which is the only identified study that analyzed a larger group of players, 10 driver shots were recorded for 285 players. These shots were recorded mainly using five 1000 Hz high speed cameras, but also the TM-launch monitor. The aim of this study was to evaluate the variability in club head presentation at impact and the resulting ball impact location on the club face, for a range of golfers with different hcps. The variability of *ClubSpeed*, *SmachFactor*, *AttackAngle*, *ClubPath*, *FaceAngle* and impact location was evaluated and compared between the different hcp groups. Statistical tests based on 10 shots from each player were used to show that overall players with lower hcps, i.e., players with hcp <=11.4, exhibited significantly less variation in all of the evaluated variables.

A rather different and interesting approach of evaluating golf player skill was taken in [7], where golf players registered real course shots in a database, using a computer. In total, 40.000 shots were registered from 130 different golfers. Each shot was then compared to a shot from a scratch player in the same situation. An interesting aspect of this study is that all parts of the games were analyzed, including the long game, short game, sand game and putting. The results show that for players with higher hcps, inconsistency was the main cause of a bad score, i.e. a few really poor shots often ruin the score. Another interesting result is that proficient players tend to be better at all parts of the game, but it is the long game, i.e. shots over 100 yards, that is the biggest influencing factor between low and high hcp players.

What all of these studies have in common is that they evaluate each parameter separately using statistical methods. To summarize the results, it is good to have a high club head speed and low variability in the presentation of the club head at impact. It is, however, not clear how low variability in the club head can be achieved or how different club head parameters relate to each other. Hence, these results demonstrate little about the difference in the swings of players with low and high hcps.

4 Method

The aim of this paper is to explain what distinguishes really proficient players from amateurs and novices. An early design choice was to model player skill on the basis of the long game, which is supposed to be the most important hcp factor for less skilled players [7]. The long game consists of both driver and iron shots and, hence, it was decided to record shots from each player with both the driver and one iron club, i.e. the 7 iron (i7). The next crucial design choice was how to discern good players from those less skilled. Since the EGA hcp system is designed to account for the skill of a golfer, it was selected as the basis of skill estimation in this study. Figure 1 shows the handicap distribution of the 277 players participating in the study. The average hcp was 12.8; the majority of players (73%) were in the hcp range of 4–18, indicating a higher skill than normal, i.e. the mean male hcp in Sweden is 21.5 and 48% of players fall into the 4–18 range [10].

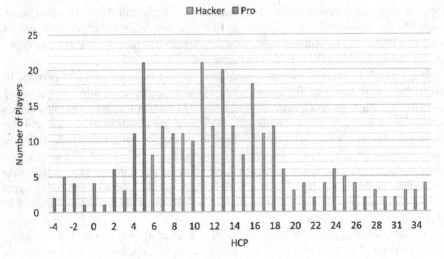

Fig. 1. Handicap distribution among players

The EGA hcp system divides players into five different categories based on their hcp. The best category has hcp numbers equal to or lower than 4.5. Hence, this was first chosen as a group of proficient players. However, to make the dataset a little less unbalanced, this group was expanded to include golfers with hcps <=5. For simplicity, players with hcps <=5 are henceforth called Pros and players with higher hcps are called Hackers. In practice, this meant that 58 players, with hcps of 5 or lower, were classified as Pros and the rest (219 players) as Hackers.

4.1 Data Collection

Most of the data was collected during 18 days in March, April and May. Due to a rather skewed sample with only a few Pros, another collection phase with only Pros was conducted, resulting in 15 additional players. All data was collected at the same training facility [11], where a special section was reserved for each day of data collection. Since the aim of this study was to find general patterns among larger groups of players, only male golfers hitting right-handed were targeted. Female and left to right stroking players only represented a small fraction of the players at the selected training facility and could hence not be recorded in sufficient numbers.

To record a player, the radar was positioned three meters behind and slightly to the right of the hitting mat. Next, the radar was aimed (using the Trackman Performance Studio software) at a flag approximately 250 m straight in front of the hitting mat. Before a player was recorded, he was first allowed to warm up, in order to reach a comfortable stroking state. Thereafter, five consecutive strokes were recorded using the players own seven iron followed by five strokes with the driver.

Naturally, an identical setting with regard to temperature and wind would have been preferable. However, this was impossible, since an indoor facility was not available. Instead, TrackMan's built-in normalization functionality was used.

When normalizing ball data, TrackMan utilizes information from the club head at impact to correct deviation caused by wind, temperature, altitude and ball type. Hence, the players were told to hit the balls in the direction of the flag using a normal full stroke, while disregarding any wind if present.

4.2 Preprocessing

Trackman Performance Studio output a total of 28 metrics, of which eight were related to the club head and twenty to the ball flight. Most metrics are measured directly, but some are calculated on the basis of other metrics. If the radar cannot measure some aspects accurately, which rarely happens but frequently enough to be an issue, it does not output any values. This typically occurs for club head related metrics, i.e. *ClubSpeed*, *AttackAngle*, *ClubPath*, *SwingPlane* and *SwingDirection*, at lower swing speeds. Ball related metrics are most often recorded properly, with the exception of *SpinRate* which is sometimes estimated instead or not reported at all. Of the 2780 shots that were recorded, 187 had at least one missing value.

One approach of obtaining representative measurements, for a single player and club, could be to use the average value of all five recorded shots. If, however, one of the shots were to be a really poor one, the average values could be quite misleading. Instead, the more robust approach, argued by Broadie in [8], of using the median value was chosen. The median value disregards both the worst and the best shots and should hence be a better estimate of normal standards. The question of how to define the median shot of a group of shots still remains. In this study, we chose the median shot based on *LengthC* of the ball, since the length of a shot is one of the most important aspects of a good shot. The distance from the target line, i.e. *SideC*, could, of course, be another alternative, but since a straight shot is not effective if it is not long enough, we settled for length in this study. In eleven cases, the median shot, i.e. the third longest shot, had some missing value. In these cases, the second best shot was used instead. If the second best longest also happened to have a missing value, the fourth best shot was used instead. For one single player all shots with the driver had at least one missing value and, hence, this player was removed from that dataset.

Since previous research has shown strong correlations between skill and consistency, the standard deviations of each of the 28 metrics were also calculated for each club using all five shots. Shots with missing values were not excluded, except in the calculation of the metric with the missing value. The average number of shots with no missing values was 4.7 for a specific club.

Another issue was how to best represent each metric for a predictive modeling technique. Most metrics, like *LengthC*, have a straightforward representation, but metrics related to angles need some extra consideration. *FaceAngle* is one example where the representation plays an important role, since the angle can be both positive and negative, i.e. representing an angle to the right or left of the target line. If no transformation is done, a big negative angle would be considered as smaller than a small positive angle. However, in relation to the target line, which is more relevant for the quality of a swing, the opposite is true. Hence, each metric related to the target line was replaced with two new variables, where the first one was the absolute value and the second was a binary variable with the same name but preceded with a *P-*, to represent whether the original angle was positive or not. Metrics related to vertical angles, i.e. *AttackAngle*, *LaunchAngle*, were not modified.

4.3   Experiments

The aim of this paper was mainly to investigate how well golf skill can be modeled using quantitative data from a TM-Radar and to understand which factors are the most important ones for a good golf swing. Naturally, this requires that the predictive models are transparent and comprehensible and, hence, WEKAs J48, which is an implementation of the famous decision tree algorithm C4.5 [12], was used in the main experiments. However, to evaluate how much predictive power the data actually contained, a Random Forest [13] was first applied as an upper benchmark.

The separation of the players into Pros and Hackers was rather unbalanced, i.e. 58 Pros vs 219 Hackers. Unbalanced data sets often result in models favoring the majority class at the cost of very few predictions for the minority class. Initial experiments confirmed that this was also the case for both the 7i- and the driver datasets in this study, resulting in true positive rates of around 35%. Hence, since the main goal was to model the proficient players, a cost of miss-classification equal to the unbalance rate was associated with the minority class. This was done for both RF and J48 using WEKA's meta *cost sensitive classifier* by assigning a cost of $219/58 = 3.78$ for miss-classifications of Pros. To keep the total weight of the instance to the original 277, WEKA, in practice, assigned a weight of 0.632 to Hackers and 2.389 to Pros.

When modeling using J48, the main goal is to describe good general swings in a comprehensible way. Hence, it was decided that at least 10% of the Pros, i.e. six players, should be present in any pure Pro leaf node. However, due to WEKAs reweighting of the instances, a minimum instance per leaf of 6 would only require three Pros. To avoid this and to ensure that in practice there were always at least six instances in a pure Pro leaf, the minimum number was instead set to $6 * 2.389 = 14$.

Another setting motivated by the class imbalance was to use *Laplace* estimates in J48, since previous studies, e.g. [14], have shown that it most often improves the probability estimates and thereby the ranking ability of the produced model.

To facilitate a comparison of the predictive power of variables related to club delivery and the ball flight, the original datasets were used to create four new ones based on four subsets of the original variables. The attribute subsets used to create the new datasets were:

- CLUB Variables related to the club delivery.
- C-STD Player standard deviations for CLUB variables.
- BALL Variables describing ball Launch and flight, Carry flat and Est. Total.
- B-STD Player standard deviations for BALL variables.

Based on these subsets, five datasets were then created; only CLUB, CLUB and C-STD, only BALL, Ball and B-STD and one final dataset containing all variables.

4.4   Model Interpretation

Since all decision trees techniques optimize some kind of information gain criteria, starting at the root, splits closer to the root are normally considered more important. Information gain is the difference in purity, e.g. *gini diversity index* (GDI) [15] or *entropy* [16], between the original dataset and the resulting subsets. The equation below defines a general way to calculate the information gain given a specific purity measure, where $P(D_i)$ is the proportion of the dataset D that is placed in the subset D_i. The split resulting in the highest purity gain is selected and the procedure is then repeated recursively for each subset in this split.

$$gain(D, S) = purity(D) - \sum_{i=1}^{s} P(D_i) * purity(D_i) \qquad (1)$$

Consequently, the importance of the final splits can be, in the same way, evaluated by considering the number of training instances affected by the split and the resulting purity of the subsets.

5   Results

The following sections present the results of the experiments. First, basic statistics are presented followed by the predictive performance of the models. Finally, a selection of models are presented and interpreted, to ensure that they are practical and based on rational relationships.

5.1   Basic Statistics

Table 1 shows the basic statistics of the players labeled as Hackers and Pros. For each attribute and club, the mean value and the standard deviation are presented. Note that the standard deviations are within each group and not for each player which is another variable used in the experiments discussed above.

The most obvious differences between Hackers and Pros are in the values for *BallFlight*, *CarryFlat* and *LengthT* variables, i.e. Pros hit the ball longer and straighter. More specifically, Pros on average hit the ball 29 m longer with the 7i and 49 m longer with the driver. However, they also hit the ball straighter than the Hackers, (4 m smaller deviation from the target line for both 7i and the driver), in spite of the longer shots. Note that since the Pros hit the ball substantially further, the difference in accuracy is essentially much greater than the 4 m deviation implies. Furthermore, the standard deviations are much smaller (for all variables) for Pros, showing that they are a more homogeneous group, in terms of how they hit the ball.

Regarding the variables related to club delivery, the arguably biggest differences (always in favor of the Pros) concern *ClubSpeed*, *AttackAngle ClubPath* and *Face-ToPath*, i.e. the Pros hit harder, more down on the ball (i7) and deliver the club and club face better in relation to the target line, resulting in longer and straighter shots.

Table 1. Basic statistics for Hackers and Pros

	i7				Driver			
	Mean		STD		Mean		STD	
	Hacker	Pro	Hacker	Pro	Hacker	Pro	Hacker	Pro
Club Delivery								
ClubSpeed	80.2	87.2	8.6	5.9	94.5	104.7	10.7	7.7
AttackAngle	−3.2	−4.8	2.4	2	−1.7	−1.1	3.5	2.9
ClubPath	4	2.9	3	2.4	3.8	3.6	3.2	2.7
P-ClubPath	0.45	0.6	0.5	0.49	0.49	0.69	0.5	0.46
SwingPlane	61.9	59.3	4.4	3.6	49.9	47.8	4.5	3.4
SwingDir.	4.8	3.5	3.4	2.6	5.6	4.8	4.1	3.6
P-SwingDir.	0.35	0.26	0.48	0.44	0.42	0.53	0.49	0.5
DynLoft	25.3	23.3	4.8	2.9	14.3	12.6	4.9	2.7
FaceAngle	3.3	2.1	2.6	1.6	4.2	2.6	3.1	1.8
P-FaceAngle	0.38	0.52	0.49	0.5	0.33	0.45	0.47	0.5
FaceToPath	4	2.5	3.4	1.7	4.6	3.4	3.7	2.4
P-FaceToPath	0.42	0.38	0.49	0.49	0.33	0.24	0.47	0.43
Ball Launch								
BallSpeed	104	116.1	11	6.7	133.1	151.8	16.5	10.4
SmashFactor	1.3	1.33	0.06	0.04	1.41	1.45	0.07	0.04
LaunchAngle	20	18.4	3.8	2.8	12.3	11.2	4.2	2.7
LaunchDir.	3	2	2.3	1.7	3.8	2.6	2.8	1.7
P-LaunchDir.	0.4	0.55	0.49	0.5	0.34	0.47	0.48	0.5
SpinRate	5470	5686	1532	847	2837	2207	1318	613
SpinAxis	6.1	3.3	5	2.3	10.7	8.2	7.8	5.4
P-SpinAxis	0.69	0.5	0.46	0.5	0.6	0.47	0.49	0.5
Ball Flight								
DistHeight	86.8	102.7	14.8	8.5	118	148.4	26.2	18.5
Height	24.7	30.1	7.2	5.7	19.6	22.8	9	6.6
SideHeight	4.8	3.2	4.1	2.9	8.1	6.4	6.3	5.1
P-SideHeight	0.45	0.53	0.5	0.5	0.39	0.47	0.49	0.5
Carry Flat								
LengthC	142.1	163.3	21.1	11.4	192.2	238.1	36.8	25.8
SideC	9	5.7	7.9	5.1	15.6	12	12	10.1
P-SideC	0.46	0.5	0.5	0.5	0.44	0.47	0.5	0.5
VertAngleC	42.3	45.9	6.7	4.6	29	29.2	9.9	6.5
BallSpeedC	54.7	56.6	3.1	2.4	65.6	68.6	7.7	4.6
Est. Total								
LengthT	153.2	172.2	21.2	11.3	223.3	271.8	36.4	24.8
SideT	9.1	5.5	8.1	4.9	17.5	13.2	13.3	11.1
P-SideT	0.46	0.5	0.5	0.5	0.46	0.5	0.5	0.5

One variable that appear to be rather similar for the Hackers and Pros is the *Swing-Plane,* which only differs by 1.6° for the 7i and 2.1 for the driver.

The longer shots of the Pros can be further explained by the Ball Launch variables. Pros have a higher *BallSpeed* which is a result from the higher *ClubSpeed* and a better *SmashFactor,* which means that more energy is transferred from the club to the ball. Another interesting variable is the *SpinRate,* where a lower spin rate promotes longer shots while higher rates give more control over the ball flight. As could be expected, Pros have a lower *SpinRate* for the driver, thus maximizing distance, but a higher *SpinRate* for the 7 iron, thus enabling more control compared to the Hackers. Another basic assumption that can be verified is that it is common among Hackers to hit the ball with a slice or fade. Slice or fade is signified by a positive *SpinAxis,* which 69% of the Hackers have. The distribution of positive and negative *SpinAxis* among the Pros is even and *SpinAxis* itself is much smaller, resulting in just a small fade or draw.

Figure 2 presents the players in a scatter plot where the y-axis is the carry distance and the x-axis is the deviation in meters from the target line. As Table 1 also shows, Pros, in general, hit longer and straighter than Hackers. However, there are many Hackers who hit as far as the Pros and the longest shot (207 m) was actually made by a Hacker (who, it transpired, was competing in the longest drive competition). The point is that some Hackers can easily be discerned on the basis of distance and side deviation, but far from all.

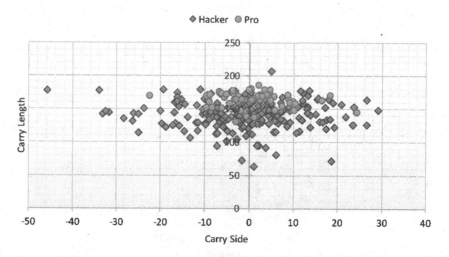

Fig. 2. i7 - Carry Length vs. Carry side

Next, Fig. 3 instead shows the standard deviation of the five recorded 7i-shots for each player. Obviously, the Pros are more consistent, i.e. deviate less, than the Hackers, in spite of hitting the ball further. Again there is no clear distinguishing boundary separating the two classes, except for the really substandard Hackers.

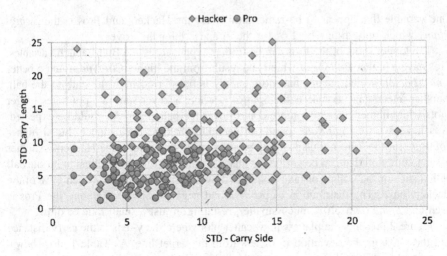

Fig. 3. i7 - STD of Carry Length vs. Carry side

The same pattern is apparent in Fig. 4, i.e. the group of Hackers has a greater variation in their *SwingPlane* and *FaceAngle,* however, only some can be easily discerned from the Pros using only these variables.

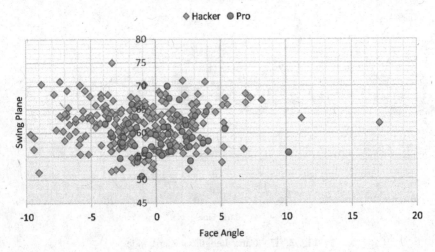

Fig. 4. i7 - SwingPlane vs. Face Angle

5.2 Predictive Performance

Table 2 below shows the results for RF, using n-fold cross validation for the different datasets. The first columns show the club that was used and the following four define the data that was present in each dataset.

Table 2. Random forest n-fold results

RF	CLUB	C-STD	BALL	B-STD	ACC	AUC	TP
i7	X				0.773	0.792	0.534
i7	X	X			0.848	0.886	0.655
i7			X		0.798	0.833	0.69
i7			X	X	0.874	0.901	0.776
i7	X	X	X	X	0.866	0.907	0.724
Driver	X				0.801	0.824	0.569
Driver	X	X			0.797	0.872	0.638
Driver			X		0.826	0.839	0.655
Driver			X	X	0.855	0.902	0.776
Driver	X	X	X	X	0.866	0.908	0.724

The first observation that can be made is that the results for datasets based on i7 and driver data are rather similar overall, even if they differ slightly for a specific dataset. Furthermore, BALL and B-STD are, in general, slightly better than the corresponding combination of CLUB and C-STD.

Using all the data, RF achieves a rather high accuracy of 86.6% for both clubs, while the naive approach of only predicting Hacker would achieve an accuracy of 79%. Due to the class imbalance, it is arguably more interesting to look at the area under the ROC curve (AUC), since it is a measure of how well the model can rank the players. Again, the RF performs well and reaches a high AUC of 0.901 for both clubs. The true positive rate (TP) for the Pro class is 72.4%, which is a reasonable level with the class imbalance in mind.

As may be expected, an analysis of the results for the attribute subsets shows that including the standard deviations for either the club or the ball flight provides extra predictive power. The second best results are achieved using datasets with BALL and B-STD, closely followed by CLUB and C-STD.

The data sets without any standard deviations, i.e. BALL and CLUB for i7 and driver, all clearly result in models with lower predictive performance. Using just BALL data, compared to BALL and B-STD, results in a drop of 8.6% in TP for 7i and 12% for the driver. Similarly, using only CLUB data results in a loss in TP of 12% for i7 and 26% for the driver, compared to using CLUB and C-STD.

Next, the results of J48 are presented in Table 3. Compared to the results of RF in Table 2, it becomes apparent that RF is superior for all datasets and metrics, except for a few cases where J48 achieves a higher TP.

The general results for J48 are also similar to those of RF, where the datasets containing the standard deviation of the ball (STD-B) again give the best results, regardless of the club that was used. This also correlates with previous research showing that consistency is a very important aspect of the swing. For both clubs, the best result is achieved using all variables, closely followed by only BALL and B-STD. The datasets containing only CLUB and C-STD variables were slightly worse, but still surprisingly accurate. An interesting detail is that adding STDs to the CLUB data only had a minimal effect for the 7i but a rather large one for the driver.

Table 3. J48 n-fold results

J48	CLUB	C-STD	BALL	B-STD	ACC	AUC	TP	SIZE
i7	X				0.773	0.755	0.741	13
i7	X	X			0.762	0.771	0.672	13
i7			X		0.765	0.797	0.69	13
i7			X	X	0.783	0.83	0.69	5
i7	X	X	X	X	0.823	0.835	0.69	9
Driver	X				0.699	0.729	0.638	11
Driver	X	X			0.83	0.778	0.759	13
Driver			X		0.71	0.732	0.724	11
Driver			X	X	0.764	0.782	0.672	13
Driver	X	X	X	X	0.815	0.835	0.621	11

The most interesting result is, however, that the J48 achieves a rather high predictive performance with relative small and simple models. Hence, it can be argued that the trees capture a substantial part of what distinguishes good swings from bad ones while still being small and comprehensible. The predictive power is, of course, higher for RF, but these models are opaque and hence of limited value for human inspection and analysis. Next, we present a few sample J48 models to evaluate how well they fit with existing golf theory and how usable they would be in a teaching situation.

5.3   Interpretation of Models

The decision trees presented below were created using data from all the players, but do otherwise use an identical setup to the main experiment. Hence, the overall accuracy of these models for new players should be judged on the results in Table 3.

The result for each leaf is, however, still presented, to show the accuracy of each rule for the existing golfers. The trees are presented in textual form where each leaf is given a number preceded with # to facilitate referencing. Leaves defining Pros and splits leading to Pro leaves are marked in green, while Hacker leaves and splits are marked in red. Splits that do not directly lead to a leaf are marked in black, since they do not define a property exclusively for Pros or Hackers. Each leaf also reports the number of golfers of the leaf class, the true positive rate (TP) of the leaf and the average hcp of all players classified by the leaf, i.e. (#players of leaf class|TP|hcp). Four trees, one based on all the data and one based on only CLUB data for each club, are discussed below. The reason for this choice is to present the most accurate trees (using all the data) and the more usable trees based on only club data.

The general result of the interpretation of the models below is that they also concur with general golf theory. Another general result is that Hackers can be identified with less splits than Pros. In practice, this means that you must master several skills to become a Pro, while just a few deficiencies in the swing are often enough to categorize a hacker. Another interesting observation is that all the trees tend to group players with similar hcps in a leaf, thus creating an implicit ranking of the players, in spite of the problem being setup as a classification task. This signifies that each split has predictive power in itself and thus represents a skill that needs to be mastered by a golfer. The contrary would apply if all the leaves relating to a particular class (Hacker or Pro) would have a similar average hcp. This would mean that all the splits leading to a rule would be needed to discern Hackers from Pros. Looking at this explains the higher AUC which exactly measures the ability to rank the players.

Model based on all data for i7

Next, Fig. 5 below, depicts a tree created from all the recorded data for the i7, which resulted in the most accurate model. Looking at the particular tree presented in Fig. 5, the first group of Hackers, i.e. rule #5, is signified by having a high STD in their launch direction. In practice, this means that they have problems controlling the starting direction of their shots. The average hcp for this large group of 115 Hackers is 17. The next group of Hackers classified by rule #1 (62 Hackers with an average hcp of 14.7) is better at controlling the *LaunchDirection* but has a lower *DistHeight* than the better golfers in leaf #3–#4. A lower *DistHeight* means that they do not hit the ball far enough, i.e. the apex and the ball trajectory are not as far away from the player, which naturally results in a shorter shot.

```
S-LaunchDirection <= 2.14
|       DistHeight <= 89.5 #1: Hacker (62|.95|14.7)
|       DistHeight > 89.5
|       |       S-SmashFactor <= 0.029 #2: Pro (39|.76|4.2)
|       |       S-SmashFactor > 0.029
|       |       |       S-DynLoft <= 1.42 #3: Pro (13|.52|7.4)
|       |       |       S-DynLoft > 1.42 #4: Hacker (18|.90|11.0)
S-LaunchDirection > 2.14 #5: Hacker (115|.99|17.0)
```

Fig. 5. Tree based on i7: CLUB, STD-C, BALL and STD-B

The first group of Pros, the largest group of 39 Pros with an average hcp of 4.2, is discerned by leaf #2. These Pros hit the ball further than the Hackers in group #1 and have a lower STD of their *SmashFactor* than players in groups #3 and #4. In essence, this means that they are more consistent in how well they hit the ball, which of course is important for controlling the length and accuracy of a shot.

The last two groups (#3 and #4) have a higher STD in their *SmashFactor* and a higher average hcp (7.4 for #3 and 11 for #4). Rule #3 defines the better golfers of these two groups which are characterized by their ability to better control the STD of their *DynLoft*. The *DynLoft* has a very strong correlation to the launch angle, which is an important factor for *DistHeight* and thereby the length of the shot. Hence, the difference between the Pros in rule #3 and the Hackers in rule #4 is that the Pros are better at controlling the length of their shots. The difference in hcp is, however, not large, which explains the low TP of .52 for rule #3.

To summarize, this tree tells us that the first skill a golfer must learn is to start the ball consistently on the target line and thereafter to hit long enough. Once mastered, the next skill to conquer is the ability to consistently hit the ball the same distance.

Models based on CLUB data for i7

Even if this tree, presented in Fig. 5, is one of the more accurate trees, it does not say much about how the swing itself should be performed, since this is mainly based on BALL-data. Hence, a model for 7i based only on CLUB-data.

The first split in this tree is based on the *DynLoft* with a split point of 29.6. This value is far from the Pros' mean value of 23.5 and the average Hacker value of 25.3 presented in Fig. 6. Hence, the 24 players that are all correctly classified as Hackers by leaf #7 have a way to high dynamic loft. The next group of players discerned by leaf #1 is again Hackers with a more reasonable *DynLoft* but a rather low *ClubSpeed* of 77.1, resulting in shorter shots. It is not a big difference from the average *ClubSpeed* for Hackers, which is 80.2, but far from the Pros at 87.2. Leaf #5 shows that the next group of Hackers has high *FaceAngle*, resulting in shots in the wrong direction, if there is no corresponding curvature of the ball (hook or slice) to counteract the initial direction. Nonetheless, swings with higher *FaceAngles* are harder to control and repeat consistently.

```
DynLoft <= 29.6
|    ClubSpeed <= 74.7 #1: Hacker (42|1.0|17.7)
|    ClubSpeed > 74.7
|    |    FaceAngle <= 4
|    |    |    ClubPath <= 4.8
|    |    |    |    ClubSpeed <= 86.2
|    |    |    |    |    SwingPlane <= 60.4 #2: Pro (13|.41|10.1)
|    |    |    |    |    SwingPlane > 60.4 #3: Hacker (32|.91|15.1)
|    |    |    |    ClubSpeed > 86.2 #4: Pro (37|.61|5.7)
|    |    |    ClubPath > 4.8 #5: Hacker (30|.91|11.6)
|    |    FaceAngle > 4 #6: Hacker (34|.94|15.3)
DynLoft > 29.6 #7: Hacker (24|1.0|17.4)
```

Fig. 6. - Tree based on i7: CLUB

Players in group #5 are again classified as Hackers who are here discerned from the remaining golfers by a rather large *ClubPath* angle (4.8) in relation to the target line. A high *ClubPath* value will also make it harder to control the ball flight, for more or less the same reasons as the *FaceAngle*. It is, however, interesting to note that *FaceAngle* is used higher up in the tree, which signifies that it is a more important factor than the *ClubPath*. This concurs with modern golf theory which has only been applied a few years.

Leaf #4 is the first leaf to classify players as Pros. Players classified by this rule (including 37 Pros and 24 Hackers) have avoided the rules leading to the leaves #1, #7, #6, #5 and thus have a reasonable swing, but also a high *ClubSpeed*, i.e. higher than 86.2. Players who have avoided the leaves #1, #7, #6, #5, but have a lower *ClubSpeed* than the Pros in #4, are classified as Pros or Hackers by leaves #2 and #3, depending on the SwingPlane. Here, a lower swing plane is favorable, which by itself is interesting, especially since Table 1 does not show any major difference in the swing plane between Hacker and Pros.

It should be noted that even if the TP rate for leaf #2 is only 0.41, it still classifies the players as Hackers due to the cost-sensitive learning applied. Nonetheless, the average hcp of this leaf is lower than all the Hacker leaves and 5 points lower than the neighboring Hacker leaf (#3). Hence, the split is still important for discerning Hackers from Pros.

Models based on all data from the driver

In the following section, models based on data from shots with the driver are presented. Figure 7 depicts a decision tree created using all the available data. The first group of Hackers, i.e. leaf #6 in Fig. 7, is selected on the basis of the STD of the *LaunchAngle* (2.89), which lies close to the Pros value of (2.7). Consequently, a large number of golfers, (93) are selected in this leaf but, surprisingly, all are correctly classified as Hackers. Next, leaf #5 selects 27 Hackers on the basis of a relatively large STD of the *FaceAngle*. More Hackers are classified in leaf #1 on the basis of a *BallSpeed* less than 128.5, which is rather low compared to the average *BallSpeed* of Pros at 151.8. Obviously, these players cannot hit the ball far enough.

```
S-LaunchAngle <= 2.89
|    S-FaceAngle <= 3.66
|    |    BallSpeed <= 128.52 #1: Hacker (26|1.0|15.1)
|    |    BallSpeed > 128.52
|    |    |    S-SmashFactor <= 0.04
|    |    |    |    SwingPlane <= 51.89 #2: Pro (52|.61|6.4)
|    |    |    |    SwingPlane > 51.89 #3: Hacker (19|.83|9.8)
|    |    |    S-SmashFactor > 0.04 #4: Hacker (19|.86|10.4)
|    S-FaceAngle > 3.66 #5: Hacker (27|1.0|17.2)
S-LaunchAngle > 2.89 #6: Hacker (93|1.0|18.2)
```

Fig. 7. Tree based on Driver: CLUB, STD-C, BALL and STD-B

Leaf #4 is characterized by a higher STD of the *SmashFactor,* which relates to how consistently the player hits the ball. The split point of 0.04 is identical to the Pros mean value and, consequently, a few Pros (3) are miss-classified as Hackers in this leaf. The final split divides Pros from Hackers on the basis of their *SwingPlane*, where it is again favorable to have a flatter plane. The chosen split point of 51.89 is higher than the average driver *SwingPlane* of both Pros and Hackers, thus discerning rather good Hackers with atypical swings, i.e. the average hcp of rule #3 is 9.8.

Models based on CLUB data from driver

The final tree presented in Fig. 8 is based on only CLUB variables for the driver. This tree selects exactly the same subset of variables as the i7 tree presented in Fig. 6, but in a slightly different order. The split point values are, however, quite different; which is natural because the driver is a longer club and designed to launch the ball at a lower angle.

The first group of Hackers in leaf #6 has a *DynLoft* at more than 18.26°, which is much too high, compared to the mean values of the Pros which are at 12.6°. A high *DynamicLoft* results in a higher *LaunchAngle* and thereby a higher and shorter shot.

```
DynLoft <= 18.26
|   FaceAngle <= 7.26
|   |   ClubSpeed <= 104.14
|   |   |   SwingPlane <= 51.89
|   |   |   |   ClubSpeed <= 89.54 #1: Hacker (22|.96|15.5)
|   |   |   |   ClubSpeed > 89.54 #2: Pro (36|.38|10.6)
|   |   |   SwingPlane > 51.89 #3: Hacker (44|1.0|15.0)
|   |   ClubSpeed > 104.14 #4: Pro (35|.59|5.6)
|   FaceAngle > 7.26 #5: Hacker (29|1.0|19.6)
DynLoft > 18.26 #6: Hacker (41|1.0|19.2)
```

Fig. 8. Tree based on Driver: CLUB

Next, leaf #5 discerns players with a high *FaceAngle*, i.e. 5° higher than that of the Pros, which results in shots in the wrong direction or curved shots that are harder to control.

The third group, defined by leaf #4, is the first to classify golfers as Pros on the basis of a *ClubSpeed* of 104.14, which is very close to the average value for Pros. Since the leaves #5 and #6 are based on rather extreme values, the main factor discerning these really proficient players, with a mean hcp at 5.5, from the rest of the golfers is high swing speed and reasonable values for *FaceAngle* and *DynLoft*. Of the remaining golfers, 44 players are classified as Hackers in leaf #3, on the basis of a rather steep swing plane. Finally, the remaining players are classified by leaves #1 and #2, again on the basis of their *ClubSpeed*. Players with club speeds lower than 89.54, which is very low compared to Pros at 104.7, are classified as Hackers and the rest as Pros. The TP rate for this last set of Pros is low (0.38), but due to the cost-sensitive training the leaf still classifies golfers as Pros. It could, however, be argued that the predictive power of this leaf is higher than indicated by this value, since the average hcp of this rule is 4.5 points lower than any leaf classifying Hackers. Obviously, players misclassified by this rule are still rather good players.

To summarize, there are two groups of Pros who all have reasonable *DynLoft* and *FaceAngle*. The best groups of Pros are, in addition, characterized by a high *Club-Speed*. The other group of Pros has a lower *ClubSpeed* but they distinguish themselves from the Hackers by a flatter *SwingPlane*.

6 Discussion and Conclusions

From the results presented above, it is clear that it is possible to model golf player skill on the basis of quantitative data from the club head at impact or the ball flight. Predictive models with high ranking ability, i.e. AUC, can be created using both RF and J48 with an advantage to RF. For the 7i datasets containing only CLUB data, there was no difference in the predictive performance of the models. Obviously, including STDs and ball data facilitates more complex relationships, which the random forest can model but not the decision tree. The models do, nonetheless, concur in the variables they consider important, which adds credibility to the found models.

It is also interesting to note that the ranking ability is high, in spite of a setup as a binary classification task. When interpreting the models, this can be seen in the fact that players in leaves longer from the root, in general, have a lower average hcp. Obviously, each split has predictive power and leaves further from the root require that more skills need to be fulfilled by a player.

Even if the random forests are more accurate, they do not give insights as actionable as the decision trees. Future work could however address this deficiency by applying a sensitivity analysis showing the relative importance of the variables. The relative importance would possibly give a teaching professional sufficient knowledge on the particular aspect of the swing that they should improve to lower a player's hcp. This is an important point, since teaching professionals are normally mainly concerned with improving a player's swing more ideal, which does not always result in a lower hcp, the goal of many Hackers.

All J48 models are, however, small, comprehensible and concur with modern swing theory. More specifically, consistency is more important than any specific value of the club head or ball flight. Looking at only the CLUB variables, it is clear that the *ClubSpeed, FaceAngle, ClubPath* and *DynLoft* are the most important variables for discerning good players from those less skilled. This also concurs with golf theory and is hence a strong result for the correctness of the models.

A more surprising and interesting result is, however, that the *SwingPlane* is also a strong indicator of skill, where proficient players tend to have flatter swings. This is surprising, since there is only a small deviation in the average *SwingPlane* of Hackers and Pros. The reason for this result is not obvious from modern golf theory and we can only speculate about the reasons; e.g., a flatter swing could possibly lead to higher *ClubSpeed* at the bottom of the swing, due to a more circular movement of the club. However, both decision tree models created from only CLUB data contradict this theory, since they split the players on the basis of *ClubSpeed* before *SwingPlane*. Hence, the *SwingPlane* is used to discern among players with rather similar *ClubSpeed*. Naturally, the flatter swings found at better players in this study is an important finding that needs to be studied in more detail. Obviously, a flatter plane gives rise to a different chain of movements in the swing, thus affecting the release pattern and the impact position. Specifically, a flatter swing plane is associated with swinging from the inside and a release leading to a lower dynamic loft and higher smash factor, which was found to be favorable in the induced models.

Finally, the J48 models show a clear distinction in the swing of Hackers and Pros. When modeled using only CLUB data, the swings of golfers classified as Pros were characterized by reasonable values for *FaceAngle, ClubPath* and *DynLoft* while having a high *ClubSpeed*. The majority of Hackers could be identified by a large deviation (from the average Pro value), for one of these variables. Better Hackers were discerned by having either a slightly lower *ClubSpeed* or a steeper *SwingPlane* than the Pros.

References

1. Wheeler, K., Nauright, J.: A global perspective on the environmental impact of golf. Sport Soc. **9**(3), 427–443 (2006)
2. Smith, A., Roberts, J., Wallace, E., Forrester, S.: Professional golf coaches' perceptions of the key technical parameters in the golf swing. Procedia Eng. **34**, 224–229 (2012)
3. TrackMan A/S. Denmark (2015)
4. Fradkin, A., Sherman, C., Finch, C.: How well does club head speed correlate with golf handicaps? J. Sci. Med. Sport **7**(4), 465–472 (2004)
5. Sweeney, M., Mills, P.M., Alderson, J., Elliott, B.C.: The influence of club-head kinematics on early ball flight characteristics in the golf drive. Sport. Biomech. **12**(3), 247–258 (2013)
6. EGA, EGA Handicap System (2012)
7. Broadie, M.: Assessing Golfer Performance Using Golfmetrics, Sci. Golf V Proc. 2008 World Sci. Congr. Golf, no. 1968, pp. 253–262 (2008)
8. Tuxen, F.: The Secret of the Straight Shot II (2009)
9. Betzler, N.F., Monk, S.A., Wallace, E.S., Otto, S.R.: Variability in clubhead presentation characteristics and ball impact location for golfers' drives. J. Sports Sci. **30**(5), 439–448 (2012)
10. SGA, Swedish Golf Association (2015). www.golf.se. Accessed 04 Mar 2015
11. World of Golf. Västra Frölunda, Sweden (2015)
12. Quinlan, J.R.: C4.5: Programs for Machine Learning, vol. 240. Morgan Kaufmann (1993)
13. Breiman, L.: Random forests. Mach. Learn. **45**, 5–32 (2001)
14. Provost, F., Domingos, P.: Tree induction for probability-based ranking. Mach. Learn. **52**(3), 199–215 (2003)
15. Breiman, L.: Classification and Regression Trees. Chapman & Hall/CRC, Boca Raton (1984)
16. Quinlan, J.R.: Induction of decision trees. Mach. Learn. **1**(1), 81–106 (1986)

Predicting Chronic Heart Failure Using Diagnoses Graphs

Saurabh Nagrecha[1], Pamela Bilo Thomas[1,2], Keith Feldman[1], and Nitesh V. Chawla[1,2(✉)]

[1] Department of Computer Science and Engineering,
Interdisciplinary Center for Network Science and Applications (iCeNSA),
University of Notre Dame, Notre Dame, IN 46556, USA
{snagrech,pthomas4,kfeldman,nchawla}@nd.edu
[2] Indiana Biosciences Research Institute,
1345 W 16th Street #300, Indianapolis, IN 46202, USA

Abstract. Predicting the onset of heart disease is of obvious importance as doctors try to improve the general health of their patients. If it were possible to identify high-risk patients before their heart failure diagnosis, doctors could use that information to implement preventative measures to keep a heart failure diagnosis from becoming a reality. Integration of Electronic Medical Records (EMRs) into clinical practice has enabled the use of computational techniques for personalized healthcare at scale. The larger goal of such modeling is to pivot from reactive medicine to preventative care and early detection of adverse conditions. In this paper, we present a trajectory-based disease progression model to detect chronic heart failure. We validate our work on a database of Medicare records of 1.1 million elderly US patients. Our supervised approach allows us to assign likelihood of chronic heart failure for an unseen patient's disease history and identify key disease progression trajectories that intensify or diminish said likelihood. This information will be a tremendous help as patients and doctors try to understand what are the most dangerous diagnoses for those who are susceptible to heart failure. Using our model, we demonstrate some of the most common disease trajectories that eventually result in the development of heart failure.

Keywords: Heart failure · Cardiovascular disease · Directed acyclic graph · Medicare · EMR · Health care

1 Introduction

Today the healthcare industry finds itself at the precipice of a significant change, as the past decade has seen the adaption and integration of electronic medical records (EMR) into clinical practice. Beyond the logistical benefits of maintaining and organizing patients' medical data, clinicians and researchers can perform novel research using these secondary data sources [1–3]. In fact EMRs

© IFIP International Federation for Information Processing 2017
Published by Springer International Publishing AG 2017. All Rights Reserved
A. Holzinger et al. (Eds.): CD-MAKE 2017, LNCS 10410, pp. 295–312, 2017.
DOI: 10.1007/978-3-319-66808-6_20

ability to provide a computationally accessible set of structured data representing the expansive healthcare feature space has fueled the emergence of a sundry of informatics tools ranging from early clinical decision support systems, to the statistical analysis of, to predictive analytics aimed at identifying patients at risk for readmission [4,5].

Building on the success of these tools, many researchers have seen healthcare informatics as the junction between another line of parallel clinical research, the shift from reactive to preventative medicine. Medical research is itself an evolving field, and has advanced in parallel with the emergence of EMR. Clinicians have put forth a strong effort in advancing the care paradigm from reactive medicine, where clinicians treat the conditions currently afflicting a patient, to preventative care where clinicians undertake courses of action "for the purpose of preventing disease or detecting it in an asymptomatic stage" [6]. As such, the early detection and treatment of adverse health conditions represents an exciting opportunity for the informatics community. Others have found that a combination of research areas, including, but not limited to, graph-based data mining, entropy-based data mining, and topological-based data mining, work best for knowledge discovery and towards an end goal of supplementing human learning with machine learning [7]. Eventually the goal is to have P4-medicine (predictive, preventative, participatory, personalized) available for all patients by using big data and the combined human computer interaction and knowledge discovery/data mining approach [7].

A number of works have built on this foundation, focusing predictive tasks from disease prediction, to the prediction of breast cancer survivability [8,9]. However, these tools suffer from a fundamental flaw, they identify patients' health conditions as isolated events, i.e. a disease will occur in a patient's future medical chart, or a patient will recover from early stage breast cancer. One must remember that an individuals' health condition does not only consist of when doctors measure them in a clinical environment. Although the rate of onset may vary, the progression of disease represents a highly fluid state. As such, it may be more valuable to view these patients' conditions as trajectories, rather than binary events.

While this seems like a significant shift in thinking, medical subfields have already established the concept of a disease trajectory, sometimes denoted as disease 'progression'. In particular, research in relation to neurodegenerative disorders such as Parkinson's and Alzheimer's have quite well established this concept [10,11]. More recently, the trajectory concept has begun expanding into the general healthcare population. Many clinicians have long postulated that an underlying progression of related diagnoses may relate to diagnoses for which we do not explicitly relate a temporal aspect. Today, the data collected through the expanding EMR now allows for researchers to examine such hypotheses in detail. Perhaps Jensen et al., have provided one of the best examples to date, where through their work they successfully extracted diagnosis trajectories by analyzing millions of longitudinal patient records and utilized a novel way of describing biological disease progression [12].

In this work, we build on this concept and present a novel graph-based diagnosis trajectory model. While recent advances have taken what effectively represent an "unsupervised" approach to trajectory discovery, we aim to provide a target based "supervised" methodology. We will begin with a discussion of the underlying methodology used in constructing the underlying diagnosis graph. From here, we will discuss utilizing the temporal relations extracted from the graph, showing that we can identify paths that significant differentiate the occurrence of the target diagnosis. Finally, we will provide a case study of the methodology in relation to patients with congestive heart failure.

2   Data Description

Electronic Medical Records (EMRs) log information on patients in the form of diagnosis codes for each of their visits. This log effectively narrates a patient's medical history as identified by medical practitioners and can predict their future health outcomes. Here we describe our data source, the data structure, how chronic heart failure appears these diagnoses logs and how prevalent it is within our patients.

Provenance. Our data comes from the Medicare records of 1,145,541 elderly patients in the United States. The accuracy and completeness of these records makes them invaluable to demographic and epidemiological research [9,13,14]. The data is completely anonymized—both in terms of the patients and the healthcare providers. For a given patient, we applied a threshold of a maximum of 5 in-patient visit, and each visit corresponds to a maximum of 10 diagnosis codes from the *International Classification of Diseases, Ninth Revision, Clinical Modification* (ICD-9-CM). These ICD-9-CM codes are designed to convey an intrinsic hierarchy of diagnosis detail—the full 5-digit code represents the specific condition, location and/or severity, and its leading 3 digits represent the medical diagnosis family. This "code collapse" [9] helps us identify the family of patients who develop heart failure in our data.

Identifying heart failure. We observe ground truth evidence of presence/absence of heart failure with ICD-9-CM diagnoses for individual patients. Diagnoses represented by the family of '428.xy' codes cover all diagnoses for heart failure. Specific examples of the 428 diagnosis family include *Systolic heart failure* (428.2); which breaks down into *Systolic heart failure, unspecified* (428.20), *Acute systolic heart failure* (428.21), *Chronic systolic heart failure* (428.22) and *Acute on chronic systolic heart failure* (428.23). We labeled as 'HF' all patients for whom we observed the '428' diagnosis family, and labeled the rest as 'NHF' for heart failure and non-heart failure respectively.

Table 1 shows a sample patient's medical history. Here we see the chronological history of the patient through each successive visit expressed in terms of full ICD-9-CM codes. For each visit, the first code is the principal diagnosis, followed by any secondary diagnoses made during that visit. The data presents these diagnoses in their full ICD-9-CM form where 733.00 represents *Osteoporosis, unspecified*. Some diagnoses, such as *Pathologic fracture* (733.1) and

Table 1. Example Patient History: Each row represents a distinct visit in chronological order. In each visit, the data shows multiple ICD-9-CM code diagnoses for our example patient. Note that the code for heart failure (428.0) appears in the fifth visit.

Visit	Vector of ICD-9-CM disease codes
1	7331 (Pathologic fracture, unspecified site), 73300 (Osteoporosis, unspecified), 2761 (Hyposmolality and/or hyponatremia), 4928 (Other emphysema), 73743 (Scoliosis associated with other conditions)
2	7331 (Pathologic fracture, unspecified site), 73300 (Osteoporosis, unspecified), 73741 (Kyphosis associated with other conditions), 73743 (Scoliosis associated with other conditions), 261 (Nutritional marasmus)
3	7331 (Pathologic fracture, unspecified site), 73300 (Osteoporosis, unspecified), 73741 (Kyphosis associated with other conditions), 73743 (Scoliosis associated with other conditions), 261 (Nutritional marasmus)
4	485 (Bronchopneumonia, organism unspecified), 2765 (Volume depletion disorder), 2769 (Electrolyte and fluid disorders not elsewhere classified), 496 (Chronic airway obstruction, not elsewhere classified),73300 (Osteoporosis, unspecified)
5	48230 (Pneumonia due to Streptococcus, unspecified) **4280 (Heart failure)**, 5119 (Unspecified pleural effusion), 2761 (Hyposmolality and/or hyponatremia), 2768 (Hypopotassemia), 73300 (Osteoporosis, unspecifie), 73741 (Kyphosis associated with other conditions), 7331 (Pathologic fracture, unspecified site)

Nutritional marasmus (261), use fewer than the maximum 5 digits in ICD-9-CM. Using Table 1 as an example, we see that in visit #5, the patient was diagnosed with *Congestive heart failure, unspecified* (428.0) and therefore belongs to the class 'HF'.

Summary Statistics. The EMR data used in this study covers 1,145,541 elderly Medicare patients over the course of 5,727,705 total visits. Over the course of these visits, the patients registered a total of 12,396 unique ICD-9-CM diagnoses codes, which represent 1,064 families of 3 digit collapsed codes. This set of patients exhibits a heart failure rate of 46.6%, which is extremely high compared to the United States, about 5.7 million (2.2%) adults have heart failure [15]. However, some have observed the overall prevalence of heart failure in elderly patients in the United States as high as 10.6 to 13.5% (Chart 20-2 [15]). Since our study focuses on patients on Medicare, this number is further amplified.

Experiments. Based on this EMR data, we group our analysis into two distinct phases—(1) building a representational model for heart failure and (2) predicting heart failure outcomes for unseen patients. First, we infer the nature of disease progression for patients with and without observed heart failure. Based on the learned model, we identify trajectories, individual diagnoses, and edges that give the best indication of heart failure. We then use this model on previously unseen patients and predict whether they will develop heart failure and validate this against observed ground truth data about these test patients.

3   Building a Representational Predictive Model

Researchers have built contemporary disease progression models using patient data with already known target outcomes. [10,11]. In contrast, our supervised approach helps contextualize disease progression trajectories against an in-situ control set of patients, i.e. our data contains trajectories followed by patients who eventually were diagnosed with Heart Failure and those who were not. This app-roach highlights the diagnosis trajectories that intensify or diminish likelihood of heart failure in patients. The identification of such divergence in diagnoses helps pinpoint signals for heart failure from overall population trends. In this section, we describe how we restructure Medicare EMR data to obtain supervised disease progression trajectories. We then merge individual trajectories in the form of a compact Directed Acyclic Graph to model class-aware patient population-wide trends in diagnoses. Using this model, we identify key differentiating diagnoses and trajectories that help separate patients who are likely to develop heart failure from those who do not.

Preprocessing. We transform the data from raw medical histories shown in Table 1 to extract class-aware trajectories for patients using the following steps. We first collapse the diagnosis codes to their 3 digit counterparts, then eliminate duplicate families of diagnoses and then decouple the diagnosis history used for prediction from the observed outcome. Table 2 shows the result of applying this preprocessing to the example history from Table 1.

1. *Removing patients who receive a heart disease diagnosis on their first visit* Out of the 46.6% of the patients in our dataset who develop heart failure, 18.0% receive a heart failure diagnosis in their very first visit. Since this study revolves around the concept of diagnoses leading up to heart failure, we consider these patients out of scope for our training and testing data. This removal of heart failure cases reduces the rate of observed heart failure in the rest of the patients down to 34.8% from the original 46.6%.
2. *Decoupling input data and target labels*—In patients with heart failure, we right-censor the diagnosis data when the first '428' code appears. This ensures that there is no "data leakage", i.e. we do not predict heart failure based on an observed diagnosis of heart failure since it is a chronic condition.
3. *Pre-pruning diagnoses and pathways*—To mitigate the impact of spuri-ous/noisy disease trajectories in our analysis, we set a minimum support threshold of 100 for the nodes and edges in our graph. By imposing this threshold, we ensure that none of the diagnoses or the pathways between them draws conclusions from a set of fewer than 100 patients out of a total sample size of 1.1M patients.
4. *Code Collapse*—The original data contains 12,396 "Minor Category" diagno-sis codes, whereas our analysis targets the "Major Category" outcome (heart

Table 2. Preprocessed Example Patient History. Using the same example data as Table 1, we derive a compact history of the patient. As a result of this preprocessing, we arrive at a set of input diagnoses (visits #1 to 4) to create a trajectory and decouple it from the labeled outcome (visit #5). Note that the diagnosis has been collapsed to its family

Visit #	ICD-9-CM codes
1	733 (Other disorders of bone and cartilage), 276 (Disorders of fluid electrolyte and acid-base balance), 492 (Emphysema), 737 (Curvature of spine)
2	261 (Nutritional marasmus)
3	NA
4	485 (Bronchopneumonia, organism unspecified), 496 (Chronic airway obstruction, not elsewhere classified)
5	**428 heart failure**

failure). Collapsing the 5-digit diagnoses codes down to their respective 3-digit major categories helps reduce the complexity of the problem and matches the granularity of the observed outcome. As a result, we now use 1,064 diagnosis families to chart patient trajectories, which is 8.6% of the original complexity.

5. *Removing duplicate diagnoses*—We only consider new and previously unobserved diagnoses in our analyses. In Table 1, this means that we consider diagnoses for *Other disorders of bone and cartilage* (733) only for their first visit. We hope to address the trade-off of dropping duplicate diagnosis in Future Work.

6. *Removing superfluous diagnoses*—ICD-9-CM diagnosis codes starting with V (Supplementary classification of factors influencing health status and contact with health services) and E (External causes of injury) reveal little about the progression of disease and were taken out of the graph.

Disease Progression for Individual Patients. For the example patient in Table 2, we can now create a disease progression history based on their diagnoses Fig. 1. Each node represents a diagnosis and each edge $(e(i, j))$ represents a potential transition from diagnosis i to j across successive patient visits. Each of these edges is strictly directed from a diagnosis in visit $(t - 1)$ to a diagnosis in visit t and nodes in the same visit do not have edges between them. This makes the graph a Directed Acyclic Graph (DAG). Each patient in our training data has an outcome label associated with them, which we use as a label for each of these patient-centric DAGs (Fig. 2).

A Class-Aware Heart Failure Model. While each patient's disease progression DAG contains signals for their eventual outcome, but a domain expert aided causal analysis for each patient would not scale to the 1.1M patients in our dataset. Instead, we aggregate these histories into a unified model across all patients to get a consensus on which diagnoses and pathways signal which

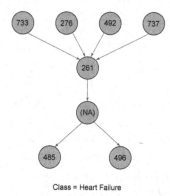

Class = Heart Failure

Fig. 1. Example Patient Disease Progression. A directed acyclic graph can model a single patient's disease progression as shown above. Each layer represents a distinct visit, and each child node belongs to the next visit. In each visit layer, we identify several unique diagnosis codes. Each individual node in the graph represents these diagnosis codes.

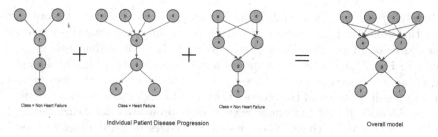

Fig. 2. Combining individual patient histories

outcome for an unseen patient. Within our patient population, we perform a 5-fold cross-validation, training on 80% of the patients and testing the model on the other 20% over 5 folds of the data. As shown in Fig. 2, we simply combine observed nodes and edges across all training set patients and create a composite DAG. The nodes at each level represent the superset of possible diagnoses at that visit and edges between each level represent the observed transitions between diagnoses.

The weight of each edge $e(i, j)$ corresponds to the observed confidence of heart failure among patients who were diagnosed with i and then j. Similarly, we assign a weight to each node n representing the observed confidence of heart failure for that node. A patient can have multiple diagnoses within the same visit, each of which adds to the support of the corresponding nodes and edges. This does not guarantee the total incoming support into a node being equal to the total outgoing support. Another salient feature of this model is that it cane distinguish the same diagnosis code between visits. For example, if one observes code '261' in visit #1 and #2 for different patients, we create nodes labeled '261_1' and '261_2'

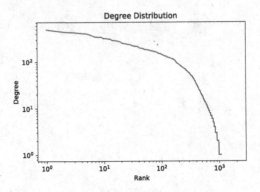

Fig. 3. Degree distribution of trained diagnosis graph

to preserve their unique trajectory histories. By this definition, it is possible for '261_1' and '261_2' to have completely different weights. In our model, we label each node's diagnosis code according to the visit it was observed in.

Model Inference. The overall trained model is an interconnected representation that contains 1,974 nodes and 26,229 edges. with an average in-degree and out-degree of 13.29. The degree distribution of the trained diagnosis graph is given in Fig. 3. A relatively few nodes and edges contain a high likelihood of heart failure as seen in Fig. 4. These high-confidence nodes and edges indicate underlying diagnoses and trajectories that lead to high rates of heart failure.

We identify nodes and edges with a high propensity for heart failure in Tables 3 and 4 respectively. These nodes and edges describe diagnostic pathways that indicate heart failure. In addition to extremely high likelihood of heart failure, we also identify diagnoses that effectively discern heart failure. For this, we use information gain (or InfoGain, for short) for successive diagnoses in patients. A higher information gain indicates a higher class polarization between

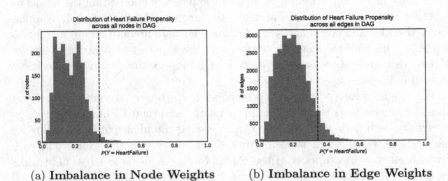

(a) **Imbalance in Node Weights**   (b) **Imbalance in Edge Weights**

Fig. 4. Heart failure trajectories are highly imbalanced: We observe that the progression of heart failure follows a minor set of nodes and edges in the learned model.

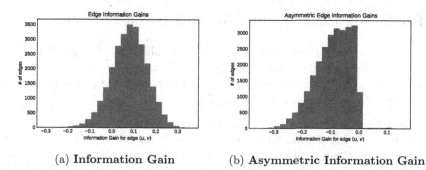

(a) **Information Gain**   (b) **Asymmetric Information Gain**

Fig. 5. Information Gain in Edges: We compute the information gain for each edge and use it as an edge attribute. By making information gain class aware, we treat non-heart failure intensifying edges as negative information gains. This makes it easier to isolate signals for heart failure intensifying paths.

heart failure and non-heart-failure. Information Gain (IG) is the *reduction* in entropy for a given edge in our model. Specifically, an edge $e(i,j)$ with high information gain indicates that the diagnosis of j after i leads to a higher confidence of arriving at either class. We compute each node's entropy from its class distribution using

$$H(i) = \sum_k -p_k(i)log(p_k(i)) \qquad H(j) = \sum_{k'} -p_{k'}(j)log(p_{k'}(j))$$

$$IG(i,j) = H(i) - H(j)$$

where i and j are the respective source and destination diagnoses, $k \in \{HF, NHF\}$, and $p_k(.)$ represents the probability of observing class k in a given node. Information Gain for $e(i,j)$ is simply $IG(i,j) = H(i) - H(j)$, where higher values of IG are more helpful in our search for heart failure propensity intensifying markers.

The sheer abundance of pathways towards non-heart-failure outcomes eclipses the relatively low InfoGain of individual edges which intensify heart failure. These are the majority of the edges which form the positive side of Fig. 5a. However, we are primarily interested in edges which intensify likelihood of heart failure. To achieve this, we artificially penalize InfoGain in edges which have a higher likelihood of non heart failure by simply making them negative. This isolates and highlights heart-failure intensifying pathways in the network. Figure 5b shows how this transformation affects the edge attributes and isolates the relatively few edges which exhibit a high InfoGain favoring heart failure.

The above steps outline how we process raw patient records into a supervised representational model. This graphical model not only amalgamates patient disease trajectories, but it also highlights key pathways leading to heart failure.

4   Predicting Heart Failure for an Unseen Patient

Now that we have a representational and interpretable model to predict heart failure, we use it to predict outcomes for our held-out test dataset. We describe how we convert a new patient's diagnosis history into predicted probabilities and how we evaluate these predicted outcomes.

How to Predict. Given a test patient's diagnosis history, we replicate the steps in the training section to arrive at a graph similar to Fig. 1. Here, we make an important assumption about the nature of our model—we assume that the probabilities at each stage obey a Bayesian model. Using the probabilities from our trained model, we can predict relative odds of heart failure and non-heart failure by simply multiplying the class-wise probabilities for each edge and normalizing them. Given a test patient with a disease progression graph G_{test}, the unnormalized value of $\mathbb{P}(Y = HF)^* = \prod_e p(e(i,j))$, $\forall e(i,j) \in G_{test}$ and $p(e(i,j)) \in G_{trained}$. We then similarly compute the unnormalized value of $\mathbb{P}(Y = NHF)^*$ and finally output the normalized value of $\mathbb{P}(Y = HF)$.

In this work, we assume a Markovian model when using the Bayesian network structure to model disease progression. This means that dependencies and graph attributes (for instance, support and confidence) do not extend beyond *immediate* descendants directly in our model, i.e. $A|B$ and $B|C$ can model disease progression, but not $A|B, C$ directly. In future work, the model can extend to include higher-order dependencies [16]. This would enable us to model dependencies of the form $A|B, C$ and beyond.

Evaluation and Baselines. We compute the above probabilities for all patients in the test set and evaluated against their true observed outcomes. We then compute the Receiver Operating Characteristics in terms of False Positive Rate and True Positive Rate for these predictions. Our key prediction metric is the area under the ROC curve (AUROC), a higher AUROC indicating superior predictive performance.

How soon can we predict Heart Failure? Each visit in our trained model is represented by a layer of nodes in the DAG. A prediction made using the first i layers of the DAG corresponds to a prediction made on i visits of an unseen test patient. Deliberately pruning the number of layers in the trained DAG is equivalent to reducing the complexity of our trained model and being able to predict our target outcome earlier. In order to see if this trade-off negatively influences predictive performance, we test the unseen patient histories on DAGs pruned to predict heart failure from 1, 2, 3 and 4 (maximum number of test visits in our data) visits and evaluate their area under the ROC curve.

5   Results

The techniques described above cover three key aspects of our research. First, we train a class-aware model of heart failure from patient history data. Second, we interpret the model to identify key diagnoses and disease progression pathways

Table 3. Top 20 confidence nodes for heart failure. These nodes represent the diagnoses with the highest likelihood of heart failure in our model.

Visit #	Diagnosis	Confidence	Support
2	Rheumatic fever with heart involvement	0.5947	882
1	Rheumatic fever with heart involvement	0.5685	690
2	Pulmonary congestion and hypostasis	0.5117	2088
1	Cardiomyopathy	0.4923	7338
1	Diseases of mitral valve	0.4746	1872
2	Cardiomyopathy	0.466	11864
1	Pulmonary congestion and hypostasis	0.4552	1046
1	Poisoning by agents primarily affecting the cardiovascular system	0.4448	679
1	Hypertensive heart and renal disease	0.4383	3784
2	Hypertensive heart and renal disease	0.4366	7624
1	Diseases of mitral and aortic valves	0.4312	8724
1	Diseases of aortic valve	0.4232	199
2	Diseases of mitral valve	0.4188	2764
2	Diseases of aortic valve	0.4097	487
1	Diseases of other endocardial structures	0.4032	3524
1	Chronic pulmonary heart disease	0.4016	4924
1	Nephrotic syndrome	0.3963	1676
2	Diseases of mitral and aortic valves	0.3949	15168
2	Chronic pulmonary heart disease	0.3918	9477
1	Hypertensive heart disease	0.375	41999

which intensify or mitigate the chances of a given patient developing heart failure. Third, we show how this model performs when predicting heart failure outcomes for a completely unseen set of patients.

Model Inference. Looking at the highest confidence nodes for heart failure in Table 3, several common themes appear in diagnoses that tend to proceed heart failure - namely, rheumatic fever, pulmonary congestion, cardiomyopathy, blood poisoning, kidney disease, hypertension, and aortic and mitral valve disease. For these diagnoses, it does not appear to matter much if one diagnoses a patient on 1 or 2 - the progression to heart disease seems to occur at about the same confidence levels. By absolute numbers in this data set, the diagnoses that lead to heart failure the most are cardiomyopathy and aortic mitral valve diseases. Rheumatic heart diseases and pulmonary congestion patients appear less than the former three in the data set, but have a higher probability of leading to heart failure.

Table 4. Highest Confidence disease progression edges in trained DAG. Top 20 diagnostic edges with extremely high confidence of heart failure. These edges represent those at the extreme right of the distribution in Fig. 4b. Visit number corresponds to source diagnosis.

Source		Destination		Conf	Supp
Visit #	Diagnosis	Visit #	Diagnosis		
1	Cardiac dysrhythmias	2	Rheumatic fever with heart involvement	0.6995	183
1	Cardiac dysrhythmias	2	Pulmonary congestion and hypostasis	0.6870	131
1	Diabetes mellitus	2	Pulmonary congestion and hypostasis	0.6798	178
1	Other forms of chronic ischemic heart disease	2	Pulmonary congestion and hypostasis	0.6486	148
1	Other diseases of lung	2	Cardiomyopathy	0.6400	150
1	Cardiomyopathy	2	Pneumonia, organism unspecified	0.6209	153
1	Cardiomyopathy	2	Acute myocardial infarction	0.6198	121
1	Conduction disorders	2	Cardiomyopathy	0.6123	325
1	Acute myocardial infarction	2	Cardiomyopathy	0.6000	180
1	Old myocardial infarction	2	Cardiomyopathy	0.5986	147
1	Cholelithiasis	2	Cardiomyopathy	0.5943	106
1	Cardiomyopathy	2	Other diseases of lung	0.5882	170
1	Diverticula of intestine	2	Cardiomyopathy	0.5847	118
1	Cardiomyopathy	2	Conduction disorders	0.5738	237
1	Cardiac dysrhythmias	2	Cardiomyopathy	0.5724	1277
1	Cardiomyopathy	2	Transcient cerebral ischemia	0.5714	105
1	Ill-defined descriptions and complications of heart disease	2	Cardiomyopathy	0.5708	212
1	Diabetes mellitus	2	Chronic pulmonary heart disease	0.5706	340
1	Essential hypertension	2	Pulmonary congestion and hypostasis	0.5610	164
1	Iron deficiency anemias	2	Cardiomyopathy	0.5577	104

Referring to the highest confidence edges for heart failure given in Table 4, we can see that may of the same destination diagnoses match the diagnoses given in the high confidence nodes in Table 3. The edges give us some idea about the diagnoses that come first that may lead to heart disease given another diagnosis. For instance, the high confidence nodes in Table 3 told us that diagnoses such as rheumatic fever, pulmonary congestion, and cardiomyopathy lead to heart

Table 5. Top 20 Information Gain edges in trained DAG. These edges represent diagnoses which go from seemingly benign to high likelihood of heart failure.

Source			Destination			InfoGain	Supp
Visit #	Diagnosis	Conf	Visit #	Diagnosis	Conf		
1	Affective psychoses	0.1541	2	Acute myocardial infarction	0.3462	0.1597	153
1	Affective psychoses	0.1541	2	Other diseases of endocardium	0.3355	0.1544	225
1	Affective psychoses	0.1541	2	Hypertensive heart disease	0.3279	0.1533	210
1	Malignant neoplasm of bladder	0.1769	2	Acute myocardial infarction	0.3462	0.1489	106
1	Other cerebral degenerations	0.1717	2	Acute myocardial infarction	0.3462	0.1324	105
1	Other cerebral degenerations	0.1717	2	Other diseases of endocardium	0.3355	0.1272	194
1	Other cerebral degenerations	0.1717	2	Hypertensive heart disease	0.3279	0.1261	141
1	Parkinson's disease	0.1795	2	Acute myocardial infarction	0.3462	0.1252	151
1	Parkinson's disease	0.1795	2	Other diseases of endocardium	0.3355	0.1200	167
1	Parkinson's disease	0.1795	2	Hypertensive heart disease	0.3279	0.1189	161
1	Neurotic disorder	0.1874	2	Acute myocardial infarction	0.3462	0.1068	249
1	Neurotic disorder	0.1874	2	Other diseases of endocardium	0.3355	0.1016	286
1	Neurotic disorder	0.1874	2	Hypertensive heart disease	0.3279	0.1005	247
2	General symptoms	0.2176	3	Cardiomyopathy	0.2980	0.1004	152
2	Other disorders of urethra and urinary tract	0.2208	3	Hypertensive heart and renal disease	0.3109	0.1004	146
2	Other disorders of urethra and urinary tract	0.2208	3	Cardiomyopathy	0.2980	0.0980	199
1	Senile and presenile organic psychotic conditions	0.1898	2	Acute myocardial infarction	0.3462	0.0979	179
1	Senile and presenile organic psychotic conditions	0.1898	2	Other diseases of endocardium	0.3355	0.0926	221
2	Other and unspecified anemias	0.2282	3	Hypertensive heart and renal disease	0.3109	0.0917	207
1	Senile and presenile organic psychotic conditions	0.1898	2	Hypertensive heart disease	0.3279	0.0915	225

failure. 14 out of the 20 top confidence edges involve cardiomyopathy, which indicates that cardiomyopathy is a strong component in leading to heart failure. Cardiac dysrhythmia is a diagnosis that is particularly deadly when combined with further diagnoses.

The findings of this graph seem to confirm the results of other studies. Others have identified cardiomyopathy and valve dysfunction as precursors for heart disease [17–19]. The American Heart Association has recommended that patients who have chronic kidney disease are in the highest risk group for development of cardiovascular disease [18]. Researchers have associated nephrotic syndrome with cardiovascular disease [18]. Pulmonary congestion is very common in patients with heart failure due to its relation to high pressure in the left ventricle of the heart. Many patients who have heart failure are also found to have fluid overload which is a common result of pulmonary congestion. Detection and treatment of pulmonary congestion can help prevent progression of heart failure [20]. The result of blood poisoning and sepsis is often multiple organ failure, including septic cardiomyopathy, which can lead to heart failure [21]. Other studies have found that chronic pulmonary heart disease is a predictor of chronic heart failure in China [22]. For many years, doctors have known that rheumatic fever can contribute to heart failure occurring later in life [23]. Hypertension is also a major contributing factor in congestive heart failure [24].

Almost all the top confidence edges involved rheumatic heart disease, pulmonary congestion and hypostasis, mitral and aortic valve disease, or cardiomyopathy, which therefore accentuates the importance of those diseases in the diagnosis of heart failure. The high confidence edges given in Table 4 let us know that diseases such as cardiac dysrhythmia, diabetes, ischemic heart disease, and lung diseases, diagnosed beforehand, can ultimately result in heart failure.

Table 5 shows us the highest information gain nodes tend to come from source diagnoses that are mental or noncardiac in nature (Affective psychoses, cerebral degeneration, malignant neoplasm of bladder, Parkinson's disease, etc.) followed by an acute myocardial infarction, endocardium diseases, or cardiomyopathy. This seems to suggest that these diagnoses are the first cardiac problems that might occur in patients with other mental or noncardiac issues. This model of information gain suggests that screening for those three diseases, since they appear as some of the first cardiac diagnosis on a trajectory that leads to heart failure.

Heart Failure Prediction. Our model can predict heart failure in patients from diagnoses from their second visit (i.e.: their first disease progression) as seen in Fig. 6. Adding diagnoses from subsequent visits makes the predictive performance plateau in comparison to the second visit. As discussed in our *Data Preprocessing* stage in Sect. 3, we only have a maximum of 4 patient visits for our prediction task.

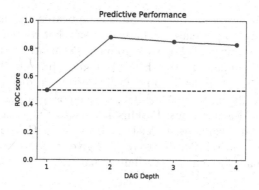

Fig. 6. Predictive performance for various number of visits. Area under the ROC curve plateaus with an increased amount of visits.

6   Discussion

Which disease progression trajectories lead to heart failure? A diagnosis of cardiomyopathy is a very common theme that appears in many high confidence edges and high information gains that lead to heart failure. Cardiomyopathy appears in 14 out of the 20 high confidence edges and 5 of the top 20 high information gains. We can therefore conclude that cardiomyopathy is an important factor in the progression of a heart failure trajectory. Monitoring patients for cardiomyopathy and intervening early is therefore important in limiting heart disease.

Besides cardiomyopathy, most of the other high information gain edges had a destination edge of acute myocardial infarction or endocardium diseases. These three appear as "gateway" diagnoses that eventually results in heart failure later in their medical record for patients who do not currently have a diagnosis of heart disease.

While cardiomyopathy is very common in the high confidence edge nodes, it does not occupy the top four high confidence edges. Cardiac dysrhythmia appears as a source diagnosis in the two top confidence edges, indicating that those with cardiac dysrhythmia should watch out for rheumatic heart disease or pulmonary congestion. Additionally, pulmonary congestion appears as a destination node for three out of the top four confidence edges, indicating that pulmonary congestion is a complication that, given other diagnoses such as cardiac dysrhythmia, diabetes, or chronic ischemic heart disease, could eventually result in heart failure.

Can we predict heart failure? Using this model, we observe we can predict heart failure using the conclusions found from this data. The ROC curve given in Fig. 6 indicates that diagnoses given in the first visit contains most of the information that leads to heart failure. We receive diminishing returns from subsequent diagnoses after that first visit. One reason could be that most of the diseases that eventually result in heart failure have already appeared by their first visit to a doctor, and rarely do patients not have diseases that are indicative of heart failure at their first visit, and then they go on to get heart failure later. Table 5 gives some examples of patients that have the highest jump in the probability of developing heart failure after their first visit. Certain cardiac events put those who were originally being treated for mental diagnoses in particular (affective psychoses, cerebral degenerations, Parkinson's disease, neurotic disorder) on a path to heart failure beginning in Visit 2. In general, the data tells us that the disease progression from Visit 1 to Visit 2 gives the most indication that a patient will eventually become a heart failure patient.

7   Conclusion

By constructing a DAG of Medicare patients and their visits, we found trends in diseases that result in an ultimate diagnosis of heart failure. We conclude that cardiomyopathy is a condition that is commonly associated with heart failure such that screening for cardiomyopathy should be a common part of preventative treatment. Additionally, we know that many patients' first diagnoses on a heart failure path are acute myocardial infarctions, endocardium diseases, and cardiomyopathy. Doctors who see patients for other medical issues, especially mental issues as observed, should know of these complications since they are often the first that show up in diagnoses that do not otherwise lead to heart failure. We also found that rheumatic heart disease, pulmonary congestion and hypostasis, cardiomyopathy, blood poisoning, and valve and aortic diseases are common comorbidities that occur before doctors diagnose patients with heart failure. Because the highest information gains in our DAG are on paths that concern mental disorders such as psychosis, cerebral degeneration, and Parkinson's, the conclusion can be made that patients being seen for these disorders should also be monitored for heart disease.

The ultimate goal of such a system is to be able to effectively predict likelihood of heart failure, which we demonstrate using our trained DAG. We show that the most indicative diagnoses belong to the first disease progression in terms of their information gain and area under the ROC curve. This underscores the usefulness of our model in extracting signals which can be used for early detection of heart failure.

References

1. Prokosch, H.U., Ganslandt, V., et al.: Perspectives for medical informatics. Meth. Inf. Med. **48**(1), 38–44 (2009)
2. Jensen, P.B., Jensen, L.J., Brunak, S.: Mining electronic health records: towards better research applications and clinical care. Nat. Rev. Genet. **13**(6), 395–405 (2012)
3. Belle, A., Thiagarajan, R., Soroushmehr, S.M., Navidi, F., Beard, D.A., Najarian, K.: Big data analytics in healthcare. BioMed. Res. Int. **2015** (2015)

4. Kawamoto, K., Houlihan, C.A., Balas, E.A., Lobach, D.F.: Improving clinical practice using clinical decision support systems: a systematic review of trials to identify features critical to success. BMJ **330**(7494), 765 (2005)
5. Nguyen, O.K., Makam, A.N., Clark, C., Zhang, S., Xie, B., Velasco, F., Amarasingham, R., Halm, E.A.: Predicting Readmissions from EHR Data. J. Hosp. Med. **7**, 473–480 (2016). doi:10.1002/jhm.2568
6. Kasl, S.V., Cobb, S.: Health behavior, illness behavior and sick role behavior: I. health and illness behavior. Arch. Environ. Health Int. J. **12**(2), 246–266 (1966)
7. Holzinger, A.: Trends in interactive knowledge discovery for personalized medicine: Cognitive science meets machine learning. IEEE Intell. Inf. Bull. **15**, 6–14 (2014)
8. Delen, D., Walker, G., Kadam, A.: Predicting breast cancer survivability: a comparison of three data mining methods. Artif. Intell. Med. **34**(2), 113–127 (2005)
9. Davis, D.A., Chawla, N.V., Christakis, N.A., Barabási, A.-L.: Time to care: a collaborative engine for practical disease prediction. Data Min. Knowl. Disc. **20**(3), 388–415 (2010)
10. Marek, K., Jennings, D., Lasch, S., Siderowf, A., Tanner, C., Simuni, T., Coffey, C., Kieburtz, K., Flagg, E., Chowdhury, S., et al.: The parkinson progression marker initiative (ppmi). Prog. Neurobiol. **95**(4), 629–635 (2011)
11. Wilkosz, P.A., Seltman, H.J., Devlin, B., Weamer, E.A., Lopez, O.L., DeKosky, S.T., Sweet, R.A.: Trajectories of cognitive decline in Alzheimer's disease. Int. Psychogeriatr. **22**(02), 281–290 (2010)
12. Jensen, A.B., Moseley, P.L., Oprea, T.I., Ellesøe, S.G., Eriksson, R., Schmock, H., Jensen, P.B., Jensen, L.J., Brunak, S.: Temporal disease trajectories condensed from population-wide registry data covering 6.2 million patients. Nat. Commun. 5 (2014)
13. Lauderdale, D.S., Furner, S.E., Miles, T.P., Goldberg, J.: Epidemiologic uses of medicare data. Epidemiol. Rev. **15**(2), 319–327 (1993)
14. Mitchell, J.B., Bubolz, T., Paul, J.E., Pashos, C.L., Escarce, J.J., Muhlbaier, L.H., Wiesman, J.M., Young, W.W., Epstein, R., Javitt, J.C.: Using medicare claims for outcomes research. Med. Care **32**(7), JS38 (1994)
15. Mozaffarian, D., Benjamin, E.J., Go, A.S., Arnett, D.K., Blaha, M.J., Cushman, M., Das, S.R., de Ferranti, S., Després, J.-P., Fullerton, H.J., et al.: Heart disease and stroke statistics2016 update. Circulation **133**(4), e38–e360 (2016)
16. Benson, A.R., Gleich, D.F., Leskovec, J.: Higher-order organization of complex networks. Science **353**(6295), 163–166 (2016)
17. McMurray, J.J., Stewart, S.: Epidemiology, aetiology, and prognosis of heart failure. Heart **83**(5), 596–602 (2000)
18. Sarnak, M.J., Levey, A.S., Schoolwerth, A.C., Coresh, J., Culleton, B., Hamm, L.L., McCullough, P.A., Kasiske, B.L., Kelepouris, E., Klag, M.J., Parfrey, P., Pfeffer, M., Raij, L., Spinosa, D.J., Wilson, P.W.: Kidney disease as a risk factor for development of cardiovascular disease. Hypertension **42**(5), 1050–1065 (2003)
19. Lloyd-Jones, D., Adams, R.J., Brown, T.M., Carnethon, M., Dai, S., De Simone, G., Ferguson, T.B., Ford, E., Furie, K., Gillespie, C., Go, A., Greenlund, K., Haase, N., Hailpern, S., Ho, P.M., Howard, V., Kissela, B., Kittner, S., Lackland, D., Lisabeth, L., Marelli, A., McDermott, M.M., Meigs, J., Mozaffarian, D., Mussolino, M., Nichol, G., Roger, V.L., Rosamond, W., Sacco, R., Sorlie, P., Stafford, R., Thom, T., Wasserthiel-Smoller, S., Wong, N.D., Wylie-Rosett, J.: Heart disease and stroke statistics-2010 update. Circulation **121**(7), e46–e215 (2010)
20. Picano, E., Gargani, L., Gheorghiade, M.: Why, when, and how to assess pulmonary congestion in heart failure: pathophysiological, clinical, and methodological implications. Heart Fail. Rev. **15**(1), 63–72 (2010)

21. Hoesel, L.M., Niederbichler, A.D., Ward, P.A.: Complement-related molecular events in sepsis leading to heart failure. Molecular Immunol. **44**(1), 95–102 (2007). XXI International Complement Workshop Beijing, China, October 22–26, 2006
22. Cao, Y.M., Hu, D.Y., Wu, Y., Wang, H.Y.: A pilot survey of the main causes of chronic heart failure in patients treated in primary hospitals in china. Zhonghua nei ke za zhi **44**(7), 487–489 (2005)
23. Bland, E.F., Jones, D.: Rheumatic fever and rheumatic heart disease. Circulation **4**(6), 836–843 (1951)
24. Levy, D., Larson, M.G., Vasan, R.S., Kannel, W.B., Ho, K.K.L.: The progression from hypertension to congestive heart failure. JAMA **275**(20), 1557–1562 (1996)

MAKE Semantics

A Declarative Semantics for P2P Systems

Luciano Caroprese$^{(\boxtimes)}$ and Ester Zumpano

DIMES, University of Calabria, 87036 Rende, Italy
{l.caroprese,e.zumpano}@dimes.unical.it

Abstract. This paper investigates the problem of data integration among Peer-to-Peer (P2P) deductive databases and presents a declarative semantics that generalizes previous proposals in the literature. Basically, by following the classical approach, the objective of a generic peer, joining a P2P system, is to enrich its knowledge by importing as much knowledge as possible while preventing inconsistency anomalies. This basic idea is extended in the present paper by allowing each peer to select between two different settings. It can either declare its local database to be sound but not complete, or declare it to be unsound. In the first case the peer considers its own knowledge more trustable than the knowledge imported from the rest of the system i.e. it gives preference to its knowledge with respect to the knowledge that can be imported from other peers. In the second case the peer considers its own knowledge as trustable as the knowledge that can be imported from the rest of the system i.e. it does not give any preference to its knowledge with respect to the knowledge that can be imported from other peers.

1 Introduction

The interaction and cooperation of peers in a P2P system allows to perform the important task of data integration. Data integration is one of the most fundamental processes in intelligent systems, from individuals to societies. In traditional data integration systems queries are submitted through a central *mediated schema*. Data is stored locally in each source and the two main formalisms managing the mapping between the mediated schema and the local sources are the *global-as-view* (GAV) and the *local-as-view* (LAV) approach [23]. The main drawbacks of traditional integration systems are due to the lack of flexibility: (i) the centralized mediated schema, that controls and manages the interaction among distributed sources, must be defined looking at the global system; (ii) the insertion of a new source or the modification of an existing one may cause a violation of the mappings to the mediated schema. Divergent or conflicting concepts were selected by hierarchical authorities or by (democratically) applying the majority criteria.

In a P2P system, ideally, there is no selection, but integration of the valuable contributions of every participant. Generally, peers can both provide or consume data and the only information a peer participating in a P2P system has is about

© IFIP International Federation for Information Processing 2017
Published by Springer International Publishing AG 2017. All Rights Reserved
A. Holzinger et al. (Eds.): CD-MAKE 2017, LNCS 10410, pp. 315–329, 2017.
DOI: 10.1007/978-3-319-66808-6_21

neighbors, i.e. information about the peers that are reachable and can provide data of interest. More specifically, each peer joining a P2P system exhibits a set of *mapping rules*, i.e. a set of semantic correspondences to a set of peers which are already part of the system (neighbors). Thus, in a P2P system the entry of a new source, *peer*, is extremely simple as it just requires the definition of the mapping rules. By using mapping rules as soon as it enters the system a peer can participate and access all data available in its neighborhood, and through its neighborhood it becomes accessible to all the other peers in the system.

The possibility for the users for sharing knowledge from a large number of informative sources, have enabled the development of new methods for data integration easily usable for processing distributed and autonomous data.

Due to this, there have been several proposals which consider the integration of information and the computation of queries in an open ended network of distributed peers [2,5–7,18] as well as the problem of schema mediation [21,22,24], query answering and query optimization in P2P environments [1,16,26]. Many of the approaches proposed in the literature investigate the data integration problem in a P2P system by considering each peer as initially consistent, therefore the introduction of inconsistency is just relied to the operation of importing data from other peers. These approaches assume, following the basic classical idea of data integration, that for each peer it is preferable to import as much knowledge as possible.

In this paper we follow the proposal in [9–12,14,15] in which a different interpretation of mapping rules, that allows importing from other peers only tuples not violating integrity constraints, has been proposed. This new interpretation of mapping rules has led to the proposal of a semantics for a P2P system defined in terms of *Preferred Weak Models*. Under this semantics only facts not making the local databases inconsistent can be imported, and the preferred weak models are the consistent scenarios in which peers import maximal sets of facts not violating the integrity constraints. Therefore, the preferred weak model semantics follows the classical strategy of importing as much knowledge as possible, but limiting this to the maximal subset that do not generate inconsistencies.

The following example, introduces the idea of importing in each peer maximal sets of atoms not violating integrity constraints.

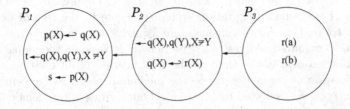

Fig. 1. A P2P system (Example 1)

Example 1. Consider the P2P system depicted in Fig. 1 consisting of three peers $\mathcal{P}_1$, $\mathcal{P}_2$ and $\mathcal{P}_3$ where

- $\mathcal{P}_3$ *contains two atoms:* $r(a)$ *and* $r(b)$,
- $\mathcal{P}_2$ *imports data from* $\mathcal{P}_3$ *using the (mapping) rule* $q(X) \hookleftarrow r(X)$[1]. *Moreover imported atoms must satisfy the constraint* $\leftarrow q(X), q(Y), X \neq Y$ *stating that the relation* q *may contain at most one tuple, and*
- $\mathcal{P}_1$ *imports data from* $\mathcal{P}_2$, *using the (mapping) rule* $p(X) \hookleftarrow q(X)$. $\mathcal{P}_1$ *also contains the rules* $s \leftarrow p(X)$ *stating that* s *is true if the relation* p *contains at least one tuple, and* $t \leftarrow p(X), p(Y), X \neq Y$, *stating that* t *is true if the relation* p *contains at least two distinct tuples.*

The intuition is that, with $r(a)$ *and* $r(b)$ *being true in* $\mathcal{P}_3$, *either* $q(a)$ *or* $q(b)$ *could be imported in* $\mathcal{P}_2$ *(but not both, otherwise the integrity constraint is violated) and, consequently, only one tuple is imported in the relation* p *of peer* $\mathcal{P}_1$. *Note that whatever is the derivation in* $\mathcal{P}_2$, s *is derived in* $\mathcal{P}_1$ *while* t *is not derived. Therefore, the atoms* s *and* t *are, respectively, true and false in* $\mathcal{P}_1$.   □

With the preferred weak model semantics in [9–12,14], each peer gives preference to local data with respect to data imported from the neighborhood. Therefore the basic assumption in this semantics is that *each peer is sound, but not complete.*

In this paper, we extend the framework in [9–12,14]. In a more general setting each peer joining the system can either (i) assume its local database to be sound, but not complete; in this case the peer considers its own knowledge more trustable than the knowledge imported from the rest of the system i.e. it gives preference to its knowledge with respect to the knowledge that can be imported other peers or (ii) assume its local knowledge to be unsound; in this case the peer considers its own knowledge as trustable as the knowledge imported from the rest of the system i.e. it does not give any preference to its knowledge with respect to the knowledge that can be imported from from other peers.

Let's now introduce another example, that will be used as a running example in the rest of the paper.

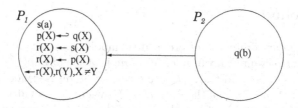

Fig. 2. A P2P system (Example 2)

Example 2. Consider the P2P system $\mathcal{PS}$ *depicted in Fig. 2.* $\mathcal{P}_2$ *contains the fact* $q(b)$, *whereas* $\mathcal{P}_1$ *contains the fact* $s(a)$, *the mapping rule* $p(X) \hookleftarrow q(X)$, *the constraint* $\leftarrow r(X), r(Y), X \neq Y$ *and the standard rules* $r(X) \leftarrow p(X)$ *and* $r(X) \leftarrow s(X)$.

---

[1] Please, note the special syntax we use for mapping rules.

- *if P_1 considers its own knowledge more trustable than the knowledge imported from P_2 (that is it gives preference to its knowledge with respect to the knowledge that can be imported from P_2), then the fact $p(b)$ cannot be imported in P_1, as it indirectly violates its integrity constraint. More specifically, $p(b)$ cannot be imported in P_1 due to the presence of the local fact $s(a)$.*
- *if P_1 considers its own knowledge as trustable as the knowledge imported from P_2 (that is if it does not give any preference to its knowledge with respect to the knowledge that can be imported from P_2), then two possible scenarios are possible: a first one in which no atom is imported from P_2, and a second one in which $q(b)$ is imported from P_2 and $s(a)$ is removed from P_1.*

In this paper we generalize the definition of P2P system in order to capture previous behavior and allow the possibility for each peer to declare either that its local knowledge is preferred with respect to the knowledge that can be imported from other peers (sound peer), or that it does not give any preference to its local knowledge with respect to the knowledge that can be extracted from the rest of the system (unsound peer). An unsound P2P system is a p2P system in which at least one peer is unsound. The semantics of an unsound P2P system is captured by the weak model semantics of a correspondent standard P2P system obtained by splitting each unsound peer into two peers.

Organization. Preliminaries are reported in Sect. 2. Section 3 introduces the syntax used for modeling a P2P system and reviews the *Preferred Weak Model* semantics, proposed in [9, 10]. Section 4 proposes a generalization of a P2P system so that each peer can declare either its preference to its own knowledge, or give no preference to its own knowledge with respect to imported knowledge. Section 5 provides results on the computational complexity of computing preferred weak models and answers to queries. Related work is discussed in Sect. 6. Conclusions are drawn in Sect. 7.

2   Background

We assume there are finite sets of predicate symbols, constants and variables. A *term* is either a constant or a variable. An *atom* is of the form $p(t_1, \ldots, t_n)$ where p is a predicate symbol and $t_1, \ldots, t_n$ are terms. A *literal* is either an atom A or its negation *not A*. A *rule* is of the form $H \leftarrow B$, where H is an atom (*head* of the rule) and B is a conjunction of literals (*body* of the rule). A program P is a finite set of rules. P is said to be positive if it is negation free. The definition of a predicate p consists of all rules having p in the head. A ground rule with empty body is a *fact*. A rule with empty head is a *constraint*. It is assumed that programs are *safe*, i.e. variables appearing in the head or in negated body literals are range restricted as they appear in some positive body literal. The ground instantiation of a program P, denoted by $ground(P)$ is built by replacing variables with constants in all possible ways. An interpretation is a set of ground atoms. The truth value of ground atoms, literals and rules with respect to an interpretation M is as follows: $val_M(A) = A \in M$, $val_M(not\ A) = not\ val_M(A)$, $val_M(L_1, \ldots, L_n) = min\{val_M(L_1), \ldots, val_M(L_n)\}$ and $val_M(A \leftarrow L_1, \ldots, L_n) = val_M(A) \geq val_M(L_1, \ldots, L_n)$, where A is an atom, $L_1, \ldots, L_n$ are literals and $true > false$. An interpretation M is a model for a program $\mathcal{P}$, if all rules in $ground(\mathcal{P})$ are $true$ w.r.t. M. A model M is said to be minimal if there is no model N such that $N \subset M$. We denote the set of minimal models of a program $\mathcal{P}$ with $\mathcal{MM}(\mathcal{P})$. Given an interpretation M and a predicate symbol g, $M[g]$ denotes the set of g-tuples in M. The semantics of a positive program $\mathcal{P}$ is given by its unique minimal model which can be computed by applying the *immediate consequence operator* $\mathbf{T}_\mathcal{P}$ until the fixpoint is reached ($\mathbf{T}_\mathcal{P}^\infty(\emptyset)$). The semantics of a program with negation $\mathcal{P}$ is given by the set of its stable models, denoted as $\mathcal{SM}(\mathcal{P})$. An interpretation M is a *stable model* (or *answer set*) of $\mathcal{P}$ if M is the unique minimal model of the positive program $\mathcal{P}^M$, where $\mathcal{P}^M$ is obtained from $ground(\mathcal{P})$ by (i) removing all rules r such that there exists a negative literal $not\ A$ in the body of r and A is in M and (ii) removing all negative literals from the remaining rules [20]. It is well known that stable models are minimal models (i.e. $\mathcal{SM}(\mathcal{P}) \subseteq \mathcal{MM}(\mathcal{P})$) and that for negation free programs, minimal and stable model semantics coincide (i.e. $\mathcal{SM}(\mathcal{P}) = \mathcal{MM}(\mathcal{P})$).

3   P2P Systems: Syntax and Semantics

This section introduces the syntax used for modeling a P2P system and reviews the *Preferred Weak Model* semantics, proposed in [9,10], in which a special interpretation of mapping rules is introduced.

3.1   Syntax

A *(peer) predicate symbol* is a pair $i : p$, where i is a *peer identifier* and p is a predicate symbol. A *(peer) atom* is of the form $i : A$, where i is a *peer identifier* and A is a standard atom. A *(peer) literal* is a peer atom $i : A$ or its negation $not\ i : A$. A conjunction $i : A_1, \ldots, i : A_m, not\ i : A_{m+1}, \ldots, not\ i : A_n, \phi$, where ϕ is a conjunction of built-in atoms[2], will be also denoted as $i : \mathcal{B}$, with $\mathcal{B}$ equals to $A_1, \ldots, A_m, not\ A_{m+1}, \ldots, not\ A_n, \phi$.
A *(peer) rule* can be of one of the following three types:

1. STANDARD RULE. It is of the form $i : H \leftarrow i : \mathcal{B}$, where $i : H$ is an atom and $i : \mathcal{B}$ is a conjunction of atoms and built-in atoms.
2. INTEGRITY CONSTRAINT. It is of the form $\leftarrow i : \mathcal{B}$, where $i : \mathcal{B}$ is a conjunction of literals and built-in atoms.
3. MAPPING RULE. It is of the form $i : H \hookleftarrow j : \mathcal{B}$, where $i : H$ is an atom, $j : \mathcal{B}$ is a conjunction of atoms and built-in atoms and $i \neq j$.

---

[2] A *built-in atom* is of the form $X\theta Y$, where X and Y are terms and θ is a comparison predicate.

In the previous rules, $i : H$ is called *head* while $i : \mathcal{B}$ (resp. $j : \mathcal{B}$) is called *body*. Negation is allowed just in the body of integrity constraints. The concepts of *ground rule* and *fact* are similar to those reported in Sect. 2. The definition of a predicate $i : p$ consists of the set of rules in whose head the predicate symbol $i : p$ occurs. A predicate can be of three different kinds: *base predicate*, *derived predicate* and *mapping predicate*. A base predicate is defined by a set of ground facts; a derived predicate is defined by a set of standard rules and a mapping predicate is defined by a set of mapping rules.

An atom $i : p(X)$ is a *base atom* (resp. *derived atom*, *mapping atom*) if $i : p$ is a base predicate (resp. standard predicate, mapping predicate). Given an interpretation M, $M[\mathcal{D}]$ (resp. $M[\mathcal{LP}]$, $M[\mathcal{MP}]$) denotes the subset of base atoms (resp. derived atoms, mapping atoms) in M.

Definition 1 P2P System. A *peer* $\mathcal{P}_i$ is a tuple $\langle \mathcal{D}_i, \mathcal{LP}_i, \mathcal{MP}_i, \mathcal{IC}_i \rangle$, where (i) $\mathcal{D}_i$ is a set of facts (*local database*); (ii) $\mathcal{LP}_i$ is a set of standard rules; (iii) $\mathcal{MP}_i$ is a set of mapping rules and (iv) $\mathcal{IC}_i$ is a set of constraints over predicates defined by $\mathcal{D}_i$, $\mathcal{LP}_i$ and $\mathcal{MP}_i$. A *P2P system* $\mathcal{PS}$ is a set of peers $\{\mathcal{P}_1, \ldots, \mathcal{P}_n\}$. □

Given a P2P system $\mathcal{PS} = \{\mathcal{P}_1, \ldots, \mathcal{P}_n\}$, where $\mathcal{P}_i = \langle \mathcal{D}_i, \mathcal{LP}_i, \mathcal{MP}_i, \mathcal{IC}_i \rangle$, $\mathcal{D}, \mathcal{LP}, \mathcal{MP}$ and $\mathcal{IC}$ denote, respectively, the global sets of ground facts, standard rules, mapping rules and integrity constraints, i.e. $\mathcal{D} = \bigcup_{i \in [1..n]} \mathcal{D}_i$, $\mathcal{LP} = \bigcup_{i \in [1..n]} \mathcal{LP}_i$, $\mathcal{MP} = \bigcup_{i \in [1..n]} \mathcal{MP}_i$ and $\mathcal{IC} = \bigcup_{i \in [1..n]} \mathcal{IC}_i$. In the rest of this paper, with a little abuse of notation, $\mathcal{PS}$ will be also denoted both with the tuple $\langle \mathcal{D}, \mathcal{LP}, \mathcal{MP}, \mathcal{IC} \rangle$ and the set $\mathcal{D} \cup \mathcal{LP} \cup \mathcal{MP} \cup \mathcal{IC}$; moreover whenever the peer is understood, the peer identifier will be omitted.

3.2 Semantics

This section reviews the *Preferred Weak Model* semantics for P2P systems [9,10] which is based on a special interpretation of mapping rules.

Observe that for each peer $\mathcal{P}_i = \langle \mathcal{D}_i, \mathcal{LP}_i, \mathcal{MP}_i, \mathcal{IC}_i \rangle$, the set $\mathcal{D}_i \cup \mathcal{LP}_i$ is a *positive normal program*, thus it admits just *one minimal model* that represents the *local knowledge* of $\mathcal{P}_i$. In this paper it is assumed that each peer is *locally consistent*, i.e. its local knowledge satisfies $\mathcal{IC}_i$ (i.e. $\mathcal{D}_i \cup \mathcal{LP}_i \models \mathcal{IC}_i$). Therefore, inconsistencies may be introduced just when the peer imports data from other peers. The intuitive meaning of a mapping rule $i : H \hookleftarrow j : \mathcal{B} \in \mathcal{MP}_i$ is that if the body conjunction $j : \mathcal{B}$ is *true* in the source peer $\mathcal{P}_j$ the atom $i : H$ can be imported in $\mathcal{P}_i$ only if it does not imply (directly or indirectly) the violation of some integrity constraint in $\mathcal{IC}_i$. The following example will clarify the meaning of mapping rules.

Example 3. Consider the P2P system in Fig. 2. If the fact $p(b)$ is imported in $\mathcal{P}_1$, the fact $r(b)$ will be derived. As $r(a)$ is already true in $\mathcal{P}_1$, because it is derived from $s(a)$, the integrity constraint is violated. Therefore, $p(b)$ cannot be imported in $\mathcal{P}_1$ as it indirectly violates an integrity constraint. □

Before formally presenting the preferred weak model semantics, some notation is introduced. Given a mapping rule $r = H \hookleftarrow \mathcal{B}$, the corresponding standard logic rule $H \leftarrow \mathcal{B}$ will be denoted as $St(r)$. Analogously, given a set of mapping rules $\mathcal{MP}$, $St(\mathcal{MP}) = \{St(r) \mid r \in \mathcal{MP}\}$ and given a P2P system $\mathcal{PS} = \mathcal{D} \cup \mathcal{LP} \cup \mathcal{MP} \cup \mathcal{IC}$, $St(\mathcal{PS}) = \mathcal{D} \cup \mathcal{LP} \cup St(\mathcal{MP}) \cup \mathcal{IC}$.

Given an interpretation M, an atom H and a conjunction of atoms $\mathcal{B}$:

- $val_M(H \leftarrow \mathcal{B}) = val_M(H) \geq val_M(\mathcal{B})$,
- $val_M(H \hookleftarrow \mathcal{B}) = val_M(H) \leq val_M(\mathcal{B})$.

Therefore, if the body is *true*, the head of a standard rule *must* be *true*, whereas the head of a mapping rule *could* be *true*.

Intuitively, a *weak model* M of a P2P system $\mathcal{PS}$ is an interpretation that satisfies all standard rules, mapping rules and constraints of $\mathcal{PS}$ and such that each atom $H \in M[\mathcal{MP}]$ (i.e. each mapping atom) is *supported* from a mapping rule $H \hookleftarrow \mathcal{B}$ whose body $\mathcal{B}$ is satisfied by M. A *preferred weak model* is a weak model that contains a maximal subset of mapping atoms. This concept is justified by the assumption that it is *preferable* to import in each peer *as much knowledge as possible*.

Definition 2 ((PREFERRED) WEAK MODEL). Given a P2P system $\mathcal{PS} = \mathcal{D} \cup \mathcal{LP} \cup \mathcal{MP} \cup \mathcal{IC}$, an interpretation M is a *weak model* for $\mathcal{PS}$ if $\{M\} = \mathcal{MM}(St(\mathcal{PS}^M))$, where $\mathcal{PS}^M$ is the program obtained from $ground(\mathcal{PS})$ by removing all mapping rules whose head is *false* w.r.t. M.

Given two weak models M and N, M is said to *preferable* to N, and is denoted as $M \sqsupseteq N$, if $M[\mathcal{MP}] \supseteq N[\mathcal{MP}]$. Moreover, if $M \sqsupseteq N$ and $N \not\sqsupseteq M$, then $M \sqsupset N$. A weak model M is said to be *preferred* if there is no weak model N such that $N \sqsupset M$.

The set of weak models for a P2P system $\mathcal{PS}$ will be denoted by $\mathcal{WM}(\mathcal{PS})$, whereas the set of preferred weak models will be denoted by $\mathcal{PWM}(\mathcal{PS})$.   □

The next theorem shows that P2P systems always admit maximal weak models.

Theorem 1. *For every consistent P2P system* $\mathcal{PS}$, $\mathcal{PWM}(\mathcal{PS}) \neq \emptyset$.

Proof. Let us consider a set M such that $\{M\} = \mathcal{MM}(\mathcal{D} \cup \mathcal{LP} \cup \mathcal{IC})$, that is the minimal model of a P2P system obtained from $\mathcal{PS}$ by deleting all mapping rules. As $\mathcal{PS}$ is initially consistent, such a model exists. Moreover, as M does not contain any mapping atoms, all the ground mapping rules have to be deleted from $ground(\mathcal{PS})$ in order to obtain $St(\mathcal{PS}^M)$. It follows that $St(\mathcal{PS}^M) = ground(\mathcal{D} \cup \mathcal{LP} \cup \mathcal{IC})$ and $\{M\} = \mathcal{MM}(St(\mathcal{PS}^M))$. This means that M is a weak model for $\mathcal{PS}$. As there is at least a weak model, then $\mathcal{PWM}(\mathcal{PS}) \neq \emptyset$.   □

Observe that in the previous definition $St(\mathcal{PS}^M)$ is a positive normal program, thus it admits just one minimal model. Moreover, note that the definition of weak model presents interesting analogies with the definition of stable model.

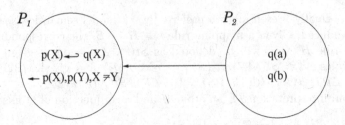

Fig. 3. The system $\mathcal{PS}$

Example 4. Consider the P2P system $\mathcal{PS}$ in Fig. 3. $\mathcal{P}_2$ contains the facts $q(a)$ and $q(b)$, whereas $\mathcal{P}_1$ contains the mapping rule $p(X) \leftharpoondown q(X)$ and the constraint $\leftarrow p(X), p(Y), X \neq Y$. The weak models of the system are $M_0 = \{q(a), q(b)\}$, $M_1 = \{q(a), q(b), p(a)\}$ and $M_2 = \{q(a), q(b), p(b)\}$, whereas the preferred weak models are M_1 and M_2 as they import the maximal set of atoms from $\mathcal{P}_2$.   □

We conclude this section showing how a classical problem can be expressed using the preferred weak model semantics.

Example 3. Three-colorability. We are given two peers $\mathcal{P}_1$, containing a set of nodes, defined by a unary relation node, and a set of colors, defined by the unary predicate color, and $\mathcal{P}_2$, containing the mapping rule

$$colored(X, C) \leftharpoondown 1 : node(X), 1 : color(C)$$

and the integrity constraints

$$\leftarrow colored(X, C_1), \; colored(X, C_2), \; C_1 \neq C_2$$
$$\leftarrow edge(X, Y), \; colored(X, C), \; colored(Y, C)$$

stating, respectively, that a node cannot be colored with two different colors and two connected nodes cannot be colored with the same color. The mapping rule states that the node x can be colored with the color c, only if in doing this no constraint is violated, that is if the node x is colored with a unique color and there is no adjacent node colored with the same color. Each preferred weak model computes a maximal subgraph which is three-colorable.   □

An alternative characterization of the preferred weak model semantics, called *Preferred Stable Model* semantics, based on the rewriting of mapping rules into prioritized rules [25] has been proposed in [9, 10].

4   A More General Framework

In previous section we introduced the *Preferred Weak Model* semantics for P2P systems [9, 10] that assumes that the knowledge of each peer of a P2P system is sound, but not complete, that is each peer (implicitly) prefers its local knowledge with respect to the knowledge that can be imported from the rest of the system. Mapping rules are therefore used to enrich the local knowledge only if imported atoms do not cause inconsistencies.

In this section we generalize the definition of P2P system so that each peer can declare either its preference to its own knowledge (sound peer), or give no preference to its own knowledge with respect to imported knowledge (unsound peer). A sound peer trusts its knowledge more than the knowledge of the rest of the system, whereas an unsound peer trusts its knowledge as much as the knowledge that can be extracted from other peers.

We first provides the definition of *P2P system* that generalizes Definition 1 by introducing a new type of peers - *the unsound peers* - giving the same priority to local data and to imported data.

Definition 3. *An unsound P2P system $\mathcal{UPS}$ is a pair $(\mathcal{PS}, \mathcal{U})$, where $\mathcal{PS} = \{\mathcal{P}_1, \ldots, \mathcal{P}_n\}$ is a (standard) P2P system and $\mathcal{U} \subseteq \mathcal{PS}$. Peers in $\mathcal{U}$ are called unsound peers.* □

The semantics of an unsound P2P system $\mathcal{UPS}$ is captured by the weak model semantics of a correspondent standard P2P system obtained from $\mathcal{UPS}$ by splitting each unsound peer $\mathcal{P}_i$ into two peers. The idea is to move the local database $\mathcal{D}_i$ from $\mathcal{P}_i$ to the new peer and to introduce in $\mathcal{P}_i$ a set of mapping rules able to import only portions of $\mathcal{D}_i$ that do not violate its integrity constraints.

Definition 4. *Let $\mathcal{UPS} = (\mathcal{PS}, \mathcal{U})$ an unsound P2P system, where $\mathcal{PS} = \{\mathcal{P}_1, \ldots, \mathcal{P}_n\}$, and $\mathcal{P}_i = \langle \mathcal{D}_i, \mathcal{LP}_i, \mathcal{MP}_i, \mathcal{IC}_i \rangle$ a peer in $\mathcal{U}$. Then, $Split(\mathcal{P}_i)$ is the set containing the following peers:*

$- \ \mathcal{P}_{(i+n)} := \langle \{(i+n) : p(X) \mid i : p(X) \in \mathcal{D}_i\}, \emptyset, \emptyset, \emptyset \rangle$

$- \ \mathcal{P}_i := \langle \emptyset, \mathcal{LP}_i, \mathcal{MP}_i \cup \{i : p(X) \leftarrow (i+n) : p(X) \mid i : p(X) \in \mathcal{D}_i\}, \mathcal{IC}_i \rangle$

Moreover:

$$Split(\mathcal{UPS}) = (\mathcal{PS} \setminus \mathcal{U}) \cup \bigcup_{\mathcal{P}_i \in \mathcal{U}} Split(\mathcal{P}_i)$$

The preferred weak models of $\mathcal{UPS}$ are obtained from those of $Split(\mathcal{UPS})$ by removing each atom $i : p(X)$ such that $i > n$. □

In previous definition, the peer $\mathcal{P}_i$ is redefined by deleting its local database $\mathcal{D}_i$ and inserting mapping rules allowing to import tuples into old base relations (which now are mapping relations) from an auxiliary peer $\mathcal{P}_{(i+n)}$. Observe that $Split(\mathcal{UPS})$ is a standard P2P system for which a preferred weak model semantics is adopted.

Example 6. Let us continue our discussion about the P2P system $\mathcal{PS}$ presented in Example 2.

- Assuming that $\mathcal{PS}$ is a sound P2P system, then $\mathcal{P}_1$ trusts its own data more than the data that can be imported from $\mathcal{P}_2$. Therefore it will not import the fact $p(b)$ because it would violate its integrity constraint. The preferred weak models of $\mathcal{PS}$ is: $M_1 = \{q(b), s(a), r(a)\}$

- Assuming that $\mathcal{PS}$ is an unsound P2P system and $\mathcal{P}_1$ is an unsound peer, $Split(\mathcal{PS})$ contains the following peers (for the sake of presentation we omit indexes for peers $\mathcal{P}_1$ and $\mathcal{P}_2$):
  - $\mathcal{P}_1 = \langle \emptyset, \mathcal{LP}_1, \mathcal{MP}_1 \cup \{s(X) \hookleftarrow 3 : s(X)\}, \mathcal{IC}_1 \rangle$
  - $\mathcal{P}_2 = \langle \{q(b)\}, \emptyset, \emptyset, \emptyset \rangle$
  - $\mathcal{P}_3 = \langle \{3 : s(a)\}, \emptyset, \emptyset, \emptyset \rangle$

  In this case, $\mathcal{P}_1$ does not give any preference to its knowledge with respect to the knowledge that can be imported from $\mathcal{P}_2$ and two possible scenarios are possible: a first one in which no atom is imported from $\mathcal{P}_2$ and $s(a)$ is imported from $\mathcal{P}_3$ - corresponding to the preferred weak model $M_1 = \{q(b), s(a), r(a)\}$, and a second one in which $q(b)$ is imported from $\mathcal{P}_2$ and $s(a)$ is not imported from $\mathcal{P}_3$ (this is equivalent to delete $s(a)$ from $\mathcal{P}_1$) - corresponding to the preferred weak model $M_2 = \{q(b), p(b), r(b)\}$. Observe that the auxiliary atom $3 : s(a)$ does not occur in the preferred weak models M_1 and M_2.   □

5 Query Answers and Complexity

We consider now the computational complexity of calculating preferred weak models and answers to queries. As a P2P system may admit more than one preferred weak model, the answer to a query is given by considering *brave* or *cautious* reasoning (also known as *possible* and *certain* semantics).

Definition 5. *Given a P2P system* $\mathcal{PS} = \{\mathcal{P}_1, \ldots, \mathcal{P}_n\}$ *and a ground peer atom* A, *then* A *is* true *under*

- *brave reasoning if* $A \in \bigcup_{M \in \mathcal{PWM}(\mathcal{PS})} M$,
- *cautious reasoning if* $A \in \bigcap_{M \in \mathcal{PWM}(\mathcal{PS})} M$.   □

Lemma 1. $\bigcup_{M \in \mathcal{PWM}(\mathcal{PS})} M = \bigcup_{N \in \mathcal{WM}(\mathcal{PS})} N$ □

The lemma states that for every P2P system $\mathcal{PS}$ an atom is *true* in some of its preferred weak models if and only if it is *true* in some of its weak models.

Theorem 2. *Let* $\mathcal{PS}$ *be a P2P system, then:*

1. *Deciding whether an interpretation* M *is a preferred weak model of* $\mathcal{PS}$ *is* $co\mathcal{NP}$ *complete.*
2. *Deciding whether a preferred weak model for* $\mathcal{PS}$ *exists is in* Σ_2^p.
3. *Deciding whether an atom* A *is* true *in some preferred weak model of* $\mathcal{PS}$ *is* Σ_2^p *complete.*
4. *Deciding whether an atom* A *is* true *in every preferred weak model of* $\mathcal{PS}$ *is* Π_2^p *complete.*

Proof.

1. **(Membership).** We prove that the complementary problem, that is the problem of checking whether M is not a preferred weak model, is in $\mathcal{NP}$. We can guess an interpretation N and verify in polynomial time that (i) N is a weak model, that is $\{N\} = \mathcal{MM}(St(\mathcal{PS}^N))$, and (ii) either M is not a weak model, that is $\{N\} \neq \mathcal{MM}(St(\mathcal{PS}^N))$, or $N \sqsupset M$, that is $N[\overline{\mathcal{MP}}] \supset M[\overline{\mathcal{MP}}]$ or $N[\overline{\mathcal{MP}}] = M[\overline{\mathcal{MP}}] \wedge N[\underline{\mathcal{MP}}] \subset M[\underline{\mathcal{MP}}]$. Therefore, the original problem is in $co\mathcal{NP}$.

   (Hardness): We will reduce the *SAT problem* to the problem of *checking whether a weak model is not preferred.*

   Let X be a set of variables and F a CNF formula over X. Then the problem that will be reduced is checking whether the QBF formula $(\exists X)$ F is *true*. We define a P2P system $\mathcal{PS}$ with two peers: $\mathcal{P}_1$ and $\mathcal{P}_2$. Peer $\mathcal{P}_1$ contains the atoms:

   $$1 : variable(x), \text{ for each } x \in X$$
   $$1 : truthValue(true)$$
   $$1 : truthValue(false)$$

   The relation $1 : variable$ stores the variables in X and the relation $1 : truthValue$ stores the truth values *true* and *false*. Peer $\mathcal{P}_2$ contains the atoms:

   $2 : variable(x)$, for each $x \in X$
   $2 : positive(x, c)$, for each $x \in X$ and clause c in F s.t. x occurs non-negated in c
   $2 : negated(x, c)$, for each $x \in X$ and clause c in F s.t. x occurs negated in c

   the mapping rule:

   $$2 : assign(X, V) \overset{\dashleftarrow}{} 1 : variable(X), 1 : truthValue(V)$$

   stating that the truth value V could be assigned to the variable X, the standard rules:

   $$2 : clause(C) \leftarrow 2 : positive(X, C)$$
   $$2 : clause(C) \leftarrow 2 : negated(X, C)$$
   $$2 : holds(C) \leftarrow 2 : positive(X, C), 2 : assign(X, true)$$
   $$2 : holds(C) \leftarrow 2 : negated(X, C), 2 : assign(X, false)$$
   $$2 : assignment \leftarrow 2 : assign(X, V)$$

   defining a *clause* from the occurrences of its positive and negated variables (first and second rule), whether a clause holds with a given assignment of values (third and fourth rule) and whether an assignment of values actually exists (fifth rule), and the integrity constraints:

   $\leftarrow 2 : assign(X, true), \ 2 : assign(X, false)$
   $\leftarrow 2 : clause(C), \ not\ 2 : holds(C), \ 2 : assignment$
   $\leftarrow 2 : variable(X), \ not\ 2 : assign(X, true), \ not\ 2 : assign(X, false),$
   $\quad 2 : assignment$

stating that two different truth values cannot be assigned to the same variable (first constraint), that if there is an assignment then there cannot be an unsatisfied clause (second constraint) and cannot be an unevaluated variable (third constraint).

Let DB the set of atoms in PS, MP the set of mapping rules in PS, LP the set of standard rules in PS and IC the set of integrity constraints in PS.

Let M be the minimal model of $DB \cup LP \cup IC$, that is the model containing no mapping atom. As PS is initially consistent, M is a weak model of PS. Observe that the integrity constraints in PS are satisfied when no mapping atom is imported in P_2 that is if no assignment of values is performed for the variables in X. If F is not satisfiable, then there is no way to import mapping atoms in P_2 preserving consistency because the second constraint will be violated. In this case M is a preferred weak model. If F is satisfiable there is a weak model N whose set of mapping atoms corresponds to an assignment of values to the variables in X that satisfies F. Clearly, as $MP[N] \supset MP[M]$, M is not a preferred weak model. Moreover, if M is not a preferred weak model there must be another weak model N whose set of mapping atoms corresponds to an assignment of values to the variables in X that satisfies F. In other words, F is satisfiable if and only if M is not a preferred weak model.

2. Let us guess an interpretation M. By (1), deciding whether M is a preferred weak model can be decided by a call to a $co\mathcal{NP}$ oracle.

3. In [9] has been shown that a PS can be modeled as a disjunction-free ($\vee - free$) prioritized logic programs. For this program deciding whether an atom is *true* in some preferred stable model is Σ_2^p complete [25].

4. In [9] has been shown that a PS can be modeled as a disjunction-free ($\vee - free$) prioritized logic programs. For this program deciding whether an atom is *true* in every preferred stable model is Π_2^p complete [25].   □

6   Related Work

The possibility for the users for sharing knowledge from a large number of informative sources, have enabled the development of new methods for data integration easily usable for processing distributed and autonomous data. The present paper is placed among the works on semantic peer data managment systems. Among the approaches that are related to ours, we mention [7,8,18,21].

In [21] the problem of schema mediation in a Peer Data Management System (PDMS) is investigated. A formalism, PPL, for mediating peer schemas, which uses the GAV and LAV formalism to specify mappings, is proposed. A FOL semantics to the global system is proposed and query answering for a PDMS is defined by extending the notion of certain answer. More specifically, certain answers for a peer are those that are true in every global instance that is consistent with local data.

In [7,8] a new semantics for a P2P system, based on epistemic logic, is proposed. The paper proposes a sound, complete and terminating procedure that returns the certain answers to a query submitted to a peer. The advantage of this framework is that certain answers of fixed conjunctive queries posed on a peer can be computed in polynomial time.

In [17–19] a characterization of P2P database systems and a model-theoretic semantics dealing with inconsistent peers is proposed. The basic idea is that if a peer does not have models all (ground) queries submitted to the peer are *true* (i.e. are *true* with respect to all models). Thus, if some databases are inconsistent it does not mean that the entire system is inconsistent. The semantics in [18] coincides with the epistemic semantics in [7,8].

Interesting semantics for data exchange systems that offer the possibility of modeling some preference criteria while performing the data integration process has been proposed in [3–5,12,13]. In [3–5] it is proposed a new semantics that allows for a cooperation among pairwise peers that related each other by means of data exchange constraints (i.e. mapping rules) and trust relationships. The decision by a peer on what other data to consider (besides its local data) does not depend only on its data exchange constraints, but also on the trust relationship that it has with other peers. Given a peer P in a P2P system a solution for P is a database instance that respects the exchange constraints and trust relationship P has with its 'immediate neighbors'. Trust relationships are of the form: $(P, less, Q)$ stating that P trusts itself less that Q, and $(P, same, Q)$ stating that P trusts itself the same as Q. This trust relationships are static and are used in the process of collecting data in order to establish preferences in the case of conflicting information.

The introduction of preference criteria among peers is out of the scope of this paper, anyhow we have proposed in recent papers extensions of the maximal weak model semantics that allows to express preferences between peers. More specifically, in [12] it is defined a mechanism that allows to set different degree of reliability for neighbor peers.

Both in [12] and in [3,5] the mechanism is *rigid* in the sense that the preference among conflicting sets of atoms that a peer can import only depends on the priorities (trust relationship) fixed at design time. To overcome static preferences, in [13] 'dynamic' preferences that allows to select among different scenarios looking at the properties of data provided by the peers is introduced. The work in [13] allows to model concepts like *"in the case of conflicting information, it is preferable to import data from the neighbor peer that can provide the maximum number of tuples"* without selecting a-priori preferred peers.

7   Conclusion

The paper introduces a logic programming based framework and a new semantics for P2P deductive databases.

The presented semantics generalizes previous proposal in the literature by allowing each peer joining the system to select between two different settings: it can either declare its local database to be sound, but not complete; in this case, if inconsistencies arise it gives preference to its knowledge with respect to the knowledge that can be imported from the rest of the system or declare its local knowledge to be unsound; in this case it does not give any preference to its knowledge with respect to the knowledge that can be imported from other peers.

References

1. Abiteboul, S., Duschka, O.M.: Complexity of answering queries using materialized views. ACM SIGMOD-SIGACT-SIGAI Symposium on Principles of Database Systems. In: PODS 1998, pp. 254–263 (1998)
2. Bernstein, P.A., Giunchiglia, F., Kementsietsidis, A., Mylopulos, J., Serafini, L., Zaihrayen, I.: Data management for peer-to-peer computing: a vision. In: WebDB, pp. 89–94 (2002)
3. Bertossi, L., Bravo, L.: Query answering in Peer-to-Peer data exchange systems. In: Lindner, W., Mesiti, M., Türker, C., Tzitzikas, Y., Vakali, A.I. (eds.) EDBT 2004. LNCS, vol. 3268, pp. 476–485. Springer, Heidelberg (2004). doi:10.1007/978-3-540-30192-9_47
4. Bertossi, L., Bravo, L.: The semantics of consistency and trust in peer data exchange systems. In: Dershowitz, N., Voronkov, A. (eds.) LPAR 2007. LNCS (LNAI), vol. 4790, pp. 107–122. Springer, Heidelberg (2007). doi:10.1007/978-3-540-75560-9_10
5. Bertossi, L., Bravo, L.: Consistency and trust in peer data exchange systems. TPLP **17**(2), 148–204 (2017)
6. Calvanese, D., Damaggio, E., Giacomo, G., Lenzerini, M., Rosati, R.: Semantic data integration in P2P systems. In: Aberer, K., Koubarakis, M., Kalogeraki, V. (eds.) DBISP2P 2003. LNCS, vol. 2944, pp. 77–90. Springer, Heidelberg (2004). doi:10.1007/978-3-540-24629-9_7
7. Calvanese, D., De Giacomo, G., Lenzerini, M., Rosati, R.: Logical foundations of Peer-to-Peer data integration. In: PODS, pp. 241–251 (2004)
8. Calvanese, D., De Giacomo, G., Lembo, D., Lenzerini, M., Rosati, R.: Inconsistency tolerance in P2P data integration: an epistemic logic approach. Inf. Syst. **33**(4–5), 360–384 (2008)
9. Caroprese, L., Greco, S., Zumpano, E.: A logic programming approach to querying and integrating P2P deductive databases. In: The International Florida AI Research Society Conference, pp. 31–36 (2006)
10. Caroprese, L., Molinaro, C., Zumpano, E.: Integrating and querying P2P deductive databases. In: International Database Engineering & Applications Symposium, pp. 285–290 (2006)
11. Caroprese, L., Zumpano, E.: Consistent data integration in P2P deductive databases. In: Prade, H., Subrahmanian, V.S. (eds.) SUM 2007. LNCS (LNAI), vol. 4772, pp. 230–243. Springer, Heidelberg (2007). doi:10.1007/978-3-540-75410-7_17
12. Caroprese, L., Zumpano, E.: Modeling cooperation in P2P data management systems. In: An, A., Matwin, S., Raś, Z.W., Ślęzak, D. (eds.) ISMIS 2008. LNCS (LNAI), vol. 4994, pp. 225–235. Springer, Heidelberg (2008). doi:10.1007/978-3-540-68123-6_25
13. Caroprese, L., Zumpano, E.: Aggregates and priorities in P2P data management systems. In: IDEAS 2011, pp. 1–7 (2011)
14. Caroprese, L., Zumpano, E.: Handling preferences in P2P systems. In: Lukasiewicz, T., Sali, A. (eds.) FoIKS 2012. LNCS, vol. 7153, pp. 91–106. Springer, Heidelberg (2012). doi:10.1007/978-3-642-28472-4_6

15. Caroprese, L., Zumpano, E.: Generalized maximal consistent answers in P2P deductive databases. In: Hartmann, S., Ma, H. (eds.) DEXA 2016. LNCS, vol. 9828, pp. 368–376. Springer, Cham (2016). doi:10.1007/978-3-319-44406-2_30
16. Fagin, R., Kolaitis, P.G., Popa, L.: Data exchange: getting to the core. ACM Trans. Database Syst. **30**(1), 174–210 (2005)
17. Franconi, E., Kuper, G.M., Lopatenko, A., Zaihrayeu, I.: Queries and updates in the coDB Peer to Peer database system. In: VLDB, pp. 1277–1280 (2004)
18. Franconi, E., Kuper, G.M., Lopatenko, A., Zaihrayeu, I.: A robust logical and computational characterisation of Perto-Peer database systems. In: DBISP2P 2003, pp. 64–76 (2003)
19. Franconi, E., Kuper, G., Lopatenko, A., Zaihrayeu, I.: A distributed algorithm for robust data sharing and updates in P2P database networks. In: Lindner, W., Mesiti, M., Türker, C., Tzitzikas, Y., Vakali, A.I. (eds.) EDBT 2004. LNCS, vol. 3268, pp. 446–455. Springer, Heidelberg (2004). doi:10.1007/978-3-540-30192-9_44
20. Gelfond, M., Lifschitz, V.: The stable model semantics for logic programming. In: ICLP/SLP 1988, pp. 1070–1080 (1988)
21. Halevy, A.Y, Ives, Z.G., Suciu, D., Tatarinov, I.: Schema mediation in peer data management systems. In: ICDT, pp. 505–516 (2003)
22. Halevy, A.Y., Ives, Z.G., Suciu, D., Tatarinov, I.: Schema mediation for large-scale semantic data sharing. VLDB J. **14**(1), 68–83 (2005)
23. Lenzerini, M.: Data integration: a theoretical perspective. In: PODS, pp. 233–246 (2002)
24. Madhavan, J., Halevy, A.Y.: Composing mappings among data sources. In: VLDB, pp. 572–583 (2003)
25. Sakama, C., Inoue, K.: Priorized logic programming and its application to commonsense reasoning. AI **123**, 185–222 (2000)
26. Tatarinov, I., Halevy, A.: Efficient query reformulation in peer data management systems. In: SIGMOD, pp. 539–550 (2004)

Improving Language-Dependent Named Entity Detection

Gerald Petz[✉] [iD], Werner Wetzlinger [iD], and Dietmar Nedbal [iD]

University of Applied Sciences Upper Austria, Steyr, Austria
{gerald.petz,werner.wetzlinger,
dietmar.nedbal}@fh-steyr.at

Abstract. Named Entity Recognition (NER) and Named Entity Linking (NEL) are two research areas that have shown big advancements in recent years. The majority of this research is based on the English language. Hence, some of these improvements are language-dependent and do not necessarily lead to better results when applied to other languages. Therefore, this paper discusses TOMO, an approach to language-aware named entity detection and evaluates it for the German language. This also required the development of a German gold standard dataset, which was based on the English dataset used by the OKE 2016 challenge. An evaluation of the named entity detection task using the web-based platform GERBIL was undertaken and results show that our approach produced higher F1 values than the other annotators did. This indicates that language-dependent features do improve the overall quality of the spotter.

Keywords: Entity recognition · Entity detection · Language-dependent · Dataset development · Gold standard · NER

1 Introduction

The recognition of named entities is an important starting point for many tasks in the area of natural language processing. Named Entity Recognition (NER) refers to methods that identify names of entities such as people, locations, organizations and products [1, 2]. It is typically broken down into the two subtasks entity detection (or "spotting") and entity classification. In many application scenarios, however, it is not only of interest which types of entities are contained in a text, but also how the entities can be semantically linked to a knowledge base. The task of correctly disambiguating and linking the recognized named entities in a text into a knowledge base with an external definition and description is referred to as Named Entity Linking (NEL) [3]. The overall goal is to make sense of data in the context of an application domain [4] (Fig. 1).

The whole pipeline (including the aforementioned tasks of NER and NEL) is strongly dependent on the knowledge base used to train the named entity extraction algorithm [5]. Most approaches for linking entities leverage on the use of Wikipedia (wikipedia.org), Dbpedia (dbpedia.org), Freebase (freebase.com) or YAGO (yago-knowledge.org) as the knowledge base. Although widely used and the largest online encyclopedia with millions of articles, Wikipedia may not be sufficient for more

A. Holzinger et al. (Eds.): CD-MAKE 2017, LNCS 10410, pp. 330–345, 2017.
DOI: 10.1007/978-3-319-66808-6_22

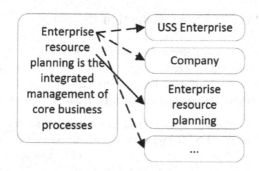

Fig. 1. Illustration for the entity linking task

specific domains and contexts. For example, in the German Wikipedia, only some large Austrian organizations are represented, names of persons are rare, etc. Moreover, the English Wikipedia does not hold this specific information either.

Among others, Piccinno and Ferragina [6] recognized that recent research tends to focus its attention on the NEL step of the pipeline by trying to improve and implement new disambiguation algorithms. However, ignoring the issues raised by entity recognition leads to the introduction of many false positives, which provoke a significant loss in the overall performance of the system. It would therefore be better to first try to improve the quality of the NER spotter.

Another problem area relates to differences in the language itself. It has been acknowledged that linguistically motivated and thus language aware spotting methods are more accurate than language independent methods [7]. The German language has a lot of differences for example in the use of upper and/or lowercase, compound nouns or hyphens to concatenate nouns. However, improvements in a certain language usually come at the expense of ease of adaptation to new languages. In addition, the established NER/NEL challenges and tasks of the scientific community like the OKE challenges [8], the NEEL challenge series [9], or the ERD challenges [10] are in the English language and therefore language-dependent improvements are often not in the focus of the research.

Moreover, the results from different tools need to be comparable against certain quality measures (cf. Sect. 4.1) based on the same dataset. Frameworks addressing the continuous evaluation of annotation tools such as GERBIL [11, 12] can be used for comparison, but evaluation datasets provided by GERBIL as "gold standards" are only available for the English language as well.

The objective of this paper therefore is to (i) develop an approach for language-aware spotting and (ii) to evaluate the proposed spotting approach for the German language.

After an analysis of the state of the art in spotting methods in general (Sect. 2), the paper focuses on possibilities to optimize the spotter for a certain language in Sect. 3. In Sect. 4, evaluation measures are discussed, followed by an analysis of available datasets for evaluation. Additionally, we show how a German dataset was developed and used for evaluation purposes. Section 5 presents results of the experiments and final conclusions are drawn in Sect. 6.

2 State of the Art in Entity Detection (Spotting)

As mentioned above the entity detection ("spotting") is an important task in the area of NEL; a couple of authors emphasize the importance of a correct entity spotting in order to avoid errors in later stages of the entity linking task. [6, 13]

Several approaches to the spotting task can be identified in the literature:

- NER tagger. Some tools and approaches rely on existing implementations of NER taggers such as Standford NER tagger or OpenNLP Named Entity Recognition in order to spot surface forms of entities [14–18]. The Standford NER tagger is an implementation of linear chain Conditional Random Field (CRF) sequence models, the OpenNLP NER is based on a Maximum Entropy model.
- POS tags and rules. A couple of authors use part of speech (POS) taggers and/or several rules in order to identify named entities [19–34]. The rules range from simple rules such as "capitalized letter" (if a word contains a capitalized letter the word will be treated as a spot), stop word lists, "At Least One Noun Selector"-rule to complex, combined rules.
- Dictionary based techniques. The majority of approaches leverage techniques based on dictionaries [6, 19, 31, 35–45]. The structure of Wikipedia provides useful features for generating dictionaries:
  - Entity pages: Each page in Wikipedia contains a title (e.g. "Barack Obama") that is very likely the most common name for an entity.
  - Redirect pages: Wikipedia contains redirect pages for each alternative name of an entity page. E.g. "Obama" is a redirect page to "Barack Obama".
  - Disambiguation pages: Disambiguation pages in Wikipedia are used to resolve conflicts with ambiguous article titles. E.g. "Enterprise" may refer to a company, to aircrafts, to Star Trek, and many more. Disambiguation pages are very useful for extracting aliases and abbreviations.
  - Bold phrases: Bold phrases in the first paragraph of a Wikipedia entry can contain useful information such as abbreviations, aliases or nicknames. E.g. the bold phrase in the page "Barack Obama" contains the full name ("Barack Hussein Obama II").
  - Hyperlinks in Wikipedia pages: Pages in Wikipedia usually contain hyperlinks to other pages; the anchor texts of these hyperlinks may provide synonyms and other name variations.
- Methods based on search engines. Some authors try to use web search engines such as Google to identify candidate entities [46–49].
- Computational techniques. A couple of authors leverage heuristic based methods or machine learning methods. Some approaches expand the surface forms by searching the textual context based on heuristic pattern matching [46, 47, 50]. Other authors use N-Grams [31, 33, 44, 51, 52], others experiment with CRF [25, 26], Topic Modeling [53, 54], Naïve Bayes and Hidden Markov Models [55]. Last but not least one can find approaches based on Finite-state machines [14, 15, 30, 34].

The majority of the papers use dictionary approaches. Nevertheless, the above mentioned approaches are usually combined, e.g. [6] leverages OpenNLP NER, a dictionary approach based on Wikipedia with utilization of several features such as anchor texts, redirect pages, etc.

The authors usually provide measures (recall, precision, F1) of the effectiveness of their approaches; unfortunately, these measures cannot be directly compared because usually different datasets are used and the approaches are optimized towards these datasets.

3 TOMO Approach to Optimize Spotter for the German Language

This section details our approach to optimizing a spotter ("TOMO") for the German language with a focus on the spotting phase within the entity linking pipeline. The base system used is Dexter [36, 37], an open-source framework (available at https://github. com/dexter/dexter) that implements a dictionary spotter using Wikipedia content. Figure 2 shows the approach comprising the construction and the annotation process using a dictionary.

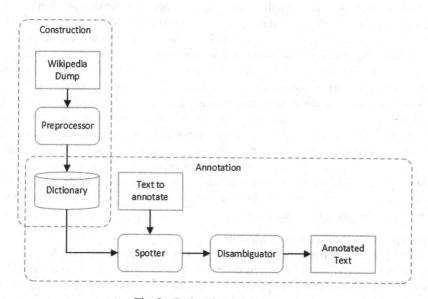

Fig. 2. Basic TOMO architecture

The annotation process involves a spotter and a disambiguator with an annotated text as output. The spotter detects a list of candidate mentions in the input text, and retrieves for each mention a list of candidate entities [36]. When spotting a text, individual fragments or words from the text ("shingles") are compared with the dictionary of up to six words ("n-grams"). Before being able to use the dictionary for NER, the dictionary needs to be filled with known entities first. Therefore, each Wikipedia article is processed using the title of the article as well as all internal links (anchors within Wikipedia) as spots for the dictionary. In addition, the measures of mention frequency (mf), link frequency (lf) and document frequency (df) are calculated and stored as well. Both in the construction of the dictionary and in the annotation of a text based on this dictionary the text fragments (shingles and known entities) go through a cleaning pipeline with a series of replacements. The cleaning pipeline in pseudocode is as follows:

```
foreach (article in knowledgebase)
  listOfSpots = preprocess(getTitle(article))
  listOfSpots = preprocess(getAnchors(article))
  calculateMeasures(listOfSpots)

preprocess(textfragment)
  clean(textfragment)
  filter(textfragment)
  map(textfragment)
```

A "cleaner" performs a simple transformation of a text fragment (e.g. transform a text to lowercase, remove symbols, remove quotes, unescape Javascript, clean parenthesis, etc.). A "filter" allows the removal of a given text fragment if it does not respect a filter constraint (e.g. delete text fragments that are below the threshold for commonness, have less than three characters, consist only of numbers or symbols, etc.). A "mapper" returns several different versions of the spot (e.g. a "quotes mapper" generates from [dave "baby" cortez] the spots [dave "baby" cortez], [baby], [dave cortez]) [56].

Moreover, for simplification purposes, many tools use lowercase filters. Full text search indices such as Lucene also imply such a lowercase behavior per default, which in many tasks (e.g. search engine querying, microblogging analysis) makes sense. In our setting, lowercase simplification is responsible for introducing several spotting errors (e.g. the sentence "the performance is worse": the word "worse" translates to "schlechter" in German and the spotter identifies this word as a candidate entry for the Wikipedia page "Carl Schlechter"). In German language, only nouns and proper names are written with capitalized initial letters.

Language-aware preprocessing pipeline
In a setting where typing errors are relatively rare (e.g. in press releases, formal documents) the application of a case sensitive setting is therefore a reliable and straightforward approach to increase the precision of the spotter for the German language [57].

Another important aspect of a language-aware approach is the correct usage of the code page. For the English language, the US-ASCII code page is the preferred setting, as it uses less space than other code pages. In the German language, many named entities contain non US-ASCII characters, like umlaut or the German eszett. Using US-ASCII filters, these characters are replaced by their English representation (umlaut a gets replaced by an "a", etc.). This sometimes changes the whole meaning of the word, as the English replacements are also used in German language and this gets even worse in combination with lowercase filtering. E.g. the sentence "we made this", with its German translation "Wir haben das gemacht": the word "made" translates to "gemacht" in German and this is disambiguated to "Gemächt" (the male genitalia). The UTF-8 code page can be used as a solution to this problem.

Additionally, some minor issues may occur due to differences in the language of the Wikipedia syntax itself. For instance, it is possible to link images within Wikipedia with the common English terms "File:" or "Image:", but the German Wikipedia additionally allows the deprecated terms "Datei:" or "Bild:" as well. Such filters therefore also need to be aware of differences in the German language in order to improve spotting.

4   Evaluation Measures and Datasets

In this section, we discuss the evaluation of spotting named entities in the German language. This includes which measures, tools and datasets to use.

4.1   Measures and Benchmarking

To ensure comparability across different NER and NEL system evaluations the most common measures are *precision, recall, F1* and *accuracy*.

Precision. Precision considers all spots that are generated by the system and determines how correct they are compared to a gold standard. Consequently, the precision of a spotting system is calculated as the fraction of correctly spotted entity mentions compared to all spotted mentions generated by a particular system.

$$precision = \frac{correctly\ spotted\ mentions}{mentions\ spotted\ by\ the\ system} \tag{1}$$

Recall. Recall is a measure that describes how many of the spots of a gold standard are correctly identified by a system. It is the fraction of correctly spotted entity mentions by a particular systems compared to the all entity mentions that should be spotted according to a selected gold standard.

$$recall = \frac{correctly\ spotted\ mentions}{manually\ annotated\ mentions} \tag{2}$$

F1. To generate a single measure for a system from recall and precision, the measure F1 was developed. It is defined as the harmonic mean of precision and recall as shown in Eq. 3.

$$F1 = \frac{2 * precision * recall}{precision + recall} \tag{3}$$

GERBIL. As also minor differences between these measures exist, we use the web-based benchmarking system GERBIL (gerbil.aksw.org) to evaluate these measures for our system and compare them with others. GERBIL is an entity annotation system that provides a web-based platform for the comparison of annotators [11]. Currently it incorporates 13 annotators and 32 datasets for evaluating the performance of systems. The evaluation is done using uniform measuring approaches and well established measures like the aforementioned recall, precision and F1 [12]. Consequently, GERBIL can be used for benchmarking different annotators. External tools can be added to the GERBIL platform by providing an URL to a REST interface of the tool. Besides the integrated datasets, GERBIL allows for the use of user-specified datasets. As GERBIL is based on Natural Language Programming Interface Format (NIF), user-specified datasets also have to be uploaded using this format. Additionally, GERBIL provides Java classes for implementing APIs for datasets and annotators to NIF. Due to these features, GERBIL is also used by challenges (e.g. OKE challenge) as platform for evaluating the performance of contestants.

4.2   Dataset

To test an entity linking system a gold standard dataset must be provided. This dataset has to include all sentences to analyze, spots to be linked and links to a knowledge base for correct disambiguation. Systems are then ranked by comparing the above-mentioned evaluation measures (recall, precision and F1) they score in relation to this dataset. There are already a number of English corpora to test entity recognition and entity linking systems. Some of them emerged from challenges that compare the results of multiple algorithms and systems to assess the performance of different approaches. For example the datasets of the OKE challenge as part of the European Semantic Web Conferences 2016 (2016.eswc-conferences.org), the NEEL challenge of the Microposts Workshop at the World Wide Web Conference 2016 (microposts2016.seas.upenn.edu), or the ERD challenge at the SIGIR 2014 Workshop ERD'14 (sigir.org/sigir2014) are publicly available.

Requirements and Review of Existing Datasets. To test the performance of our approach to spot entities in the German language we had to select or develop a dataset. For this task, we defined the following requirements:

- The dataset has to be available in German to test the performance of the spotter for German texts.
- The dataset should be testable via the GERBIL web service. Thus, it should be already available in GERBIL or encoded in NIF format.
- The dataset should be widely used, specifically by new systems, to be able to compare our results with leading systems and approaches.
- The dataset should be independent of a certain domain (e.g. only articles about economics).
- The content of the dataset should be comprised of natural language in encyclopedia entries or news. Specific content like tweets or queries were not of interest, since these datasets often have just very few spots with average entries per documents lower than 2.0.

- The dataset should include co-references to evaluate the performance improvements of future enhancements of our system.

We examined existing datasets and their suitability for our requirements. Table 1 shows the results of this literature review which showed that nearly all available datasets are for the English language.

Table 1. Comparison of gold standard datasets

Datasets	Type	Lang	Co-Refs	Docs	Linked Entities	Avg. Entity/Doc
ACE2004	news	en		57	257	4.44
AIDA-Yago2/CoNLL	news	en		231	4485	19.97
AQUAINT	news	en		50	727	14.54
Dbpedia Spotlight	news	en		58	330	5.69
Derczynski - Broad Twitter Corpus	tweets	en		9551	12117	1.27
ERD2014	queries	en		91	59	0.65
GERDAQ	queries	en		992	1706	1.72
IITB	webpages	en		103	11249	109.22
KORE50	news	en		50	144	2.86
MSNBC	news	en		20	658	32.50
Microposts2014 test dataset	tweets	en		1165	1458	1.25
Microposts2015 test dataset	tweets	en		2027	2382	1.18
Microposts2016 test dataset	tweets	en		3164	738	2.46
N3-RSS-500	news	en		500	1000	1.00
N3-Reuters-128	news	en		128	880	4.85
OKE 2015 Task 1 evaluation dataset	encyclopedia	en	x	101	664	6.57
OKE 2015 Task 2 evaluation dataset	encyclopedia	en	x	99	99	1.00
OKE 2016 Task 1 evaluation dataset	encyclopedia	en	x	55	340	6.18
OKE 2016 Task 2 evaluation dataset	encyclopedia	en		50	50	1.00
N3-News-100	news	de		100	1547	15.47
Meij	tweets	en		502	812	1.87
LinkedTV	news	de		150	1346	8.97
GerNED	news	de		2468	1664	0.67
Ritter	tweets	en		2394	1672	0.70

The three German datasets found were not appropriate for our requirements because they were too domain specific (News-100, LinkedTV), possess only the "classic" named entities (persons, locations, etc.), had no co-references defined, and/or are not publicly accessible (GerNED). Since none of these datasets fitted our requirements, we decided to develop a new dataset to evaluate the spotter against German texts.

Development of a German Gold Standard Dataset. We chose to develop a new German dataset based on the evaluation dataset of the OKE challenge 2016 ("OKE 2016 Task 1 evaluation dataset") for several reasons. Since the content of this dataset originated from Wikipedia articles, it covers a wide range of topics. Therefore, it also consists of natural language and not of tweets or search queries. Furthermore, documents are long enough to contain multiple spots (6.18 average entities per document) and they include co-references as well. Additionally, the English version of the dataset is coded in NIF format and is already integrated in GERBIL. Finally, with 55 documents and 340 entities, we considered this dataset to be of an appropriate length.

To develop the new dataset based on the dataset, we conducted a multi-step approach that consisted of the following tasks:

1. Identify all documents and included spots in the NIF file of the OKE 2016 Task 1 evaluation dataset.
2. Translate all documents in this dataset using Google Translate (translate.google. com)
3. Adjust the initial Google translation by improving German grammar, word order, etc. by native speakers.
4. Identify all English spots of dataset in the German translation.
5. Identify the corresponding entities in the German knowledge base (de.wikipedia. org).
6. Link the spots to the identified knowledge base entities using links in a HTML file.
7. Transform the HTML file to NIF using a converter.

This process was not straightforward and a number of problems occurred that were mainly based on ambiguities in steps 5 and 6:

- Because the English Wikipedia is more than twice as large as the German Wikipedia, some spots had no representation in the German knowledge base. This was mainly the case with persons (e.g. Andrew McCollum, James Alexander Hendler) and organizations (e.g. Kirkcaldy High School, American Association for Artificial Intelligence).
- Literal translation by Google Translate led to surface forms that were wrong or unusual (e.g. "artificial intelligence researcher" was translated to "künstlicher Intelligenzforscher").
- Translation by Google Translate led to a sentence structure and grammar that was sometimes unusual or incorrect for German sentences.
- In some cases, it was not clear which term was the correct German translation of the English term in the specific context of sentences (e.g. "independent contractor" was translated to "unabhängiger Auftragnehmer" by Google Translate, but "freier Mitarbeiter" was considered to be the correct translation for the context of the sentence).

- In a few cases, it was not clear to which entity in the German knowledge base an entity should be linked (e.g. the English term "treasury" can be translated based on traditional British or American interpretations of the word as "Finanzministerium" or "Schatzamt", but is now also used in its English form as a department of corporations.)

In order to cope with these uncertainties, three researchers (German native speakers) independently identified the corresponding German surface form for the spot based on the translated text. For every spot that led to different surface forms or links the different solutions from the three authors were discussed and a majority decision was made by voting.

As a result, some spots were not available in the German knowledge base and therefore the resulting dataset has fewer spots than the original. Since not all systems currently support co-references, we developed two versions of the dataset. One with co-references and one without co-references (15 documents incorporated a total of 24 co-references). The resulting corpus can be downloaded here: https://github.com/HCSolutionsGesmbH/OKE-Challenge-German.

5   Experiments and Results

Based on the discussion described in Sect. 4 we built different test cases to evaluate the changes between a language independent (n/a) and an explicit German language (de) setting. In addition, we considered case sensitivity as a test case for our experiments and built a model based on a case sensitive (cs) and case insensitive (cis) setting. These model characteristics led to the four different test cases shown in Fig. 3.

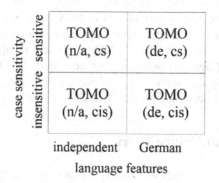

Fig. 3. Test cases

Using the German case sensitive model, we experimented with the commonness threshold. We cut out 0%, 5%, 10%, 15% and 20% of spots with the lowest commonness and evaluated the resulting F1 scores. Results showed that using all spots (i.e. not cutting out any) led to the highest F1 score. Thus, this setting resulted in the highest recall without lowering the precision too much.

Table 2. Evaluation of spotting results

Annotator	Recall	Precision	F1
TOMO (n/a, cis)	0.8447	0.4575	0.5684
TOMO (n/a, cs)	0.8599	0.4707	0.5823
TOMO (de, cis)	0.8447	0.4575	0.5684
TOMO (de, cs)	0.8569	0.4811	**0.5866**
AIDA	0.3109	0.6516	0.3983
Babelfy	0.4336	0.3599	0.3689
DBpedia Spotlight	0.4139	0.5077	0.4197
Dexter	0.3537	0.6176	0.4236
Entityclassifier.eu NER	0.767	0.4888	0.5689
FOX	0.4523	**0.6777**	0.4996
FRED	**0.9519**	0.1878	0.303
FREME NER	0.2353	0.3485	0.2643
Kea	0.541	0.5953	0.5399
WAT	0.495	0.6442	0.5163

Consequently, we tested all four test cases using this setting in GERBIL with our developed dataset that is based on the recent German Wikipedia dump from 2017/05/01. Table 2 shows the resulting scores for recall, precision and F1.

The annotators TagMe 2, xLisa-NER and xLisa-NGRAM of GERBIL did not produce any results (the GERBIL experiment reported: "The annotator caused too many single errors.") and could not be evaluated. FRED produced the highest recall. As FRED aims at producing formal structure graphs from natural language text and is based on a dictionary comprising different knowledge bases including WordNet aims at a high recall. On the other side it automatically translates the input text beforehand which may lead to a decrease in precision [45]. FOX combines the results of several state-of-the-art NER tools by using a decision-tree-based algorithm which performed best on the precision measure [58, 59]. In addition, the tool is capable of automatically detecting German language text input. Results also show that the TOMO approach using the German language setting in combination with the case sensitive model achieved the highest F1 score among all tested annotators.

6   Conclusions and Future Work

The paper discusses an approach for language-aware spotting and evaluates the proposed spotting approach for the German language. The results indicate that language-dependent features do improve the overall quality of the spotter. This is necessary, because errors introduced in the spotting phase have an effect on the disambiguation step and can hardly be corrected. A limitation of this work is that the performance metrics of TOMO vs. other systems are only partially comparable, because the annotators were either developed only for the English language or do not take into account any language specifics. However, we were able to show that language-dependent features improve spotting quality. With the availability of a dataset in German and English language, it is possible to directly compare the performances of the systems for different languages.

When the authors of this paper developed the German corpus a lot of discussions about which surface forms should be linked to the knowledge base arose. For example this text (taken from OKE 2016 Task 1 evaluation dataset) contains several links (shown as underlined words): "Ray Kurzweil grew up in the New York City borough of Queens. He was born to secular Jewish parents who had emigrated from Austria just before the onset of World War II." It is not quite clear, why "parents" are linked to an entity, but some text fragments that are probably more in need of explanation such as "Jewish" or "World War II" are not spots. Wikipedia contains a separate page that provides guidelines for linking. These guidelines suggest for example, not to link everyday words, but to link to other articles that will help the reader to understand the context more fully [60]. However, every gold standard obviously represents a certain way of thinking. Furthermore, performing well on a certain gold standard just means the system replicates a certain way of thinking very well.

Further research work should include a discussion and development of guidelines or rules which terms should be annotated in a gold standard dataset in order to align the different evaluation datasets. Furthermore, a population of a cross-language and cross-domain gold standard in order to evaluate annotation systems for different purposes would be of value for the community.

Acknowledgements. This research was supported by HC Solutions GesmbH, Linz, Austria. We have to express out appreciation to Florian Wurzer, Reinhard Schwab and Manfred Kain for discussing these topics with us.

The TOMO Named Entity Linking is part of TOMO ® (http://www.tomo-base.at), a big data platform for aggregating content, analyzing and visualizing content.

References

1. Petasis, G., Spiliotopoulos, D., Tsirakis, N., Tsantilas, P.: Large-scale sentiment analysis for reputation management. In: Gindl, S., Remus, R., Wiegand, M. (eds.) 2nd Workshop on Practice and Theory of Opinion Mining and Sentiment Analysis (2013)
2. Derczynski, L., Maynard, D., Rizzo, G., van Erp, M., Gorrell, G., Troncy, R., Petrak, J., Bontcheva, K.: Analysis of Named Entity Recognition and Linking for Tweets. Preprint submitted to Elsevier (2014)
3. Rizzo, G., van Erp, M., Troncy, R.: Benchmarking the extraction and disambiguation of named entities on the semantic web. In: 9th International Conference on Language Resources and Evaluation (LREC 2014), pp. 4593–4600 (2014)
4. Holzinger, A.: Introduction to machine learning and knowledge extraction (MAKE). Mach. Learn. Knowl. Extr. **1**, 1–20 (2017)
5. Rizzo, G., Troncy, R., Hellmann, S., Brümmer, M.: NERD meets NIF: lifting NLP extraction results to the linked data cloud. In: LDOW, 5th Workshop on Linked Data on the Web, 16 April 2012, Lyon, France (2012)

6. Piccinno, F., Ferragina, P.: From TagME to WAT: a new entity annotator. In: Proceedings of the First International Workshop on Entity Recognition & Disambiguation, pp. 55–62. ACM, New York (2014)

7. Daiber, J., Jakob, M., Hokamp, C., Mendes, P.N.: improving efficiency and accuracy in multilingual entity extraction. In: Proceedings of the 9th International Conference on Semantic Systems, pp. 121–124. ACM, New York (2013)

8. Nuzzolese, A.G., Gentile, A.L., Presutti, V., Gangemi, A., Garigliotti, D., Navigli, R.: Open knowledge extraction challenge. In: Gandon, F., Cabrio, E., Stankovic, M., Zimmermann, A. (eds.) SemWebEval 2015. CCIS, vol. 548, pp. 3–15. Springer, Cham (2015). doi:10.1007/978-3-319-25518-7_1

9. Rizzo, G., Pereira, B., Varga, A., van Erp, M., Cano Basave, A.E.: Lessons learnt from the named entity rEcognition and linking (NEEL) challenge series. Semantic Web J. (2017, in press)

10. Carmel, D., Chang, M.-W., Gabrilovich, E., Hsu, B.-J., Wang, K.: ERD 2014: entity recognition and disambiguation challenge. SIGIR Forum **48**, 63–77 (2014)

11. Usbeck, R., Röder, M., Ngonga Ngomo, A.-C.: GERBIL – General Entity Annotator Benchmarking Framework (2015)

12. Röder, M., Usbeck, R., Ngonga Ngomo, A.-C.: GERBIL's New Stunts: Semantic Annotation Benchmarking Improved (2016)

13. Hachey, B., Radford, W., Nothman, J., Honnibal, M., Curran, J.R.: Evaluating entity linking with wikipedia. Artif. Intell. **194**, 130–150 (2013)

14. Mendes, P.N., Jakob, M., Garcia-Silva, A., Bizer, C.: DBpedia spotlight: shedding light on the web of documents. In: Proceedings of the 7th International Conference on Semantic Systems, pp. 1–8. ACM, New York (2011)

15. Mendes, P.N., Jakob, M., Bizer, C.: DBpedia: a multilingual cross-domain knowledge base. In: Proceedings of the International Conference on Language Resources and Evaluation (LREC), pp. 1813–1817 (2012)

16. Rizzo, G., Troncy, R.: NERD: evaluating named entity recognition tools in the web of data. In: ISWC 2011, Workshop on Web Scale Knowledge Extraction (WEKEX 2011), 23–27 October 2011, Bonn, Germany (2011)

17. Hoffart, J., Yosef, M.A., Bordino, I., Fürstenau, H., Pinkal, M., Spaniol, M., Taneva, B., Thater, S., Weikum, G.: Robust disambiguation of named entities in text. In: Proceedings of the Conference on Empirical Methods in Natural Language Processing, pp. 782–792. Association for Computational Linguistics, Stroudsburg, PA, USA (2011)

18. Charton, E., Gagnon, M., Ozell, B.: Automatic semantic web annotation of named entities. In: Butz, C., Lingras, P. (eds.) AI 2011. LNCS, vol. 6657, pp. 74–85. Springer, Heidelberg (2011). doi:10.1007/978-3-642-21043-3_10

19. Eckhardt, A., Hreško, J., Procházka, J., Smrž, O.: Entity Recognition Based on the Co-occurrence Graph and Entity Probability (2014)

20. Zhao, S., Li, C., Ma, S., Ma, T., Ma, D.: Combining POS tagging, lucene search and similarity metrics for entity linking. In: Lin, X., Manolopoulos, Y., Srivastava, D., Huang, G. (eds.) WISE 2013. LNCS, vol. 8180, pp. 503–509. Springer, Heidelberg (2013). doi:10.1007/978-3-642-41230-1_44

21. Zhang, L., Dong, Y., Rettinger, A.: Towards Entity Correctness, Completeness and Emergence for Entity Recognition (2015)

22. Moro, A., Raganato, A., Navigli, R.: Entity linking meets word sense disambiguation: a unified approach. Trans. Assoc. Comput. Linguist. **2**, 231–244 (2014)

23. Leaman, R., Gonzalez, G.: BANNER: an executable survey of advances in biomedical named entity recognition. In: Pacific Symposium on Biocomputing, vol. 13, pp. 652–663 (2008)

24. Cucerzan, S.: Large-scale named entity disambiguation based on wikipedia data. In: Proceedings of the 2007 Joint Conference on Empirical Methods in Natural Language Processing and Computational Natural Language Learning (EMNLP-CoNLL), pp. 708–716. Association for Computational Linguistics, Prague, Czech Republic (2007)

25. Dojchinovski, M., Kliegr, T.: Entityclassifier.eu: Real-Time Classification of Entities in Text with Wikipedia. In: Blockeel, H., Kersting, K., Nijssen, S., Železný, F. (eds.) ECML PKDD 2013. LNCS, vol. 8190, pp. 654–658. Springer, Heidelberg (2013). doi:10.1007/978-3-642-40994-3_48

26. Kliegr, T.: Linked hypernyms: Enriching DBpedia with Targeted Hypernym Discovery. Web Semantics: Science, Services and Agents on the World Wide Web (2014)

27. Tonelli, S., Giuliano, C., Tymoshenko, K.: Wikipedia-based WSD for multilingual frame annotation. Artif. Intell. **194**, 203–221 (2013)

28. Goudas, T., Louizos, C., Petasis, G., Karkaletsis, V.: Argument Extraction from News, Blogs, and Social Media. In: Likas, A., Blekas, K., Kalles, D. (eds.) SETN 2014. LNCS, vol. 8445, pp. 287–299. Springer, Cham (2014). doi:10.1007/978-3-319-07064-3_23

29. Ritter, A., Clark, S., Mausam, Etzioni, O.: Named entity recognition in Tweets: An Experimental Study. In: Proceedings of the Conference on Empirical Methods in Natural Language Processing, pp. 1524–1534. Association for Computational Linguistics, Stroudsburg, PA, USA (2011)

30. Olieman, A., Azarbonyad, H., Dehghani, M., Kamps, J., Marx, M.: Entity linking by focusing DBpedia candidate entities. In: Carmel, D., Chang, M.-W., Gabrilovich, E., Hsu, B.-J., Wang, K. (eds.) The First International Workshop, pp. 13–24 (2014)

31. Chiu, Y.-P., Shih, Y.-S., Lee, Y.-Y., Shao, C.-C., Cai, M.-L., Wei, S.-L., Chen, H.-H.: NTUNLP approaches to recognizing and disambiguating entities in long and short text at the ERD challenge 2014. In: Carmel, D., Chang, M.-W., Gabrilovich, E., Hsu, B.-J., Wang, K. (eds.) The First International Workshop, pp. 3–12

32. Barrena, A., Agirre, E., Soroa, A.: UBC entity recognition and disambiguation at ERD 2014. In: Carmel, D., Chang, M.-W., Gabrilovich, E., Hsu, B.-J., Wang, K. (eds.) The First International Workshop, pp. 79–82 (2014)

33. Noraset, T., Bhagavatula, C., Downey, D.: WebSAIL wikifier at ERD 2014. In: Carmel, D., Chang, M.-W., Gabrilovich, E., Hsu, B.-J., Wang, K. (eds.) The First International Workshop, pp. 119–124 (2014)

34. Lipczak, M., Koushkestani, A., Milios, E.: Tulip: lightweight entity recognition and disambiguation using wikipedia-based topic centroids. In: Carmel, D., Chang, M.-W., Gabrilovich, E., Hsu, B.-J., Wang, K. (eds.) The First International Workshop, pp. 31–36 (2014)

35. Petasis, G., Spiliotopoulos, D., Tsirakis, N., Tsantilas, P.: Sentiment Analysis for Reputation Management: Mining the Greek Web. In: Likas, A., Blekas, K., Kalles, D. (eds.) SETN 2014. LNCS, vol. 8445, pp. 327–340. Springer, Cham (2014). doi:10.1007/978-3-319-07064-3_26

36. Ceccarelli, D., Lucchese, C., Orlando, S., Perego, R., Trani, S.: Dexter: an open source framework for entity linking. In: Proceedings of the Sixth International Workshop on Exploiting Semantic Annotations in Information Retrieval, pp. 17–20. ACM, New York (2013)

37. Ceccarelli, D., Lucchese, C., Orlando, S., Perego, R., Trani, S.: Dexter 2.0 - an open source tool for semantically enriching data. In: Horridge, M., Rospocher, M., van Ossenbruggen, J. (eds.) Proceedings of the ISWC 2014 Posters & Demonstrations Track, pp. 417–420 (2014)

38. Ferragina, P., Scaiella, U.: TAGME: On-the-fly annotation of short text fragments (by Wikipedia Entities). In: Proceedings of the 19th ACM International Conference on Information and Knowledge Management, pp. 1625–1628. ACM, New York (2010)

39. Mihalcea, R., Csomai, A.: Wikify!: linking documents to encyclopedic knowledge. In: Proceedings of the Sixteenth ACM Conference on Conference on Information and Knowledge Management, pp. 233–241. ACM, New York (2007)

40. Ratinov, L., Roth, D., Downey, D., Anderson, M.: Local and global algorithms for disambiguation to wikipedia. In: Proceedings of the 49th Annual Meeting of the Association for Computational Linguistics: Human Language Technologies, vol. 1, pp. 1375–1384. Association for Computational Linguistics, Stroudsburg, PA, USA (2011)

41. Agirre, E., Soroa, A.: Personalizing PageRank for word sense disambiguation. In: Proceedings of the 12th Conference of the European Chapter of the Association for Computational Linguistics, pp. 33–41. Association for Computational Linguistics, Athens, Greece (2009)

42. Agirre, E., de Lacalle, O.L., Soroa, A.: Random walks for knowledge-based word sense disambiguation. Comput. Linguist. **40**, 57–84 (2014)

43. Milne, D., Witten, I.H.: An open-source toolkit for mining Wikipedia. Artif. Intell. Wikipedia Semi-Struct. Res. **194**, 222–239 (2013)

44. Kemmerer, S., Großmann, B., Müller, C., Adolphs, P., Ehrig, H.: The neofonie NERD system at the ERD challenge 2014. In: Carmel, D., Chang, M.-W., Gabrilovich, E., Hsu, B.-J., Wang, K. (eds.) The First International Workshop, pp. 83–88 (2014)

45. Gangemi, A., Presutti, V., Reforgiato Recupero, D., Nuzzolese, A.G., Draicchio, F., Mongiovì, M., Alani, H.: Semantic Web machine reading with FRED. In: SW, pp.1–21 (2016)

46. Lehmann, J., Monahan, S., Nezda, L., Jung, A., Shi, Y.: LCC approaches to knowledge base population at TAC 2010. In: TAC 2010 Proceedings Papers (2010)

47. Han, X., Zhao, J.: NLPR_KBP in TAC 2009 KBP track: a two-stage method to entity linking. In: TAC 2009 Workshop (2009)

48. Dredze, M., McNamee, P., Rao, D., Gerber, A., Finin, T.: Entity disambiguation for knowledge base population. In: Proceedings of the 23rd International Conference on Computational Linguistics, Coling 2010, pp. 277–285 (2010)

49. Monahan, S., Lehmann, J., Nyberg, T., Plymale, J., Jung, A.: cross-lingual cross-document coreference with entity linking. In: Proceedings of the Text Analysis Conference. (2011)

50. Jain, A., Cucerzan, S., Azzam, S.: Acronym-expansion recognition and ranking on the web. In: 2007 IEEE International Conference on Information Reuse and Integration, pp. 209–214. IEEE (2007)

51. Hakimov, S., Oto, S.A., Dogdu, E.: Named entity recognition and disambiguation using linked data and graph-based centrality scoring. In: Proceedings of the 4th International Workshop on Semantic Web Information Management, p. 4. ACM, New York (2012)

52. Milne, D., Witten, I.H.: Learning to link with wikipedia. In: Proceedings of the 17th ACM Conference on Information and Knowledge Management, pp. 509–518. ACM, New York (2008)

53. Han, X., Le S.: A generative entity-mention model for linking entities with knowledge base. In: Proceedings of the 49th Annual Meeting of the Association for Computational Linguistics: Human Language Technologies, vol. 1, pp. 945–954. Association for Computational Linguistics, Stroudsburg, PA, USA (2011)

54. Han, X., Le S.: An entity-topic model for entity linking. In: Proceedings of the 2012 Joint Conference on Empirical Methods in Natural Language Processing and Computational Natural Language Learning, pp. 105–115. Association for Computational Linguistics, Stroudsburg, PA, USA (2012)

55. Carpenter, B.: Phrasal queries with LingPipe and Lucene: ad hoc genomics text retrieval. In: Voorhees, E.M., Buckland, L.P. (eds.) Proceedings of the Thirteenth Text REtrieval Conference, TREC 2004. National Institute of Standards and Technology (NIST) (2004)

56. Ceccarelli, D., Lucchese, C., Orlando, S., Perego, R., Trani, S.: SpotManager, https://github.com/dexter/dexter/blob/eeced3782f958f070f2448413f413e10e9df2281/dexter-core/src/main/java/it/cnr/isti/hpc/dexter/spot/clean/SpotManager.java

57. Neumann, G., Backofen, R., Baur, J., Becker, M., Braun, C.: An information extraction core system for real world German text processing. In: Grishman, R. (ed.) The Fifth Conference, pp. 209–216

58. Speck, R., Ngonga Ngomo, A.-C.: Named entity recognition using FOX. In: International Semantic Web Conference 2014 (ISWC2014), Demos & Posters (2014)

59. Speck, R., Ngonga Ngomo, A.-C.: Ensemble learning for named entity recognition. In: Mika, P., et al. (eds.) ISWC 2014. LNCS, vol. 8796, pp. 519–534. Springer, Cham (2014). doi:10.1007/978-3-319-11964-9_33

60. Wikipedia: Manual of Style/Linking. https://en.wikipedia.org/wiki/Wikipedia:Manual_of_Style/Linking

Towards the Automatic Detection of Nutritional Incompatibilities Based on Recipe Titles

Nadia Clairet[1,2,3]([✉]) and Mathieu Lafourcade[1]

[1] LIRMM (Laboratoire d'Informatique,
de Robotique et de Microélectronique de Montpellier)/860 rue de St Priest,
34000 Montpellier, France
{clairet,mathieu.lafourcade}@lirmm.fr
[2] LIMICS (Laboratoire d'Informatique Médicale et d'Ingénieurie des Connaissances
en e-Santé)/74 rue Marcel Cachin, 93017 Bobigny, France
[3] Lingua et Machina/7 Boulevard Anatole France,
92100 Boulogne-Billancourt, France

Abstract. The present paper reports experimental work on the automatic detection of nutritional incompatibilities of cooking recipes based on their titles. Such incompatibilities viewed as medical or cultural issues became a major concern in western societies. The gastronomy language represents an important challenge because of its elusiveness, its metaphors, and sometimes its catchy style. The recipe title processing brings together the analysis of short and domain-specific texts. We tackle these issues by building our algorithm on the basis of a common knowledge lexical semantic network. The experiment is reproducible. It uses freely available resources.

1 Introduction

The analysis of cooking recipes is a very challenging task when it comes to automatically detect the compatibility of a dish with a diet. Indeed, performing such detection given the dish title as it can be found in a restaurant menu implies solving the following issues:

- short text analysis: how to overcome the context scarcity?
- domain specific text analysis: how to select the relevant information for the processing?
- qualified output structure: how to reflect the shades of the nutritional incompatibility as it may be strict or calibrated (forbidden, undesirable, small quantity authorized, fully authorized ingredients)?

We shall tackle these issues by immersing domain specific knowledge into a large general knowledge lexical semantic network, then by building our algorithm on top of it. In terms of structure, the network we use is a directed

A. Holzinger et al. (Eds.): CD-MAKE 2017, LNCS 10410, pp. 346–366, 2017.
DOI: 10.1007/978-3-319-66808-6_23

graph where nodes may represent simple or compound terms, linguistic information, phrasal expressions, and sense refinements[1]. The arcs of the graph are directed, weighted, and typed according to the ontological, semantic, lexical associations between the nodes. They also may be semantically annotated (e.g. *malignant tumor* $\xrightarrow{characteristic/frequent}$ *poor prognosis*) which is useful for working with domain specific expert knowledge. During the traversal (interpretation) of the graph, the nodes and the arcs are referred to as respectively *terms* and *relationships*. Thus, in our discourse, a relationship is a quadruplet $R = \{term_{source}, type, weight, term_{target}\}$. The weight can be understood as an association force of the relationship between two terms of the network.

The aim of the present graph browsing experience is to obtain probabilistic incompatibility scores given a list of raw recipe titles and a lexical semantic network (directed, weighted, and typed graph). The paper will be structured as follows. First, we will evoke main state-of-the-art achievements related to short text analysis, cooking recipe analysis, and specific applications for the nutrition domain. Second, we will introduce our experimental setup. Third, we will describe our method. Finally, we will present and discuss the output of our system and sketch some possible evolutions and applications of the method.

2   State of the Art

Recipe titles can be viewed as short texts on a particular domain. In terms of semantic information required for the analysis and methodology, the processing of recipe titles can be considered as a possible specialization of some general method for short text analysis. Two approaches to short text processing will be highlighted in this section: knowledge based distributional method and logic based distributional method. The methods proposed for the analysis of domain specific texts (cooking recipes) are also relevant as they point out the selection of relevant information for domain specific text analysis. We will detail the main approaches to the analysis of cooking recipes and conclude this section by discussing the domain specific systems and the way the cooking recipes can be represented in order to facilitate their semantic processing.

An interesting example of a knowledge-based method for the short text analysis is the method developed by [11] in the framework of the Probase[2] lexical semantic network. As a knowledge resource, Probase is positioned as a graph database helping to better understand human communication and resolve ambiguities related to the human common sense knowledge. The Probase-based tools allow obtaining a concept distribution based on different scoring functions

---

[1] Unlike the dictionary sense, the sense refinement reflects the typical use of a term, its sense activated by a particular context.

[2] https://www.microsoft.com/en-us/research/project/probase/.

(conditional probability distribution[3], point-wise mutual information[4] etc.). In terms of relationship type representation, the publicly available Probase release only provides the *is-a* relationship data mined from billions of web pages. In the recent years, the research experiments using Probase has been focusing on segmentation, concept mapping, and sense disambiguation. As part of this work, [11] introduced a method for short text analysis that has been tested for analyzing queries. Prior to the analysis of short texts, the authors acquire knowledge from web corpus, Probase network as well as a verb and adjective dictionary It is stored as a set of resources such as co-occurrence network, *is-a* network, concept clusters, vocabularies etc. They solve the segmentation task by introducing a multi-fold heuristic for simple and multi-word term detection. It takes into account the presence of *is-a* and *co-occurrence* relationships between the candidate terms. Then, the terms are typed according to different categories: part of speech, concept/entity distinction etc. Finally, the disambiguation is done using the weighted vote (conceptual connections of the candidate term considering the "vote of context"). This method seems to be relevant for queries, however it would be difficult to apply it for the analysis of recipe titles and the detection of nutritional incompatibilities. The main difficulty comes from the fact that it is concept driven. Indeed, for a term such as "creme brulee", we obtain the concept distribution scores shown in the Table 1. Due to underlying semantic relationship types (*is-a; gloss* or *relatedness*), these examples bring very few information about the composition and the semantic environment (that needs considering relationship types expressing *part-whole, location, instrument, sensory characteristic* relationships) of the recipes and one can hardly qualify some of the returned scores (e.g. *off beat flavor*) in order to approximate the underlying relationship type. An improvement of the knowledge based distributional method could be made using an additional semantic resource containing a rich part-whole semantics[5] such as WordNet [9]. This type of resource could be used as a reference for a part-whole relationship discovery from large web corpus. There has been a number of proposals in the recent years and among them the semi-automatic approach proposed by [10]. A different kind of methods for short text analysis may rely on general-purpose first order probabilistic logic as shows the approach developed by [4]. In the framework of this hybrid method, the distributional semantics is used to represent the meaning of words. Some of the

---

[3] Conditional probability distribution of two discrete variables (words)

$$P(A|B) = \frac{P(A) \cap (B)}{P(B)} .$$

[4] Point-wise Mutual Information is calculated according to the formula:

$$PMI(x; y) = \log \frac{P(x,y)}{P(x)P(y)} .$$

[5] The WordNet part-whole relation splits into three more specific relationships: *member-of*, *stuff-of*, and *part-of*.

lexical and semantic relations such as synonymy and hyponymy can be predicted. The authors use them to generate an on-the-fly ontology that contains only the relevant information related to some current semantic analysis task. They argue that the first-order logic has a binary nature and thus cannot be graded. Therefore, they adopt probabilistic logic as it allows weighted first order logic formulas. The weight of the formulas corresponds to a certainty measure estimated from the distributional semantics. First, natural language sentences are mapped to a logical form (using the Boxer tool [5][6]). Second, the ontology is built and encoded in the form of weighted inference rules describing the semantic relations (the authors mention *hyponymy, synonymy, antonymy, contextonymy* i.e. the relation between "hospital" and "doctor"). Third, a probabilistic logic program answering the target task is created. Such program contains the evidence set, the rule base (RB, weighted first order logical expressions), and a query. It calculates the conditional probability $P(Query|Evidence, RB)$. This approach has been tested on the SICK[7] data for the tasks of semantic textual similarity detection and textual entailment recognizing. The results showed a good performance of this method over distributional only and logic only methods. This kind of approach rather considers lexical relations (revealing some linguistic phenomena), than purely semantic (language independent, world knowledge phenomena) relations. As the knowledge based distributional method, it suffers from the difficulty to qualify the relationships as it uses mainly the co-occurrence analysis.

Table 1. Concept distribution for *creme brulee* (Probase conceptualization tool)

Term (concept)	Score by MI	Score by $P(concept|entity)$
dessert	0.386	0.446
authentic bistro dish	0.164	0.12
off beat flavor	0.047	0.06
homemade dessert	0.046	0.048
dairy based dessert	0.04	0.036

---

[6] Boxer [5] is a semantic parser for English texts based on Discourse Representation Theory.

[7] *Sentences Involving Compositional Knowledge.* This dataset includes a large number of sentence pairs that are rich in the lexical, syntactic and semantic phenomena (e.g., contextual synonymy and other lexical variation phenomena, active/passive and other syntactic alternations, impact of negation, determiners and other grammatical elements). Each sentence pair was annotated for relatedness and entailment by means of crowd-sourcing techniques. http://clic.cimec.unitn.it/composes/sick.html.

The analysis of cooking recipes is a flourishing research area. Besides the approaches focused on flavor networks which consider cooking recipes as "bags of ingredients" with a remarkable contribution of [1], the existing approaches to the recipe analysis concentrate on recipes taken as a sequence of instructions that can be mapped to a series of actions. Numerous publications report the implementation supervised learning methods. For instance, [18] use the annotated data to extract predicate-argument structures from cooking instructions in Japanese in order to represent the recipe as a work flow. The first steps of this process are words segmentation and entity type recognition. The latter is based on the following entity types: Food, Quantity, Tool, Duration, State, chef's action, and foods' action. Therefore, this task is similar to the conceptualization process proposed by [11] in the framework of knowledge based short text analysis and discussed earlier in this section. Entity type recognition is followed by syntactic analysis that outputs a dependency tree. The final step aims at extracting predicate-argument triples from the disambiguated (through segmentation, entity type recognition, and dependency parsing) recipe text. In this approach, the semantic information that could be attached to the arcs is attached to the nodes. The node type together with the syntactic markers (i.e. case marker) helps determining the nature of the predicate argument relation. This method yields modest results and could be improved by using more annotations and also by adopting a more versatile graph structure (i.e. a structure with typed arcs). [13] proposed a similar approach as part of an unsupervised technique for mapping recipe instructions to actions based on a hard Expectation Maximization algorithm and a restricted set of verb argument types (*location, object*).

In the paradigm of semantic role labeling, the approach of [17] use a Markov decision process where ingredients and utensils are propagated over the temporal order of instructions and where the context information is stored in a latent vector which disambiguates and augments the instruction statement under analysis. In this approach, the context information corresponds to the state of the kitchen and integrates the changes of this state according to the evolving recipe instructions. The changes are only partially observed (the authors assume that some instruction details may be omitted in the recipe text) and the resulting model is object-oriented. Each world state corresponds to a set of objects (i.e. ingredients, containers) along with predicates (quantity, location, and condition) of each object. Each action of the process is represented by a verb with its various arguments (semantic roles). Such representation indicates how to transform the state. The model also uses a simple cooking simulator able to produce a new state from a stream of low-level instructions to reflect the world dynamics model $p(State_t | State_{t-1}, Action_t)$.

In the case based reasoning paradigm, [8] represent the cooking instructions as a work-flow and thus propose a method for the automatic acquisition of a rich case representation of cooking recipes for process-oriented case-based reasoning from free recipe text. The cooking process is represented using the Allen [3] algebra extended with relations over interval durations. After applying classical NLP tools for segmentation, part-of speech tagging, syntactic analysis, the extraction process from texts focuses on the anaphora resolution and verb argument analysis. The actions are modeled on the basis of the instructional text *without* considering the implicit information proper to the cooking recipes. The underlying knowledge resource is the case-based reasoning system Taaable [7].

Despite the variety of their theoretical background, the existing methods of cuisine texts analysis converge on the necessity to have a richer context around the terms present in the input text. Such context can be obtained using the following approaches:

- specific meta-language such as MILK[8], proposed as a part of the SOUR CREAM project [23], SIMMR [12][9]. SOUR CREAM stands for "System to Organize and Understand Recipes, Capacitating Relatively Exciting Applications Meanwhile". MILK has been proposed as a machine-readable target language to create sets of instructions that represent the actions demanded by the recipe statements. It is based on first-order logic, but allows handling the temporal order as well as creation/deletion of ingredients. A small corpus of 250 recipes has been manually annotated using MILK (CURD (Carnegie Mellon University Recipe Database)). Similarly, SIMMR [12] allows to represent a recipe as a dependency tree. The leaves of the tree are the recipe ingredients and its internal nodes are the recipe instructions. Such representation supports semantic parsing. MILK tags have been used to construct the SIMMR trees. The authors also propose a parser to generate SIMMR trees from the raw recipe text. Machine learning methods (SVM classification) have then been used for instruction-ingredient linking, instruction-instruction linking using SIMMR;
- dynamic structures such as latent vector used by [17] and described earlier in this section;
- graph-shaped resources (ontologies, semantic networks) and their use by projection on the text under scope (as described earlier in this section).

Among the projects centered on building specific resources and applications for the food and nutrition domain, the PIPS[10] project and the OASIS[11] project appeared as pioneering large-scale European ventures dedicated to the promotion of healthy food practices and to the building of counseling systems for the nutrition field. The PIPS project proposed a food ontology for the diabetes control whereas the OASIS project focused on nutritional practices of elderly people. Later on, some work has been centered on menu generation considered as a multi-level optimization issue (MenuGene [20])[12]. Other authors introduced the proposal of alternative menus (Semanticook [2]). The case-based reasoning Taaable [7][13] system evolved in the same direction and has been provided with

---

[8] *Minimal Instruction Language for the Kitchen.*
[9] *Simplified Ingredient Merging Map in Recipes.*
[10] http://cordis.europa.eu/project/rcn/71245_en.html. Concepts such as *diet, nutrient, calories* have been modeled in the framework of this project.
[11] http://www.oasis-project.eu/.
[12] http://www.menugene.com/.
[13] http://wikitaaable.loria.fr.

nutritional values as well as nutritional restrictions and geographical features related to the recipes stored in the case base. However, in this paradigm, a formal representation of recipes in terms of semantic properties (directed acyclic graph) is mandatory. The Taaable knowledge repository and the formal framework of this system allow the representation of incompatibilities based on nutritional values and the subsumption relation i.e. *alcohol free, cholesterol free, gluten free, gout, vegan, vegetarian, nut free.*

We briefly introduced the main approaches capable of handling recipe title analysis. Nevertheless, to our knowledge, there has been no proposals of a system designed for recipes or recipe titles analysis in order to determine nutritional incompatibilities against a list of diets (medical or cultural). In the next section, we will propose this kind of system based on a general knowledge lexical semantic network.

3   Experimental Setup

3.1   Problem Statement

The problem can be stated as follows: how to detect nutritional restrictions from raw data using a background knowledge resource (lexical semantic network), rank the obtained incompatibility scores, and maximize the confidence about the scores. We leave the last point for future work.

3.2   Nutritional Incompatibility Representation

For our experiment, we use the recipe representation shared by the recipe content owners and available at schema.org[14]. In the scope of technical and semantic interoperability, we focus on the property *suitableForDiet* which concerns the concept *Recipe* and, subsequently the type *RestrictableDiet* and its instances defined as follows: *DiabeticDiet, GlutenFreeDiet, HalalDiet, HinduDiet, KosherDiet, LowCalorieDiet, LowFatDiet, LowLactoseDiet, LowSaltDiet, VeganDiet, VegetarianDiet.* Thus, our results may be easily encoded in the widely shared format in order to enhance the existing recipe representation. For these diets, we automatically extracted and manually validated an initial set of approximately 200 forbidden ingredients. We used domain-specific resources (lists of ingredients) found on the Web for this step. These ingredients (if not already present in our graph-based knowledge resource) have been encoded as nodes and linked to the nodes representing the diets listed above by the arcs typed *r_incompatible.* The nutritional restrictions differ in terms of their semantic structure which may rely on nutritional composition (*part-whole* relation), cutting types (*holonymy* etc.), cooking state (i.e. boiled carrots are undesirable in case of diabetes). Basically, the incompatibility detection is a non linear classification problem as one recipe may be incompatible with several diets and with a different "degree" of incompatibility. Therefore, it needs a qualifying approach as

---

[14] schema.org/Recipe.

in some cases (i.e. diabetes, low salt) a food may be not strictly forbidden but rather taken with caution.

3.3   Corpus

For our experiment we used a set of 5 000 recipe titles in French, which corresponds to a corpus[15] . of 19 000 words and a vocabulary of 2 900 terms (after removing stop words and irrelevant expressions such as "tarte tatin *à ma façon*", *tarte tatin my way*). This data mirrors the French urban culinary tradition as well as the established practice of searching the Web for recipes. The most important terms (and their number of occurrences in the corpus) are salade *salad* (157); tarte, poulet *tart, chicken* (124); soupe *soup* (112); facile *easy* (93); chocolat *chocolate* (89); saumon, gâteau *salmon, pastry* (87); légume, confiture *vegetable, jam* (86). These occurrences highlight the terms for which we need to have more details in our knowledge resource to perform the analysis.

3.4   Knowledge Resource

Why Using a Large General Knowledge Resource? The data scarcity proper to the recipe titles is an important obstacle to their processing. If we focus on a plain co-occurrence analysis and compare our corpus to the list of forbidden ingredients, we only obtain 998 straightforward incompatibilities i.e. for which the forbidden ingredient is part of the recipe title and no specific analysis is needed to detect it. Distributional scores used by [4,11] may be interesting in terms of flavor associations, but they also demonstrate that we need to know more about the most likely semantic neighborhood of the term to handle the part-whole semantics and incompatibility analysis.

Enhancing the Knowledge Resource for the Analysis. The semantic resource we use for the experiments is the RezoJDM lexical semantic network for French[16]. This resource stems from the game with a purpose AI project JeuxDeMots [14]. Built and constantly improved by crowd-sourcing (games with a purpose, direct contribution), RezoJDM is a directed, typed, and weighted graph. Today it contains 1.4 M nodes and 90 M relations divided into more than 100 types. The structural properties of the network have been detailed in [15] and later in [6], its inference and annotation mechanisms respectively by [22,24]. The ever ending process of graph population[17] is carried on using different techniques including games with a purpose, crowd-sourcing, mapping to other semantic and

---

[15] The corpus has been collected from the following Web resources : *15%* www. cuisineaz.fr, *20%* www.cuisinelibre.org *et 65%* www.allrecipe.fr.

[16] http://www.jeuxdemots.org/jdm-about.php.

[17] The process of either inferring new relationships from the terms and relationships already present in the network or sourcing new terms and relationships through user contribution or by automatically identifying and retrieving lexical and semantic relationships from texts or other semantic resources.

knowledge resources such as Wikipedia or BabelNet [19]. In addition, endogenous inference mechanisms, introduced by [24] are also used to populate the graph. They rely on the transitivity of the *is-a*, *hyponym*, and *synonym* relationships and are built for handling polysemy. In addition to the hierarchical relation types (*is-a* relation, *part-whole* relations), RezoJDM contains grammatical relations (*part-of-speech*), causal, thematic relations as well as relations of generativist flavor (ex. *telic role*). This resource is considered as a closed world i.e. every information that is not present in the graph is assumed as false. Therefore, the domain specific subgraph of the resource related to food and nutrition has been populated in order to allow cuisine text analysis.

It has been demonstrated by [22] that, for the sake of precision, general and domain specific knowledge should not be separated. Thus, for our experiment we do not build any specific knowledge resource dedicated to the recipe analysis. Instead, we immerse nutrition, sensory, technical knowledge into RezoJDM to enhance the coverage of the graph. This has been done partly through the direct contribution. External resources such as domain specific lexicons and terminological resources have been used. In particular, some equivalence and synonym relation triples have been extracted from IATE[18] term base[19]. The Agrovoc[20] thesaurus provided only a few new terms; it contained no relevant relations. Additionally, as RezoJDM can be enhanced using crowd-sourcing methods and, in particular, games with a purpose, specific game with a purpose assignments have been given to the JeuxDeMots (contribution interface for RezoJDM) players. Today (June 2017) the domain specific subgraph corresponds to 40 K terms (approximately 2.8% of the RezoJDM). The overall adaptation process took about 3 weeks.

In the framework of our experiment, we use *taxonomy* relations, *part-whole* relations, *object-mater* relations and, in some cases, *hyponymy* and *characteristic* relations. Running the experiment involves preprocessing steps (identifying multi-word terms, lemmatization, disambiguation using the *refinement scheme* [14] of our resource), browsing the graph following path constraints, scoring possible incompatibilities, and finally normalizing scores. Among other approaches using a similar plot, [21] use ConceptNet [16] network for the semantic analysis task.

4   Method

In this section, we shall detail the pre-processing steps, describe how we move from plain text to the graph-based representation,detail the graph browsing strategy for nutritional incompatibility detection, detail our the method evaluation and discuss the current results yielded by our system.

---

[18] http://iate.europa.eu/switchLang.do?success=mainPage\&lang=fr.

[19] The part of the IATE resource that has been used corresponds to the subject field 6006, French.

[20] http://aims.fao.org/fr/agrovoc.

Table 2. Pre-processed recipe titles. Expressions relevant for the domain (i.e. 1, 2) as well as multi-word terms (i.e. 3, 4), and phrases (i.e. 5) are detected, spaces are replaced by the underscore symbol to facilitate the further processing. Sometimes, two segmentations are possible for the same input: *confiture_de_cerises* and *cerises_noires*. In such cases, the contrast is favored: *black_cherry* is more informative than *cherry_jam* as the semantics of *jam* is independent from the semantics of *cherry* or *cherry_jam*. In our resource, semantics can be explored by looking at the outgoing semantic relationships of *confiture* compared to that of *confiture_de_cerises* or at least by looking at the *out* degree of the nodes corresponding to these two segments. In this particular case, the concordance between *cerises* and *noires* (both in plural) helps to consolidate the choice guided by semantics.

French (*English*)
1. Carpe à_la_forestière
(*Forest_style carp*)
2. Carré d'agneau dans_son_jus
(*Rack of lamb in_its_own_jus*)
3. Waterzoí de lieu_noir
(*Coley waterzooí*)
4. Verrines de lentilles au saumon_fumé
(*Lentil and smoked_salmon verrines*)
5. Gâteau_basque à la confiture de cerises_noires
(*Basque_cake with black_cherry jam*)

4.1 Pre-processing

The preprocessing step includes text segmentation which relies on the multi-word lexical entities detection, followed by stop-words removal. The multi-word term detection is done in two steps. First, the recipe titles are cut into n-grams using a dynamic-length sliding window ($2 \leq 4$). Second, the segments are compared to the lexical entries present in RezoJDM which is therefore used as a dictionary. In RezoJDM, the multi-word terms are related to their "parts" by the relation typed *locution* (or "phrase"). This relation is useful for compound terms analysis. Bi-grams and trigrams are the most frequent structures in the domain-specific subgraph as well as in RezoJDM. Indeed, they represent respectively 28% and 16% of the overall set of multi-word terms and expressions (300 K units). For our experiment, we often opted for trigrams which turned out to be more informative (i.e. correspond to nodes with a higher out degree). The preprocessed text examples are given in the Table 2.

We used a dump RezoJDM[21] stored as a Neo4j[22] graph database. It is also possible to use special purpose API targeted at real time browsing of RezoJDM, Requeter Rezo[23].

4.2 From Text to Graph

Starting from a sequence $w_1, w_2, ...w_n$ of n terms, we build a "context" namely the lemmatized and disambiguated representation of the recipe title under scope. Such context is the entry point to our knowledge resource.

A context C is a sequence of nodes (the text order is preserved): $C_{w_1,w_2,...w_n} = n_{w_1}, n_{w_2}, ...n_{w_n}$ where the node n_{w_n} is the most precise syntactic and semantic representation of the surface form available in our resource. To obtain such representation we search for the node corresponding to the surface form if it exists[24]. Then, we yield its refinement (usage) if the term is polysemic. The irrelevant refinements are discriminated using a list of key terms that define our domain (i.e. thematic subgraph within a lexical semantic network). The identification of the refinement is done through the cascade processing of relationships of a node typed *refinement*, *domain*, and *meaning*. The choice between several lemmas (i.e. multiple POS problem) is handled by stating[25]: $\forall a \forall b \forall c \forall x, lemma'(b,a) \land lemma''(c,a) \land pos(x,a) \land pos(x,b) \Rightarrow Lemma(b,a)$. For a term a having multiple lemmas such as b and c, we check whether the part of speech (represented as a relationship typed r_pos) for b and c is the same as the part of speech for a. We choose the lemma with the same part of speech as the term a. The context creation function returns for *quiche au thon et aux tomates* (*quiche with tuna and tomatos*) the result *[quiche (préparation culinaire), thon (poisson,chair), tomate légume-fruit]*, respectively: "quiche (preparation), tuna (fish flesh), tomato (fruit-vegetable)".

For each node $n_i \in C$ we explore paths $S = ((n_1 a_r n_2), (n_2 a_r n_3), (n_{m-1} a_r n_m))$. The type of relationships we choose for the graph traversal depends on the local category of the node:

1. If $isa("preparation", n_i)$[26], $r \in \{hypo, part - whole, matter\}$.
   This is the case of mixtures, dishes and other complex ingredients;
2. If $isa("ingredient", n_i)$ (see Footnote 26), $r \in \{isa, syn, part - whole, matter, charac\}$.
   It is the case of plain ingredients like *tomato*.

---

[21] http://www.jeuxdemots.org/jdm-about.php.

[22] https://neo4j.com/docs/java-reference/current/javadocs/.

[23] https://github.com/lirmm-texte/RequeterRezo.

[24] In the opposite case the acquisition process through external resources like Wikipedia, Web and through crowd-sourcing (Games with a purpose) may be triggered (if an open world hypothesis is favored).

[25] First Order Logic notation.

[26] *idem.*

The weight of all relations we traverse must be strictly positive. We traverse the graph testing a range of conditions: relevance to the domain of interest D_{alim} (food domain), existence of a path of a certain length (≤ 2) and type between the candidate node and the rest of the context under analysis, co-meronymy relation etc.

To obtain relevant results, two conditions are to be fulfilled. First, there must be a disambiguation strategy and a domain filtering. Second, the similarity has to be handled between the *preparation* and its hyponyms. Indeed, the exploration of the *part-whole* relations of the network refers to *all the possible* ingredients and constituents of the *preparation*. If the *preparation* has a conceptual role (i.e. "cake"), the *part-whole* relations analysis will output a lot of noise. In our example, it is important to grasp the absence of *pork (meat)* and the presence of *tuna (fish)* in the *quiche* under scope. Therefore, instead of directly exploring the *part-whole* relations of the *quiche(preparation)*, we rather try to find similar *quiche(preparation)* hyponyms for the context $C=$ "quiche (preparation), tuna (fish flesh), tomato (fruit-vegetable)" and yield the typical parts they have in common with the generic *quiche(preparation)*. Our function finds the hyponym which maximizes the similarity score. This score is a normalized Jaccard index over all the positive outgoing *part-whole, isa, matter* relations.

$$J(S_C, S_{C_{hypo}}) = \frac{S_C \cap S_{C_{hypo}}}{S_C \cup S_{C_{hypo}}}$$ where C_{hypo} is the hyponym context built on the go.

Different threshold values have been experimented. Empirically, the threshold fixed at 0.30 allows capturing generic similarities such as (for our example) *quiche saumon courgette* ("quiche salmon zucchini") score = 0.32, a quiche with some fish and a vegetable. More precise similarity corresponds to higher scores.

Using the described strategy, the irrelevant recipes such as *quiche lorraine* (score = 0.20) are efficiently discriminated. Once the relevant hyponym is identified, its *part-whole* neighbors can be grasped. A specific graph traversal strategy is used for the LowSalt diet. It includes exploring the *characteristic* relation type for the *preparation* and its parts.

4.3   From Graph to Associations

The incompatibility calculation takes as input the list of diets and the queue F containing terms related to main context. This function looks for an incompatibility path S_{inc} such that $N' \in F \wedge S_{inc} = ((N', r_{type}, N), (N, r_{inc}, N_{DIET})) \wedge type \in (holo|isa|haspart|substance|hypo)$.

Algorithm 1. Creation of diet incompatibility scores

Input : text *RecipeTitle*, lexical semantic network *RezoJDM*, node *Régime*
Output : Key-value pair *Result* ← ∅
Local variables : list *LContext, LNodes, LProcessed, LSkip, LRelationTypes, LResult*, float[] *score*
Local functions : makeContext, relatedToContext, lookupIncompatible
/* Initialize general lists */
LSkip ← ListOfNodes (à éviter)
/*too general terms i.e. *aliment*("food") */
LRelationsContexte ← {r_lemma, r_raff, r_domain, r_meaning}
LRelationTypes ← {r_isa, r_syn, r_part, r_matter, r_holo,r_hypo}
/* Initialize local lists */
LContext ← makeContext(*RecipeTitle*)
LNodes← relatedToContext (*LContext*,

$x \in \{ContextNode \xrightarrow{R} x > 0\}$, R ∈ *LRelationTypes*)
/* incompatibility */
for all *Node* ∈ *LNodes* **do**
    LResult ← lookupIncompatible (*LNodes*, $x \in \{Node \xrightarrow{R} x > 0\}$,
    R ∈ *LRelationTypes* && $x \xrightarrow{R_{incompatible}} Diet$), score
    LProcessed ← *LProcessed* · *Node*
end for
/*appending RecipeTitle and its scores*/
Result[RecipeTitle][] ← LResult
Return Result

The output is a key value pair (*diet, score*). The score depends on the distance in the RezoJDM graph and on the relation type between the diet and the incompatible node in the context. Besides the *refinement* relation type[27], it is calculated as follows for the distance $d : \frac{1}{1+d}$. The score for the whole context corresponds to the addition of the individual scores of the context nodes. It is adapted in order to bring it closer to a probability distribution and allow further statistical or predictive processing. Starting from the precited context, our system first obtains a list of nodes linked to the context. Then, after following a traversal strategy, it comes up with a list of probabilistic scores for each part of the context. I.e. (w corresponds to *weight* and d corresponds to *distance*) :

```
recipe : quiche thon tomate
context size 3
[quiche>preparation,thon>poisson,tomate>legume]
processing incompatible for quiche>preparation
r_hypo quiche lorraine d=1 w=76
simcontext [quiche,lorraine]
Jaccard index [quiche,lorraine] 0.20
isSimilar=false
```

---

[27] Which participates to the disambiguation process.

Further similarity processing as described in Sect. 4.2, then processing of parts shared by quiche and its hyponyms similar to the context. For each part, the *isa, part-whole, mater* and *characteristic* relations are further explored

```
r_has_part pte d=1 w=6 *dough*
r_has_part gruyere rape d=1 w=105 *grated Gruyere*
r_has_part oeufs d=1 w=105 *eggs*
r_has_part creme d=1 w=105 *cream*
etc.

raw incompatibility scores quiche>preparation
Diabetes 1.3, LowLactose 3.0, Halal 0.0,
Kosher 0.3, LowCalories 1.5, LowSalt 0.5,
LowGluten 1.8, Hindu 0.5, LowFat 0.8,
Vegan 0.5, Vegetarian 0.3
```

LowLactose incompatibility detected. LowSalt, LowCalories, Kosher, Hindu, Vegetarian and Vegan incompatibilities suspected.

```
processing incompatible for thon>poisson
r_similar bonite d=1 w=26 *skipjack*
r_object_mater poisson>chair d=1 w=30 *fish (flesh)*
r_carac sal d=1 w=36 *salted*
r_carac cru>171869 d=1 w=1 *raw*
r_carac en conserve d=1 w=35 *canned*
r_carac savoureux>got d=1 w=34 *delicious (taste)*
r_isa ltre vivant d=1 w=82 *living being*
r_isa poisson d=1 w=192 *fish*
etc.

raw incompatibility scores for thon>poisson *tuna (fish)*
Diabetes 0.0, LowLactose 0.0, Halal 0.0,
Kosher 0.0, LowCalories 0.0, LowSalt 2.0,
LowGluten 0.0, Hindu 3.0, LowFat 0.0,
Vegan 3.0, Vegetarian 3.0
```

Vegetarian and Vegan incompatibility confirmed, LowSalt detected, Hindu incompatibility detected. No incompatibilities have been detected for *tomato*.

The output can be "normalized" in a probabilistic fashion according to the following rule applied to the raw score $s \in L_s$ (raw list of scores) in order to produce a probabilistic score s_p : if $s \geq 0.5$, $s_p \leftarrow 1$, if $s \leq 0.5$, $s_p \leftarrow 0.5$. The range of this new score is restricted to three possible values: compatible (0), uncertain (0.5), and incompatible (1).

```
final probabilistic scores
Diabetes 0.5, LowLactose 1.0, Halal 0.0,
Kosher 0.5, LowCalories 1.0, LowSalt 1.0,
LowGluten 1.0, Hindu 1.0, LowFat 1.0,
Vegan 1.0, Vegetarian 1.0
```

Thus, if we imagine a restaurant scenario, where a client would be informed about the strict incompatibility or compatibility of a dish with his or her nutritional restrictions and alerted about some potential incompatibilities that would need further information from the caterer to be confirmed or denied. Given a list of diets, for some of them, we can only output a probabilistic score. Indeed, in our example, we highly suspect the Diabetes incompatibility and the LowCalories incompatibility but nothing in the semantic environment gives us a full confidence.

The list of terms that are not present in the resource (for example, *sibnekh*, *zwiebelkuchen*) is output by the system. It serves to the further improvement of the RezoJDM graph from external resources. The incompatibility scores are also used for the ever ending learning process as they may form candidate terms for RezoJDM, influence the weight of the existing relations etc.

4.4   Evaluation and Discussion

The system has been evaluated using a incompatibility annotated corpus of 1 500 recipe titles. The evaluation data has been partially collected using structured document retrieval simultaneously with the raw corpus constitution. Relevant meta-tags (HTML tags present in micro-formats[28]) have been used to pre-build incompatibility scores. The overlap between the different diets (vegan recipes are compatible with a vegetarian diet, low fat recipes are convenient for the low calories diet etc.) has been taken into account. The labels have been adjusted and enriched (LowSalt, Kosher diets) by hand by the authors of the system because the structured meta-tags do not contain such information. The obtained evaluation scores are binary. For now, as our system is under improvement, we estimated that the score returned by the system should be ≥ 0.5 to be ranked as acceptable. Later, a finer grained evaluation will be adopted.

Our results are listed in the Table 3. It is expressed in terms of precision, recall and f-measure (F1 score)[29]. The most important score is the precision as, for an allergic or intolerant restaurant customer, even a very small quantity of

---

[28] Micro-formats(μF) refer to standardized semantic markup of web-pages.

[29] F1 score is calculated as follows

$$F_1 = 2 \cdot \frac{Precision \times Recall}{Precision + Recall}$$

where *Precision* corresponds to all relevant answers returned by the search and *Recall* to all relevant documents that are successfully retrieved.

Table 3. Corpus-based evaluation. We specify the repartition between the 3 possible probabilistic scores in the whole corpus and detail the quality of our scoring for an sub-corpus annotated for evaluation. The evaluation set is a subset of our corpus annotated in incompatibilities. We totally ignore the annotations during the processing.

Diet and scores	Corpus			Evaluation set		
	0	0.5	1	Precision	Recall	F-score
diabetes	344	1667	2989	92%	92%	92%
low lactose	1410	1856	1733	71%	73%	72%
halal	1629	3140	231	65%	75%	70%
kosher	1307	3453	240	67%	60%	63%
low calories	2540	122	2338	60%	75%	67%
low salt	3491	1312	197	88%	65%	75%
low gluten	589	2961	1450	80%	73%	76%
hindu	568	3939	493	86%	80%	83%
low fat	2161	2636	203	67%	70%	68%
vegan	454	4261	285	80%	90%	85%
vegetarian	360	1655	2985	83%	90%	86%
macro-average				**76%**	**77%**	**76%**
totals	**14 852**	**27 004**	**13 144**			

a forbidden product may be dangerous. The average value correspond to the macro-average[30].

For the halal diet, there are very few terms in the graph that point to this diet. The LowCalories and Vegetarian diets are well known among the RezoJDM community and well represented in the graph. In 13% of cases, the graph traversal did not return any result as the terms corresponding to the words of the context do not exist in the graph. It was the case of borrowings (such as *quinotto*) or lexical creations[31] (i.e. *anti-tiramisu* as our analysis scheme doesn't take into account morphology). The average number of incompatibility scores $\neq 0$ per recipe title is of about 3.8. Traditional diets (such as halal diet and kosher diet) have been very challenging as the nature of nutritional restriction for them may concern food associations. The low salt diet incompatibility detection is still difficult because salt is everywhere and it is sometimes difficult to find a criterion to separate the property from the possibility of being salted.

---

[30] Macro average refers to the arithmetic mean, $AM = \frac{1}{n}(a_1 + a_2 + ... + a_n)$, F-score average is therefore the harmonic mean of precision average rate and recall average rate.

[31] The term *lexical creation* refers to the neology (creation of new terms). The commonly established general typology of neology distinguishes *denominative* and *expressive* neology. Denominative neology is used to refer to the creation of new lexical units to denominate new concepts, objects, and realities. The expressive neology refers to the use of lexical creation to introduce different subjective nuances.

Table 4. Mean values per diet (evaluation)

Diet	Mean (M)	Standard deviation (SD)	Comment
diabetes	0.785	0.295	$M \geq 0.5$ and $SD \leq 0.5 \implies$ confidence about the incompatibility
low lactose	0.200	0.215	$M \leq 0.5$ and $SD \leq 0.5 \implies$ uniform scores but low confidence
halal	0.240	0.239	$M \leq 0.5$ and $SD \leq 0.5 \implies$ uniform scores but low confidence
kosher	0.275	0.243	$M \leq 0.5$ and $SD \leq 0.5 \implies$ uniform scores but low confidence
low calories	0.487	0.484	M and SD close to 0.5 $\implies$ confident but sparse (scores may be very low or quite high), the data is unequally distributed in the resource, more relationship types should be explored
low salt	0.031	0.094	very few incompatibilities detected with low confidence, finer grained approach is needed (i.e. relationship annotation)
low gluten	0.549	0.349	good confidence but scores vary a lot, knowledge consolidation needed
hindu	0.447	0.244	M close to 0.5 and $SD \leq 0.5 \implies$ uniform scores, satisfactory confidence at the consolidation stage
low fat	0.380	0.202	$M \leq 0.5$ and $SD \leq 0.5 \implies$ uncertain scores
vegan	0.406	0.219	$M \leq 0.5$ and $SD \leq 0.5 \implies$ uncertain scores
vegetarian	0.809	0.253	$M \geq 0.5$ and $SD \leq 0.5 \implies$ confidence about the incompatibility, benchmark result
overall	**0.406**	0.219	low confidence but uniform scores

Given the specificity of our resource, a low score may depend on the lack of some relevant information in the graph. Thus, the output may be considered as correct (at least at the development stage) but with a low "confidence" which corresponds to a lower mean[32] value.

The mean and standard deviation values reveal this confidence issue (Table 4). A lower mean value together with a low deviation indicates that there were too many uncertain scores (≤ 0.5) among the resulting scores of a particular diet. To maximize the confidence related to the score, the knowledge resource must be continuously enhanced. Today this is achieved using two main strategies: exogenous and endogenous. The first one may include term extraction from corpora, relationship identification based on word embeddings, direct contribution, specific games with a purpose assignments. The second one refers to propagation of the relations already existing in the graph using inference schemes based

---

[32] The mean, as it is understood here, weights each score s_i according to its probability given the dataset, s_i. Thus, $\mu = \sum s_i p_i$.

on the transitivity of the *isa, part-whole*, and *synonym* semantic relations as proposed by [24].

4.5   Discussion

Using a lexical semantic network for text processing offers some clear advantages. First, the background knowledge management is handy as there is no need to use multiple data structures (lists, vocabularies, taxonomies, ontologies) during the processing. Second, the graph structure supports encoding various kinds of information that can be useful for text processing tasks. Every piece of information encoded using the graph formalism is machine interpretable and can be accessed during the traversal. Thus, the graph interpretation algorithms can be more accessible to domain specialists. Finally, the graph based analysis strategy has an explanatory feature, it is always possible to know why the system returned some particular output. However, two main issues must be tackled: the knowledge resource **population** method and the **filtering** strategy while traversing the resource. Our resource is only available for French. To test the **interoperability of the system**, we run our approach using the ConceptNet common knowledge network and tested it on a restricted set of recipe titles in English that are also available in the French culinary tradition (here we cite the examples of *veal blanquette* and *banana bread*). Then, the obtained probabilistic incompatibility scores have been compared across languages. The values are given as follows: "score for French [score for English]".

```
"blanquette de veau" ["veal blanquette"]
Vegan 1.0[0.5],Vegetarian 1.0[0.5]
Hindu 1.0[0.5],Diabetes 0.6[0.0],
LowLactose 0.5[0.0],Kosher 0.4[0.0],
LowFat 0.4[0.0], LowSalt 0.4[0.0]

"cake à la banane" ["banana bread"]
Diabetes 1.0[1.0], LowLactose 0.5[0.0]
LowGluten 0.5[0.0], LowFat 0.5[0.0]
Vegan 0.5[0.5]
```

We can see that the some incompatibilities have been detected using subsumption and hierarchical relations To grasp the *kosher* incompatibility (meat cooked into a creamy sauce) or the LowLactose incompatibility (banana bread may contain some butter), we would need to either extend or specify the *part-whole* relation in order to cover the *matter/substance* relation. We probably need finer grained relations such as *patient, receivesAction* etc. This additional testing showed that the approach introduced here is a generic approach, further performance improvement mainly depends on the data contained in the resource.

5   Conclusion

We introduced the use of a lexical-semantic network for nutritional incompatibility detection based on recipe titles. The scores obtained by our system can be used for building specific resources for machine learning tasks such as classifier training. Our experiments showed the implementation of a graph browsing strategy for incompatibility detection. Knowledge resource projection on raw text is a relevant method for short text analysis. Among the perspectives of the approach, we can list:

- exogenous approaches (using external resources and processes to populate the graph) for the graph population;
- endogenous approaches to the graph population (i.e. propagating the relevant relationships over the RezoJDM graph, relationship annotation);
- mapping the resource to other existing semantic resources (domain specific ontologies, other wide-coverage semantic resources such as BabelNet [19]);
- making the system evolve towards a multilingual (language independent?) nutritional incompatibility detection.

An important advantage of the system over purely statistical approaches is its explanatory feature, we can always know how the system came to its decision and thus can constantly improve it. The limitations of our contribution are linked to its improvement model which is based on contribution work and the necessity to (weakly) validate the new relations.

References

1. Ahn, Y.Y., Ahnert, S.E., Bagrow, J.P., Barabási, A.L.: Flavor network and the principles of food pairing. CoRR abs/1111.6074 (2011)
2. Akkoç, E., Cicekli, N.K.: Semanticook: a web application for nutrition consultancy for diabetics. In: García-Barriocanal, E., Cebeci, Z., Okur, M.C., Öztürk, A. (eds.) MTSR 2011. CCIS, vol. 240, pp. 215–224. Springer, Heidelberg (2011). doi:10.1007/978-3-642-24731-6_23
3. Allen, J.F.: An interval-based representation of temporal knowledge. In: Proceedings of the 7th International Joint Conference on Artificial Intelligence, IJCAI 1981, Vancouver, BC, Canada, 24–28 August, 1981, pp. 221–226 (1981). http://ijcai.org/Proceedings/81-1/Papers/045.pdf
4. Beltagy, I., Erk, K., Mooney, R.: Semantic parsing using distributional semantics and probabilistic logic. In: Proceedings of ACL 2014 Workshop on Semantic Parsing (SP-2014), Baltimore, MD, pp. 7–11, June 2014. http://www.cs.utexas.edu/users/ai-lab/pub-view.php?PubID=127440
5. Bos, J.: Open-domain semantic parsing with boxer. In: Proceedings of the 20th Nordic Conference of Computational Linguistics, NODALIDA, 11–13 May 2015, Institute of the Lithuanian Language, Vilnius, Lithuania, pp. 301–304 (2015). http://aclweb.org/anthology/W/W15/W15-1841.pdf
6. Chatzikyriakidis, S., Lafourcade, M., Ramadier, L., Zarrouk, M.: Type theories and lexical networks: using serious games as the basis for multi-sorted typed systems. In: ESSLLI: European Summer School in Logic, Language and Information, Barcelona, Spain, August 2015. https://hal.archives-ouvertes.fr/hal-01216589

7. Cordier, A., Dufour-Lussier, V., Lieber, J., Nauer, E., Badra, F., Cojan, J., Gaillard, E., Infante-Blanco, L., Molli, P., Napoli, A., Skaf-Molli, H.: Taaable: a case-based system for personalized cooking. In: Montani, S., Jain, L.C. (eds.) Successful Case-Based Reasoning Applications-2. SCI, vol. 494, pp. 121–162. Springer, Heidelberg (2014). doi:10.1007/978-3-642-38736-4_7
8. Dufour-Lussier, V., Ber, F.L., Lieber, J., Meilender, T., Nauer, E.: Semi-automatic annotation process for procedural texts: An application on cooking recipes. CoRR abs/1209.5663 (2012). http://arxiv.org/abs/1209.5663
9. Fellbaum, C. (ed.): WordNet An Electronic Lexical Database. The MIT Press, Cambridge, May 1998. http://mitpress.mit.edu/catalog/item/default.asp?ttype=2&tid=8106
10. Girju, R., Badulescu, A., Moldovan, D.I.: Automatic discovery of part-whole relations. Comput. Linguist. **32**(1), 83–135 (2006). https://doi.org/10.1162/coli.2006.32.1.83
11. Hua, W., Wang, Z., Wang, H., Zheng, K., Zhou, X.: Short text understanding through lexical-semantic analysis. In: International Conference on Data Engineering (ICDE), April 2015. https://www.microsoft.com/en-us/research/publication/short-text-understanding-through-lexical-semantic-analysis/
12. Jermsurawong, J., Habash, N.: Predicting the structure of cooking recipes. In: Màrquez, L., Callison-Burch, C., Su, J., Pighin, D., Marton, Y. (eds.) EMNLP, pp. 781–786. The Association for Computational Linguistics (2015)
13. Kiddon, C., Ponnuraj, G., Zettlemoyer, L., Choi, Y.: Mise en place: Unsupervised interpretation of instructional recipes, pp. 982–992. Association for Computational Linguistics (ACL) (2015)
14. Lafourcade, M.: Making people play for lexical acquisition with the JeuxDeMots prototype. In: SNLP 2007: 7th International Symposium on Natural Language Processing, p. 7. Pattaya, Chonburi, Thailand, December 2007. https://hal-lirmm.ccsd.cnrs.fr/lirmm-00200883
15. Lafourcade, M.: Lexicon and semantic analysis of texts - structures, acquisition, computation and games with words. Habilitation à diriger des recherches, Université Montpellier II - Sciences et Techniques du Languedoc, December 2011. https://tel.archives-ouvertes.fr/tel-00649851
16. Liu, H., Singh, P.: Conceptnet – a practical commonsense reasoning tool-kit. BT Technol. J. **22**(4), 211–226 (2004)
17. Malmaud, J., Wagner, E., Chang, N., Murphy, K.: Cooking with semantics. In: Proceedings of the ACL 2014 Workshop on Semantic Parsing, pp. 33–38. Association for Computational Linguistics, Baltimore, June 2014. http://www.aclweb.org/anthology/W/W14/W14-2407
18. Mori, S., Sasada, T., Yamakata, Y., Yoshino, K.: A machine learning approach to recipe text processing (2012)
19. Navigli, R., Ponzetto, S.P.: BabelNet: the automatic construction, evaluation and application of a wide-coverage multilingual semantic network. Artif. Intell. **193**, 217–250 (2012)
20. Pinter, B., Vassányi, I., Gaál, B., Mák, E., Kozmann, G.: Personalized nutrition counseling expert system. In: Jobbágy, Á. (eds.) 5th European Conference of the International Federation for Medical and Biological Engineering. IFMBE Proceedings, vol 37, pp. 957–960. Springer, Heidelberg (2012)
21. Poria, S., Agarwal, B., Gelbukh, A., Hussain, A., Howard, N.: Dependency-based semantic parsing for concept-level text analysis. In: Gelbukh, A. (ed.) CICLing 2014. LNCS, vol. 8403, pp. 113–127. Springer, Heidelberg (2014). doi:10.1007/978-3-642-54906-9_10

22. Ramadier, L.: Indexation and learning of terms and relations from reports of radiology. Theses, Université de Montpellier. https://hal-lirmm.ccsd.cnrs.fr/tel-01479769
23. Tasse, D., Smith, N.A.: Sour cream: toward semantic processing of recipes. T.R. CMU-LTI-08-005, p. 9, May 2008
24. Zarrouk, M., Lafourcade, M., Joubert, A.: Inference and reconciliation in a crowd-sourced lexical-semantic network. In: CICLING: International Conference on Intelligent Text Processing and Computational Linguistics. No. 14th, Samos, Greece, March 2013. https://hal-lirmm.ccsd.cnrs.fr/lirmm-00816230

The More the Merrier - Federated Learning from Local Sphere Recommendations

Bernd Malle[1,2], Nicola Giuliani[1], Peter Kieseberg[1,2],
and Andreas Holzinger[1(✉)]

[1] Holzinger Group HCI-KDD Institute for Medical Informatics,
Statistics and Documentation, Medical University Graz, Graz, Austria
{b.malle,a.holzinger}@hci-kdd.org
[2] SBA Research GmbH, Favoritenstrae 16, 1040 Wien, Austria
PKieseberg@sba-research.org

Abstract. With Google's *Federated Learning* & Facebook's introduction of client-side NLP into their chat service, the era of client-side Machine Learning is upon us. While interesting ML approaches beyond the realm of toy examples were hitherto confined to large data-centers and powerful GPU's, exponential trends in technology and the introduction of billions of smartphones enable sophisticated processing swarms of even hand-held devices. Such approaches hold several promises: 1. Without the need for powerful server infrastructures, even small companies could be scalable to millions of users easily and cost-efficiently; 2. Since data only used in the learning process never need to leave the client, personal information can be used free of privacy and data security concerns; 3. Since privacy is preserved automatically, the full range of personal information on the client device can be utilized for learning; and 4. without round-trips to the server, results like recommendations can be made available to users much faster, resulting in enhanced user experience. In this paper we propose an architecture for federated learning from personalized, graph based recommendations computed on client devices, collectively creating & enhancing a global knowledge graph. In this network, individual users will 'train' their local recommender engines, while a server-based voting mechanism aggregates the developing client-side models, preventing over-fitting on highly subjective data from tarnishing the global model.

Keywords: Machine Learning · Federated ML · Interactive ML · The local sphere · Graph based personalized recommenders · Distributed bagging

1 Introduction and Motivation

A 2006 paper [1] examined recommender networks crystallizing from purchases based upon previously received product recommendations by employing an

Published by Springer International Publishing AG 2017. All Rights Reserved
A. Holzinger et al. (Eds.): CD-MAKE 2017, LNCS 10410, pp. 367–373, 2017.
DOI: 10.1007/978-3-319-66808-6_24

online shopping system observing purchases and recommendations of several product categories. Users of the platform were modeled as nodes in a graph with recommendations connecting them. This resulted in a collection of fragmented subgraphs representing series of so called *recommendation cascades*. Their analysis revealed that an overwhelming percentage of all relevant recommendations originated from a subgraph with a diameter of only ∼1.2, that is a node's immediate vicinity. Similar findings were also reported out of the blogosphere [2].

Observing an seemingly unrelated field of Software Development, the early 2010 s have yielded new Web frameworks bringing the power of publish/subscribe systems within reach of even single developers. These mechanisms work by reconciling two potentially conflicting interests in a set-theoretic way: The set of all data-points a client wishes to receive and the set of all data-points a server is allowed to publish. This intersection is then pushed down to the client and constantly kept up to date, obviating the need for a client to permanently send new data/update requests. This leads to a certain sub-sample of global data permanently residing on the client device; in the case of a graph structure this sub-sample would (at minimum) contain a node's immediate neighborhood.

Combining these two developments, we arrived at the definition of a *local sphere* residing on a client device, representing a subset of the globally available information within a system. As for most recommendations those data points are seemingly the only ones relevant, we conjecture a new system architecture based on client-side recommenders whose interaction with the user results in modifications of the local sphere, which by means of publish/subscribe are propagated throughout the system, in turn triggering possible actions by other users.

We therefore challenge the traditional notion of Machine Learning as happening on powerful, centralized servers and would like to replace them by a

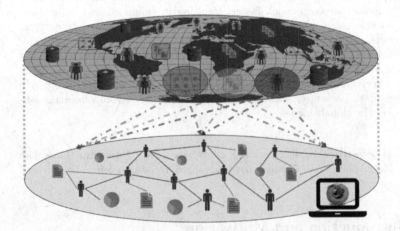

Fig. 1. Publish-subscribe mechanism used by a client to constantly synchronize a subsample of a *global database* to constitute what we term the *local sphere*. Note that the local sphere is a superset of the user's data - it may contain items a user is not actually requesting, but might be significant for computing relevant recommendations.

collective of mundane personal devices. We see this as a logical solution especially to the problems of large-scale graph analysis [3] as well as a continuation of a long-running trend towards employing commodity hardware for even the most demanding applications [4]. Ultimately, it could provide a globally distributed web of personalized knowledge extraction agents [5].

2 Theoretical Building Blocks

Aside from the engineering effort necessary to realize an architecture as we propose, we have identified 4 main theoretical aspects, or building blocks, that could make it a target for novel scientific research, the confirmation and refinement of current theories, or even the formulation of new conjectures.

2.1 Client-Side Machine Learning

... holds the promise of extreme scalability even for the smallest of startup companies. Because computations are mostly transferred to the client, organizations can limit their investment to the bare minimum of running any common Web-Site: Some servers transmitting snippets of client-side code as well as a sufficient database infrastructure. While there are still many challenges to overcome until client-side ML becomes ubiquitous, progress is already under way: Two teams [6,7] report on a new distributed NN model that needs much less communication than synchronized SGD. As nodes in such a federated approach have but a tiny sub-sample of a traditional, global database, new algorithms are being devised for this setting [8]. Because client-side computations might utilize personal information available only on a phone or tablet and model updates could inadvertently contain fragments of such information, secure server-side model aggregation has to be developed [9].

2.2 Privacy and Security

Privacy aware Machine Learning has been a hot topic for years [10] with its importance increasing dramatically due to ever intensifying limitations imposed by government regulations as well as public demand. One dramatic advantage of a distributed, client-side ML platform as we suggest it would be the isolation of privacy-endangering information within each user's personal device, rendering transfer of such information unnecessary, thereby effortlessly satisfying data protection regulations. On the other hand, learning on very small, subjective subsets of 'reality' could be seen as a profound distortion of data, and algorithms will have to be tested for suitability as well as stability in such scenarios [11].

2.3 Interactive Machine Learning (iML)

Interactive ML algorithms adapt their models not just via feedback after their learning phase, but by continuously interacting with an outside *oracle* (assumed to be omniscient), drawing positive/negative reinforcement from this interaction [12]. Such systems are especially desirable in areas requiring highly-personalized predictions or decision support [13]; moreover human brains are known to be very good at approximating solutions and learning from a very small set of samples, thus enabling us to 'intuit' solutions that exact algorithms need (super)exponential time to resolve [14,18].

Since client-side recommenders in our proposed architecture would continuously compute & provide users with individual recommendations which they can accept or reject, one could interpret this platform as a distributed system of interactive Machine Learning. As a consequence, one could transfer models learned by one user to new users of similar characteristic (however we obtain this information), thereby solving the notorious *cold start* problem well known in the recommender community.

2.4   Distributed Bagging

Another intriguing aspect to our proposal comes from the field of ensemble learning, where Leo Breiman conceived the technique of *Bagging* [15] in 1994. In Bagging (short for 'bootstrap aggregating') a global population is randomly sampled into several bags, so that each bag holds its own view of reality. Subsequently predictors are trained on these isolated sub-samples with the consequence of overfitting on their respective, local data. Finally an aggregation mechanism fuses the local models back together, producing a much more stable global predictor.

Our local sphere approach might be seen as analogous to the idea of bagging, potentially distributed over billions of devices and with access to data not permissible in a central dataset. The overlapping of local spheres produces the same effect as sampling with replacement does for Bagging; the main difference of our strategy being the lack of randomness, since user-data are not actually 'sampled' from global knowledge. It remains to be seen if this difference presents a major drawback or actually an advantage.

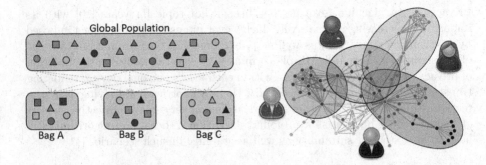

Fig. 2. Bagging vs. Spheres: To the left we depict the traditional bootstrap approach. To the right we see a global graph with user-defined *local spheres*, which influence each other via their overlapping segments (albeit each residing on their respective client). The graph visualization was generated using D3.js [16]

3   Proposed Workflow

In order to organize a perfect interplay of the components described above, we suggest the following sequence of interactions between the server (global sphere), client (local sphere), user (actually relevant data plus secure personal information) as well as the 'world' (all the information available on the Web or specialized online services):

1. The client defines a subscription for all data which might interest the user.
2. The server computes a local sphere by reconciling the client's request with it's own security/publication policy and pushes it down to the client.
3. Once the local sphere is instantiated, the actually relevant user data are prepared & visualized; the whole local sphere is instantiated within a client-side graph library in the background.
4. Client-side recommender algorithms continuously check the local sphere that is not already part of the user data for possible new information and recommend them on occasion.
5. Client-side *gatherers* (web crawlers) utilize the users personal information accessible via their local device or social media account, scanning the web for suitable information items on every user interaction with the local sphere. Any extracted information items are again recommended to the user on a regular basis. Users' private data might even act as personalized ontologies and be combined with well-known knowledge extraction methods [17].
6. The user interacts with their data via adding, connecting or re-arranging items. Each time new information is introduced into a local sphere it is synchronized to the server and - via it's overlapping segments with other local spheres - to those respective clients as well.

As a consequence of this interactive workflow, it might even be possible to renounce the idea of a centrally curated global graph demanding tremendous computational power, energy as well as financial resources. Apart from occasional server-side sampling for reasons of security and general prudence, a global graph would emerge, be sustained and developed purely through the growth and/or modification of all the local spheres that fabricate it.

4   Conclusion

In this paper, we have welcomed the era of client-side machine learning and introduced the concept of the *local sphere* as a logical building block for future collective (federated) machine learning systems. We have derived the local sphere idea for graph-based recommendations from earlier works and defined the 4 theoretical building blocks of our proposed system, describing the advantage each of their underlying approaches contributes to the system. Finally, we presented a possible workflow architecture which would allow a global graph to exist entirely as an abstract, logical layer on top of a multitude of local sphere's interaction with one another and the rest of the world.

References

1. Leskovec, J., Singh, A., Kleinberg, J.: Patterns of influence in a recommendation network. In: Ng, W.-K., Kitsuregawa, M., Li, J., Chang, K. (eds.) PAKDD 2006. LNCS, vol. 3918, pp. 380–389. Springer, Heidelberg (2006). doi:10.1007/11731139_44
2. Leskovec, J., McGlohon, M., Faloutsos, C., Glance, N., Hurst, M.: Patterns of cascading behavior in large blog graphs. In: Proceedings of the 2007 SIAM International Conference on Data Mining, pp. 551–556. SIAM (2007)
3. Leskovec, J., Faloutsos, C.: Sampling from large graphs. In: Proceedings of the 12th ACM SIGKDD International Conference on Knowledge Discovery and Data Mining, pp. 631–636. ACM (2006)
4. Al-Fares, M., Loukissas, A., Vahdat, A.: A scalable, commodity data center network architecture. In: ACM SIGCOMM Computer Communication Review, vol. 38, pp. 63–74. ACM (2008)
5. Holzinger, A.: Introduction to machine learning & knowledge extraction (make). Mach. Learn. Knowl. Extr. 1(1), 1–20 (2017)
6. McMahan, H.B., Moore, E., Ramage, D., Hampson, S. et al.: Communication-efficient learning of deep networks from decentralized data. arXiv preprint arXiv:1602.05629 (2016)
7. Konečný, J., McMahan, H.B., Yu, F.X., Richtárik, P., Suresh, A.T., Bacon, D.: Federated learning: strategies for improving communication efficiency. arXiv preprint arXiv:1610.05492 (2016)
8. Konečný, J., McMahan, H.B., Ramage, D., Richtárik, P.: Federated optimization: distributed machine learning for on-device intelligence. arXiv preprint arXiv:1610.02527 (2016)
9. Bonawitz, K., Ivanov, V., Kreuter, B., Marcedone, A., McMahan, H.B., Patel, S., Ramage, D., Segal, A., Seth, K.: Practical secure aggregation for privacy preserving machine learning. Cryptology ePrint Archive, Report 2017/281 (2017). http://eprint.iacr.org/2017/281
10. Wainwright, M.J., Jordan, M.I., Duchi, J.C.: Privacy Aware Learning. In: Advances in Neural Information Processing Systems, pp. 1430–1438 (2012)
11. Malle, B., Kieseberg, P., Weippl, E., Holzinger, A.: The right to be forgotten: towards machine learning on perturbed knowledge bases. In: Buccafurri, F., Holzinger, A., Kieseberg, P., Tjoa, A.M., Weippl, E. (eds.) CD-ARES 2016. LNCS, vol. 9817, pp. 251–266. Springer, Cham (2016). doi:10.1007/978-3-319-45507-5_17
12. Holzinger, A.: Interactive machine learning for health informatics: when do we need the human-in-the-loop? Springer Brain Inform. (BRIN) 3(2), 119–131 (2016)
13. Kieseberg, P., Malle, B., Frhwirt, P., Weippl, E., Holzinger, A.: A tamper-proof audit and control system for the doctor in the loop. Brain Inform. 3(4), 1–11 (2016)
14. Holzinger, A., Plass, M., Holzinger, K., Crişan, G.C., Pintea, C.-M., Palade, V.: Towards interactive Machine Learning (iML): applying ant colony algorithms to solve the traveling salesman problem with the human-in-the-loop approach. In: Buccafurri, F., Holzinger, A., Kieseberg, P., Tjoa, A.M., Weippl, E. (eds.) CD-ARES 2016. LNCS, vol. 9817, pp. 81–95. Springer, Heidelberg (2016). doi:10.1007/978-3-319-45507-5_6
15. Breiman, L.: Bagging predictors. Mach. Learn. 24(2), 123–140 (1996)
16. Zhu, N.Q.: Data visualization with D3. Js cookbook. Packt Publishing Ltd, UK (2013)

17. Alani, H., Kim, S., Millard, D.E., Weal, M.J., Hall, W., Lewis, P.H., Shadbolt, N.R.: Automatic ontology-based knowledge extraction from web documents. IEEE Intell. Syst. **18**(1), 14–21 (2003)
18. Holzinger, A., Plass, M., Holzinger, K., Crisan, G.C., Pintea, C.-M., Palade, V.: A glass-box interactive machine learning approach for solving NP-hard problems with the human-in-the-loop. arXiv preprint arXiv:1708.01104 (2017)

Author Index